Approaches and Methodologies in the Social Sciences

A revolutionary new textbook introducing masters and doctoral students to the major research approaches and methodologies in the social sciences. Written by an outstanding set of scholars, and derived from successful course teaching, this volume will empower students to choose their own approach to research, to justify this approach and to situate it within the discipline. It addresses questions of ontology, epistemology and philosophy of social science, and proceeds to issues of methodology and research design essential for producing a good research proposal. It also introduces researchers to the main issues of debate and contention in the methodology of social sciences, identifying commonalities, historic continuities and genuine differences.

Donatella della Porta is Professor of Sociology in the Department of Political and Social Sciences at the European University Institute, Florence, and Professor of Political Science at the University of Florence.

Michael Keating is Professor of Politics in the Department of Politics and International Relations at the University of Aberdeen.

Approaches and Methodologies in the Social Sciences

A Pluralist Perspective

Edited by

Donatella della Porta and Michael Keating

CAMBRIDGE
UNIVERSITY PRESS

CAMBRIDGE UNIVERSITY PRESS
Cambridge, New York, Melbourne, Madrid, Cape Town, Singapore, São Paulo,
Delhi, Tokyo, Mexico City

Cambridge University Press
The Edinburgh Building, Cambridge CB2 8RU, UK

Published in the United States of America by Cambridge University Press, New York

www.cambridge.org
Information on this title: www.cambridge.org/9780521709668

© Cambridge University Press 2008

First published 2008
3rd printing 2011

Printed in the United Kingdom at the University Press, Cambridge

A catalogue record for this publication is available from the British Library

ISBN   978-0-521-88322-1 Hardback
ISBN   978-0-521-70966-8 Paperback

I have lived among people of letters, who have written history without being involved in practical affairs, and among politicians, who have spent all their time making things happen, without thinking about describing them. I have always noticed that the former see general causes everywhere while the latter, living among the unconnected facts of everyday life, believe that everything must be attributed to specific incidents and that the little forces that they play in their hands must be the same as those that move the world. It is to be believed that both are mistaken.

Alexis de Tocqeville, *Souvenirs*

Contents

Figures

Tables

Contributors

Rainer Bauböck Professor of Social and Political Theory at the European University Institute

Zoe Bray Freelance artist and researcher and former doctoral and post-doctoral researcher at the European University Institute

Christine Chwaszcza Professor of Social and Political Theory at the European University Institute

Donatella della Porta Professor of Sociology at the European University Institute, and Professor of Political Science at the University of Florence

Mark Franklin Professor of Comparative Politics at the European University Institute

Adrienne Héritier Professor of Public Policy at the European University Institute

Michael Keating Professor of Politics at the University of Aberdeen

Friedrich Kratochwil Professor of International Relations at the European University Institute

Peter Mair Professor of Comparative Politics at the European University Institute

Alessandro Pizzorno Emeritus Professor and Professorial Fellow in Sociology at the European University Institute

Philippe Schmitter Emeritus Professor and Professorial Fellow in Comparative Politics at the European University Institute

Sven Steinmo Professor of Public Policy at the European University Institute

Pascal Vennesson Professor of International Relations and Security Policy at the European University Institute

Preface

The genesis of this book lies in the early 2000s, at the European University Institute (EUI), where a number of PhD researchers started to complain about the neglect of 'qualitative methods'. As only a minority of the faculty worked principally with quantitative methods, we had assumed that the rest were qualitative in the way that Molière's M. Jourdain was a speaker of prose. A series of discussions and debates revealed that in most cases they were talking about something else, a specific form of epistemology rather than a method, and one whose meaning was being continually stretched across the discipline. While it was difficult to tie down exactly what was meant by 'qualitative', it seemed to be defined in opposition to 'positivist', another description that most professors found difficult to accept for themselves and which was also subject to considerable stretching.

The EUI was not alone here, for this was merely the latest expression of a Manicheanism in which social scientists seem to be driven to define themselves into opposing camps. The fact that we could never find a shared name or vocabulary for the two approaches suggested that the question was altogether more complicated. It was also apparent that most of the issues at stake were not new but echoed debates in philosophy, sociology and political science going back to classical times. Rather than succumb to the culture wars that have wracked too many social science faculties, especially in the United States, we decided to launch a debate among various schools and approaches and an exploration of the issues at stake. A minimum requirement for PhD students in the social sciences, we believe, is a familiarity with current debates and an ability to read critically a piece of work and understand its perspective, whatever its provenance. They should also be conscious of, and able to defend, the perspective they have chosen in their own work. If they criticize other perspectives, it should be from a position of knowledge. Finally, they should know how, and how far, it is possible to combine different perspectives in a coherent research design.

The result was a common first-year seminar for doctoral students in political science, sociology, international relations and political and social theory.

These students have been our most demanding critics, insisting on clarity and coherence and urging the faculty to debate with each other. If the immediate effect of the seminar was to confuse and complicate their ideas about research, we hope that at the end they have a clearer idea of where they stand, as well as an understanding that the issues at stake are perhaps fewer than first appeared. The tendency of academics to invent new concepts, to stretch old ones, to relabel others and to divide themselves into warring factions has only increased over time, and the present generation of graduate students are perhaps the victims.

It was at the suggestion of Helen Wallace, then director of the Robert Schuman Centre for Advanced Studies at the EUI, that we converted a course into a book. This forced us to think much more carefully about content and coherence, but we believe that the experience of the authors working together for two years has helped us to clarify the issues. We do not offer a single approach to social sciences, or even attempt to synthesize existing ones into a whole. The enterprise is a pluralistic one, informed by a belief that there is no single 'best way', and by a commitment to diversity and tolerance of different approaches. We do believe, however, that a debate among these approaches, using common standards of argumentation, is possible; and we have sought to present such a debate in these pages.

Some characteristics of the European University Institute made this debate, if not unique, more challenging. Not only is the Department of Political and Social Sciences deeply interdisciplinary, with political science, sociology, international relations and political and social theory as essential components; it is also a European institution, with PhD students coming from all EU member-states and beyond. They bring with them rich and various backgrounds, with knowledge not only of their own countries, but also of the specific contributions to the various disciplines in those countries. As a result, they constantly stimulate and challenge us to go not only beyond our own individual backgrounds, but also beyond the mainstream Anglophone social science literature. They push us to learn other languages, to read other languages and to link ideas coming from the various national traditions; and they help build, in everyday interactions, a truly transnational approach to the social sciences.

This makes our enterprise a quintessentially European one. This is not to say that there is a single European way of doing social science that might be contrasted with an American one. Exponents of rational choice, of constructivism or of historical institutionalism are much the same on both sides of the Atlantic. In Europe, however, there is a greater plurality of approaches.

National intellectual traditions are multiple, and there is less of a tendency for one approach to dominate at any time or in any institution. As with the European project itself, different perspectives and expectations must live together in greater or lesser harmony.

To press the analogy further, we can identify three broad attitudes to difference. There are those who are wedded to a specific approach and think that everyone should conform to it. Others have their preferred approach and would like it to prevail, but realize that this is not practical and that if there were a single approach it would perhaps not be their own; these are the pragmatic pluralists. Finally, there are those who see pluralism as positive in itself, since intellectual pluralism can enrich the experience of research by encouraging us to learn and borrow from each other. It is this last perspective that motivated us to bring together this collection. We believe that social science must never become prisoner of any orthodoxy and must continually renew itself by learning from other disciplines and from new developments, and by revisiting its own past. This is not to say that we believe that 'anything goes' or that researchers can mix and match any idea, approach, theory or method according to whim. Methodology is important, intellectual rigour is essential within all approaches, and clarity and consistency are vital.

We are grateful to Yves Mény, president of the EUI, for support in this project, to Sarah Tarrow for editing the contributions and to our PhD researchers for inspiration and criticism.

1 Introduction

Donatella della Porta and Michael Keating

This book is an introduction to approaches and methodologies in the social sciences. 'Approaches' is a general term, wider than theory or methodology. It includes epistemology or questions about the theory of knowledge; the purposes of research, whether understanding, explanation or normative evaluation; and the 'meta-theories' within which particular theories are located. It takes in basic assumptions about human behaviour; whether the unit of analysis is the individual or the social group; and the role of ideas and interests. The first part of the book outlines some of these approaches, their development and the key issues they address. It is, in the spirit of the project as a whole, pluralistic, and readers should not expect the chapters to build into a single picture. Rather, they present different research traditions and orientations, some of which overlap while others are more starkly opposed.

The second part moves into questions of methodology, of how we turn a research problem into a workable design and of the basic choices to be made about methods. It does not go into detail on methods themselves; for this, students must turn to the numerous manuals available. The chapters should, however, help them to read and understand research based on different methodologies as well as help to guide their own choices. Readers will not find a road map leading step-by-step to their final goal. Instead, we present a map of the terrain over which they must travel, noting the main landmarks and turning points on their way. The various contributions follow different styles, reflecting individual and national preferences but also the ways in which the various approaches have developed, sometimes in interaction with each other. Authors present different mixes of rules and illustrations, reviews of sophisticated methodological debates and concrete 'how-to' suggestions in the various steps of a research design and its implementation.

Big questions

A number of big questions run through the whole collection. One is the fundamental question of epistemology, of what we know and how we know it. This is one of the oldest issues in philosophy and can never be resolved to the satisfaction of all. Fortunately, we can make progress without always having to return to these foundational issues; but nonetheless, it is important to be clear just which epistemological assumptions we are making in our research. Social scientists work much of the time with concepts, which are more or less abstract representations of the social world they are studying. Indeed, without basic notions such as class, state and society it is difficult to see how we could get anywhere; but when we use these concepts in radically different ways, common knowledge and even informed disagreement become impossible.

Another important issue is that of the units of analysis. One tradition in the social sciences, that of individualism, holds that only individuals really exist (ontological individualism) or that only individuals can act and, therefore, social science is the study of what individuals do (methodological individualism). Most versions of rational choice theory start from the individual and explain broader processes as the aggregation of individual acts. Other approaches, however, use larger units of analysis, including collectivities and institutions such as classes, ethnic groups or states. Related to this is the issue of the level of analysis: whether we are interested only in micro-level behaviour and infer broader social processes and change (the macro level) from that, or whether we can reason at the level of social aggregates. For example, international relations scholars may be interested in the behaviour of individual states, or may think of the pattern of international relations as composing a system with its own logic; critics of the 'realist' approach insist that the states themselves are not unitary actors. Whereas unit of analysis is a choice of empirical items to study, level of analysis is concerned with theory and the level at which explanations are postulated to work. The authors in this book take different views on this matter and the micro–macro link, and it is important that the reader note this.

A recurrent debate in social science concerns theories of action: why people do as they do. Some social scientists take an individualist perspective, adding the assumption that individuals are motivated by self-interest and will do what maximizes their own benefits – the logic of consequentialism. This supposition underlies most rational choice theory, although some proponents of rational choice stretch the idea of self-interest to include altruistic behaviour. Critics see this assumption as untenable and, when stretched to include all behaviour, tautological. An alternative explanation for behaviour is that it is the product of learned norms and socialization. Institutions play a role here, both in setting the incentives for rational choice and for providing the socialization mechanisms. In addition, people may act based on what they consider to be right according to ideology or ethical criteria. In recent years, there has been a renewed interest in the role of ideas as opposed to interests in social and political life; and in the way that perceptions of interests are conditioned by ideas.

The purposes of social science research are often contested. For some, the aim is explanation of social behaviour, on the assumption that it has causes that are knowable and measurable. Few people now think that social science works like Newtonian mechanics, with fixed mechanisms that are predictable. Some social scientists, however, do aim to approximate this; if they do not always succeed, it is because there is missing information which, in principle, could be supplied. Other scholars prefer the analogy of biology, with social behaviour evolving over time in response to learning and adaptation. Some of the work in historical institutionalism is informed by this idea. Yet some social scientists disclaim the idea of explanation and causation altogether, seeking rather to understand the motivations and calculations of actors who are not pre-determined in their behaviour. This breaks altogether with the natural science analogy and is closer to the approach and methodology of historians. Expressed in modern social science as the choice between agency and structural explanations, this dilemma corresponds in many ways to the old philosophical debate as to how far human beings are possessed of free will.

There is a persistent division in the social sciences between those who prefer to break their material up into variables and those who prefer dealing with whole cases. In our experience, there are few causes of greater confusion among graduate social scientists, many of whom insist on speaking in the language of variables while working with whole cases, or occasionally vice versa. The difference will be evident in the chapters to follow, with some authors insisting on a variable-based approach and others favouring holistic methods. Donatella della Porta addresses the argument more explicitly. Our view is that there is not one 'right' way to do analysis. Both variable-driven and case-driven research are the products of prior conceptualization and theorization, since neither cases nor variables exist as objects. If we are interested in parsimonious explanations and generalization as to what causes what, then it is useful to isolate variables and examine their effects across cases. If we are interested in context and in the complexity of outcomes, then whole cases may yield more insight. So one approach may explain part of the outcome in a large number of cases, while another may explain most of the outcome in a small number of cases.

Methods, too, divide social scientists. In a very general sense, we can talk of a distinction between hard methods (usually based on a positivist epistemology and a belief in the reality of social concepts) and soft methods (relying more on interpretation). Yet matters are in practice a great deal more complicated, with different forms of information being suitable for different forms of analysis. There is scope for combining methods through triangulation, but, in order to do this, we need to be clear of the assumptions that underlie each and to ensure that they are not incompatible.

Most sciences have an agreed-upon set of concepts and a shared vocabulary so that, even where there is no agreement on substance, at least we know what the disagreement is about. In the social sciences, concepts are often unclear or contested – think of the different meanings of globalization, capitalism or Europeanization. Concepts are contested when people use them in different ways. They are 'essentially contested' when there is no possibility of common meaning because they are based on different epistemological premises or underpin radically different world-views. Even where concepts are not consciously contested, there is often no shared vocabulary, and the same word may be used differently in different disciplines or even within the same discipline. This is confusing enough where words have quite distinct meanings. It is even more confusing where meanings only partially agree and overlap. Readers should be alert to this problem, and we have provided a glossary of the meanings of some key terms at the end of the book.

Finally, there is the issue of norms and values in social sciences. One school of thought seeks rigorously value-free social science, again on the natural science model. Norms might be a subject for study in themselves, insofar as they can be operationalized and measured; but the social scientist should set his or her own values aside. Others disagree, arguing that many concepts and much of our language has a normative content – think of terms like peace, democracy or legitimacy – and cannot be understood without it. Some go further and argue that, until the twentieth century, the social sciences were concerned with the conditions for improving the human lot and that this, rather than explanation and prediction, is what the human sciences are good at, and that they should return to it.

National traditions and cross-national influences

Social sciences (as opposed to philosophy) emerged in the nineteenth and twentieth centuries alongside the nation-state. They often remained bound by national assumptions and experiences; even political and social data tend to come in national sets. The result is a certain 'methodological nationalism', which takes two forms. One is a tendency to generalize from one's own country, often presented as the harbinger of modernity and the model for the future. The other is the myth of exceptionalism, according to which one's own country is the exception to the general rules of development and thus deserving of particular interest. For example, in most countries there exists a school of thought to the effect that the particular country is exceptional in never having had a real 'bourgeois revolution'. Paradoxically, one thing that nearly all countries do have in common is the notion that they are exceptional.

Speaking of national traditions risks reifying them and suggesting a uniformity that does not exist, yet certain ideas continue to be stressed in particular countries, as do specific approaches. For example, the concept of the state has a meaning in France and Germany that is difficult to convey in the United States or the United Kingdom. By contrast, American scholars, while downplaying the concept of the state in domestic politics, often give it supreme importance in international relations. French social science traditionally tends to an abstraction that contrasts with the empiricism of the English-speaking world. As emerging disciplines in the late nineteenth and early twentieth centuries, political science and sociology were linked in some countries to the older disciplines of history and law and these legacies are still visible. In many countries, international relations emerged as a discipline separate from comparative politics. The division between political science and sociology is sharper in the United Kingdom and the United States than in France or Italy. Sometimes these contrasts reflect differences in the political and social realities of the countries concerned. France has traditionally had a strong state. American politics has revolved around interest-group pluralism within a rather narrowly defined value system (at least until the revival of the religious cleavage). Yet the difference in intellectual emphasis does not always reflect an underlying social reality, as opposed to different ways of thinking about politics and society. There is thus great value in taking the concepts and ideas from one country and seeking to apply them comparatively, and more generally in seeking concepts that travel, both as an aid to comparative research and as an antidote to methodological nationalism.

There had always been an international market in ideas, peaking at times such as the Renaissance or the eighteenth-century Enlightenment; but in the twentieth century, this intensified greatly. The existence of a common language, successively Latin, French and English, encourages this, but itself may shape the ideas and their reception. For our purposes, two arenas are important: the market of ideas within Europe, and transatlantic trade as the United States has ascended to a dominant position within the social science research world. For example, the 'behavioural revolution' in the 1960s was American in origin but powerfully affected European thinking from the 1970s onwards, emphasizing universalism, quantification and rigour. Rational choice theory, so influential from the 1980s, was not an American monopoly but was strongest there and was powerfully aided by the strength of US social science in the global market. Other ideas have more complex histories. Organizational analysis was imported from the United States in the 1950s by Michel Crozier and others, who transformed it into a particularly French form of science, the 'sociology of organizations'. This in turn was taken up by British scholars and brought back into the English-speaking world. Here it encountered the 'new institutionalism', which had been working with similar ideas, starting from a different basis, as a reaction to behaviourism and rational choice. European sociology was influenced by American approaches, but also developed and then diffused new ideas of its own. Among others, French sociologist Alain Touraine was influenced by Parsonian functionalism when developing his theory of society, and European ethno-methodologists by Erwin Goffman. In all these fields, ideas developed by European scholars travelled to the other side of the Atlantic, with particularly strong impacts on theorization and research on such issues as power (Foucault), communication (Habermas) and culture (Bourdieu).

There has been a similar recycling over time as ideas have come and gone. The study of institutions has emerged, faded away and returned in a new form. So have the study of history, and cultural approaches in both politics and sociology. Normative theory, marginalized during the behaviouralist revolution, has made a strong comeback. Much confusion is caused by the habit of re-inventing old ideas but giving them new labels. There is also a tendency for those advancing new ideas (or often just new terms) to present a simplified caricature of their predecessors, thus preventing us from building on past knowledge and advancing theoretically and methodologically.

As editors of this collection, we do not believe that a unified global social science is possible or, given the nature of the matters addressed, desirable. Yet there are better opportunities for cross-fertilization and synthesis than there have been for some time, as scholars grow weary of debates in which the protagonists just talk past each other. We hope to show how the various approaches intersect, and the points in common as well as the points of difference. The chapters that follow do not read as a unified or continuous whole. We have encouraged authors to emphasize the distinctive features of the approach they are describing, and readers will appreciate that each is bringing his/her own interpretation and perspective.

The chapters

The next chapter, by della Porta and Keating, asks how many approaches there are in the social sciences and how compatible they are with each other. We distinguish among ontologies and epistemologies, or how we know the social world; methodologies, in the form of coherent research designs; and methods, the tools of the trade. While these are linked, there is no one-to-one connection from choices at one level to those at the others. Epistemological debates often pit positivists or realists, who believe in the concrete reality of social phenomena, against constructivists or interpretivists, who emphasize human perception and interpretation. We argue that matters are more complicated, with a spectrum of positions between these extremes. Methodological debates are often framed as a confrontation between the quantitative methodologies used by positivists and the qualitative ones used by constructivists and interpretivists. There is indeed a school of positivist scholars wedded to hard data and quantification, and another school that uses softer data for interpretation; but many social scientists combine approaches. As for methods, these are merely ways of acquiring information. Tools such as surveys, interviews and analysis of texts are used for a variety of purposes and with different epistemological bases. We conclude the chapter by showing how different approaches and methodologies can and cannot be combined, a question to which we return in the final chapter.

For much of the twentieth century, social science sought theories of politics and society that could explain outcomes in a rigorous causal manner, eliminating all value judgements. Questions of values and the 'good society' were relegated to philosophy, where they were addressed in an abstract manner. This contrasts with an earlier tradition in which some of the classical sociologists and political analysts were consciously seeking ways to improve social institutions. Rainer Bauböck, in Chapter 3, shows how normative considerations have come back into social science in recent decades, starting with theories of social justice and moving into other concerns such as self-determination and competing conceptions of liberalism and democracy. He argues that normative questions are unavoidable in social science, since concepts are often normatively charged, especially when dealing with questions of power and its legitimation. Bauböck goes on to explain how normative theory and empirical research can be combined, in the empirical study of attitudes and beliefs; in institutionally embedded norms; in qualitative case studies including legal judgments; and in quantitative comparative cases. He concludes with some remarks on the ethics of normative theorizing and the position of the political theorist in present-day political debates.

The next two chapters address what are often considered as polar-opposite approaches. Adrienne Héritier starts from positivist premises in presenting an account of causal analysis in social science, which seeks to create generalizable knowledge about the world on the assumption that the world is real, ordered, structured and knowable. Antecedent events are taken as the cause of subsequent ones and we can, through accumulated knowledge, discover how particular causes will be followed by particular effects. Often this knowledge is probabilistic in that there are other factors at work, but in principle these could be known and accounted for if all the necessary information were available. Sometimes theories are built up from the accumulation of knowledge of particular cases, but most social science will start with a theory, expressed as a hypothesis as to what will follow a particular cause, which is then tested against reality. Such hypotheses should be internally consistent, logically complete and falsifiable. Once an association between a cause and an effect has been established, there are ways to flesh out the causal mechanisms. Another form of causal analysis works backwards from a known outcome and seeks complex explanations through modules, each of which explains part of the outcome.

Critically discussing some of the assumptions of causal analysis, Friedrich Kratochwil takes up one of the key questions posed in Chapter 1, about what we know and how we know it. In the constructivist perspective, social scientists deal not with a given, objective and undisputed real world, but with concepts. Concepts and theories can never be disproved by reference to a separate reality; rather, they are confronted by other concepts and theories. This does *not* entail two further propositions sometimes attributed to constructivists – that the physical world is merely the product of our imagination, and that any proposition can be asserted to be as valid as any other without need for proof or demonstration. On the contrary, it is incumbent upon social scientists to specify the frames within which they make truth claims. In explaining social behaviour, attention must be paid to the perceptions and motivations of actors. Explanations of social behaviour may be multiple, operating at different levels and asking different sorts of questions – about proximate causes, actor motivation, large structures or causal chains, for example.

The history of social science, we have argued, is not a matter of progressing to ever better theories and methods, but rather of successive efforts to capture the social world and to answer questions that themselves may be different. It is not a search for a complete set of concepts that would be inclusive, in covering the entire world, and exclusive, in the sense of not overlapping with each other. Concepts, rather, overlap, and the same thing may be explained using various different tools. At one time, the concept of culture was used rather carelessly to explain differences between national societies. During the behavioural revolution, this approach was downplayed as scholars sought universal patterns and context-free knowledge, pushing cultural explanations to the margins with a view to eliminating them altogether. In recent years, it has made something of a comeback as a way of resolving some of the big questions outlined above. Michael Keating argues that it addresses the relationship of the individual to the collective level, of ideas to interests and of the past to the present and the future. It does not provide an explanation for everything, and it overlaps with other concepts. Culture is located neither at the level of the individual nor at that of a reified society, but at the inter-subjective level, where it provides a means for identifying group boundaries, interpreting events and according value. It is not amenable to the positivist language of independent and dependent variables. It is not primordial or unchanging, but adapts to events even as it shapes them. Culture is notoriously difficult to measure. Surveys can capture value differences among individuals but are not always reliable when we move to the collective level. Stereotypes may get in the way of understanding how societies really work. The best approaches consist of a triangulation of survey methods, ethnographic studies and case work.

The following chapters address some main theoretical developments in the social sciences. Sven Steinmo charts the rise of the new institutionalism as a corrective to the universalizing, behaviouralist accounts of the 1960s. While 'old' institutionalists (including many European social scientists) took institutions as sets of binding rules, new institutionalists have a more sociological conception. There are three varieties of new institutionalism. For rational choice institutionalists, institutions shape the patterns of incentives and sanctions available to individuals making decisions. Sociological institutionalists see people as being socialized by institutions, so that their behaviour is shaped by what they have learnt to see as appropriate. Historical institutionalists can accept both of these accounts, but emphasize the importance of context and of the historical order of events. History is not a chain of independent events but a sequence in which one happening influences the next. In this way, these scholars seek to account for both continuity and change over time. Although they use various methodologies, historical institutionalists share the methodological challenge of bringing history back into the social sciences. They are sceptical of the idea of independent variables that can be isolated to measure the effect of each, since factors constantly interact with each other. If there is a scientific analogy, it is with biology rather than physics. Historical institutionalists are interested in specific cases and the comparison of a small number of cases rather than generalizations over large numbers of cases.

Two chapters examine theories of action. We have not included a separate chapter on rational choice theory. The older debates about rational choice theory have become rather exhausted, and rational choice theory itself has become more sophisticated and variegated over the years. The classic objection is that the rational choice assumption that people are rationally calculating utility-maximizers is either wrong (since some people are altruistic) or tautological (if utility is stretched to include altruistic behaviour). Debating this issue would not take us much further. Instead, Christine Chwaszcza takes us into game theory. She starts from the classic assumptions of rational choice theory – consequentialism, utility theory and methodological individualism. Individualist rational choice approaches to explanation have been criticized for their demanding assumptions about how individuals actually make decisions, and for failing to take context and the actions of others into account. Game theory seeks to get around these problems by factoring in other actors and relaxing the assumption that all try to maximize their goals. Instead, the criterion of rational choice in game theory is the equilibrium principle, which takes into account the actions of others. This still depends, however, on strictly consequentialist thinking with the result that actors can find themselves in paradoxes such as the prisoners' dilemma, in which each actor will choose the option that leaves both of them worse off. Sometimes there are two equilibria, each of which would maximize overall welfare (such as choosing to drive on the left or on the right); but rational choice and game theory in themselves do not indicate which one the individual actor should choose. More complicated still are cases with multiple equilibria in which the benefits to the various parties are unequal. Ways out of this problem include iterated games, in which the actors learn how to react, and evolutionary game theory, in which actors signal and learn and adapt to their environment. This takes us into more socially embedded forms of action in which institutions and norms help shape the actions of individuals. By taking the argument in this direction, Chwaszcza shows how rational choice and game-theoretical approaches can link into other approaches discussed in the book, including historical institutionalism (Steinmo) and cultural approaches (Keating). Game theory, while not providing a complete account of social behaviour, remains valuable as a tool of analysis in specific settings, a mode of reasoning and a way of generating hypotheses and research questions.

Alessandro Pizzorno takes the problem of motivation and action in another direction. He acknowledges a move in social sciences away from seeking *causes* of action, to seeking *reasons*, which involves looking at the individual who takes the decision to act. Yet he takes issue with the idea that reason can be reduced to individualistic self-regarding motives and stresses the characteristic of the human being as an essentially relational actor, together with the need to consider preferences, interest and identities as endogenous to social science analysis. That is, they should not be taken for granted, as already existing, but be put at the core of a sociological analysis. Instead of assuming that human beings are isolated and interested only in their own utility, Pizzorno places them in a social context, where the opinion of others becomes an essential part of their own welfare calculations. Thus, rationality is a function not merely of the intention preceding the action, but also of ways in which an action is received and interpreted in the culture in which it takes place. This chapter focuses in particular on reconstructing the intellectual background of a theory of recognition, locating it in the role Adam Smith gave to the anticipation of the favourable judgement of a neutral 'other', in Rousseauian attention to the *regard des autres*, Hegel's focus on interpersonal relations as the basis of the structure of subjectivity, Weber's theory of social action and Durkheim's focus on the 'social forces' that constrain individual action. Like several other contributions in the book, it seeks to establish a link between the micro analysis of individual behaviour, and the macro level of social change.

The second part of the book takes us beyond these general questions of modes of understanding, towards research design.

Peter Mair addresses a matter discussed earlier by Friedrich Kratochwil, the question of concepts and conceptualization. Kratochwil problematizes the notion of concepts, showing how they arise from the interpretation of the observer and exist for analytical purposes – they do not correspond to 'things' in the real world. Mair moves in the other direction, towards operationalization and classification. Kratochwil addresses an epistemological question, from a constructivist perspective, whereas Mair proceeds on more positivist assumptions. Yet they meet on the intermediate or 'meso' level of analysis in that both argue that social science is built on concepts and that conceptual clarity is essential to research and argumentation. Concepts, in Mair's treatment, are categories, so that each variable or item is an instance of something more general. Categories can be organized according to Sartori's ladder of abstraction so that two items which at one level are instances of different things, at another level can be in the same category; for example, apples and pears are different but are both fruit. Categories are exclusive, so that no item can belong to two classes at the same level of abstraction, and exhaustive, so that all items are located somewhere. Researchers can choose the level of abstraction according to the research question. The most fruitful abstractions, Mair argues, are often done at the middle level. Not all concepts, however, can be arranged so neatly. In some cases, different properties may constitute the category, not all of which are necessary or sufficient. In this case, instead of taxonomies, social scientists may use ideal types, abstract categories containing all the necessary attributes. Real cases can be identified according to whether they have any of the properties, generating radial categories. An alternative is Wittgenstein's family resemblances, in which each member shares at least one feature with each other member but there is not necessarily a single feature common to them all.

Donatella della Porta addresses the choice between variable-based and case-based approaches in comparative research. After recalling the way in which the debate on methodology developed within comparative politics, della Porta presents the different logics of research in the work of Durkheim and Weber, focusing on the methodological assumptions underlying variable-oriented and case-oriented strategies. She warns against considering variable-oriented research as setting the standard to which all social science research has to conform. Accepting shared standards does not mean adopting the same rules. The chapter addresses some of the main methodological choices: the relevant unit of analysis; the number of cases; the trade-off between most-similar and most-different designs; the ways of addressing the time dimension. It also discusses recent attempts to bridge the gap between the two approaches, in particular with qualitative comparative analysis (QCA) and recent reflections on the case-oriented strategy. Conditions that might influence the choice of one logic or the other include environmental conditions (such as stages in a research cycle or types of data available) and researchers' epistemological preferences as to approach and their methodological skills.

The case study has often been disparaged in social science as being descriptive and contributing nothing to theory or wider understanding. Case studies, in this view, might be useful only as a supplement to comparative or statistical analysis. Pascal Vennesson argues that this is mistaken and that, properly done, case studies represent a significant contribution to knowledge. There are five forms of case study: descriptive/configurative; interpretive, using theory to explain a case and then refining theory; hypothesis-generating, providing a basis for further work; deviant-case, to suggest new hypotheses and theories; and theory-evaluating. Cases themselves are not given by the world, but are themselves the product of theory and conceptualization – as when we ask what something is a case of, set the boundaries of the case or use conceptual tools to understand it. Case studies may be undertaken through process tracing, otherwise known as analytic narrative, which links the events to explain the outcome. Importantly, Vennesson notes that this can be done within either a positivist or an interpretivist framework. A positivist would identify variables as causal mechanisms, to fill in the void (the 'black box') left when general effects are imputed to general causes. An interpretivist would examine the understandings and motivations of actors; assumptions like rational utility-maximization can here be subject to critical scrutiny. Sometimes positivist and interpretivist approaches may be combined. Vennesson then discusses practical questions about doing case studies, including the use of theory; empirical sources; and the cognitive biases of the researcher.

The next three chapters take us further into the practicalities of research, although none of them intends to be a complete account of how to undertake it. Mark Franklin addresses quantitative analysis. The approach is positivist, based on causal logic. The idea is to establish, using a large number of cases, linkages between causes (independent variables) and effects (dependent variables). Franklin takes us in steps through the logic, vocabulary and practice of quantitative analysis. First are the sources and quality of the data. Then the data are arranged and ordered in a set. Interval, ordinal, nominal and dummy variables are defined. He then discusses units and levels of analysis and the common problems posed in these, and the significance of findings and how this is assessed. Next, Franklin takes us through multivariate and regression analysis. Finally, he warns of some common pitfalls in quantitative research.

Philippe Schmitter's chapter takes us into the process of research from a substantially positivist perspective, following the logic of causal analysis although not presenting this as the only possible aim of research. In a more didactic style than the other chapters, it identifies the main steps in a 'research cycle', leading us from an idea to its transformation into a topic, considered relevant enough to focus our energies upon, and also suitable for transformation into a feasible project. It highlights a series of strategic choices to be followed in order to translate the topic from a problem (or puzzle) into a project. Using the metaphor of a clock, Schmitter traces the whole process of a research project, from the singling out of a scientific problem (or an object of study) to the conceptualization of the main dimensions (or variables) to be analysed and their definition and operationalization, the choice of cases and methods, and the collection of data and their interpretation. In the course of this, he includes choices about the aim of the research, which might be exploring normative issues, understanding, explanation or causal analysis. As Schmitter himself stresses, it is rare that a single researcher follows all these steps in the course of a single PhD thesis or travels all the way to twelve o'clock. Indeed, within the scope of a doctoral project, this is impossible, so that those interested in causal analysis might need to short-cut the earlier steps by using existing theories and concepts. Others might be interested precisely in reconceptualization, normative issues, or understanding as opposed to explanation (as explained in Chapter 2). So readers should not get the impression that this chapter is laying down 'one best way' for all research designs; they will notice that Schmitter's insistence on always using variables rather than cases is not supported by, among others, della Porta, Vennesson and Bray in their chapters. Most readers, however, can benefit from Schmitter's lists of things that researchers should bear in mind and fallacies that they should avoid.

Zoe Bray introduces a different approach to collecting and analysing data, the ethnological or ethnographic method, linked to interpretation and the search for meaning. Ethnography is usually associated with anthropology, but Bray argues that the underlying approach and the methods can have wider application in the social sciences. The ethnographic approach looks at social phenomena from the micro-perspective, although this may be a complement to, rather than a substitute for, the macro-perspective. It focuses on the meanings that actors give to their actions, rather than making prior assumptions about motivation. It is contextual, examining whole social situations rather than breaking them down into discrete variables whose effects are separate. Theory is important for research, but it is not imposed on the situation and is developed in the course of the research. The researcher should be open to new interpretations and thinking. There are three phases to the research itself. First, the researcher selects cases based on their theoretical or practical relevance. Second, the case is studied in detail, often by a long period of immersion, bearing in mind the risk of the researcher him/herself becoming part of the situation under study. Third, ethnographic writing involves note-taking and analytical writing of the final report. Methods include participant observation, interviewing and recording in the form of oral records or notes. This approach is thus distinct from that of positivist and variable-based social science. It looks at whole cases, and it stresses depth (understanding a lot about one case) over breadth (understanding a little about many cases). Yet it is scientific, with its own standards of evidence, subject to affirmation or disproof, with its own procedures and research ethics. Even if we do not adopt the ethnographic approach wholesale, it may be a valuable counterpart to more positivistic approaches. For example, survey research generates apparently hard data, but these are dependent on the question asked, which in turn stems from the theoretical assumptions and biases of those devising the questions. Ethnographic research can be valuable in interpreting the answers that people give to these questions and in designing better ones. Ethnographic approaches have also been used in the study of political processes and institutions, where they complement institutional and rational choice analysis.

In the concluding chapter, we return to the question of how many logics exist and how they can be combined. We identify points of commonality and complementarity among the approaches discussed, highlighting the key differences.

Part I

Epistemology and philosophy of the social sciences

2 How many approaches in the social sciences? An epistemological introduction

Donatella della Porta and Michael Keating

Paradigms in the social sciences

Partisans articulate their positions with passion and intensity, yet the nature of what divides them is hard to pin down. At times we hear of a stand-off between 'qualitative' scholars, who make use of archival research, ethnology, textual criticism, and discourse analysis; and 'quantitative' scholars, who deploy mathematics, game theory, and statistics. Scholars in the former tradition supposedly disdain the new, hyper-numerate, approaches to political science as opaque and overly abstract, while scholars of the latter stripe deride the 'old' ways of studying politics as impressionistic and lacking in rigor. At other times the schism is portrayed as being about the proper aspiration of the discipline – between those who believe that a scientific explanation of political life is possible, that we can derive something akin to physical laws of human behavior, and those who believe it is not . . . at still other times the rivals are portrayed as 'rational choice theorists,' whose work is animated by the assumption that individuals are rational maximizers of self-interest (often economics, sometimes not), and those who allow for a richer range of human motivations (Shapiro, Smith and Masoud 2004a: 1).

This quotation from the introduction to a recent volume on *Problems and Methods in the Study of Politics* addresses a core methodological issue for the social sciences in general: how many approaches/methods are available for students in the discipline? And what are the main cleavages along which they are divided?

In *The Structure of Scientific Revolutions*, Thomas Kuhn (1962) suggested that mature scientific disciplines rely upon a paradigm that defines what to study (relevance of social phenomena), why to study (formulating explanatory hypotheses) and how to study (through which methods). In normal times the presence of a paradigm, based upon previous acquisitions in a discipline, allows for the accumulation of knowledge. In times of turbulence, scientific revolutions produce changes of paradigm. An important element of a paradigm is that it is accepted by the whole community of scientists active in a certain discipline. According to Kuhn, in the 1960s the existence of a paradigm in the social sciences was an open question; in the 2000s, it remains so.

Some social scientists insist that there is only one approach (and thus one paradigm) in the social sciences. King, Keohane and Verba (1994: 6) synthesized the 'ideal to which any actual quantitative and qualitative research' should aim in the following definition of 'scientific research':

1   The goal is inference. Scientific research is designed to make descriptive or explanatory inferences on the bases of empirical information about the world . . .
2   The procedures are public. Scientific research uses explicit, codified, and public methods to generate and analyse data whose reliability can therefore be assessed . . .
3   The conclusions are uncertain . . .
4   The content is the method. . . . scientific research adheres to a set of rules of inference on which its validity depends.

Not all social scientists, however, share all these assumptions or even believe in the possibility of a common definition of scientific research. Some think that social science is pre-paradigmatic, still in search of a set of unifying principles and standards; others believe that it is post-paradigmatic, having shed a set of scientistic assumptions tied to a particular conception of modernity (the post-modern approach). Yet others believe that it is non-paradigmatic, in that there can never be one hegemonic approach and set of standards, but that the social world is to be understood in multiple ways, each of which may be valid for specific purposes; or even that it is multiparadigmatic, with different paradigms either struggling against each other or ignoring each other.

Some social scientists are specifically concerned with this issue, specializing in the philosophy of social science and the theory of knowledge. Others take the basic issues for granted and concentrate on empirical research. We agree that not all social scientists need to be philosophers, and certainly most social science research would never get off the ground if we had first to resolve the fundamental questions about being and knowing. Nevertheless, some reflection on the foundations of knowledge is necessary as a preliminary to all research.

We argue that it is possible to encompass much of the field, not by imposing a single truth, but by setting certain standards of argumentation and debate while recognizing that there are differences in approaches and types of evidence. Although these do not inevitably constitute fundamentally different world-views, they are not necessarily all compatible. Researchers need to be aware of the various approaches, the differences among them, and the extent to which they can be combined.

Disputes over approaches are often presented in a rhetorical form based upon a dualist opposition of two main approaches (usually positivistic versus humanist, or quantitative versus qualitative) (Cresswell 1994). Others follow a more nuanced 'two-plus-one' approach, with two more extreme positions and a more moderate version of one of them (as in Corbetta 2003). In what follows, we have constructed some simplified ideal types of rival approaches in order to explore their inherent logic. Such devices are inescapable if we are to understand clearly the main issues at stake, although in practice social science research is more complex and different approaches are mixed in various ways. We do not claim that any social scientists follow precisely these formulations, but many of the issues discussed below provide relevant guidelines for the methodological choices we often have to make in our research.

What can we know and how? Ontologies and epistemologies in the social sciences

Usually, competing approaches in the social sciences are contrasted on (a) their *ontological* base, related to the existence of a real and objective world; (b) their *epistemological* base, related to the possibility of knowing this world and the forms this knowledge would take; (c) their *methodological* base, referring to the technical instruments that are used in order to acquire that knowledge (Corbetta 2003: 12–13).

The ontological question is about *what* we study, that is, the object of investigation. Disputes about the existence of a physical world go back to the ancients. This is not the point at issue here, since few people now bother to dispute the existence of physical objects.[1] Rather, the question is how the world fits together and how we make sense of it. The natural sciences are still home to arguments about how we identify natural phenomena, for example whether taxonomies of species really exist in nature or are the product of scientific classification. For *nominalists*, categories only exist because we arbitrarily create them. For *realists*,[2] the categories are there to be discovered. Again, we should not overstate this point. There are certain categories that are unchallenged and others that everyone accepts are the product of convention.

Almost everyone accepts a distinction between living forms and inert objects, and most accept a distinction between human beings and other animals. On the other hand, there was an argument in 2006 about the definition of a planet following the discovery of objects in the solar system larger than Pluto, which had been accepted as a planet for years. This was not an argument about facts (the existence or size of the new body), but a purely nominalist argument about definitions (Kratochwil, ch. 5, uses the same example).

Most disputes between nominalists and realists in the natural sciences are at the margins, where conventional categories and labels can be challenged on the grounds that they are misleading or that they reify what should properly be seen as concepts rather than objects. In the social sciences there are much wider differences about the degree to which the world of social phenomena is real and objective, endowed with an autonomous existence outside the human mind and independent of the interpretation given to it by the subject (Corbetta 2003). For some, the only 'real' object is the individual person, with all other units being mere artefacts. This is the basis for 'methodological individualism' and for most, but not all, rational choice approaches.[3] Most social scientists, however, use larger categories such as class, gender or ethnicity, provoking disputes about the extent to which these are real objective distinctions, the product of our own categorization, or just concepts.[4]

Epistemology is about *how* we know things. It is a branch of philosophy that addresses the question of the 'nature, sources and limits of knowledge' (Klein 2005). Knowledge here is *propositional* knowledge – distinct from 'belief' in that it requires that we give reasons for saying that something is so and can potentially convince others. Again, the question arises also in the natural sciences; but they have shared standards of evidence, argument and logic. This is not so in the social sciences, with some social scientists calling for objective evidence akin to that of the natural sciences, while others insist that other forms of knowledge are possible. For example, a common device in positive social science is to contrast 'myth', as widely shared belief, with 'reality', revealed by empirical research; the task of the social scientist is to expose this falsehood and discard what is not empirically verifiable or falsifiable. Many anthropologists, however, would reject this way of proceeding, on the grounds that myths and beliefs are data as valid as any other and that we have no business telling other people (especially in other cultures) that their construction of the world is wrong, as opposed to merely different. Less radically, many social scientists would agree that myths are important factors in themselves and their role in social behaviour is independent of whether they are true or false. Of course, social science itself can be charged with existing on myths, for example the

Table 2.1. How many ontologies and epistemologies in the social sciences?

	Positivist	Post-positivist	Interpretivist	Humanistic
Ontological issues				
Does social reality exist?	Objective; realism	Objective, critical realism	Objective and subjective as intrinsically linked	Subjective: science of the spirit
Is reality knowable?	Yes, and easy to capture	Yes, but not easy to capture	Somewhat, but not as separate from human subjectivity	No; focus on human subjectivity
Epistemological issues				
Relationship between the scholar and his/her object	Dualism: scholar and object are two separate things; inductive procedures	Knowledge is influenced by the scholar; deductive procedures	Aims at understanding subjective knowledge	No objective knowledge is possible
Forms of knowledge	Natural laws (causal)	Probabilistic law	Contextual knowledge	Empathetic knowledge

myth of rationalized institutions that – according to neoinstitutional analysis of organizations – dominates in modern societies (Meyer and Rowan 1983: 27). As in other domains, this modernist myth is challenged by other discourses stressing the post-modern character of contemporary societies.

Taking these two dimensions together, we can identify four broad approaches (Table 2.1). Again, these should not be taken as hard categories (or fixed labels), but rather as positions on a spectrum from the most positivistic to the most humanistic.

The traditional approach in *positivism* (as represented in the work of Comte, Spencer and, according to some, Durkheim)[5] is that social sciences are in many ways similar to other (physical) sciences. The world exists as an objective entity, outside of the mind of the observer, and in principle it is knowable in its entirety. The task of the researcher is to describe and analyse this reality. Positivist approaches share the assumption that, in natural as in social sciences, the researcher can be separated from the object of his/her research and therefore observe it in a neutral way and without affecting the observed object. As in the natural sciences, there are systematic rules and regularities governing the object of study, which are also amenable to empirical research. In the words of Emil Durkheim (1982: 159), 'Since the law of causality has been verified in other domains of nature and has progressively extended its authority from the physical and chemical world to the biological world, and from the latter to the psychological world, one may justifiably grant that it is likewise true for the social world.'

In *neo-positivism* and then *post-positivism*, these assumptions are relaxed. Reality is still considered to be objective (external to human minds), but it is only imperfectly knowable. The positivist trust in causal knowledge is modified by the admission that some phenomena are not governed by causal laws but, at best, by probabilistic ones. This does not represent a sharp break with the natural sciences but follows modern scientific developments (Delanty 1999). If positivism closely resembles the traditional scientific method (or Newtonian physics) in its search for regularities, post-positivism is closer to modern scientific approaches, which accept a degree of uncertainty. *Critical realist* epistemology holds that there is a real material world but that our knowledge of it is often socially conditioned and subject to challenge and reinterpretation.[6] There are mechanisms governing human affairs that may be unobserved and unobservable, but these are not therefore to be discounted. Again, this is also true in the natural sciences, where theories have often been formulated and applied before the underlying causal mechanisms have been explicated.

Similar ideas are present in *(social) constructionism* (sometimes called constructivism[7]). This approach does not, as is sometimes thought, argue that the physical world itself is the product of the imagination of the social scientist; rather, it is he/she who puts order onto it. As Hacking (1999: 33) explains: 'Social constructionists tend to maintain that classifications are not determined by how the world is but are convenient ways to represent it.' Theories are not descriptions to be evaluated by their literal correspondence to some discoverable reality, but partial ways of understanding the world, which should be compared with each other for their explanatory power (Kratochwil, ch. 5). The world is not just there to be discovered by empirical research; rather, knowledge is filtered through the theory the researcher adopts.

These ontologies and epistemologies shade into the *interpretivist* approach. Here, objective and subjective meanings are deeply intertwined. This approach also stresses the limits of mechanical laws and emphasizes human volition. Since human beings are 'meaningful' actors, scholars must aim at discovering the meanings that motivate their actions rather than relying on universal laws external to the actors. Subjective meaning is at the core of this knowledge. It is therefore impossible to understand historical events or social phenomena without looking at the perceptions individuals have of the world outside. Interpretation in various forms has long characterized the study of history as a world of actors with imperfect knowledge and complex motivations, themselves formed through complex cultural and social influences, but retaining a degree of free will and judgement.[8]

Historians also recognize that the interpretation is often dependent on the values and concerns of the historian him/herself and that reinterpretation of the past (revisionism) is often stimulated by the political agenda of the present. Such traditional forms of interpretation have been joined by a newer school of interpretivism derived from post-modernist premises (Bevir and Rhodes 2003). This school casts doubts on the epistemological constants of much social science, which it sees as unduly influenced by modernist assumptions about order, causation and progress (themselves in turn derived from nineteenth-century natural science). Interpretation works at two levels. The world can be understood not as an objective reality, but as a series of interpretations that people within society give of their position; the social scientist, in turn, interprets these interpretations. In a further reflexive turn, social scientists' interpretations feed back to the people through literature and media, influencing them yet again in what Giddens (1976) calls the 'double hermeneutic'. This is one reason why relationships that may have held in the past might not hold in the future (Hay 2002).

The *humanistic* approaches shift the emphasis further towards the subjective. In this perspective, what distinguishes human science from natural sciences is that human behaviour is always filtered by the subjective understandings of external reality on the part of the people being studied and the researcher him/herself. Social science is therefore, in the often-quoted definition proposed by Clifford Geertz (1973: 5), 'Not an experimental science in search of laws but an interpretative science in search of meaning'. In the most radical versions of this approach, reality does not exist beyond the (relative and partial) images the various actors have of it. Knowing the reality is therefore impossible, and scholars should focus on the meaning through empathetic knowledge.

How many methodologies in the social sciences?

The methodological question refers to the instruments and techniques we use to acquire knowledge. At one level, this is independent of the ontological and epistemological questions just discussed, since there are multiple ways of acquiring each type of knowledge. In practice, they tend to be linked, since positivistic social science lends itself naturally to 'hard' methods, seeking unambiguous data, concrete evidence and rules and regularities, while more interpretive approaches require 'softer' methods allowing for ambiguity and contingency and recognizing the interplay between the researcher and the object of research (but see below). All these differences are linked with the differing final scope of the research.

In the positivist tradition, research aims at singling out causal explanations, on the assumption of a cause–effect relationship between variables (see Héritier, ch. 4). Researchers aim at an explanation that is structural and context-free, allowing generalization and the discovery of universal laws of behaviour. Such laws may be discovered in two ways. The *inductive* approach, which is associated with pragmatism or behaviourism (Hay 2002), involves deriving generalizations from specific observations in a large number of cases. Positivists in the more scientific tradition, however, would insist that one start with a theory, which then generates hypotheses (an expected state of affairs) which are then subjected to the test of hard facts and only accepted if they survive the ordeal (see Héritier, ch. 4).[9] This is the *hypothetico-deductive* (deductive-empirical) method,[10] in which the study of social reality utilizes the conceptual framework, techniques of observation and measurement, instruments of mathematical analysis and procedures of inference of the natural sciences (Corbetta 2003: 13). Since it is rarely possible in the social sciences to conduct experiments, large datasets and statistical analyses are used in order to identify and isolate causes and effects in a rigorous manner and arrive at a single explanation. This is not to say that positivists use only quantitative methods; but where they use other (qualitative) methods, they follow the same logic of inference. The main aim is 'identifying, assessing and eliminating rival explanations' (Collier, Brady and Seawright 2004a: 229).

By contrast, interpretive/qualitative research aims at understanding events by discovering the meanings human beings attribute to their behaviour and the external world. The focus is not on discovering laws about causal relationships between variables, but on understanding human nature, including the diversity of societies and cultures. More specifically, following Weber, this type of social science aims at understanding (*verstehen*) the motivations that lie behind human behaviour, a matter that cannot be reduced to any predefined element but must be placed within a cultural perspective, where culture denotes a web of shared meanings and values (see della Porta, ch. 11, and Keating, ch. 6). Theory is important, but is not always established prior to the research as in the deductive-empirical approach. In the form of 'grounded theory', it may be built up in the course of the research, but then be available for further research and the study of other cases. Cases are not broken down into variables but considered as interdependent wholes; generalization is achieved by assigning cases to classes and approximating them to ideal types. Context is considered as most important since research on human activity must consider an individual's situational self-interpretation (Flyvbjerg 2001: 47). Predictability is impossible since human beings change in time and space and, in the words of Bourdieu (1977: 109), 'practice has a logic, which is not that of logic'. The outcome of the research then takes the form of specific explanations of cases, but also of refined concepts for the analysis of future cases.

This type of research, like the positivist approach, seeks explanations for social outcomes but does not expect to derive these from universal rules. Rather, explanation comes from the interpretation of people's motives for their actions. Ferejohn (2004: 146) clarifies this distinction by contrasting 'externalist' and 'internalist' explanations:

Externalists explain action by pointing to its causes; internalists explain action by showing it as justified or best from an agent's perspective. Externalist explanations are positivist and predictive; internalist explanations are normative or hermeneutic. Externalists tend to call themselves political scientists; internalists, political theorists. And, both externalists and internalists agree, if they agree on little else, that they are engaged in different enterprises.

Sometimes this difference is presented as a contrast between quantitative (positivist) and qualitative (interpretive) methods (Creswell 1994; Corbetta 2003). This is a source of considerable confusion, conflating ontology and epistemology on the one hand with methods and methodology on the other. The quantitative method refers to sophisticated data analysis using large numbers; there is certainly a stream in social science that is both positivist and quantitative in approach. Brady, Collier and Seawright (2004) describe a 'mainstream quantitative method' as an approach based upon the use of regression analysis and related techniques aiming at measuring causal inference; but note that work in the positivist tradition also makes use of non-quantitative material such as case studies, paired comparisons, interview records and even ethnographic approaches in field research and interpretation. King, Keohane and Verba (1994), leading exponents of the positivist approach, accept that qualitative methods may be used as a supplement to quantitative methods as long as they follow the same logic. The chapters in Brady and Collier (2004) argue that qualitative methods can tackle questions that quantitative methods cannot encompass, but remain within the same positivist epistemological framework. Even participant observation is often used within 'theory-driven' research designs (Lichterman 2002). Laitin (2003) likewise admits to the validity of narrative approaches but only as part of a tri-partite approach in conjunction with statistics and formal modelling. For Laitin, narratives can provide plausibility tests for formal models, mechanisms that link dependent and independent variables, and ideas for searching for new specifications of variables that have yet to be modelled.

There is, however, another rather different, more specific meaning often given to the term qualitative methods, linked to the interpretive approach derived from ethnography and anthropology and which has now arrived in other areas of the social sciences. As defined by Denzin and Lincoln (2000: 3):

Qualitative research is a situated activity that locates the observer in the world. It consists of a set of interpretive practices that make the world visible. These practices transform the world. They turn the world into a series of representations, including field notes, interviews, conversations, photographs, recordings and memos to the self. At this level, qualitative research involves an interpretive, naturalistic approach to the world. This means that qualitative researchers study things in their natural settings, attempting to make sense of, or to interpret, phenomena in terms of the meanings people bring to them.

Favoured methods for this are unstructured interviews, focus groups, textual analysis and content analysis (see Bray, ch. 15). However, just as positivists may make use of interviews, case studies and even participant observation, so interpretivists sometimes use quantitative techniques. Sophisticated computer software is available for analysis of the content of speech and texts to identify key words, patterns of symbols, codes and references. This shows once again that we should not confuse issues of epistemology with those of methodology or research technique.

From methodology to method

It would therefore be a great simplification to say that there is a distinction between quantitative and qualitative methods corresponding to the distinction between positivist and interpretivist epistemologies. Methods are no more than ways of acquiring data. Questions about methods do, however, come together with epistemology and theory in discussions about *methodology*, which refers to the way in which methods are used. Here we face choices pointing in the direction of more or less formally structured approaches and 'harder' or 'softer' methods.[11] To explore them, we first present a simplified set of choices to be made in research design and in method selection (see also della Porta, ch. 11).

The first choice is in the framing of the research question. Positivists will usually start with a hypothesis deductively derived from theory and previous knowledge. Typically, this will postulate some expected state of affairs or causal relationship and be empirically falsifiable. By this we do not mean that it is actually false, merely that the conditions under which it can be rejected are specified. If it is not falsified, then it can be taken as true, not only for the cases in question but for all cases with the same characteristics. Interpretivists (or qualitative researchers in the restricted sense) work more inductively, build up the research question in the course of the research and are prepared to modify the design while the research is in progress. There is thus no clear time distinction between the research design and its implementation, as they are interlinked with continuous feedbacks. Positivists take care to operationalize their concepts and hypotheses in scientific and general terms, while interpretivists let the concepts emerge from the work itself.

Another difference refers to the number of cases analysed, as well as the criteria for selecting them. Positivists will often choose a large number of cases to achieve the maximum generalizability and capture most sources of variation. Alternatively, they will choose a small number of cases, but rigorously select them in such a way that their differences can be specified precisely. In J. S. Mill's (1974) classic formulation, two cases should be chosen such that they share only one attribute in common, or so that they differ in only one attribute. In this approach, numbers are not necessarily used, and cases can be few: the logic is, however, the approximation to a statistical type of analysis, with concerns with (statistical) representativity, validity and reliability. Non-quantitative techniques must thus follow the same logical structure and rules for scientific inference (King, Keohane and Verba 1994).[12] Interpretivists, on the other hand, will select cases on the basis of their inherent interest (for example, paradigmatic cases), not because they are typical of a category but for what they tell us about complex social processes.

Positivists usually employ the language of variables. That is, they are not interested in cases as such, but in the properties of those cases that cause them to differ. Since they are concerned with general or universal laws, they want to know what factors cause which outcomes in social life, for example what is the causal relationship between economic growth and democratization. This requires that they develop an operational definition of economic growth and

cause–effaction relationships

of democratization and ways of measuring them. These then become the variables in the analysis, with economic growth as the 'independent' or causal variable and democratization as the 'dependent' or caused variable. Of course, it is rarely the case that one independent variable will everywhere and always produce the same effects on the dependent variable, but this merely means that more variables need to be added so that, eventually, all variation is accounted for. In the words of Przeworski and Teune (1970), the aim is ultimately to 'eliminate proper names' – that is, to account for social processes by reference to general rules without talking about individual cases, since these will all be accounted for within the general rules (Corbetta 2003). Context for these social scientists merely consists of variables that have yet to be specified adequately (Laitin 2003).

Neo-positivist approaches have relaxed the assumption that knowledge is context-free and that the same relationships among variables will hold everywhere and at all times. Instead, there is more emphasis on the particular and the local, and on the way in which factors may combine in different circumstances. To capture this contextual effect, researchers have increasingly resorted to the idea of institutions as bearers of distinct patterns of incentives and sanctions, and on the way that decisions taken at one time constrain what can be done later. These institutional factors may be expressed in the form of variables, but an important role is played by comparative study of a small number of cases, where the variation is the institutional structure and its historical evolution (see Steinmo, ch. 7). Neo-positivists seek to express the effect of context in the form of institutional structures and try to avoid the concept of culture as impossible to operationalize and inimical to general theorizing. Others, however, have moved from institutions into culture, providing a bridge between interpretivist and positivist approaches (see Keating, ch. 6).

Interpretive analyses keep a holistic focus, emphasizing cases (which could be an individual, a community or other social collectivity) as complex entities (della Porta, ch. 11) and stressing the importance of context. Concepts are orientative and can be improved during the research. The presentation of the data is usually in the form of thick narratives, with excerpts from texts (interviews, documents and ethnographic notes) presented as illustration. The assumption of mutual influence among the many factors at work in any case discourages any attempt to reason about causes and effects or to generalize. Understanding reality implies 'immersing ourselves in information about the actors in question, and using both empathy and imagination to construct credible accounts of their senses of identity' (Smith 2004: 43). In such an enterprise, methods generally labelled as qualitative – such as interpretative textual analyses, ethnographic fieldwork, biographical studies or participant observation – are key (see Bray, ch. 15).

Another difference is in the relationship of the researcher to the research object: how much participation is permissible in the situation to be observed? How much of a stranger should the researcher be? And how sympathetic towards the point of view of the object of his/her research? The positivist sets up a complete separation between the observer and what is observed, taking care not to 'contaminate' the research by becoming part of it. S/he will prefer standardized questionnaires and interview schedules, anonymized surveys, rigorous coding of responses and, often, quantitative techniques. The interpretivist will tend, on the contrary, to immerse him/herself in the situation to be studied, to empathize with the population and to see things from their perspective. Anthropologists spend long periods in the field seeking to gain an inside knowledge. The sociology of intervention (as pioneered by Alain Touraine) involves the researchers working with social movements and the activists they study in a common path, with the aim of helping the latter to interpret the situation and engaging in mutual learning. In the most radical understanding, all statements about the external world have such strong subjective elements that no shared observation can exist. The acknowledgement of the role of interactions between researchers and the object of the research poses many ethical issues; among others, whom to accept as a sponsor, how much to reveal about the research to the interviewees, how to protect their privacy, how to compensate them for their collaboration, how to keep them informed about the results of the research and how to avoid manipulation.

Another critical question that differentiates approaches concerns value-neutrality. In the positivist perspective, the researcher brings no normative, ideological or political perspectives to bear on the research. S/he is merely seeking the unadorned truth. Critics would argue that this often conceals a normative agenda and indeed that the founding assumptions of positivism themselves reflect a value choice.[13] Positivists counter that, if this is the case, then all such normative tendencies should be declared in advance. Normative work as such is, according to this perspective, a separate endeavour, which belongs in the field of ethical philosophy. Interpretivists would tend not to make such a sharp distinction between empirical and normative work; taken to its fullest, this approach denies the distinction between facts and values altogether. More moderate versions argue that most language and speech acts have both descriptive and normative elements within them, that concepts themselves usually have some normative content, and that the researcher should be aware of this. Recently, there have been conscious efforts to pull

Table 2.2. How many methodologies in the social sciences?

	Positivist	Post-positivist	Interpretivist	Humanistic
Which methodology?	Empiricist, aiming at knowing the reality	Mainly empiricist, recognizing context	Relative focus on meanings, context	Focus on values, meaning and purposes
Which method/s?	Imitating the natural method (experiments, mathematical models, statistical analysis)	Based upon approximations to the natural method (experiments, statistical analysis, quantitative interviews)	Seeking meaning (textual analysis, discourse analysis)	Empathetic interactions between researchers and object of research

together normative work derived from philosophy with empirical research (see Bauböck, ch. 3). While in one sense new, this also represents a return to the classical era of social thought. Flyvbjerg (2001) has controversially suggested that, since the social sciences can never gain the explanatory power of the natural sciences because of the nature of the world, they should return to this earlier age and seek to provide reflexive analysis and discussions of values and interests aimed at praxis, that is, to contribute to the realization of a better society. This in turn has sparked some critical rejoinders (Laitin 2003).

Returning to our fourfold classification, and with the caveats already mentioned, we can summarize some main methodological assumptions (Table 2.2).

How many ways to knowledge?

How exclusive must be our methodological choices? Should we leave space for epistemological anarchism, and trust exchanges with scholars working within the other 'paradigm'? Even switching between the two? Or is the building of knowledge only possible within one paradigm? Is the combination of approaches/methods useful to overcome the limits of each methodology? Or would it risk undermining the soundness of the empirical results?

Three approaches to these issues can be singled out in the social sciences:

(a) *Paradigmatic, exclusive approach.* In the light of Kuhn's conception of the role of paradigm, some social scientists aim at a paradigmatic science, where only one paradigm is considered as the right one, combining theory, methods and standards together, usually in an inextricable mixture (Kuhn 1962: 109). Those who see the social sciences as paradigmatic stress the importance of converging on (or imposing) one single way to knowledge.

(b) *Anarchist, hyper-pluralistic approach.* At the other extreme, there is an 'inclusive' position that combines scepticism about a 'true' knowledge with enthusiasm for experimentation with different paths to knowledge. Those who subscribe to this position to various extents support Feyerabend's anarchism and his belief that:

the world we want to explore is a largely unknown entity. We must therefore keep our options open . . . Epistemological prescriptions may look splendid when compared with other epistemological prescriptions . . . but how can we guarantee that they are the best way to discover, not just a few isolated 'facts', but also some deep-lying secrets of nature? (Feyerabend 1975: 20).

(c) *The search for commensurable knowledge.* Between those two extremes, there are positions that admit the differences in the paths to knowledge and deny the existence of a 'better one', but still aim at rendering differences compatible.

Within this third perspective – which we tend to follow in this volume – it is important to compare the advantages and disadvantages of each method and methodology but also be aware that not all are compatible. Goals that cannot be maximized at the same time include seeking precise communication as opposed to fertility in the application of concepts, parsimonious explanations as opposed to thick descriptions, and generalizability as opposed to simplicity (Collier, Brady and Seawright 2004a: 222). It may therefore be necessary to trade off one advantage against another. This choice will be made on the basis of the fundamental question the researcher is trying to answer – for example, whether he/she is trying to explain a particular case; to gain nomothetic knowledge (discovering general rules); or seeking ways to achieve a better society. It depends on the preferences of the researcher, and on the sorts of data that are available, including reliable statistical data or detailed field data requiring long immersion in the field.

The choice of approach is linked to another choice in social science research: whether to start with a theory, a method or a problem. Those aiming at a paradigmatic social science will often start with a theory, seeking to test it with a view to proving, disproving or modifying it and so contributing to universal knowledge. This is often tied to a particular methodology to allow studies to be reproduced and compared. Those interested in a specific problem, on the other hand, will tend to look for the method and approach that seems to offer more by way of understanding of the case. Exponents of the first approach are accused of studying methods for their own sake and choosing only issues that are amenable to that method – summed up in the old adage that if the only tool you have is a hammer, every problem starts to look like a nail (Green and Shapiro 1994; Shapiro 2004). Those who focus on problems, in contrast, are accused of adding nothing to the writings of historians and journalists (Shapiro, Smith and Masoud 2004a).

Ways of combining knowledge can be characterized as synthesis, triangulation, multiple perspectives and cross-fertilization. Synthesis involves merging elements of different approaches into a single whole and can be done at various levels. Synthesizing different epistemologies is virtually impossible, since they rest on different assumptions about social reality and knowledge. Methodologies may be easier to synthesize since, as we have seen, they are not necessarily tied to specific epistemological assumptions. Techniques and methods are most easily combined since, as we have noted, many of them can be adapted to different research purposes. So comparative history and historical institutionalism have adopted and adapted techniques from comparative politics, history and sociology to gain new insight into processes of change.

Triangulation is about using different research methods to complement one another. Again, it is difficult to triangulate distinct epistemologies, easier with methodologies and very common with methods. So positivists can incorporate interviews and textual analysis into their research designs, although using these as hard data rather than in the manner of interpretivists. Case studies are frequently used to complement large-N statistical analyses as ways of opening the 'black box' of explanation (see Héritier, ch. 4). Survey research may be complemented by ethnographic work, which explores the way in which questions are understood and the meanings of the responses.

Multiple perspectives implies that a situation may have more than one interpretation according to how we view it. De Tocqueville (1999) wrote that in his life he had met theorists who believed that events in the world owed everything to general causes, and practical people who imagined that daily events and actions were those that moved the world – he added that both were mistaken. Allison's (1971) study of the Cuban Missile Crisis examined the same events using different frames to come up with different explanations.

It has been said that everyone is born either an Aristotelian or a Platonist (Hacking 1999: 84), yet hardly any social scientist now is a naïve empiricist who believes that the world represents itself to us without interpretation.

Conversely, nobody in mainstream social science denies the existence of the physical world or maintains that reality is entirely subjective and in our minds. This encourages a cross-fertilization in a large middle ground.

Concepts often arise in the social sciences by different tracks, derived from slightly different starting points but ending in similar places. For example, the concept of 'framing', widely used in policy analysis to indicate the different ways in which people will define and conceptualize a policy issue or problem, can be derived from an anti-positivist and interpretivist position (Fischer 2003) but also from a positivist one. It has been used in social movement research since long before the so-called 'cultural turn' by scholars interested in strategic action by collective actors (such as David Snow), but also by others more interested in the micro-dynamics of cognition (such as William Gamson). In all cases, the idea is that situations can be interpreted differently and presented differently to evoke different reactions from the same set of facts. The differences are in exactly how much weight is given to the objective world and how much to its interpretation. The concept of culture, much used by interpretivists, is rejected by positivists and rational choice analysts but then often brought back in as normative institutionalism or shared meanings and understandings that underpin policy communities (see Keating, ch. 6). Context is central to ethnographic and interpretivist approaches, where it is deeply textured and rich, but is also used in neoinstitutionalist analysis and even features in the hardest regression analyses (where difficult whole cases are expressed as dummy variables). New institutionalism has come into the social sciences through several doors: in political science, where it is a response to decontextualized rational choice approaches; in sociology, where it draws on organizational theory; and in economics, where it draws on economic sociology. The result is a set of concepts that are very similar but, because of their distinct origins and vocabulary, never quite identical.

There is also a large crossover in ways of developing and using theory. As mentioned, *grounded theory* does not start with a deductively produced hypothesis but with experience; nevertheless, it does then go on to build up general theory of wider applicability. It owes a lot to the American pragmatist tradition, with roots in a 'realist' ontology, but it has been extended and elaborated in more interpretivist approaches. Meanwhile, in the United States, that same realist ontology has evolved into varieties of rational choice approaches, based supposedly on the solid foundation of the individual person, but in practice using an ideal-type construct and models derived from deductive reasoning. Indeed, rational choice approaches themselves seem to be compatible both with determinism (on the assumption that preferences are knowable and outcomes predictable from individual self-maximization) and with free will (in that the individual does choose). A great deal of social science proceeds by going back and forth between theory and cases, using the one to develop and deepen understanding of the other.

Sometimes the cross-fertilization is explicitly acknowledged. In a contribution to a volume significantly titled *Rethinking Social Inquiry. Diverse Tools, Shared Standards*, Collier, Seawright and Munck (2004) stress the importance of good theories and empirical methods, but also appreciate the contribution of interpretive work to concept formation and fine-grained description. Many of the classic works in sociology and political science have taken the form of interpretive case studies from which general theories have been developed by example, replication and extension (Van Langenhove 2007). Examples are Alexis de Tocqueville's *De la démocracie en Amérique* and *L'ancien régime et la révolution*, but also more recent historical sociology in the school of Barrington Moore Jr. Qualitative analysis has also been used to highlight causal effects by focusing on striking cases where the impact is clearest and the detailed mechanisms can be examined. In this way, social scientists can proceed from correlation, where the same causes are associated with the same effects, to explanations of why and how.

Influences come not only from within the discipline but also from other areas of science. Newtonian physics, with its search for laws and constants, has been an inspiration for positivist social science, while its opponents have drawn attention to the uncertainties underlying modern physics and the huge epistemological assumptions among which scientists have to choose (such as the existence of one or parallel universes). Evolutionary biology now provides inspiration for historical institutionalists (see Steinmo, ch. 7).[14] Rational choice scholars are inspired by neoclassical economists, while institutional economists learn from sociology. History long provided the model and tools for the study of politics in Britain, while law was its basis in many European countries. After a period in which the social sciences insisted on their own specificity, many scholars are now turning back to history, while developments in legal scholarship (including law in context, critical legal theory and constitutionalism) are linking back to concerns in political science and sociology. Literature has helped inspire the 'sociological imagination' by portraying dramatic situations that need to be explained and resolved and drawing attention to the conflicts within the individual mind.

Cross-fertilization, however, is inhibited by the existence or closing up of research communities, groups of scholars in regular contact and discussion, who may define their common interest by substantive topic, methodology, or both (Sil 2004). These are reified and perpetuated by processes which them-selves are worthy of sociological analysis, including the existence of journals wedded to particular approaches, the orientation of individual departments or sections, patterns of graduate supervision and discipleship, routinized assessment procedures, and routes to career advancement. When research communities are defined both by substantive topic and by method, barriers may be very high and knowledge remain limited to the problems each method is best fit to tackle, secluded from external stimuli and challenges. On the other hand, when barriers are more fluid, the problem emerges of the commensu-rability of different forms of knowledge, as well as 'fuzzy' and ill-defined stan-dards (Ruggie 1998). This makes it all the more important for researchers to know the field and to be able to compare standards and arguments with those from different communities. This is what Sil (2004) suggests under the label of eclecticism, where problems of incommensurability are not absolute and comparisons can be made across fields to the advantage of both empirical knowledge and theoretical innovation.

Further problems are caused by the tendency for concepts or expressions to become fashionable and then stretched beyond their original or indeed any useful meaning. In recent years, for example, the use of the word 'governance' has exploded. For some scholars, this is a specific phenomenon distinct from government and capable of operationalization, but for others it is used inter-changeably with government. Still others see it as less than government, refer-ring to a specific way of governing through networks, alongside traditional institutional government. Others see it as a broader category of social regula-tion, of which government is a subcategory. Some see it as an alternative to government – that we are moving from a world of government to one of gov-ernance. 'Construction' or 'social construction' are similarly stretched to cover almost everything (Hacking 1999) as, for a while, was the term 'invention'. Discourse analysis is sometimes used as a specific methodology, with its own ontology (speech acts themselves) and its own techniques; at other times it is applied to any technique that involves using texts and interviews. Sometimes the blame for all this confusion lies with scholars thinking that they need to get inside the current paradigm in order to make their point; often it is merely a matter of publishers looking for a trendy title.

Of course, not everything is methodologically healthy, and the label of eclec-ticism should not be used to justify hybrids that violate, if not rules, at least codes of conduct of what we have presented here as main approaches. Although the triangulation of various methods and methodologies within the same research project often increases reliability and improves our understanding, the different parts of the enterprise must respect internal coherence. If an 'eclectic knowledge' of qualitative and quantitative techniques enriches a researcher's curriculum, human limits, together with the increasing sophistication of most qualitative and quantitative techniques, impose some specialization. The following chapters offer differing approaches in ontology, epistemology and methodology but also indicate points of commonality and overlap.

NOTES

1 This is either because they accept the material world, or because it is a question that cannot and need not be answered and is therefore futile to debate.

2 This is one of the terms in social science that has a multiplicity of meanings. In international relations it has a rather different meaning from the one given here (see Kratochwil, ch. 5).

3 In fact, even the individualist solution, reducing the ontology to the individual human being, does not answer this question definitively, as one might argue that even the self-regarding rational individual is an artefact of social science methodology and not something that occurs naturally, since the original condition of human beings is the group. This is argued in Adam Ferguson's (1966) Enlightenment classic, *Essay on the History of Civil Society*, of 1767.

4 A classic example of this is the case of gender. While nobody denies the existence of sexual differences, there is a big dispute over the category of gender, which includes a lot of other attributes and roles which have been mapped onto sex differences.

5 Van Langenhove (2007) claims that late twentieth-century social scientists have often portrayed the classical sociologists as more simplistically positivist than they really were.

6 Critical realism has been defined as 'a philosophical view of science and/or theology which asserts that our knowledge of the world refers to the-way-things-really-are, but in a partial fashion which will necessarily be revised as that knowledge develops'. Christopher Southgate, www.meta-library.net/.

7 For a discussion of the difference, see Hacking (1999: 47–9). He recommends leaving the term 'constructivism' to the mathematicians.

8 This taps into a long-standing division in philosophy between determinists and those emphasizing free will. While for St Augustine and John Calvin, determinism was a matter of divine selection, for modern social scientists it is a matter either of genetic programming, social conditioning or a predictable response to institutional incentives. Believers in free will cannot by definition be certain about how another actor will behave, no matter what constraints they are under.

9 In practice, social scientists often go back and forth between inductive and theory-driven approaches as they seek to frame their projects.

10 This is not to be confused with the pure deductive method, in which conclusions are derived from premises by pure reasoning, with no empirical research involved. Héritier (ch.4) explains the link between induction and deduction in the positivist tradition.

11 These terms are not used in a value-laden way to suggest that one is better than the other. Hard methods correspond to the view that social science can be made to resemble the physical sciences; soft methods to the view that social reality is more elusive.

12 For example, case studies can be accepted either to disconfirm a hypothesis (since it only takes one case to disprove a rule) or as a basis for formulating hypotheses for general testing. They are not valuable in themselves.

13 This is perhaps most obviously so in rational choice analysis, which claims a strictly positivist basis but includes some strong assumptions and tends to lead to highly normative conclusions.

14 This is not to say that the unity of the natural and social sciences can thereby be restored, as many people insist that the specificity of the latter is that the objects of study are endowed with consciousness and can act on their own volition.

3 Normative political theory and empirical research

Rainer Bauböck

Introduction

Normative theory and empirical research have become separate branches of social science. Yet, as I will suggest, empirical research can be guided by normative theory; and normative theory can be improved by empirical research. This is not always well done. Empirical researchers resort too often to *ad hoc* normative assumptions. On the other side, some theorists studying social problems still rely on hypothetical arguments in spite of available empirical evidence, while others interpret empirical research naïvely without the necessary critical knowledge (Favell and Modood 2003).

We should not, moreover, erase the difference altogether. Normative problems can never be fully resolved through analytical explanation or hermeneutical interpretation, nor can deep disagreement within normative theory be overcome by testing the empirical presuppositions. The goal of a unified political theory is not merely illusory but profoundly misunderstands the nature of this enterprise. Normative political theory mirrors political disagreements among citizens that cannot be resolved through conceptual analysis nor by inference from empirical evidence, but only through politics itself. The contribution of political theory to political debates is not to settle disputes but to clarify arguments and to highlight the values involved in political choices. Such theory should be supported by social science research to specify the real-world conditions and consequences of the choices that its normative propositions advocate.

The first section of this chapter argues that developments within the liberal mainstream of normative theory have prepared the ground for a rapprochement by comparing political institutions in different cultural and historical contexts. The second part explains the specific salience of normative questions within political science (understood as the study of power relations) and explores how the divide between normative theory, on the one hand, and explanatory models and historical perspectives, on the other, looks from both sides. The third part illustrates how a certain normative question can guide the search for empirical methodologies and data. I conclude with reflections on the ethical challenges of normative theory that arise from crossing the boundaries between academic argument and political intervention.

The normative (re)turn in political theory

What is normative political theory? Instead of offering a definition, it is more useful to describe it as an academic discipline that uses specific modes of argument in order to address a specific set of questions.

Ways of 'doing normative theory' vary greatly, from narrative styles to techniques borrowed from analytical philosophy. Their common ground is that prescriptive or evaluative statements are treated as sets of *propositions* that must be internally consistent and must be defended against opposing views, rather than as subjective *opinions* whose validity cannot be established through argument.

Since its origins in Ancient Greece, the core questions of the discipline have been about the common good realized through political community, the legitimacy of political authority, the rights and freedoms of those living under such authority and the nature and binding force of political obligations. Until the rise of sociology as a distinct discipline during the nineteenth century, nearly all important works in political theory combined normative and empirical claims. Take Aristotle: 'Our purpose is to consider what form of political community is best of all for those who are most able to realize their ideal in life. We must therefore examine not only this but other constitutions, both such as actually exist in well-governed states, and any theoretical forms which are held in esteem, so that what is good and useful may be brought to light' (Aristotle 1999, book II.1: 30–1). The goal to discover the best form of government is a normative one, but in order to find it, we need comparative political science.[1]

In the early twentieth century, the rise of positivism in law and in the social sciences shrank the space for normative political theory and prepared the ground for empirically oriented, behaviouralist political science and for theoretical paradigms whose explicit goal was to explain social and political facts without making value judgements. Within political science, normative theories were often regarded as a legacy of the past, to be studied by the subdiscipline of history of ideas. The turning point in this development was John Rawls' *A Theory of Justice* in 1971, which oriented normative political theory towards the ongoing task of justifying or criticizing political institutions within liberal democratic societies. The debate about social justice in the 1970s and 1980s spilled over into neighbouring disciplines, especially into economics, where some of Rawls' ideas about just distributions were tested empirically (Frohlich and Oppenheimer 1992). Among political theorists, the initial reaction was much more focused on philosophical foundations than on empirical applications (Nozick 1974; Sandel 1982). In the American mainstream, these debates firmly re-established normative theory as a core field within political science.

European developments have gradually converged with American ones. In Germany, the so-called positivism dispute (*Positivismusstreit*) of the 1960s divided sociologists between critical rationalists and the followers of the Frankfurt school represented by Theodor W. Adorno, Max Horkheimer and Jürgen Habermas. The former camp defended Karl Popper's view that, like all other scientific theories, social science theories must be built around empirically falsifiable hypotheses. The Frankfurt school highlighted instead the inescapability of value judgements in social science and urged theorists to adopt a critical perspective focusing on the basic structures of late capitalist societies. Jürgen Habermas, who initially represented the second generation of the Frankfurt school, subsequently developed a synthetic theory of communicative action (1981) that served as a foundation for his later move towards moral philosophy (1983) and political and legal theory (1992). Today, Habermasian and Rawlsian perspectives are used as alternative theoretical frameworks by normative theorists on both sides of the Atlantic.

An institutionalist and contextualist turn

In the 1990s, when the debate about principles and their philosophical foundations appeared to have reached a dead end, bridges across the normative–empirical divide were built by political theorists who turned towards what can be properly called applied normative theory. An institutionalist focus had already been announced in Rawls' proclamation that 'justice is the first virtue of social institutions' (Rawls 1971: 1), which shifted the emphasis away from moral philosophies that consider justice primarily as a virtue of individual human actions. Yet Rawlsian theory was constructed deductively and remained at a very general level when describing social and political institutions. The new institutionalist approaches in normative theory were more concerned with examining actual institutional arrangements in liberal democracies, and they attempted to distil in an inductive manner generalizable norms from these institutions' responses to new challenges.

This institutionalist turn led naturally to stronger attention to contextual variation.[2] In the past, the only contextual consideration for prescriptive theories of justice and democracy had often been the level of economic development; now, much more attention was paid to historical traditions and culturally specific norms and world-views. In his late writings, Rawls distinguished between conceptions of justice in liberal and in decent non-liberal societies (Rawls 1993, 1999). Yet the new applied normative theories were not so much inspired by Rawls' shifting interpretations of his own theory as by perceived limitations of his approach. Examining some important contributions of the 1990s, we can see how they focus on questions that Rawls had put aside or neglected. I will list here four such themes that have become prominent in post-Rawlsian liberal egalitarian theory.

Non-ideal theory

Rawls deliberately started with 'ideal theory', that is, conditions where everybody fully complies with what justice requires.[3] He argued that one first needs to establish what justice means under ideal conditions before moving to problems that arise from partial compliance, such as criminal and compensatory justice or just wars (Rawls 1971: 8). This priority for ideal theory meant that the controversies of the 1970s and 1980s were about themes that explanatory political theorists, who focus on non-ideal worlds, found largely irrelevant. Rawls' proposal for a strict sequence between the tasks of ideal and non-ideal theory was challenged by Joseph Carens (1996), who argued for alternating between idealistic and realistic approaches. The former respond to the question: 'what does justice require?', and may lead to a fundamental critique of basic institutions. Carens suggests, for example, that from a global perspective, citizenship in the modern state system is like a feudal status of inherited privilege or disadvantage and thus incompatible with liberal ideals of equal dignity and opportunity. In contrast, realistic approaches respond to the question: 'what ought we to do, all things considered?' In order to answer this latter question, many circumstances must be accepted as given. These two lines of normative inquiry should not be artificially separated from each other. When considering a controversial theme, such as a just immigration policy, the theorist should instead move back and forth between them in an attempt to unsettle convictions articulated at either level.

Global justice

Rawls starts with an account of domestic justice and moves from there towards a much thinner conception of international justice that yields a short list of universal human rights (Rawls 1999). In this view, humanitarian concerns about the basic needs and rights of members of other societies are essentially different from egalitarian justice among citizens living under a common government (see also Dworkin 2000; Nagel 2005). A number of critics have rejected this two-stage approach, insisting that liberalism requires extending equal respect and concern to human beings globally (Beitz 1979; Pogge 1988). At first glance, it seems that this critique takes a step away from realistic approaches by designing principles of global justice addressed to a world government that simply does not exist. Yet the increasing interdependence of societies and density of political and economic institutions involved in transnational governance may also create institutional preconditions for addressing problems of global justice. Some theorists argue that global justice requires not merely redistribution across states but also democratic legitimacy for political decisions with global impact (Held 1995; Held and Archibugi 1995). In response to charges of idealism, arguments for distributive justice as well as for democratic accountability on a global scale have shifted from an assertion of principle to empirically grounded advocacy of reform.

Closed societies

Rawls had assumed that societies were organized as sovereign states, and that citizens lived their whole lives within the territorial borders. This counterfactual assumption enabled Rawls to model such societies as intergenerational schemes of co-operation. When he later addressed the problem of immigration, he framed it again as a question of international justice between states rather than of global justice among individuals. The implication is that liberal states are free to restrict immigration to preserve their public culture and to prevent some peoples' 'mak[ing] up for their irresponsibility in caring for their land and its natural resources . . . by migrating into other people's territory without their consent' (Rawls 1999: 39). This view contrasts sharply with arguments for open borders as a requirement of liberal justice (see Carens 1987; Bader 2005). One such argument regards migration as a possible substitute for global redistribution: 'If we cannot move enough money to where the needy people are, then we will have to count on moving as many of the needy people as possible to where the money is' (Goodin 1992: 8). Others argue instead that free movement is a basic liberty – constraints on which need to be justified also to would-be immigrants – yet accept that economically motivated migration may be restricted in order to preserve domestic conditions for democratic citizenship and social justice (Bauböck 1997). The former argument thus defends free movement as a means of flattening disparities between countries, whereas for the latter reduced disparities are a condition for free movement. If both were right, they might form a virtuous circle, with open borders creating conditions under which migration would no longer be a problem. Yet this rather sanguine view cannot be supported merely by theoretical speculation without studying the economic and political impact of migration on societies of origin and of destination, the capacity of states to regulate migration as well as the different types of admission claims raised by refugees, family reunification and economic immigration.

Self-determination and minority rights

Rawls' theory places great value on collective self-government of independe peoples (Macedo 2005). This explains his reluctance to challenge the syst of sovereign states, to require equal opportunities and redistribution acr borders, or to consider free movement as at least potentially a universal rig Even if one accepts all these constraints on the scope of justice, there remai the puzzling question of who are the peoples that have a right to govern then selves. Although Rawls distinguishes peoples from states in their moral natur and interests, he assumes that the borders of peoples and states coincide. I the real world, however, territorial borders and national identities are often contested. Self-determination struggles are endemic, not only in authoritarian regimes but also in liberal states with large national or indigenous minorities. The breakup of socialist federations in the early 1990s triggered a wave of normative theories of minority rights and secession. For libertarians, the right to secede and the autonomy of cultural minorities follows simply from defending the freedom of association against state power (Beran 1984; Kukathas 1992; Gauthier 1994). Against these, liberal egalitarians have claimed that democratic government needs territorial integrity and that secession is therefore a strictly remedial right, justified only in response to severe grievances of an oppressed group (Buchanan 1991). A third group are liberal nationalists. They consider national self-determination important because membership in a nation provides individuals with cultural resources for their autonomy (Tamir 1993; Kymlicka 1995; Gans 2003) or because the congruence between nation and state is a precondition for solidarity among citizens and for their compliance with the requirements of social justice (Miller 1995). Kymlicka's work illustrates best the move from a universalistic theory of justice in multicultural societies to a comparative and contextualist approach that acknowledges the historic preconditions of liberal models of minority accommodation and the difficulties in exporting these to societies where ethnocultural minority rights are still perceived as a threat to state security (Kymlicka 2007). The most important device in liberal accommodation of large and territorially concentrated national minorities has been a devolution of power to autonomous institutions of government dominated by the minority. The debate about plurinational federalism (Gagnon and Tully 2001; Keating 2001) has since revealed another blind spot in Rawls' concept of peoples. Constellations of federally nested peoples in plurinational states or in the supranational European Union raise novel questions that straddle the division between domestic and international justice, which appears all too clear-cut in Rawlsian theory.

My list of themes discovered in post-Rawlsian normative theory during the 1990s is meant to illustrate the institutionalist and contextualist turn without being exhaustive. Other themes could be added. For example, feminist theorist Susan Okin challenged Rawls' division between public and private spheres and his apparent shielding of internal relations within families from the application of principles of justice (Okin 1989). Carol Gilligan's work (1982) inspired communitarian feminists who complained that Rawls' conception of justice as impartiality behind a veil of ignorance neglects a female ethic of care and relational justice between interdependent persons.

Rawls' theory is certainly not the only important reference point for the institutionalist and contextualist turn in normative theory. Habermas has had a strong influence on the burgeoning literature on deliberative democracy (Benhabib 1996; Bohman 1996; Gutmann and Thompson 1996; Dryzek 2000). This approach provides an alternative to mainstream theories of democracy, including Joseph Schumpeter's elite rotation (1942) and Anthony Downs' electoral markets (1957), as well as to pluralist theories focusing on the representation of organized interests (Dahl 1971) or elite co-operation in divided societies (Lijphart 1977). Against the former, theories of deliberative democracy argue that individual preferences of citizens and their representatives can be transformed in the process of exchanging arguments; against the latter, they maintain that sectional interests may be transcended if the democratic process includes the voices of all affected by collectively binding decisions. Instead of focusing on substantive issues of justice, deliberative democrats have more often argued for procedures that would provide stronger legitimacy for political institutions and decisions. Yet the trend in this field seems to be still the same as in post-Rawlsian theory: a move from a discussion of principles derived from an 'ideal speech situation' towards concrete and policy-oriented reform proposals that promote actual deliberation among citizens or their representatives in various institutional settings (Ackerman and Fishkin 2004).

I have presented the trend towards applied normative theory as emerging from unresolved problems and disagreements in the theories of justice of the 1970s and 1980s. Yet this endogenous development was reinforced by simultaneous changes in the political environment. The period after the collapse of Eastern European communist regimes has disconfirmed expectations of convergence towards a single model of liberal society (Fukuyama 1992) and has witnessed a loss of confidence in the problem-solving capacities of representative democracy. Normative theorists as well as social scientists are not merely members of academic communities but also participants in politicized discourses about challenges to which liberal principles and democratic procedures do not provide ready-made answers. It might thus be a sense of political urgency that motivates theorists to address real-world problems and empirical researchers to raise normative questions.

Normative theory and the social sciences: can the gap be bridged?

The institutionalist and contextualist turn in normative theory has made those who work in this field more open towards the comparative and historical knowledge provided by the respective subdisciplines of political science. Yet not everybody on the other side of the normative–explanatory divide favours narrowing the gap. Some may fear that normative questions will inappropriately be exported into their domains and undermine the status of the discipline as a science.

An initial response to this charge is that normative theory may not be science, but is certainly more than a mere articulation of the theorist's ethical preferences. It shares soft and hard features with most other social sciences. Like these (and unlike neoclassical economics), it is an internally pluralistic and eclectic subject (Vincent 2004) without a core methodology and unifying paradigm. Although liberalism can be identified as the mainstream, the discord among its various schools seems often as great as the differences with its main rivals. However, as in the social sciences generally, this internal diversity does not mean that normative theory is not a discipline in the original sense of the term: a practice or art that obeys specific rules and that can be studied and learned. As citizens, we all have moral convictions and intuitions as well as some empirical knowledge and practical understanding of politics. As political theorists, however, we must try to make our normative judgements coherent and defensible within an ongoing academic discourse, in much the same way that we must expose our social science explanations to empirically grounded objections and our interpretations to alternative perspectives.

While normative theory is a specific subdiscipline, normative questions arise unavoidably in the social sciences in three different ways. First, all scientific research has to face ethical questions about the selection of research objects, the impact of its methods on individuals, society or the environment, and the possible uses and abuses of its research results. Second, in social research these ethical challenges are compounded by the fact that research objects cannot be clinically isolated. When studying a social phenomenon empirically, the researcher is him/herself involved in a social relation with that phenomenon and contributes directly to its perception in the wider society. This is not only true for direct interaction with individuals in field research. The analysis of statistical data on, say, unemployed youth is implicated in constructing the social categories and meanings of 'youth' and 'unemployment'.[4] All such categories and interpretations are normatively loaded, because they create prescriptive expectations about human behaviour and the performance of social institutions. Third, as I will now argue more extensively, there is a specific challenge for political science, which must deal with normative questions about the legitimacy of political power and authority as a matter of its research *content*, and not merely of its societal research *context*. For all these reasons, the attempt to purify the social sciences of normative questions is misguided.

John Gerring and Joshua Yesnowitz argue that the gap between normative and empirical analysis is an artificial one. '[N]ormative theorizing must deal in facts just as empirical work must deal in values; they do not inhabit different worlds' (Gerring and Yesnowitz 2006: 108). While the first part of this statement will be generally supported by applied normative theorists, the second part may be protested by positivist social scientists. The latter are certainly committed to values that guide academic teaching and research, and they may also analyse values empirically as facts of social life, that is, as beliefs held by individuals or as principles and goals proclaimed by organizations; but they do not think that values should determine their empirical research design or their theoretical inferences from the data.[5] Positivists generally do not dispute, however, that values inevitably and legitimately play a role in the social scientist's choice of topic. Gerring and Yesnowitz repeat the old argument of the Frankfurt school in the *Positivismusstreit* by postulating a norm of social relevance that *ought* to guide this choice. 'Empirical study in the social sciences is meaningless if it has no normative import. It simply does not matter. Empirical study is misleading if its normative import is present but ambiguous. It matters, but we do not know how' (Gerring and Yesnowitz 2006: 133). Social science should not merely focus on relevant problems but should also be explicit about the implications of its findings for addressing these problems. This statement echoes Ian Shapiro and Donald Green's call for problem-driven instead of method-driven political science (Green and Shapiro 1994). Even if this norm were generally accepted (which it is not), it would still not commit empirically oriented social scientists to engage in normative analysis or to advocate specific solutions to a problem.

We must therefore consider whether political science has a specific normative thrust that distinguishes it from other social sciences and humanities. Robert Nozick rightly mocked the idea of a normative sociology studying 'what the causes of problems *ought* to be' (Nozick 1974: 247). Why is it less absurd to conceive of normative analysis as an integral part of political science?

Gerring and Yesnowitz's answer has a venerable Aristotelian tradition. They define politics as 'decisional action oriented towards, or judged according to, some normative ideal pertaining to the entire community' (Gerring and Yesnowitz 2006: 113). '[I]t is impossible to think about politics without also considering the impact . . . on the commonweal' (114). Political science is, then, the study of actions oriented towards a conception of the common good. Since political scientists are themselves members of societies and since their findings feed into a public discourse about the common good, their research should also be guided by an explicit conception of the common good.

A possible objection against Gerring and Yesnowitz's definition of politics is that it does not apply to totalitarian regimes like those of Hitler or Stalin, who pursued ideals pertaining to the entire community that can hardly be understood as versions of the common good. Yet totalitarianism is in many ways a denial of politics. The relevance of some conception of the common good as a background for the study of politics shows in the difficulty of analysing such regimes without passing any value judgement about their impact on the societies in question. A more serious problem with the proposed definition concerns ordinary politics in democratic regimes. While it is easy to agree on the common bad of totalitarianism, it is notoriously difficult to agree on the common good in liberal and pluralistic societies. Even if we assume that this deep disagreement can be overcome at some level,[6] there remains the question whether politics can be *explained* by reference to a shared conception of the common good. Politicians may pay lip-service to such ideals, but their actions can be better explained by looking at their interest in power or at the particular interests in society whose representation they use as a vehicle for accumulating power. Shapiro has therefore cautioned against invoking the common good as the unifying object, even for theories of democracy. 'Rather than seeing democracy as a device for discovering or manufacturing the common good, democracy can be understood as a device for managing the power dimensions of activities people engage in as they pursue their own – individual or shared – conceptions of the good' (Shapiro 2002: 240).

Three views of political power

Political power is the core phenomenon studied by political science, but its various schools seem to have almost diametrically opposed perspectives on power. Nevertheless, as will be argued in this section, each of the main views of power tends to generate a set of normative attitudes or questions.

As Hannah Arendt has pointed out, political power should not be equated with force and violence. The latter are instrumental in coercing others to act according to one's will, whereas power is the manifestation of a society's capacity for collective action and is thus inherently in need of legitimation (Arendt 1970). Even where it is manifestly not directed towards the common good, political power is always established through a normative discourse of legitimacy. On this much, social scientists should be able to agree. What distinguishes normative theorists not only from explanatory and interpretive approaches but also from many political philosophers is the question of whether power should always be viewed sceptically or also affirmatively, in the sense that political theory can spell out conditions under which political authority may be regarded as legitimate. We can roughly identify three different answers to this question.

The first one could be called the 'dark view of political power'. All politics is driven by a quest for power, but power is inherently unpredictable, irresponsible and pervasive in its impact. Discursive legitimation is an essential condition for successful exercise of power, and it blinds those subjected to the fact of their subjection. Every normative account of political power is ideological in the sense of being itself engaged in the quest for power (rather than for other values such as truth, justice or the common good). There is thus no escape route for normative theorists, who merely help to accumulate or stabilize political power by providing arguments that can become tools of ideological hegemony. This view has been articulated most prominently by Michel Foucault, but traces and lineages can be found in many authors from Niccolò Machiavelli to Antonio Gramsci.

In its Gramscian and Foucauldian versions, this view cannot deny a normative impetus. It reveals itself in political sympathies for movements that attempt to unsettle existing power structures. Even if revolutionary hopes and projects have been abandoned, the theorist who is convinced that established power can never be normatively legitimate makes an ethical choice to side with resistance and new social movements and to focus on subversive and transgressive phenomena (Connolly 2004: 344–5).

The second view can be labelled 'rationalist'. The pursuit of political power is guided by instrumental rationality of individual or collective agents. Power is primarily a tool for the satisfaction of preferences, and political action can be understood as a means towards that end. Alternatively, rational agents may seek power for its own sake if exercising power happens to be one of their strong preferences or – in the case of collective agents such as political parties – their organizational purpose. Maximizing power under conditions of competition for this scarce good may then serve as an *explanans* for their actions.[7] Rational interest thus provides generalizable explanations for human behaviour and social institutions that can be stated coherently within a scientific theory. These explanations are superior to the discursive justification offered by political agents themselves. Both those who seek power in order to advance their particularistic interests as well as those who seek power for its own sake are likely to appeal to notions of the common good in order to gain popular support or to achieve wider compliance with their exercise of political authority. In this rationalist view, discursive legitimation is thus either irrelevant or directly misleading for explanatory purposes.

As with the dark view of power, however, the rationalist one need not refrain from normative argument. In economics, as in political science, rational choice analysis has often been used prescriptively in arguing for public policies that resolve collective action dilemmas or that generate Pareto-optimal outcomes by regulating competition between self-interested rational agents. When scholars move from explaining existing political institutions through rational interests towards justifying them or towards designing alternative ones, they implicitly accept that political decisions and institutional reform are not merely the result of actions based on given preferences, but can actually be influenced by arguments that appeal to some version of the common good.

This latter kind of belief explicitly grounds the third view of political power, which can be properly called a normative one, in a more comprehensive sense than the other two. While it would be naïve to assume that political power is generally oriented towards the common good, normative political theorists must at least assume that power is potentially capable of being justified in these terms and that it therefore makes sense to examine the conditions under which it may be regarded as legitimate.

This view is minimally based on the Hobbesian conviction that the absence or breakdown of political power is worse than most (even if certainly not all) forms of institutionalized power. And it is guided by the idea that political power *ought* to be organized in ways that serve the common good. What this common good consists of is disputed among various schools of thought. The concept should really be seen as a placeholder for some combination of values that can only be realized in a well-ordered polity. Among these, I would count the basic human interests in well-being, in individual autonomy and in collective self-rule. As mentioned above, normative theorists must concede that there have been political regimes whose modes of legitimation were based on norms that are abhorrent and cannot possibly provide legitimacy, but they contest the generalization of the dark view into a feature of the human condition. Many normative theorists will also largely agree with a rationalist account of power, but will emphasize that the normative principles that can make political power legitimate should not themselves be seen as an object of rational choice by self-interested agents[8] and require therefore a different type of political theory.

Problem-driven and tradition-driven approaches

So far, I have contrasted normative with explanatory theory and have argued that the institutionalist and contextualist turn has narrowed the gap by making normative theory strongly problem-driven. Yet many scholarly analyses could be called tradition-driven rather than either method-driven or problem-driven. This pertains particularly to the study of the history of political ideas. Every discipline consists not only of methodologies but also of traditions. The study of the history of the discipline is an essential subdiscipline in all social sciences. In contrast with anthropology or sociology, which have emerged as disciplines only over the last two hundred years, the study of politics has a much longer pedigree and provides historians with a rich body of records.

With regard to methodology, the history of political ideas is much closer to the humanities since its goal is generally not explanatory, but interpretive. Ideas are interpreted either synchronically within their context of origin, or diachronically by relating them to earlier and later ideas and thus identifying traditions and their evolution over time.

Engaging with the history of ideas is important not only for professional historians, but for all scholars. It allows them to build on earlier insight and prevents them from reinventing the wheel. Since progress in social sciences is cumulative but never linear, even the theoretical modelling of a social problem using advanced mathematical methods may be improved by considering hypotheses and conclusions in the light of ideas articulated in an earlier historical period. For most social scientists, however, the purpose of engaging with traditions is not to defend them. The competitive nature of scientific inquiry means that the prize goes to innovation rather than to restating earlier ideas. The value of traditions lies in the inspiration they provide for new interpretations that move beyond tradition.

From this perspective, the study of history of ideas can be just as much problem-driven as that of contemporary societies. This may be less obvious for the Leo Straussian approach, which has been dominant in the United States. There, the focus is very much on textual exegesis and immanent interpretation, although it is generally not difficult to identify contemporary concerns lurking behind sophisticated discussions of the meaning of a certain concept in the texts of Plato or Aristotle. The Cambridge school of historians, whose most prominent members are John Pocock and Quentin Skinner, reads the historical texts of the canon much more as interventions in a problem-driven dialogue among contemporaries. In a similar manner, the history of concepts and of collective memory initiated by the German historian Reinhard Koselleck is mainly interested in reconstructing the genealogy and context of origin of political ideas that have ongoing relevance in contemporary societies.

Yet there remains a significant difference between historians of ideas and normative political theorists. The historian's style and ambition is hermeneutic rather than normative. Abolishing this difference would lead to writing counterfactual histories, which may be a worthwhile task for novelists,[9] but hardly for historians. Just as it does not make sense to discuss what the causes of social problems ought to be, so it makes little sense to theorize about what decisions ought to have been taken by a political regime that no longer exists. I said 'little' rather than no sense, because doing so might at least make us aware of the inherent contingency of all historical development and thus inoculate us against historical determinism. But beyond this cautionary effect a normative theory of the past would be rather pointless, since it lacks an addressee for its prescriptions.

In contrast with historians of ideas, applied political theorists are driven by problems of contemporary societies. Their interest in past ideas resembles the mindset of a gold-digger who looks for the nugget and cannot be bothered too much by a mineralogist's account of the origin of the mountain. Yet without some basic knowledge of mineralogy, the gold-digger is unlikely to find the right spot in which to dig, and he might still mistake a worthless mineral for gold. Therefore, without abandoning their particular goals, normative theorists should listen carefully to historians of ideas. And because the pre-nineteenth century tradition of political science is so overwhelmingly and explicitly normative, they have a lot to learn.

Let us now consider again how the divide looks from the other side. Do historians of ideas regard normative theorists as performing a complementary task to their own, as rivals who are inclined to transgress into their own domains, or as illegitimate squatters who are already there and ought to be chased from a terrain that rightfully belongs to the scholars of history? One attempt to do so is Kari Palonen's assertion that the historical school represented by Kosselleck and Skinner is engaged in 'indirect political theorizing' that is fundamentally subversive of normative theory by focusing on 'the explication and the tacit normative content in the use of concepts' (Palonen 2002: 91). '[W]hat is rejected by a political theory appealing for contingency, contestation and change concerns any and all attempts to define what is worth striving for in substantial terms' (103).

This seems to me an implausible view of the relation between normative theory and the history of ideas. Instead of undermining the former task altogether, studying the historic contingency, contestation and change of political concepts and norms will reinforce the contextualist turn outlined above. Normative theorists should not merely examine how principles change colour when travelling across political and cultural boundaries, but also when their present interpretation is compared with their historic origins. They might then, for example, refrain from interpreting universal human rights as a timeless concept and see them instead as responses to standard threats from the abuse of modern state power (Shue 1980) and as a specific interpretation of what respect for human dignity requires in the context of a highly developed and interdependent global society and state system. As this example shows, such historical contextualization need not in any way diminish the validity of normative judgements for contemporary society. On the contrary, it can help to demonstrate how a proposed interpretation of a norm responds to specific conditions and problems of our time.

Historians of ideas, on the other side, are often motivated to recover lost strands of political thought because they are convinced that these still carry some relevance today. Yet it is not the historian's task to reformulate such ideas as a coherent normative theory. From a problem-driven perspective, the two agendas should then clearly be seen as complementary rather than substitutive.

How to combine normative theory and empirical research

There are many possible answers to this question. What will be demonstrated briefly in this section is how normative questions can inform the choice of specific empirical research topics and methodologies.

The empirical study of normative attitudes and beliefs

Social, political and legal norms can be an object of empirical studies whose goal is not to defend normative propositions. In particular, normative beliefs held by citizens can be researched without endorsing or criticizing them.[10] Yet, empirical investigations of this kind may also be important for normative theories. If a communitarian theory suggests that its interpretation of a certain norm is grounded in shared meanings and understandings within a particular community, then it will be helpful if empirical evidence can show that many members of this community actually endorse that interpretation.[11] If theorists of deliberative democracy propose that a certain institutional setting or procedure will produce a reflexive change of beliefs through deliberation, then this again involves empirical claims that can be tested. Even a more minimalist theory of democracy that suggests merely that political decisions ought to be more responsive to citizens' given normative preferences should also gather some empirical evidence on the presumed discrepancy. In each of these cases, the choice of the right kind of empirical methodology is a question on which the normative theorist has no special expertise to offer. All we can say is that normative ideas involve complex and contested concepts. And for this reason there is a particularly strong trade-off between achieving greater representativity through large-N quantitative surveys and attaining greater validity through qualitative methods that are more sensitive to subjective interpretations.

Studying institutionally embedded norms

Norms exist not only as ideas in the mind but also as institutional patterns that constrain or promote specific types of human actions.[12] Democracy or economic markets can be described as sets of institutionally embedded norms whose effectiveness in regulating human action is relatively independent[13] of subjective individual beliefs in, and support for, these norms.

Institutionalized norms are explicit and formal or implicit and informal, in which case they can only be inferred from observing empirically how institutions operate. Contemporary applied normative theory, therefore, often relies on inductive reasoning about the evolution of implicit norms derived from the operations of institutions that are seen as crucial for the legitimacy of political authority, such as democratic constitutions or public international law. Consider the norm of self-determination of peoples in international law, which stands in obvious tension with the equally important norm of the territorial integrity of states. Traditionally, these two norms were reconciled by conceiving of peoples as the total populations of states or colonies (Cassese 1995). Practices of state recognition after the breakup of Yugoslavia and self-determination claims by national minorities and indigenous peoples have, however, initiated an evolution of this norm of which the outcome is yet uncertain (Ratner 1996; Buchanan 2004).

Comparative empirical studies of institutions across time and across societies are essential in order to support claims that a certain norm is not merely morally defensible, but also operationally effective. Even where the normative argument suggests that current institutions are morally defective, it may be important to show how they could be transformed to live up to some normative ideal; this requires, again, empirical knowledge about their historical evolution and current variations.

Qualitative case studies

When discussing empirical applications, most normative political theorists use a case study approach. They illustrate their normative arguments with a particular case, often reduced to a few aspects that are considered relevant. Judicial decisions are particularly attractive for political theorists since in deciding complex cases, judges have to fine-tune legal norms and balance them against each other. The difference is that normative theorists will be more interested in establishing the validity of a specific norm (which is taken for granted in legal positivist thinking) than in the particular decision. Take, for example, the decision of the US Supreme Court in *Yoder* v. *Wisconsin* (1972), which granted orthodox Amish parents an exemption from the last two years of compulsory schooling so that their children would not become alienated from their religious community's pre-modern way of life. This judgment triggered a whole normative literature on how to balance the freedom of religious exercise with the state's duty to educate future citizens.[14] The methodological point is that both judges and normative theorists must consider the details of the case at hand, the former in order to reach a verdict, the latter in order to illustrate their preferred interpretation of the norms involved. Contextualists go one step further. They believe that case studies should not merely serve to underpin a pre-established normative argument, but should really be the starting point for generating new normative insights. Joseph Carens has argued that thick descriptions (Geertz 1973) of strange and unfamiliar cases can help the normative theorist to overcome cultural biases in his or her normative judgements (Carens 2000: 4–6, 200–59).[15]

Quantitative comparative studies

Only rarely have political theorists supported normative conjectures with findings from large-N social research. This is partly due to a lack of training in social science research methodologies among political theorists who have studied philosophy and the history of ideas. Some of the fault also lies, however, with method-driven social sciences. While there is little common ground, or need for communication, between philosophers concerned with meta-ethical issues and method-driven positivist sciences, problem-driven social science starts from research questions that link explanatory tasks (what is the cause of the problem?) with normative ones (how to respond to it?). These two aspects of problem-driven social science are hard to separate. When applied normative theory leads to policy prescriptions, it must take into account real-world conditions for implementing such policies. Insofar as quantitative empirical research results in valid generalizations about the conditions for winning support for a proposed policy, or about its likely (and often unintended) side-effects, it will be relevant for applied normative theory. All too often, normative theorists are tempted merely to speculate about the real-world implications of a policy that they want to propose or criticize.

A rare attempt to test empirically some hypotheses raised in the normative literature is Keith Banting and Will Kymlicka's study of the effects of multi-cultural public policies on welfare regimes (Banting and Kymlicka 2007). Kymlicka is a proponent of multicultural policies in response to ethno-national diversity. Such policies have recently come under attack from liberal egalitarians. They are said to divert attention from the fight against social inequalities, to misinterpret social marginalization as an effect of cultural domination, and to undermine support for redistribution through empha-sizing difference and compartmentalizing society into cultural segments. Banting and Kymlicka call these, respectively, the crowding-out, the misdiag-nosis and the corroding effects. Each of these challenges can be discussed at length in terms of its theoretical plausibility. Yet they may also be tested empirically by examining whether the strength of multicultural policies cor-relates with growing inequality or with diminishing support for redistribu-tion. Comparative research of this kind is notoriously plagued by problems involving the operationalization of independent and dependent variables, statistical inference from small numbers of cases, and causal interpretations of observed correlations.[16] Empirical studies like these can therefore hardly ever resolve a normative dispute. The results of Banting and Kymlicka's study – which show no systematic negative effect of multicultural policies on redistribution – may be contested on methodological grounds. Alternatively, normative theorists may accept the evidence but restate their critique of multiculturalism in different terms, which already represents progress in nor-mative debates.

The ethics of normative theorizing

Instead of a summary, I will conclude with a caveat about the ethics of applied normative theorizing. Political scientists who engage in this activity are often accused by their colleagues of abandoning value-free explanation as the only true scientific goal and turning instead towards policy advocacy. If we examine public interventions of political scientists in the mass media we will, however, find that normative theorists are hardly overrepresented. The difference might be that the latter do not think of their core academic work as something entirely separate from the ongoing political discourse in civil society. An article in a political theory journal will be addressed to a different audience than, and thus be written in a different style from, an op-ed comment. Yet if the former elaborates a normative argument defending or criticizing a public policy, it will quite naturally be translatable into a political intervention. The advantage of the normative theorist in this field is that her academic discipline teaches her to state her normative preferences explicitly and to address the strongest objections against them. This should help her to avoid normative 'adhocery' and inconsistency, which can be found in abundance in policy conclusions drawn from empirical research.

The danger is to assume that the philosopher-king should have a privileged voice in political decisions. Problem-driven social science and normative theory are both contributing in important ways to political discourses, the former by providing theoretical explanations and empirical knowledge, the latter by clarifying the principles and arguments involved. Social scientists have a quite powerful influence, which can be measured as the popularization of academic concepts, such as the prisoners' dilemma and zero-sum games, or ethnicity and gender. Their primary task outside academia is to promote greater reflexivity in civil society, not to give policy advice to rulers. If they give such advice, they should do it publicly, speaking as citizens to fellow-citizens in order to convince them of the policy they propose. This is what democratic modesty requires.

Yet this very role of the public intellectual who keeps a distance from political power raises an ethical problem for the normative theorist. Politicians and holders of public office should follow what Max Weber called an 'ethics of responsibility' in considering all implications of their decisions and in accepting that their career may be tied to the success or failure of the policies they endorse. The normative theorist's interventions may instead be guided by *Gesinnungsethik* (an ethic of good intentions and conscience), which defends an ideal without attention to the trade-offs and dilemmas involved in translating it into political decisions. The theorist is generally not held accountable for her advocacy of policies that lead to disaster. Nor should she be, since chasing her out of academia would severely restrict the freedom of thought that is the essence of academic life. The proper remedy for this dilemma is not to abandon normative theory altogether or to confine it to an arcane academic discourse, but to expose it instead to the full force of critique from explanatory theory and empirically grounded research that analyse the application context for normative ideas. For the normative theorist who wants to pre-empt such critique, the advice is simple: try to learn as much as possible from the other branches of social science and integrate their insights into your work.

NOTES

1 Aristotle took the comparative task quite seriously. Among the work carried out by him or by his students is a collection of 158 Greek constitutions.

2 See Steinmo (ch. 7) for parallel developments in comparative political science.

3 Ideal normative theory in this sense is different from utopias in which there is little need for principles of justice because of an abundance of means to satisfy human desires or a transformation of human nature itself.

4 See also Kratochwil (ch. 5).

5 For a statement on why causal explanation should be value-free, see Héritier (ch. 4).

6 Gerring and Yesnowitz believe that disagreement is deep only at the level of philosophical principle, but that there is much agreement about desirable policy outcomes such as economic growth, racial equality or human development (Gerring and Yesnowitz 2006: 129).

7 But see Chwaszcza (ch. 8) for an argument that game-theoretical models, which are often used in political science, do not assume that outcomes of strategic interactions are determined by individual utility maximization.

8 See Gauthier (1986) for an attempt to derive moral principles from agreement among rational self-interested agents in a fair initial bargaining position. For a critique, see Barry (1989: 360–2).

9 For a recent example, see Roth (2004).

10 An influential example is Kaase and Newton (1998).

11 A classic example of applied communitarian research is Bellah (1985).

12 See Steinmo (ch. 7).

13 Institutional norms are only relatively independent, since institutions would break down if a majority of individual agents actively rejected the underlying norms and acted accordingly.

14 For contrasting views, see Arneson and Shapiro (1996) and Galston (2002).

15 See della Porta (ch. 11), Vennesson (ch. 12) and Bray (ch. 15) for arguments about why single or small-N case studies can also be attractive for some explanatory purposes.

16 See Héritier (ch. 4), Mair (ch. 10) and Franklin (ch. 13).

4 Causal explanation

Adrienne Héritier

Introduction

This chapter presents a set of approaches to systematic explanation of specific empirical political and social phenomena. These approaches strive to create theoretical, generalizable knowledge with respect to the phenomena in question. In the search for terms of generalization, they differ from research that seeks an in-depth understanding and an idiographic description of the unique and singular aspects of a given empirical political or social phenomenon (see Bray, ch. 15). Rather, they concentrate on theory development and the use of empirical cases or observations as illustrations or as a way of testing hypotheses and theories (Von Wright 1971: 19). This type of social science strives to provide answers to 'why' questions by seeking to identify one or several antecedent factors (*explanans*) that are responsible for the occurrence of the event or behaviour in question (*explanandum*) (Nachmias and Frankfort-Nachmias 1976). As Gerring (2005: 170) puts it: 'to be causal, the cause in question must generate, create, or produce the supposed effect'.

The procedures of explanation discussed here are all based on the *ontological* (unproven) assumptions that there are recognizable regularities and a recognizable order in the world 'out there'. No causal argument can be made without making a number of assumptions about how the world works – 'that there is a degree of order and structure and that change itself is patterned and can be understood' (Nachmias and Frankfort-Nachmias 1976: 6–7). It is further assumed 'that we strive for knowledge of the humanly created world that is systematic, empirical, falsifiable, replicable and, in some sense, "objective"' (Gerring 2005: 169).[1] The claims for 'truth' made in scientific knowledge must be demonstrated objectively and in a transparent way (Nachmias and Frankfort-Nachmias 1976: 8). Knowledge that is used to support the validity of scientific claims must be empirical, relying on perceptions, experience and observations. The latter, in turn, are guided by existing points of view and theoretical notions (Popper 1961: 106).

All of the approaches to causal explanation discussed here strive for regularity and generalization, reliability and replicability, validity, prediction and parsimony, although to differing degrees as regards the latter two. *Regularity and generalization* refer to relations between concepts (see Mair, ch. 10). These relations are stated as hypotheses or propositions of a link between an independent and a dependent variable, a variable being the empirically measurable aspect of a concept that describes a causal sequence[2] (Nachmias and Frankfort-Nachmias 1976; King, Keohane and Verba 1994). These hypotheses may be formulated as probability statements, laws, or necessary and sufficient conditions (Ragin 1987), clearly stating to which universe of cases the claims purport to apply. The *reliability and replicability* rule refers to the need to explicate the steps by which the hypotheses are subject to empirical assessment. This should be done in such a way as to make it possible to follow these steps, replicate the study and reassess the outcomes. The *validity* rule relates to internal and external generalization: do the indicators used to measure the empirical values of the variables measure what they intend to measure (internal validity)? Can the claims made for one case be generalized to other cases, and to what extent (external validity)?[3] *Prognostication or prediction* – under *ceteris paribus* assumptions – uses conclusions from existing confirmed hypotheses and extends them to other unobserved phenomena. *Parsimony* postulates that the number and complexity of causal hypotheses used should be limited and they should not be deducible from each other (Nachmias and Frankfort-Nachmias 1976).[4]

While the goal of formulating general claims as to the causes of a particular phenomenon and systematically subjecting these claims to empirical scrutiny is common to all the approaches discussed here, they nevertheless differ as to the specific procedures used. The following important ways of proceeding appear particularly useful when seeking to explain complex political and social phenomena:

- deductive and inductive approaches;
- comparative statics;
- causal mechanisms;
- explanatory frameworks and modular explanations;
- causal reconstruction.

Deductive and inductive approaches

In identifying causal relationships to account for a particular *explanandum*, one may choose to proceed *deductively* or *inductively*. If the choice is to proceed *deductively*, an explanation of an event is derived from a theoretical hypothesis about the processes that brought it about (Little 1991: 7). Existing theories are scrutinized for possible answers to the research question. These answers are formulated as hypotheses which establish a relationship between two concepts, accounting for the phenomenon at issue.[5] From the theories considered as possible candidates for the explanatory purpose at hand, a theory is selected that shows the 'best fit'.[6] In other words, the hypothetical answers it offers directly aim at the phenomenon to be accounted for, rather than being related only somewhat loosely to the *explanandum*.

The hypotheses derived from a theory should also be *internally consistent*, *logically complete* and *falsifiable* (Nachmias and Frankfort-Nachmias 1976; King, Keohane and Verba 1994). A theory is internally consistent if the hypotheses it comprises do not contradict each other. It is logically complete when its hypotheses logically derive from the mutually consistent assumptions that are taken as given (Nachmias and Frankfort-Nachmias 1976). To offer an example, it would be logically inconsistent to start out from the behavioural assumption of perfect information *and* the assumption of incomplete contracts and then go on to study the lack of compliance with a contract during application. Actors with perfect information would foresee this danger and anticipate it, considering it in the *ex-ante* designing of the rule (Karagiannis 2007).

In proceeding deductively, it is important to bear in mind that the goal of theoretical analysis is the model and not the one-to-one reflection of reality. In other words, the objective is not to describe minutely a situation given in reality in all its details, but to focus on what one deems the most important aspects of the situation. This presupposes some prior, theory-guided conceptualization of the situation. This conceptualization is translated into a model whose components are assumed to incorporate the essential elements of the concrete empirical situation to be explained. In doing so, the results of the theoretical analysis will also shed light on the real-world situation the model is intended to explain (Hedström and Swedberg 1998: 13–14).

The alternative to an explanatory model is not to use no model at all, but to use an alternative model based on an alternative theory (Hedström and Swedberg 1998: 14).[7] If the main hypotheses of such an explanatory exercise are empirically disconfirmed, we still may retain the theory, but will need to modify and specify the model and its hypotheses by adding an additional variable. This means that the scope of the explanatory claim has been reduced: it explains less (Little 1991; King, Keohane and Verba 1994).

For a theory to be falsifiable, it should not be tautological and should allow for the deduction of hypotheses concrete enough to be accessible to empirical disconfirmation. When the theoretical explanation has been translated into a model as described above, it enables the formulation of empirically testable propositions regarding the nature of these relationships (Nachmias and Frankfort-Nachmias 1976: 43–4). The propositions should be clear, specific and value-free.[8] In order to validate a hypothesis empirically, all variables mentioned in the hypothesis need to be defined and operationalized, specifying among other things the time and space conditions under which the proposition is expected to hold. It also identifies the unit of analysis, the element of investigation to which they refer, such as states, persons or institutional rules (Nachmias and Frankfort-Nachmias 1976: 52). Hypotheses should be value-free in order to be amenable to a causal analysis. Thus, the proposition 'a political system should be governed according to democratic institutional rules' cannot be subject to empirical verification.

By specifying the limits in time and space under which our hypotheses may hold, we recognize that they do not have the nature of 'universal laws' (David Hume). Deterministic statements, in the sense of 'if event X occurs, then event or behaviour Y will always follow', are rare in social science. When stating a hypothesis subject to time and space conditions, we must scrutinize whether these conditions hold in the case of an empirical object in question (Hedström and Swedberg 1998: 8). The limited (or middle-range) scope (Sartori 1970) of our theoretical claims is taken into account when theories claim validity only under clearly specified conditions, such as the conditions found in a Western parliamentary democracy. To give an example: given the necessary condition of a Western parliamentary democracy, the number of veto players in a Western parliamentary democracy may be considered as the sufficient condition for a specific policy outcome; in a parliamentary democracy polity with few veto players, a high degree of policy innovation is expected, and vice versa.

An *inductive approach*, as opposed to a *deductive approach* to theory-guided empirical research, starts from an empirical investigation of the phenomenon of interest (Merton 1968). The objective is to gain a new view of what is relevant in the empirical area of study by seeing it from the perspective of the actors involved. Using diverse data sources, empirical regularities are carefully described. In a further step, the empirical information is interpreted conceptually, i.e. it is attributed to concepts that help bundle and measure the data so that systematic patterns of variation may be identified. The latter may then be posited in the form of hypotheses that may be systematically linked and subject to a standard method of hypothesis testing (Glaser and Strauss 1967; Nachmias and Frankfort-Nachmias 1976: 47). Well-known examples of limited-scope, inductively developed theories of the complex functioning of particular political systems are the Westminster model of British parliamentarism (Wilson 1994); the consociational model of Swiss or Dutch democracy (Lehmbruch 1967, 1974); the pluralist model of American politics (Dahl 1967); the joint-decision model of German federalism (Scharpf, Reissert and Schnabel 1976; Scharpf 1988); and the neocorporatist model of interest intermediation in Austria and the Scandinavian countries (Schmitter and Lehmbruch 1979; Scharpf 1997: 32).

Frequently, an iterative procedure between deduction and induction is applied. This method tries to link both processes by first developing hypotheses from existing theories and then engaging in explorative field research to gain 'inspiration' for the generation of new hypotheses. The latter are then confronted with the existing stock of relevant theories, possibly leading to a modification of the pre-existing hypotheses and situating the inductively gained hypotheses within a larger theoretical framework. These modified hypotheses are then subject to systematic empirical validation with *new* data. This procedure, iterating between deduction and induction, has been called 'abduction'.

Whatever the approach, if we seek to explain a particular political or social outcome as extensively as possible – as opposed to assessing the explanatory power of a particular theory or hypothesis – we are faced with the problem of multiple explanations. As a rule, several theories lend themselves to accounting for the phenomenon in question, and it is rare that only one may plausibly be used to explain an outcome. This raises the difficult question of the logical relationship between the different theories and the issue of their commensurability (Jupille, Caporaso and Checkel 2003: 18). Jupille, Caporaso and Checkel emphasize that in order to compare theories, we need to guarantee the use of concepts that are mutually intelligible: the dependent and independent variables are conceptualized in such a way as to allow for comparison (Jupille, Caporaso and Checkel 2003: 19).[9]

Assuming a sufficient amount of commensurability of theories and their concepts, the authors distinguish three important modes of dialogue between theories: (a) competitive empirical assessment, (b) additive relationship based on complementary domains of application and the sequencing of theories, and (c) relationship of subsumption (Jupille, Caporaso and Checkel 2003: 19). Under a *competitive relationship*, the propositions are set up in such a way as to compete with one another (Campbell and Stanley 1963; Jupille, Caporaso and Checkel 2003: 20). The assessment of the empirical power of the two theories is based on the observation of the outcome – whether the outcome predicted by theory A or the outcome predicted by theory B can be observed. Under a *complementary relationship*, the respective domains under which two theories hold are identified. For example, the outcome of decision-making in policy areas with clear-cut redistributive stakes may be more amenable to a rational institutionalist bargaining explanation. The outcome of policy-making in an area like abortion may be more susceptible to a socio-logical institutionalist explanation based on social norms. *Sequencing* of theoretical explanations means that one theoretical account temporally depends on the other to explain a given outcome. Thus, a given formal treaty provision in the European Union may be accounted for by liberal intergovernmentalist theory (Moravcsik 1993). The following phase of the application of the formal rules may lead to the emergence of informal rules substantively changing the formal ones. This phase may be captured by a theory of endogenous institutional change based on bargaining (Farrell and Héritier 2003; Héritier 2007). *Subsumption* shows that one theoretical account can be logically incorporated into another (Jupille, Caporaso and Checkel 2003: 23). Thus, it has been argued by sociological institutionalists that a utility-maximizing behaviour may be considered as a subform of value-guided behaviour. Or conversely, rational choice theorists have argued that the invoking of ideas and values may serve as an instrument for pursuing particular policy goals and hence be subsumed under a rational strategy.

Whether we are proceeding deductively or inductively, based on a one-theory explanation or a multiple-factor (theories) explanation, there is a variety of procedures to account for a particular *explanandum*. We may apply an exercise of comparative statics, identify causal mechanisms or engage in modular theoretical explanations or causal reconstruction.

Comparative statics

The goal of social-scientific inquiry typically is to explain outcomes and observe trends or events. As emphasized, due to their complexity, most of the phenomena investigated by political scientists and sociologists require the assessment of several independent explanatory factors or variables. One independent variable will explain a certain part of the variation in the dependent variable, the phenomenon to be accounted for. For instance, if we want to account for political participation, it may be submitted that social class plays a crucial role; but gender and education may be equally important explanatory factors. Accordingly, more independent variables are introduced to account for more of the variation of the *explanandum*.[10]

In dealing with this problem of multifactor explanation, comparative statics uses a thought experiment or a conceptual experiment based on the comparison of two cases. The underlying idea is to vary one feature while holding constant all the other features of the selected cases, assessing how this variation impacts upon the outcome.[11] If the outcome changes, one concludes that this was caused by the variation of the feature of the independent variable in question. To give an example: under a strategic rational choice approach based on the assumption of actors trying to maximize their utility, we would ask how an outcome might be affected by changes either in an actor's preferences or in the environment, available actions and information condensed in existing institutional rules. One conceptual experiment varies the properties of preferences or the actors' beliefs (about the preferences of others), holding constant the environmental attributes (information/institutions) in which they interact, in order to assess the empirical impact of the variation of preferences. The other, more frequently used conceptual experiment varies features of the environment, institutional rules, and holds the attributes of actors' preferences constant in order to empirically assess how a variation in institutional rules impacts upon the outcome (Lake and Powell 1999: 9–12). The underlying logic of comparative statics is that not all possible influence factors can simultaneously be brought into play, that is vary, when explaining outcomes. All but one must be held constant (Gourevitch 1999: 137).

By holding all aspects constant except for one explanatory variable of interest, we use control variables to reduce the risk of attributing explanatory power to independent variables that in fact are *not* responsible for the occurrence of the variation in the dependent variable; these would be spurious relationships.[12] If the effects of all relevant variables are eliminated (or controlled for) and the empirical relation between the independent variable and the dependent variable is maintained, then the relationship is considered non-spurious (Nachmias and Frankfort-Nachmias 1976: 56). This has some similarity with the 'most-similar systems design' in comparative political research (without the strategic interaction aspect of comparative statics) in which, when comparing two cases, all aspects are held constant except for the one whose explanatory power we would like to assess empirically (see also

J. S. Mill's method of agreement).[13] To give an example: assuming diversity of actors' preferences, we would expect that less innovative policies would be adopted in a polity governed by a system with many formal veto players than in a political system with few formal veto players. In empirically assessing the impact of the institutional rule across a number of cases, we would need to control for other potentially influential factors such as the level of economic development or exogenous shocks.

In applying comparative statics in an explanatory exercise, 'unit homogeneity' (or conditional independence) of the units of analysis should be observed, and endogeneity and multicollinearity should be avoided. When observing *unit homogeneity*, we assume that when comparing several cases with varying values, the expected values of the dependent variables of each case are the same when our explanatory variable takes on a particular value or, less strictly, that there is at least a 'constant effect' (King, Keohane and Verba 1994).[14]

Endogeneity denotes the problem that the causal effect may go in both directions. The independent variable may be influenced by the dependent variable. This is linked to the fact that the world around us is – to a large extent – shaped by human actors. Przeworski discusses the example of the impact of democracies as compared to dictatorships on economic growth; he argues these factors are not independent of each other because democracies are much more vulnerable to economic crises than are dictatorships. To assess empirically the effect political regimes have on economic growth, we must consider that empirical observations may not be exogenously caused. 'Given endogeneity, you are unlikely to observe poor economic performance in democracies, particularly in poor democracies . . . When democracies face bad economic conditions, they die, and we do not observe them anymore' (Przeworski 2004: 10). In the observed cases, democracies do better; but this is because they are more sensitive to economic crises. We are faced with a selection bias that we can only correct by using counterfactuals to fill the unobserved, truncated part of the distribution (Przeworski 2004: 10). The counterfactual thought experiment should help determine what economic growth in democracies would have been, had they experienced conditions of dictatorship (Przeworski 2004: 10).

Avoiding *multicollinearity* means that the various explanatory factors used to account for an *explanandum* should not be predictable from each other or derived from each other. If they are clearly related, they can be collapsed into one explanatory variable (King, Keohane and Verba 1994). For example: the number of veto players and the presence of an independent central bank may be considered as important factors explaining why a polity easily or less easily adopts domestic policy reforms. A system with several formal veto players is expected to adopt less innovative policies innovation than a polity with few veto players. Here, the existence of an independent central bank may be considered as correlated to the number of veto players and simply collapsed under the value of several veto players on the side of the independent variable.[15]

Experiments in comparative statics may be driven *deductively* – derived from an existing theory – or *inductively* – initially suggested from existing empirical observations and then subject to systematic empirical assessment.

Causal mechanisms

Assuming that we have empirically observed a systematic relationship between a cause and a particular outcome, we might wish to go further and scrutinize the nature of the process linking the independent to the dependent variable, thereby identifying the underlying causal mechanism (Elster 1989: 3–10; Little 1991). For example: if we have found a valid relationship between a particular institutional rule and a specific policy outcome such as between a unanimity rule and lack of innovation in policy outcomes, we might want to know more about the underlying process leading to this outcome to form a theory describing this process and its structures (Little 1991: 7).[16] Bargaining theory may explain the particular outcome in question: assuming divergent preferences, the greater the number of actors who have to agree under a unanimity rule, the less they will be able to produce innovative policy outcomes, because each actor will have to consent to the decision. The advantage of this 'mechanism approach' is that it helps distinguish between 'genuine causality and coincidental association, and it increases the understanding of why we observe what we observe' (Hedström and Swedberg 1998: 8–9). As Elster put it, 'understanding the details of the causal story reduces the risk of spurious explanations (of mistaking correlation for causation)' (Elster 1998: 49).[17]

This mode of explanation clearly departs from Hempel's (1965) covering-law, probabilistic model of explanation, based on a 'black-box explanation' that minimizes the importance of the mechanism linking causal factors and outcomes (Little 1991: 15–17; Hedström and Swedberg 1998: 10). We cannot couch causal mechanisms in the form of 'If p, then sometimes q' (Elster 1998: 52). The most systematic form of 'black-box explanation', causal modelling (Duncan 1975), relies on regression analysis linking X, Y and Z to W and regression coefficients measuring the effects of several relevant variables on an outcome. As such, it tends to pay little attention to explanatory mechanisms (Von Wright 1971: 7; Hedström and Swedberg 1998: 7).

However, as Gerring rightly emphasizes, the difference should not be overstated, since all mechanisms may also be regarded as causes (or intermediate variables) (Lazarsfeld 1972; King, Keohane and Verba 1994) and, moreover, a causal mechanism argument without any appeal to covariational patterns between *explanans* and *explanandum* would be futile (Gerring 2005: 166). Correlation refers to a pattern of covariation between cause and effect, while mechanisms refers to the connecting process between the purported cause and its effect, and the question is, rather, whether a causal explanation focuses *only* on the associational patterns between X and Y, without consideration of what might link them; or focuses *only* on causal mechanisms, ignoring patterns of association between cause and effect. Either is rare. Some correlational-style analyses do not mention causal mechanisms because it seems obvious and in no need of explicit examination. Conversely, a causal mechanism argument without reference to covariation between X and Y does not make any sense. Moreover, the suggested causal mechanism may be decomposed into patterns of association among a set of intermediate variables (which, however, may not be directly observable) (Gerring 2005: 166).

When identifying the underlying causal mechanism between a causal factor and an outcome, simply developing an *ad hoc* story fitting a specific case will not be adequate. Rather, we need to propose an explanation of some generality (Hedström and Swedberg 1998: 10) and, for this purpose, resort to existing theories (Boudon 1976). To discuss an example used by Hedström and Swedberg, the causal link between social class and health has been repeatedly empirically confirmed, but the correlation says nothing about why this is so. One causal mechanism underlying the relationship may refer to income-dependent consumption and living conditions and their impact upon health. Another may relate to working conditions and their impact upon health; yet another could be increased health awareness due to better education.

Causal mechanisms, as underlying structures and mechanisms, may be theorized and hypothesized to produce the *explanandum*. Causal mechanisms are unobserved analytical constructs which, through invoking causal agents, make a relationship intelligible by accentuating some aspects of a process and omitting others (Little 1991; Elster 1998). The principle of methodological individualism is closely linked with the core idea of causal mechanisms (Hedström and Swedberg 1998: 46). While a strict version of methodological individualism does not accept explanations based on social aggregates as explanatory factors, the less rigorous version does consider social aggregates (not connected back to individual action) such as collective institutional rules and corporate-actor behaviour.[18] Many political science explanations based on legal rules or political organization could not be undertaken if the causal history of each of these macro-rules or corporate actors/organizations first had to be traced back to the original micro-actors' behaviour – as claimed by the strict version of methodological individualism.

A well-known causal mechanism is the threshold theory of collective action developed by Granovetter (1978). An individual's decision whether or not to partake in collective action often depends in part on how many other actors are already participating. The argument is that actors differ as to the number of others who must already be participating before they decide to take part themselves. This individual threshold describes the proportion of the group that must join before the actor in question is willing to do so. It can be shown that even slight differences in thresholds can produce vastly different collective outcomes (Hedström and Swedberg 1998: 19). Another well-known theoretical causal mechanism, much discussed in the literature, is the self-fulfilling prophecy described by Merton (1968), where an individual perception of an event triggers an individual behaviour which in its aggregate effect brings about the consequences that the individual expected in the first place. The example frequently mentioned in this context is an individual's belief in the likely insolvency of a bank, which induces her to withdraw her deposits, which in turn indeed leads to the failure of the bank (Merton 1968).

Coleman (1986) distinguished between different levels of causal mechanism for collective action: macro-micro and micro-macro mechanisms. Macro-micro models focus on how macro-level factors influence individual behaviour, such as the impact of unanimous decision-making, through the causal mechanism of bargaining, on the likelihood of policy innovation. Instances of a micro-macro causal mechanism are the self-fulfilling prophecy of a bank-run, or the threshold model of participation in a particular collective action mentioned earlier. Another famous example of such a micro-macro causal mechanism is the 'tragedy of the commons' (Hardin 1968), where individual rational behaviour in the use of natural limited resources – given accessibility and rival consumption – may lead to the depletion of these resources at the macro level (Ostrom 1990). This micro-macro mechanism shows how individuals – micro-actors – in given conditions, through their actions because of mechanism X will produce a certain outcome at the macro level (Gambetta 1988), producing a transformational impact that may be intended or unintended (Hedström and Swedberg 1998: 23).[19] (See also Chwaszcza, ch. 8).

Elster points to a problem that needs to be taken into account when using causal mechanisms. He emphasizes that mechanisms often come in pairs and distinguishes between different types. The first pair (which he calls type A) implies that the two causal mechanisms are mutually exclusive. Discussing the example of individual wishful thinking when faced with an aspect of the world that is different from what one would wish, he points out that the individual reaction can either be to engage in wishful thinking or to resort to the 'sour grapes mechanism' – that is, to adjust one's preferences by degrading the specific aspect of the world and making it appear less desirable. The two reactions are mutually exclusive. But, *ex ante*, we do not know which one will come to bear.

In another pair of causal mechanisms (which Elster calls type B), two mechanisms may operate simultaneously, with opposite effects on the dependent variable (Elster 1998). To give an example discussed by Le Grand: a high marginal tax rate on the one hand lowers the opportunity costs (or price) of leisure and encourages people to consume more leisure and work less (substitution effect). On the other hand, it also lowers individual incomes and may therefore induce people to work harder in order to maintain their standard of living (income effect). While they are not mutually exclusive, the two mechanisms work in opposite directions, and their joint effect cannot be predicted from the theory alone (Le Grand 1982: 148). Other examples of type B mechanisms are offered by spillover effects. The expectation that if people participate in decision-making at their workplace, they will also tend to participate in politics (Pateman 1970, cited in Elster 1998: 54) may be confirmed. But participation at the workplace may also produce just the opposite impact, the crowding-out effect: given limited time, participation at the workplace will occur at the expense of the other (Elster 1998: 55).

The general implication is that causal mechanisms may have an aspect of indeterminacy. The indeterminacy aspect linked to causal mechanisms implies that under the type A mechanism, we do not know, *ex ante*, which mechanism will be triggered. However, by measuring intermediate variables (Lazarsfeld 1972), we may be able to identify whether it is one or the other. In the case of the type B mechanism, we may only be able to assess the net effect of the two opposing mechanisms (Elster 1998: 50). But again, by measuring intermediate variables for the ongoing processes, we may be able to identify the relative importance of one or the other mechanism in producing a joint effect.

Causal mechanisms are important building-blocks of the procedure of modular explanations developed by Scharpf, to be discussed in the next section.

Explanatory frameworks and modular explanations

If we aim to explain policy outcomes where we know what the solution of a policy problem has been, we will have to account for the policy outcomes in question to the largest extent possible, rather than building upon the explanatory power of *one* theory or factor. To identify the relevant factors causing the specific policy outcome, we would have to go backwards in time. Moreover, we would have to look for the factors that are amenable to political influence. This implies a backward-looking approach as opposed to a forward-looking one that investigates the effects of a particular explanatory variable, as for instance under comparative statics (Scharpf 1997: 24). In political science policy research, the questions asked are frequently of this backward-looking nature, starting from the *explanandum* and trying to explain the outcome of a particular policy choice from a political feasibility perspective. The chain of causation must be long enough to include the entire range, from the dependent variable to 'pragmatically useful independent variables, that is, to variables that permit explanations that either identify causal factors that can be politically manipulated or that show that the outcome is/was beyond political control' (Scharpf 1997: 25). With increasing length of the chain of causation, the number of relevant causal and intervening variables increases.

Given this multiplicity of factors accounting for policy outcomes, it is difficult to derive hypotheses from one theory that is specific enough to yield hypotheses to be directly applied to empirical phenomena. Scharpf follows the approach outlined by Elinor Ostrom (Keohane and Ostrom 1995; Ostrom 1996), who starts from an analytical framework that lists all variables at the micro, meso and macro levels of policy interaction, the particular properties of the policy problem (type) at hand, the external situation, the institutional setting, the actors involved and their modality of interaction. To give an example, Ostrom lists all explanatory variables that could account for the provision of a common pool resource threatened by overuse. The list systematically describes all variables and their potential relationships, as well as the multiple 'partial theories or more limited causal mechanisms at work' (Scharpf 1997: 30) that may account for the complex phenomenon.

Since each causal mechanism is of only limited scope, we have to link various partial theories in a modular construct to account for a complex political phenomenon (Scharpf 1997: 31). The linkages between these modules may be established by narratives, or – if possible – again by a partial theory (Scharpf 1997: 30). As discussed in the section on causal mechanisms, Scharpf also refers to mechanisms of a rational strategic interaction,[20] such as Granovetter's (1978) 'bandwagon/threshold model' and the 'tragedy of the commons' based on a prisoners' dilemma (Hardin 1968), as well as his own causal mechanism of the 'joint-decision-trap' describing what is likely to happen when high-conflict constellations must be resolved through compulsory negotiations (Scharpf 1997: 31).

To illustrate the approach of modular explanation, Scharpf discusses his comparative analysis (1991) of the success and lack of success of an anti-inflation policy in the 1980s. He shows that in accounting for the policy outcomes, he could not rely on one causal mechanism but had to build on five different theoretical modules, all characterized by specific actor constellations, modes of interaction and institutional restrictions. The central module is the interaction between government and trade unions. In an additional module, the strategic interaction among unions (the 'union–union' module) is theorized either as a competing or as a co-ordinating interaction mode, since unions do not constitute a unitary actor. Further, in a 'voluntary-organization' module the process within unions is theoretically captured, focusing on the difficulties that unions face in maintaining the loyalty of their members ('intra-union' module). Moreover, interactions were conceptualized in a 'government–central bank' module characterized by different actor constellations, different modes of interaction and different institutional settings. In the final module, the preferences of 'the government' are conceptualized as being strongly influenced by a three-cornered 'electoral game' with the voting public (Scharpf 1997: 32).

The upshot is a composite explanation of political or policy outcomes, building on various theoretical modules; some were already well established in the existing literature, while others had to be newly developed. All yield empirically testable theoretical statements. Raising the question of how the different modules then link together, Scharpf proposes connecting them either via a narrative or – more elegantly – via a theory linking several or all of the causal mechanisms, essentially amounting to a theory of strategic interaction across multiple levels (Scharpf 1997: 32).[21]

Given such a composite module-based explanation of an outcome, the empirical *disconfirmation* in a particular case (treated as a crucial case) (Eckstein 1975)[22] allows for several conclusions: a necessary element, a theoretical module, may be missing; or the link between two theoretical modules was not correctly specified. This does not necessarily call into question the entire composite model. Rather, we might look for additional factors distinguishing this case from previously explained cases. However, restricting the validity of the original hypothesis is only acceptable if the additional factual evidence is based on the 'identification of a causal mechanism that could *generally* produce the different outcome' (Scharpf 1997: 34, emphasis added). If we cannot define a general hypothesis that would justify the exception, our original hypothesis is falsified.

Causal reconstruction

The aim of what Mayntz calls 'causal reconstruction' is not abstraction and maximum simplification, but concretization and necessary complexity. Causal reconstruction – as an explanatory programme similar to approaches of complex process tracing (Hall 2003; George and Bennet 2005; Vennesson, ch. 12) – questions a political ontology assuming unit homogeneity, independence of variables, the absence of multicollinearity and endogeneity as described above, but emphasizes that political outcomes are the result of complex interaction effects and various forms of multicausality (see also Hall 2003). This method is appropriate when the number of cases is small, the explanatory factors are highly dependent on each other and there are interaction effects among the variables (Hall 2003).

Causal reconstruction seeks to account for a macro-phenomenon by identifying the processes and interdependencies of factors at its origin (Mayntz 2002: 13). For this purpose it requires in-depth and detailed knowledge of the subject under investigation. Acquiring this knowledge begins with the study of so-called 'existence propositions', propositions regarding the existence of a particular phenomenon, as well as 'individual propositions' describing the individual phenomenon and their relationship to 'general propositions' (which have been the object of our discussion so far). The less we know about a particular area under study, the more important are such 'existence propositions' and 'individual propositions' (Mayntz 2002: 14). This first step of conceptualizing a macro-phenomenon in highly complex areas of political and social investigation, particularly when it is not immediately identifiable as a unity (such as globalization or governance), constitutes a demanding enterprise (Mayntz 2002: 15).

In accounting for a complex political or social macro-phenomenon, several causal factors need to be taken into account. Moreover, these factors may be causally linked. In a second step, the explanatory programme of causal reconstruction identifies particular, contingent conditions under which complex causal structures of interdependent variables come to bear. Thereby, causal reconstruction clearly differs from comparative statics which, when comparing macro-phenomena, relies on an assumption holding all aspects constant except the one considered to be the relevant causal factor. In contrast, causal reconstruction seeks to open the black box of *ceteris paribus* assumptions. In a similar argument, Peter Hall emphasizes that for many topics of social science research – even when the claim is that one factor, *ceteris paribus*, has an impact on a specific outcome – an effect may be mediated by complex interactions with other variables (Hall 2003: 388–91).

Once a complex causal interdependence under certain contingent conditions has been identified, the question of generalization arises. Only by comparing several cases may general causal patterns or causal equivalences be identified and the specific contingent conditions and their scope conditions be expressed in more general terms (Mayntz 2002: 22–3) Causal reconstruction describing structures and processes occurring under specific conditions also refers to 'causal mechanisms'. However, in contrast to Elster (1989) and Little (1991), Mayntz emphasizes the distinction between process and mechanism. While 'process' focuses on the time dimension and the dynamic character of cause–effect relationships, 'mechanism' refers to its 'mechanics', to the 'how' by which a cause, step by step, leads to a particular effect. Moreover, 'mechanisms' describe generalizable cause–effect relationships, while a concrete 'process' may also be unique (Mayntz 2002: 25).

Macro-phenomena may be influenced through one process or mechanism or through several interdependent factors. If a macro-phenomenon is the result of several partial processes or mechanisms, the question arises of whether the partial processes can be subsumed under a mega-model and be presented as a complex contingent cause–effect system? If this is the case, an overall theoretical model can account for the outcome. If there is no discernible pattern producing a *joint* effect of the different partial processes, we are faced with 'interference' (Mayntz 2002) or coincidental effects, or what Boudon (1984: 168, 183, quoted in Mayntz 2002: 36) called Cournot effects. This coincidental or conjunctural explanation of an outcome emphasizes that a specific linking of structural causes and events may produce unique outcomes that may not be repeated (Paige 1999: 782, cited in Mayntz 2002: 36n32).

Interference as a form of multicausality, Mayntz argues, can typically be found in the context of highly differentiated macro-systems. They are generated by the fact that processes in different sectors and at different levels of a macro-system function according to different logics, entering into unexpected and uncoordinated causal relationships. They may result from a coincidental crossing of two effects from within the social system, but also by a crossing with an exogenous external effect. Interferences, while not precluding systematic explanation, set close limits to the explanation of social macro-phenomena based on social regularities. However, the explanatory programme of causal reconstruction that aims not only for generalizations but also for the satisfactory explanation of concrete macro-phenomena must include the identification of coincidental effects (Mayntz 2002: 37).

Conclusion

In considering the different procedures for explaining a political or social outcome described in this chapter, the question arises of which one is best. The answer would be: it depends. It depends on the particular outcome to be accounted for and its complexity. But it also depends on an even earlier decision: is the research to be problem-driven or theory-driven? Does the researcher want to account for a particular political or social problem to the largest extent possible, or does she want to test how far a particular, well-defined theory carries us in explaining an outcome?

Viewed from the position of this initial basic choice, an approach based on linked modules of partial theories/causal mechanisms and causal reconstruction would appear better suited for problem-driven explanatory purposes than would comparative statics, operating with fewer explanatory variables and controlling for all other intervening variables. The latter lends itself more easily to theory-driven research where the foremost concern is to assess empirically how far the explanatory power of one theory can take us. Each choice implies a trade-off: what is gained in extensiveness of explanation in the first case is paid for with greater complexity of the explanatory attempt; what is gained in parsimony of explanation in the second case is paid for with the partial nature of the explanation.

NOTES

1 Social science focuses on human action that is shaped not only by objective conditions but also by the actor's perception of these conditions and by the actor's preferences (Scharpf 2006: 7). Since actors' perceptions and preferences are subjective and not mutually directly observable, institutions play an important role in social science analysis. Institutions make actors' perceptions and preferences mutually predictable, and are therefore crucial for explaining human behaviour (Scharpf 2006: 8).

2 Or conditions of persistence or efficiency of structures.

3 This raises the thorny problem of the indeterminacy of an explanation. How many cases do I need to empirically assess the external validity of my claim? In the situation of a large number of cases, a random sample selection and a multiple regression analysis will generally help answer the question of validity. In the situation of a small number of cases and an intentional design, the problem of having more explanatory variables than cases must be avoided. The number of cases may be multiplied longitudinally across different time periods, or by incorporating (e.g. territorial) subunits, by multiplying the values of the dependent variables specifying what else could be predicted or by reducing the number of explanatory variables to a smaller number of key variables (King, Keohane and Verba 1994).

4 Gerring enlarges the number of criteria a causal argument has to satisfy: (i) specification, (ii) precision, (iii) breadth, (iv) boundedness, (v) completeness, (vi) parsimony, (vii) differentiation, (viii) priority, (ix) independence, (x) contingency, (xi) mechanism, (xii) analytical utility, (xiii) intelligibility, (xiv) relevance, (xv) innovation, (xvi) comparison (Gerring 2005: 170).

5 Each hypothesis derived from a theory contains abstract concepts that need to be defined in more concrete or operationalized terms.

6 To be truthful, researchers often start out with a notion of the theory that they deem to be particularly useful in accounting for a specific empirical phenomenon. Nevertheless, they should also take alternative explanatory programmes into account.

7 A standard critique of analytical models of explanation questions the empirical accuracy of the assumptions made. This critique commits the logical fallacy of mistaking the abstract for the concrete. There will always be many analytical models that can be used to describe a given social situation. All models, by definition, select features from the reality they mean to describe. Therefore, the selection of one model cannot be based on the 'truth value' of the assumptions made, but rather on the usefulness of the model for the purpose at hand (Hedström and Swedberg 1998: 14–15).

8 Value premises inherent in concrete research should be stated very explicitly (Myrdal 1944: 1043). Value judgements may often be involved in our choice of a particular topic in that we consider it to be of political and social importance. The concepts we use carry value elements as well. Thus, the concept of democracy implies positive societal values.

9 The authors argue that theories are comparable to different language systems with limited mutual translatability. Words (or scientific terms) relate to different observables in different theories. 'They slice and package the empirical world in different ways. Each theory does its own work at the data level – determining what are relevant data' (Jupille, Caporaso and Checkel 2003: 18). Moreover, theories (like languages) also contain 'referential aspects', i.e. they establish networks of significance and rules about relations among terms and referents (19).

10 This presupposes the basic decision to seek to account for as much of the variance as possible.

11 When focusing on the estimate of the effect of one cause on a dependent variable, we need to be aware of the bias of omission, i.e. leaving out an important factor that may have an influence on the outcome (King, Keohane and Verba 1994).

12 A spurious relationship is a relationship that can be explained by other variables.

13 The 'most-different systems design' (Przeworski and Teune 1970) allows us to identify out of a diversity of independent variables for a large number of cases a common set of

explanatory factors. It allows us to exclude causal factors if they are consistently not present when particular outcomes occur (Rogowski 2004).

14 For a critique of the assumption of unit homogeneity, see Collier, Brady and Seawright (2004b).

15 Collier, Brady and Seawright, however, caution that an 'excessive concern with these objectives [of avoiding multicollinearity] may push analysts toward redesigning theory to be conveniently testable' (Collier, Brady and Seawright 2004b: 8).

16 The opposite of a mechanism is a scientific law. The latter asserts that given certain initial conditions, an event of a given type (the cause) will always produce an event of some other type (the effect) (Elster 1998).

17 However, 'the plea for mechanisms is not an argument against the idea that when such explanations fail . . . we must fall back on narrative and description' (Elster 1998: 49).

18 The strong version is demanding to apply because social phenomena have long and complicated causal histories (Hedström and Swedberg 1998: 12). The weak version 'agrees with the strong version in assuming that all social institutions in principle can be explained by only the intended and unintended consequences of individuals' actions. But faced with a world consisting of causal histories of nearly infinite length, in practice we can only hope to provide information on their most recent history . . . By taking certain macro-level states as given and incorporating them into the explanation, the realism and the precision of the proposed explanation is greatly improved' (Hedström and Swedberg 1998: 13).

19 A third mechanism is located at the micro level, showing how specific combinations of individual desires, beliefs and action opportunities generate a specific action. These are psychological and socio-psychological mechanisms such as the theory of cognitive dissonance (Hedström and Swedberg 1998: 23).

20 As applied in game theory.

21 This 'also means that the composite explanation itself remains vulnerable to charges of being ad hoc' (Scharpf 1997: 32). 'Though there have been promising efforts (Putnam, 1988; Tsebelis, 1990), it seems fair to say that good theoretical models of "connected games" (also referred to as "two-level" or "nested games") are not yet generally available' (Scharpf 1997: 32).

22 A crucial case represents all the relevant variables of a theory and in this sense is 'crucial' for the validation of the theory. If the case allows the confirmation of the theory, it is considered as valid; if not, it is disproven.

5 Constructivism: what it is (not) and how it matters

Friedrich Kratochwil

Introduction

One of the fundamental issues in social science is about what we know and how we know it (see della Porta and Keating, ch. 2). Constructivism addresses these issues in a distinctive way, but one that is often misunderstood. For a long time, constructivists were sequestered to the margins of social science, along with other 'reflexivists',[1] because they had not used the conventional methodological tools. On the other hand, they are not to be confused with 'deconstructionists'[2] in denying truth or preaching relativism. Now they are admonished to seize the middle ground (Adler 1997: 319–63) and to demonstrate by their commitment to science that they are doing neither. This all raises sensitive issues about the nature of reality and the possibility of creating warranted knowledge, as well as the nature of proofs or tests.

Obviously, we need to sort out some things before we understand what constructivism is, as opposed to some other post-modern approaches such as deconstruction, and before we can show how a particular research project might profit from a constructivist perspective. Therefore, I will clear some ground in the remainder of this section before I attempt a more detailed examination of constructivism. The following sections are devoted to some major issues in social theory (concept formation and explanation) when addressed from a constructivist perspective.

Idola fori et theatri

In order to provide the grounds on which the constructivist challenge rests, I want to dispose of some misconceptions. *First*, constructivism is neither a theory, nor even an approach to politics, any more than empiricism is.[3] Rather, in both cases a meta-theoretical issue is raised: whether things are simply given and correctly perceived by our senses (empiricism), or whether the things we perceive are rather the product of our conceptualizations (constructivism). They answer questions like 'how do you know?' more than questions about which issues, variables, institutions, and so on are the elements out of which we build our theories of a certain subject matter. Thus an empiricist will point to the operationalization and measurement of the theoretical terms in order to justify what he is doing. The constructivist, on the other hand, might point out that social phenomena such as money or authority are not natural kinds but utterly conventional. The answers are couched on a different level and point more towards meta-theoretical than theoretical issues – although they have implications both for our substantive theories and for the methods we choose.

From this, a *second* and equally important problem can be sorted out: the issue of truth and relativism. The simplest case of a truth claim is something that follows by necessity, such as when we state the analytical truth that bachelors are unmarried men. But even in geometry, the question arises of whether the sentence 'the straight line is the shortest distance between two points' is still purely analytical. These problems have been hotly debated in philosophy and in discussions concerning the foundations of logic, but need not concern us here. For us, the relevant lesson is that several difficulties arise when we try to use logic in our theories about the real world. Here the principle of the excluded middle – either something exists or it does not exist, there is no other possibility – is of particular importance, as experimental science relies on this principle. We all hope that by asking nature a clear question it will answer back unequivocally in accordance with this binary scheme.

A related issue concerns the inference based on logic alone to the existence of something in the real world (deductive rigour notwithstanding). Descartes' proof of the existence of God is a case in point. He deduces that because I can think of a most perfect being, it has to exist (Descartes 1980). Of course no such thing follows, as my thinking of a Pegasus does not bring it into existence. The equivocation of the term 'existing' relates to two different semantic systems. Insofar as my thinking is concerned, that which I think exists (*qua* thought). Yet there remains a difference between my imagination and the ontological status (or actual existence) of the thing of which I am thinking. Model-builders try to deal with this problem by making predictions about states of the world which then supposedly bear out their logical constructs, forgetting sometimes that events and actions might be overdetermined and thus (mistakenly) warrant truth claims that are false.

These rather abstract considerations are helpful in clarifying issues of truth and relativism. As the above example shows, things or objects cannot be 'true'; only *assertions about objects* can. To that extent, truth is not a property of the 'world out there' but, with the exception of purely analytical statements, is always relative to a semantic system. But even in the latter case, the truth will then depend on the conventions of language that make certain assertions analytical – if we want to keep this distinction of analytical and synthetic statements to begin with.[4] Yet from this relativity none of the alleged fatalities follow: neither are we throwing ourselves into the abyss of arbitrariness or idiosyncrasies, nor are we ending up in the general denial of truth. Far from justifying the inference that 'anything goes', we simply have to be careful in specifying the frames within which we argue and make truth claims.[5]

The mistake in the Descartes example above precisely derives from the failure to examine the issue of the semantic system to which an assertion relates. Although Descartes knew very well that the true epistemological problem consisted precisely in the issue of how the system of thought relates to the world, his answer remains, notwithstanding his critical intent, thoroughly theological. He adduces God as the guarantor that our concepts and the world out there indeed match.[6] Only because we need not worry that we are systematically deceived by an evil daemon can we be sure that what we clearly and distinctly perceive is true, and, by extension, so are the conclusions we draw when we follow his method.

A *third* problem needs to be addressed in this context. Although we think that we pose clear questions to nature when we test or conduct experiments, our hope for unequivocal answers is actually quite optimistic. For one, even if we have no reason to believe that nature wants to cheat us, it cannot answer us unless it, so to speak, uses a language. This language, of course, is provided by our concepts and theories, and because of this theory-dependence of our questions, we never directly test against nature. There is simply no going behind our concepts or theories, and no direct appeal to the things themselves. Rather, we can reflect on the questions and experiments only if we use different theories or different concepts. Then the blind spots of other conceptualizations come to the fore and we become aware that what we took for a direct answer actually means something quite different. Recognizing this dilemma is, of course, not the same as denying the independent existence of the world. It means, instead, that very little follows from this latter acknowledgement. In order not only to know that the world – or, to use Kant's terminology, the 'thing in itself' – *exists*, but also to decide *what it is*, we need concepts and theories, which are our creations and not some neutral description of how things are.

So while, in logic, no third possibility exists, in actual research, things get quickly more complicated. Issues arise not only of the interpretation of data, but also of undecidability, as the physicist and philosopher John Ziman (1978) suggests. Tests are frequently far from conclusive in justifying an exclusive attribution to either the 'is' or the 'is not' class. Consequently, the evidence has to be weighed and debated. Arguments ensue, relying on a variety of authoritative sources ranging from metaphysical convictions (such as Einstein's objection to quantum theory: that God does not play dice!), to analogies, to best practices, or to authorities in the field or peer-group review. Quite obviously, such arguments and debates are different from the straightforward demonstrations (complicated as they might be) familiar from logic and mathematics, or from the belief in proofs by empirical test.

Rather, in these debates both theoretical and meta-theoretical arguments interact and usually cannot be settled by looking harder at the facts. Consequently, the community of practitioners plays a decisive role in determining what counts as knowledge (Knorr-Cetina 1981; Fuller 1991). To that extent, disagreements abound, and actual science is quite a different enterprise from the notion of a self-justifying set of incontrovertible, atemporal and universal truths – located in a Third World (Popper 1972: ch. 3) – which are ready for inspection and open to anybody who follows the right method. Here, the history of science, Kuhn's critique on the textbook conception of science (1970) and sociological theories of how knowledge is produced (see Bourdieu 2004) have been useful correctives in that they showed that the picture of science that is often invoked is that of a science that never was (see Toulmin 2001).

The constructivist perspective

We can now turn to a closer examination of constructivism itself. Precisely because it is not a specific theory, it is heir to many of the traditional epistemological debates. Here we could mention the humanist critique of Descartes' project by Giambattista Vico (1999), who suggested that the preoccupation with certainty would have deleterious consequences for a reflective understanding of practice and of the historical world. Another strand is Kant's attempt to ground knowledge neither in the things themselves – as in the ontological tradition from Plato to the scholastics – nor in a Cartesian or Leibnitzian belief of the parallelism between our mind and the world (fixed by God), nor in blind empiricism that uncritically invoked habits and psychological factors in the manner of Hume. For Kant, only reason could provide an absolute foundation because it served as its own court (with a judge leading the inquisition, *bestallter Richter*) and thus established critically what could count as knowledge (Kant 1787: B xiii). Far from specifying a single scientific method – a problem that had to be solved by the sciences themselves – it nevertheless provided criteria for understanding how science is possible (Hoeffe 1994).

In the last century, constructivism was deeply influenced by cybernetics and modern systems theory, which severed the link between determinism and predictability/uniqueness. As foreshadowed by Poincaré's solution of the three-body problem (Toulmin 2001), the same result might be realized by a different path, or the same path might produce a different result, with obvious implications for our understanding of 'causal necessity'. Similarly, the idea of an absolute foundation, so dear to traditional epistemology, had to be given up. Absolute foundations could no longer be found in things, as traditional ontology pretended, since the things themselves were productions and not unchangeable and eternal entities. It also could not be understood in terms of categories of the mind of the observing subject (Kant), because the categorical frames are not simply natural, but the result of specific conceptual developments. As soon as even space and time could be shown not to be simply given, any attempt at founding our understanding on atemporal and universal categories of reason had to be abandoned, even though we could understand the enterprise of science as a whole in terms of a non-teleological notion of evolution (Luhmann 1997).

Thus, in contrast to former notions of successive enlightenment and progress, modern systems thinking dispensed with preordained end-states or teleologies and allowed for equivalent but different solutions. It is, however, important to note that this new unity in scientific understanding is no longer based on applying the theories and methods derived from the hard sciences to social phenomena, but through a focus on information and communication that lies across the old matter v. mind divide. Thus, as in nature, different possibilities exist for social systems to ensure reproduction. The whole process is not the result of a simple mechanical sameness, based on causally produced identical elements, but rather one of increasing differentiation through evolutionary jumps.

Since cybernetics focused on information, rather than on the tangible elements of a system, such as Waltz's units (usually conceptualized as analogous to mass and force; 1979: ch. 5), it did not submit to physics envy, so familiar from the social sciences. It also dispensed with the traditional distinction of material and ideal factors, as we have seen, and with the fruitless debates of what really is the basis for everything. Since the reproduction of a system – that is, its ability to go on, rather than its existence in equilibrium – became the central puzzle, the old vocabulary got in the way, as it led to impasses and could not illuminate how systems accomplish the tasks of reproduction. Similarly, efficient causality and general laws were no longer very helpful in explaining how systems functioned. Instead, we had to turn our attention to the reception and translation of external stimuli into the logic of the system, and its ability to handle these irritations and come up with new responses. The first issue is exemplified by the blow to the eye: it produces light effects in the eye that could not be grasped if we focused exclusively on the physicalist account, which would stress the *actio est reactio* dimension but provide no further heuristic clues to explain the actual functioning of the system.

It was perhaps no accident that the original push for a constructivist perspective did not come from the social sciences but was pioneered in biology (Maturana and Varela 1992) and only later introduced to the social sciences by the sociologist Niklas Luhmann. He thereby provided a radically different perspective on society from that of Talcott Parsons, who had elaborated his social system within the old systems perspective (Parsons 1968). Parsons had started with the elements (actors and actions) and attempted to solve the Hobbesian problem of order through the classical devices of utilizing the system and subsystem division and assigning them specific functions.

The important differences between these two system conceptions need not preoccupy us here. After all, most of the later adherents of a constructivist perspective did not encounter constructivism via the new formulation of cybernetics and systems theory, but through the criticism of Parsons' work, through the symbolic interactionism pioneered by Mead (1934) and the fascinating micro studies of Goffmann (1990). Particularly influential were also the sociological manifestos of Berger and Luckmann on the *Social Construction of Reality* (1967), which John Searle answered with his *Construction of Social Reality*, introducing speech acts to a wider audience. Finally, there was a general linguistic turn in philosophy and social analysis due to the influence of the late Wittgenstein and the historical and pragmatist critique of the dominant understanding of science as a mirror of nature (Rorty 1980).

Those familiar with the social science literature in the constructivist mode will, of course, recognize that these various sources of constructivism impacted differently on different authors. Given the wide variety of theoretical approaches and methodologies, one might indeed wonder what all these writers share, whether there is indeed some core belief or commitment that inspires such theorizing. I think two basic commitments can be identified as the minimal core of constructivism. One is that agency matters in social life and, therefore, agents are not simple throughputs of structures – material or ideal – working behind their backs. While, of course, the former is represented by vulgar Marxism, the latter focuses on the properly socialized individual acting according to the rules. Here the conflict school in sociology (see Dahrendorf 1959) and Goffmann's studies on the strategic manipulations in everyday social life (1971, 1980) were an important antidote to Parsons' argument about normative integration, which had made the actors more or less simple implementers of normative scripts. A similar criticism could be mounted against the Stanford school of sociology, representing the newest version of the belief in modernity (Thomas, Boli, Ramirez *et al.* 1987). It is true that all states have to choose the same organizational forms if they want to be taken as serious players in the international political game. But this tells us very little about actual politics, as we have learned from the political development literature and from the experiences of failed states. Similarly, precisely because these adoptions might not resonate with local traditions, they are likely to engender resistance and thus, most certainly, do not foreshadow the 'end of history' as suggested by the fundamentalist challenge to both the Western political project and the alleged universalism of human rights.

A second core belief of constructivists is that if we accept that the human world is one of artifice, then the notions the actors have about their actions matter. They cannot be left exogenous to the descriptions and explanations of actions, nor can they be solved by assumption, precisely because the latter often amounts to a naturalizing move contradicting the first commitment. This should also help us to end the entirely fruitless debate of whether interest or ideas are primary. After all, interests are neither universal nor self-explanatory,[7] since much depends on which game the actors are involved in. Even what counts as a resource changes dramatically, depending on the framing conditions. For example, bodily strength and size might be an asset if one is playing football, but they are rather a hindrance in tennis and simply irrelevant for playing chess.

Hobbes – whose naturalism we usually admire, as he seemed to found politics on the avoidance of a commonly accepted evil (violent death) – knew that this naturalizing move was highly problematic. Nevertheless, it was part of a persuasive strategy to convert cantankerous and fundamentalist believers,[8] engaged in risking their lives for honour and other ultimate values, into proper subjects dedicated to the pursuit of happiness, property and consumption. The fact that his strategy of persuasion was successful, so as even to hide its character as a *political project* and make it appear as natural, should not blind us to the fact that, after all it remained a project. If adopted, it results in certain types of actors and political structures whose co-constitution is usually overlooked. It also makes it appear that the success of this process is a triumph of reason over irrationality. Other political projects then become simple stepping-stones to modernity, or they are reactionary, harking back to times long bygone. In addition, rationality, reduced to purely instrumental thinking, is then considered the only legitimate form of reflection on action – never mind its limitations, which threaten to make rational fools of us, to use Sen's (1999) terminology.

These brief remarks on the non-natural constructed foundations of Hobbes and his concept of rationality also show why rational choice approaches (see Chwaszcza, ch. 8) and constructivism differ despite their common emphasis on choice and the production of social reality. While adherents of rational choice share with constructivists the first commitment, their ways part rather remarkably at the second crossing.[9] And although constructivists usually share these two commitments, there exist significant differences among them. Some constructivists, such as Wendt, apparently believe that scientific realism is compatible with a constructivist perspective (Wendt 1999: ch. 2), which seems incoherent to me. Aside from the fact that scientific realists are quite a motley crew, they have to espouse the position that there is one true description of how things are. While they no longer use terms like 'essence', there is nevertheless a foundationalist belief in being able to go to the things themselves and capture them by some hard data.

Here, I certainly do not want to inveigh against empirical research or claim that quantitative analyses can never be useful since they do not ask the deep questions that, of course, have always to do with epistemology and philosophical issues. A good antidote to the hypertrophic concern with epistemology and with positioning oneself within certain camps would be the realization that not all deep questions can be answered. 'Why is there something and not nothing?' is certainly deep but unanswerable. Similarly, not all questions have to be asked every time around, since we usually do not move in incommensurable universes. Most of the time we can make sense out of each other's work, criticize and sometimes even improve it without addressing these ultimate questions. The belief that we constantly have to wear a badge identifying us as bona fide members of an exclusive club or party strikes me as definitely odd.

Nevertheless, I do maintain that hard data are also constructions based on conceptual choices that, therefore, cannot speak for themselves.

Consequently, extreme care has to be taken not to treat them as if they were natural facts. In a way, practitioners of comparative research have always cautioned that treating such presumably natural facts as age as universally given in any social system is likely to court disaster. As we all know, a forty-year-old New York socialite is probably at the height of her power and influence, while for a peasant woman in Bolivia life might be over as she has virtually no choices left. Similarly, the sociologist Ulrich Beck has warned of using 'zombie concepts', such as the nation-state, which have largely lost their power but, like zombies, still populate the well-trodden paths of theory and go through the motions as if they were alive (Willms and Beck 2004: conversation 1).

This brief discussion shows that the role of language, of concept formation, meaning and interpretation cannot be circumvented by opting for a thin version of constructivism. While constructivism is certainly neither a theory nor a methodology, taking this perspective does enable and constrain our research designs and our choice of the tools in making our case. In the following, I want to discuss several areas of particular importance in this respect. First, I will deal with issues of concept formation and the meaning of our theoretical terms. Contrary to the traditional issues of operationalization, taxonomic rigour and clear reference, I shall argue that most of the recommendations flowing from these criteria have to be taken with a grain of salt: descriptions of things as they are do not exist; the logic of concept formation does not follow the classical taxonomic criteria; and finally, most concepts are therefore contestable, particularly in the social sciences. They are not observer-neutral, but involve self-reference; thus their meaning is not disclosed by simple observation and accurate description but by understanding their grammar, their function within a larger semantic field and their use. Second, I want to address issues of explanation, when considered from a constructivist perspective.

Problems of description, classification and operationalization

According to the standards of the scientific method, we first have to describe our objects, clearly separating accidental properties (such as colour) from those that determine what a thing is, such as 'dog' or 'house'. Subsequently, we have to classify them according to the usual taxonomic requirements (such as exclusivity of the classes allowing for unequivocal attribution) and, finally, if there are no clear points of reference – as when we deal with such abstract problems as democracy or sovereignty – we have to operationalize the concept, showing by what type of operations we want to define or measure it. Since in the latter case we have to make qualitative judgements in which our values play a role – my democracy might be your fascism – the scientific canon requires a neutral observational stance. This means not letting one's preferences or values get ahead of one's task, but also relying on empirical data and objective measurements. The following three examples, however, show the problematic nature of this account. Quite aside from the fact that the strict separation into ascending steps is difficult to maintain in practice, the idea of a neutral description, free from theoretical or value contamination, is unachievable. This impossibility has little to do with the interference of values or personal preferences that are not susceptible to a scientific treatment (*de gustibus non est disputandum*). Finally, the assumption that conceptual difficulties can be circumvented by clear operational definitions is similarly mistaken.

Let us begin with the procedure of matching a concept to phenomena of the outer world, bringing it under the appropriate description. I shall use as a foil the concept of a planet, as it seems to provide a straightforward case of matching a *res extensa* of the world with a concept of the *res cogitans*. Although all heavenly bodies exhibit mass, some seem to be fixed in place, while others roam. Even if fixed heavenly bodies are not actually fixed as the universe expands, the distinction still holds and provides important information as to the observable behaviour of these two classes of body. Consequently, the class of planets contains bodies like Venus and Earth as well as some comets that wander around. But what about asteroids or moons? Do they also belong here, or are they in a different class? In the case of moons, we could say that their distinguishing characteristic is that they are 'trabants', while asteroids are simply chaff or debris flying around in space. In the latter case, is size the important characteristic? But then, how big has the mass to be in order to qualify as a planet? Making size the important dimension and choosing a more or less arbitrary but agreed upon limit seems to take care of these puzzles and to provide an objective and empirically sound operationalization of the concept.

However, as shown by the proposals and discussions of the International Astronomic Union to agree on a definition of a planet (August 2006 meeting in Prague), things are a bit more complicated.[10] Under the new definition, comets are no longer planets, but are treated as asteroids – officially called 'small objects within the solar system'. Some moons, like ours, remain within that class; however, Charon, Pluto's moon, would become a planet, while Pluto itself would no longer enjoy that status. The reason is that in the former case, the gravitational centre lies within one of the two bodies of the Earth/Moon system, while this is not the case with Pluto and Charon. All is not lost for our moon, since in a few million years it will be promoted to planet too. By then it will have moved away from Earth – a movement of about 3 cm a year, as ascertained by laser measurements – and its revolution will take forty-seven instead of the present twenty-eight days.

This story drives home the fact that naming a thing is not akin to a simple empirical matching operation, but depends on the theoretical assumptions guiding our observations. Furthermore, while size remains an important dimension, there is a certain unease with this classification: how small (or how big) have objects to be, in order to be classified accordingly, raises an important theoretical issue. A consensus definition is certainly helpful, since it avoids classificatory confusions; the example of moons shows, however, that we seek theoretically more informative distinctions. After all, classifications reflect an important theoretical element (gravitational centre) on which the distinctions are based. In short, what is desirable is not a clear reference to the properties of objects, but rather a *theoretically relevant* distinction.

Note that such determinations and the controversies surrounding them have little to do with whether or not measurements are objectively recording factual matters, or with the alleged indeterminacy of values that might get in the way. As conventionally argued, the latter are simple personal preferences that have nothing to do with science and must be avoided at all costs. But putting the problem this way is essentially misleading. What counts descriptively as big or small is not determinable by looking harder at the facts. It depends on, perhaps not always explicitly formulated, but nevertheless important, field-dependent criteria. While a millimetre might be a big deviation for a watchmaker or a producer of microchips, it is of no importance – owing to its smallness – to the architect or engineer who is building a fifty-storey office tower. Outside a field of reference there is simply no fact of the matter, as philosophers would say. Again, the example shows that the meaning of a concept – even if it presumably only describes – is hardly provided by its direct reference, but by its position within a larger semantic field.

In the same vein, consider the following situation. You enter my study and see, aside from the desk, chairs and a lamp, several paperweights keeping down some papers. Why do you perceive paperweights rather than two pieces of granite or Murano glass? Obviously, the identification has little to do with immediate perception.[11] Would it then be more correct to say that there are two stones or pieces of glass on my table? Hardly, because it would hide the function of these objects, which stones in nature do not have. Neither would it be correct to say that the accurate description would be 'paperweight' if they no longer serve that specific purpose. In general, would it be sensible to argue that these objects are susceptible to one and only one accurate description? What these objects are is obviously not independent of their usage; the accurate description depends on the familiarity of the observer with the customs and habits of a given culture, rather than on their material properties. Anyone familiar with the embarrassment of having treated a bidet as a urinal will be able to attest to these 'facts'.

Consequently, arguing that the only true description consists in the material substratum seems rather silly. If it were true – that we always have to go back to the material givens – we could never perceive a 'broom' but would have to use circumlocutions such as: 'I see a handle with some bristles and a wire holding them together'. Again, we notice here that meaning is *use rather than reference*. We use a term because we name an object according to a specific use; it does not matter whether the handle consists of wood or metal, the bristles are plastic or natural fibres, and the device holding it together is of wire or string.

These considerations are of even greater importance when we deal with contested concepts such as democracy or sovereignty. But why are they any more contested than the disagreements we have encountered in classifying planets? The short and simple answer is that terms like democracy and sovereignty are not referring to objects of the world out there. Neither democracy nor the international system nor sovereignty runs around like a black dog so that the only question remaining is whether it is a labrador, black shepherd, or some other mutt. Even though the use of a noun mistakenly suggests a similarity to designating objects, the only reference we can make out, after some reflection, is to *an assembly of practices and actions.*

However, since we do make a distinction between an event and an action – the former being just the result of some natural forces such as an earthquake or a rainstorm – our vocabularies differ quite significantly in the two cases (Conolly 1983). In the case of actions, issues of praise or blame, of responsibility, of failing, of making a mistake, perhaps even of super-rogation shape our discourse, while of course no such concerns are part of our vocabulary for events. Thus, when we describe an action by saying that someone abandoned another person – instead of just noticing that someone opened the door, walked through it and left – we want to call attention to the special character of the action. Stating what is generally true (that one has to open doors before one leaves) would be entirely beside the point.

Submitting blindly to the search for generalizations, or cleansing our language of all (value-laden) points of view might miss what is of the greatest interest to us when we interact with one another and assess actions.[12] While generalizations insure against idiosyncrasies or adhocery, they are not a potent antidote to irrelevance in both description and appraisal. Traditional social analysis has therefore warned against engaging too readily in generalizations, particularly in a comparative context, since the more general concepts are, the less informative they become (Sartori 1970: 1033–53). Consequently, there is virtue in using middle-range concepts and middle-range theories. (See here Mair, ch. 10 who comes to the same conclusion based on a different position.) Besides, such a procedure is also well in tune with how we form concepts. As the cognitive revolution in social psychology suggests (Lakoff 1987), we reason from a paradigmatic best example and move from there by analogous reasoning to other cases (Davis 2005). This inevitably leads to fuzzier concepts than classical taxonomies would allow, posing new challenges to analysis; but such a strategy does not entail the deleterious consequences that are usually associated with unclear concepts.[13]

But let us return to the example of sovereignty which, as we said, is not a thing but represents certain practices and actions, or rather *the entitlements* to certain practices and actions. Consequently, sovereignty cannot be conceptualized as a homogeneous quantity or position, as when we naïvely ask where sovereignty is now located after a transfer to Brussels. It is an ascription of a *status*, of certain enabling rights and constraining obligations that allow an actor to do things that he could not do without it. Only states can send ambassadors or make treaties, only universities can confer degrees, and actions done in the name of a corporation are quite different from those done by the same persons in their unofficial capacity. In short, looking at the facts will not tell us much. This explains that sovereignty might be attributed to failed states, those whose exercise of public power is highly contested and where no single power-holder can claim supremacy (Jackson 1990), or to governments in exile that are not even pretending to be in power.

Is Norway more sovereign than France because the latter is in the EU, while the former has not joined? Has Switzerland been less sovereign than Italy since the former could not freely contract alliances because it had been neutralized by the Great Powers? Was Luxembourg ever really sovereign, since it could hardly ever defend its borders? All of these questions are puzzling only if we assume that sovereignty stands for something that is treated like a thing that we can observe. But even in that case simple observation will not do, since we must distinguish among admissions (the waiver of my right to exclude), violations (illegal entry) and failures to assert this right. All problems require *appraisals* rather than simple observations.

Even on a common-sense level, there is something odd here about the obsession with observation and measurement. Is a nation that has no contacts with others and does not participate in any social undertakings more sovereign than one that is deeply embedded in a web of relations and which can (also therefore) call the shots? That, of course, is the old Robinson Crusoe problem, since Robinson was nearly totally free from interference. Or is, for us, freedom not intrinsically linked to the notions of meaningful choices, to agency, autonomy, respect, standing and membership (Berlin 2002: 188–217)? In short, the meaning of these terms *does not consist in their constative capacity* but in the links they forge to other concepts and the boundaries they draw. Consequently, they can only be understood through the rules by which they are constituted, not through the events or phenomena of the outer world. A goal is a goal only if I understand soccer; and that means that there is not a goal every time the ball enters the net! Offsides, fouls and mistakes of a referee (empowered to make this determination) clearly demonstrate that it is not observations but shared understandings that constitute the relevant facts.

These examples raise several problems turning on issues of interpretation, as the following example of the sign 'No dogs on the escalator' shows. If I take my dog, Ulysses, on the escalator and the officer writes a ticket, can I claim that the rule does not apply because only dogs and not a dog are prohibited? The official will probably be unimpressed, but the next day I find a new sign: 'No dog of any kind allowed on the escalator'. Fortunately, I have my little pet puma Mao with me and I argue again for the irrelevance of the rule. Mao is certainly not a dog. Exasperated, the official issues me a ticket explaining that obviously the meaning of the rule was to prevent harm, citing the experience that animals have caught their claws in the grooves of the steps and have panicked. Finally, on the third day, I see a sign: 'No animals on the escalator'; but fortunately, I am in the company of my tame boa constrictor Sling-sling which lazily hangs around my shoulders. She is certainly an animal but arguably not on the escalator, nor do the functional arguments of yesterday apply. Besides, I see in front of me a woman with a budgerigar in a cage, who passes by the inspector without any problem.

We could go on with further absurdities, but they are absurd only because we well know that the meaning of a rule is not simply a matter of descriptive content and that we all share in inter-subjective understandings telling us what is the case and how we can go on. Thus, while rules are indispensable for the reproduction of the social system, this reproduction is never automatic, issuing in identical or iconic reproductions. Rather, precisely because of the need for interpretation, we can adjust to new circumstances before even having to invent a new rule. In this way, stability and change can be accommodated in this reproductive process. Note also that the rule's scope is not enhanced through generalizations (or restricted through simple classificatory devices), but through analogies and exceptions whereby careful attention to how facts and norms interact plays a significant role. Thus while a gun or a knife, or an ice pick, are weapons in our commonsensical understanding, we very well understand that a pencil (not all pencils) is a weapon when an enraged student attacks his teacher with it, or that a soda pop released into the eyes of a shopkeeper at the moment he opens his cash register is used as a weapon by the youngsters who attempt to rob him. Similarly, in a traditional society where people live in huts with thatched roofs, the person who is spreading sparks might be considered the cause of a fire and be held liable. In an industrial society in which sparks from cars, locomotives, power lines, and aircraft abound, the house-owner, insisting on a thatched roof, might be held liable, since his use of flammable materials causes fire.

Issues of explanation

The last remarks lead us directly to the problem of explanation. Allegedly, all scientific explanations have to exhibit a specific form in order to qualify. Here, subsumption under a general law or the identification of a causal mechanism are the most common specifications. But while the controversy between adherents of the subsumption model and those emphasizing causal mechanisms (see Héritier, ch. 4) is already subverting the idea that scientific explanations are all of one cloth, recent arguments about constitutive explanations cast further doubt on efforts to canonize certain forms of explanation. Thus, when I show that a token serves as money, I am not elaborating on a cause, but I am showing how it functions in a society and how the practices of saving, purchasing and transferring are related to it. Also, contrary to logical positivisms which postulate that all scientific explanations have to assert the logical equivalence between explanation and prediction, the theory of evolution in biology is explanatory but cannot predict. Changes occur through random variations in reproduction and selection mechanisms in which often seemingly unviable species survive through symbiosis or finding niches.

Finally, we ask for explanations in a variety of contexts, making it difficult to argue that only one type of explanation is the true one. For example, both the coroner and the prosecutor at a murder trial proffer accounts of what caused the death of the victim, the coroner focusing on the wounds inflicted by the murder weapon and the prosecutor on the murderer's motives and the evidence placing him at the scene. While we might be inclined to admit that different types of explanation exist, we may still want to reserve the term 'scientific explanation' to those that use laws and efficient causes, while dropping the requirement of the logical equivalence of prediction and explanations.[14] The problem with such a stipulation is not only that it does not take care of constitutive explanation but also that it eliminates highly important issues of interest to us (such as guilt or responsibility). This at least indirectly shows why the notion of cause has to be wider.

As we have seen, rules and rights might provide reasons for action, but they do not work like efficient causes. This leads often to the postulation that material factors or self-explanatory interests are assumed to do the explaining. But even some of the adamant structuralists cast doubt on such constructions. Thus Waltz speaks of permissive causes (1959: 233), adding one more category to the traditional dichotomy between necessary and sufficient. But recognizing that the restriction to efficient causality is not viable supports the Aristotelian strategy of treating causation as a cluster-concept of different types (efficient, material, final or formal) rather than restricting causality to one type. Similarly, Wendt (1999) recently attempted to show that explanations are of two types: one explaining the possible (how is action X possible), the other explaining the actual (what brought X about rather than Y). It addresses the old explaining/understanding controversy by adducing structural explanations for the analysis of the possible, where understanding is required, while the actual is reserved for traditional modes of analysis. But this is too simple. The problem is again one of privileging necessary and sufficient conditions, and efficient causes for explaining actual choices. But is a finalistic explanation (any 'in order to' argument), which we commonly use, no explanation, because it does not entail efficient causes? This, of course, has implications for case studies and the explanations that are used in the single in-depth analysis they provide (see Venesson, ch. 12).

Besides, consider in this context the following case. When we try to ascertain what caused a fire in a building, we proceed through a variety of steps that link natural facts and actions, with the result that the final finding resembles more a narrative than a simple causal account. For example, the source of the fire was an electric coffee machine that was not switched off. However, it would not have caused the fire, had the window not been open and had the curtain, moved by the wind, not touched the hot plate (since I had not placed the coffee-pot there but had left it in the sink). But even the curtain would not have been able to cause further damage had the initial flames not reached a pile of old papers atop the cupboard, and had the sprinkler system actually worked instead of being deactivated by a faulty sensor. In other words, instead of arguing with necessary and sufficient conditions, we are only able to make much more contingent claims.

As Mackie (1976) has shown, we usually face situations in which explanations are of the INUS type. The identified cause or causes is an insufficient but non-redundant element of a complex which is itself unnecessary but sufficient for the production of a result. While certainly causal laws are somewhere at work, covering the combustibility and flashpoints of various materials, they do relatively little for the question in which we are interested; in addition, not much would be gained if we now engaged in the search for generalizations (explaining all fires? or only those in which natural causes and actions interact? or only certain types, such as electrical fires?). The latter questions are certainly worth pursuing if I am interested in establishing the likelihood of fires, designing better products or creating redundant systems that make the outbreak of fires less likely. But these cases have not much to do with explanations of such an event, but rather with the managing of risks that have been identified on the basis of examining real or hypothetical processes.

Students of historical cases (see also Steinmo, ch. 7) and of process tracing will, of course, recognize the similarity of the difficulties they face when explaining a complex phenomenon such as the outbreak of a war or the genesis of a crisis. Take the example of the outbreak of the First World War. We would have to account for the interaction of weapons and transportation systems (remember that Kaiser Wilhelm could not rescind the mobilization as insufficient troops would then be on the Eastern front, endangering the Schlieffen plan); misperceptions (why did Great Britain not stay neutral?); and contingencies like declaring *Nibelungentreue* (unconditional loyalty) to Austria, so giving it a free hand. Explaining such an occurrence makes it necessary to understand the technical as well as the social conditions and institutional practices, such as war and diplomacy or the role of an actor's attempt to perform within a system (Great Britain as a balancer). In such a case it will not do to stay at the level of plausible causal accounts or of *prima facie* reasons for actions, as we try to enhance the credibility of one explanation sketch by comparing it with others, using counterfactuals and analogical reasoning in establishing what was the case.[15]

Thus, we have to realize that there are many more than merely two stories to tell, as the recent understanding/explaining controversy between Smith/Hollis and Wendt suggests. As Heikki Patomäki pointed out:

We can distinguish between different 'How is action X possible?' questions. When we are concerned with the identity of X, we need an account of relevant constitutive rules. This analysis freezes, so to speak, the social world in question. Then we can move to the world of historical . . . interaction and ask: what are the INUS conditions that made that action possible? At this level we are analysing processual complexes in open systems, and thus we cannot find general necessary conditions of X. Instead, we are interested in the actual constellation of conditions that made X *contingently possible*. Other constellations could have made it contingently possible as well. After this we can ask: what made X actual rather than Y? When posing this question, we are interested in reasons, justifications and the like, organized as discourses, as well as in the interactive actions of various actors. Finally, we can pose this genealogical query: how was X's identity and the relevant constitutive rules produced in the course of historical interaction? (1996: 126)

Admitting the plurality of possible interpretations allows us to free ourselves from the mistaken identification of explanation with one of its forms. It allows us to ask interesting questions instead of eliminating them from the research programme because of a problematic understanding of science.

Indeed, it seems to be one of the ironies of social analysis that we have attempted as much as possible to naturalize our subject matter, paying little attention to the constituent elements of the social world. But actions are not events, reasons are not causes (in the sense of efficient causes), systems are not simple throughputs in which stimuli call forth responses according to the law of *actio est reactio*, values function differently from desires or tastes, power is not a simple function of palpable things and the role of institutions is not limited to or akin to constraints. The social world is of our making, and it requires an *episteme* that takes the questions of our world-making seriously and does not impede an inquiry on the basis of a dogmatic conception of science or of method.

NOTES

1 This rather strange characterization was used by Robert Keohane in lumping together constructivists and Marxists; see Keohane (1988: 379–96).

2 The latter had already devastated several comparative literature departments by releasing the Derridian bug, treating everything as 'texts', while denying the possibility of an authoritative reading of them and attacking the 'logo-centrism' of modernity. See Derrida (1982).

3 See the interesting discussion of this problem by Guzzini (2000: 147–82).

4 See the denial of the distinction by Quine (1953).

5 For a more extensive discussion, see Kratochwil (2007: 1–15).

6 See Descartes (1980), particularly the Fifth Meditation.

7 See the discussion by Mansbridge (1990: ch. l).

8 See, therefore, the modern Hobbes interpretations that stress the persuasive dimension of Hobbes' work, rather than his attempts to found a science '*more geometrico*'. See Johnston (1986) and Skinner (2002).

9 However, 'hard' rational choice advocates consider the real issue to be not choice, but rather 'getting the incentives right' so that the actual outcome follows by necessity and is no longer a choice at all. See Satz and Ferejohn (1994: 71–87).

10 See the article 'Flexibler Mond', *Frankfurter Allgemeine Zeitung*, 23 August 2006, p. N2.

11 For a further discussion, see Searle (2001), especially chs. 2–4.

12 This point is also powerfully made by Rorty (1994: ch. 3).

13 Here Charles Ragin's work is of particular interest. See Ragin (2000).

14 This was the crucial argument for the 'covering-law model' of Popper and Hempel. See Popper (1965), particularly ch. 3, and Hempel (1965).

15 On counterfactuals, see Tetlock, Lebow and Parker (2006); see also Tetlock and Belkin (1996).

6 Culture and social science

Michael Keating

Do we need a concept of culture?

The social sciences face four enduring problems in understanding and explaining behaviour. First is how to account for both continuities and change over time within societies. Second is to explain the connection between micro-level changes and the larger, macro level. Third, and related, is how to explain the connection between individual decisions and the aggregate behaviour of a society as a whole. Fourth is the relationship between the hard facts of the social world and the way in which these are interpreted by people. Several chapters of this book broach these issues. Methodological individualism focuses on the individual and seeks to account for collective behaviour as the sum of individual actions. Chwaszcza's chapter shows how this is done through game theory, but also the limitations of this form of explanation. Pizzorno takes a different approach, by locating the individual within society in a set of reciprocal understandings. Kratochwil argues that our understanding of the world is shaped by the conceptual apparatus that we use.

This chapter seeks to make the link through the concept of culture. Cultural explanations of social phenomena go directly to the collective level, they are essentially social and in many respects (but not quite all) they represent a challenge to methodological individualism. They also seek to bridge external explanation, by reference to the social world, and internalist explanations, which rely on individual interpretation and decision. Yet if culture allows us to identify and explain differences in behaviour among groups – be these nations, classes, genders or localities – it is an extremely elusive and slippery idea, prone to all manner of abuse. Indeed, so difficult is it to use that many social scientists have abandoned it altogether as meaningless or as an excuse for lazy thinking. The argument of this chapter is that culture can help to understand and explain social and political institutions and behaviour, but only if it is understood in a sophisticated way. Although there are numerous difficulties in operationalizing and measuring it, these are not totally insurmountable.

In the nineteenth century, it was common to ascribe differences in political behaviour and institutions among states to 'national character'. This was an ingrained set of attitudes persisting over long periods and explaining the behaviour both of individuals and of states. So the English (sometimes confounded with the British) were pragmatic and committed to gradual change, while the French were dogmatic and prone to revolution. Germans were aggressive and domineering, while Italians were disorganized and Spaniards proud and stubborn. These stereotypical visions have mostly been abandoned as unscientific, overgeneralized and unmeasurable (but see Galtung 1988 for an amusing set of stereotypes about national academic styles). Often they were no more than propaganda on the part of nationalist intellectuals keen on praising or damning according to taste, or rationalizations for events that could not be explained otherwise. The *ex post* nature of the explanation is seen in the rapid changes of stereotypes in the course of the nineteenth century, with the Swiss going from warring highlanders to peaceful and compromising citizens, and the Germans from scholars to aggressive warriors. Yet while these kinds of characterization are easy to dismiss, they are surprisingly resilient and continue to creep in even to social science works.

A more sophisticated concept of culture was used in the classical sociology of Weber and (to some degree) Durkheim, who did not suggest that recognition of cultural factors is incompatible with a broadly positivist ontology or with analytical rigour. Yet the modernization theory that derived from nineteenth-century sociology tended to emphasize one form of rational instrumental action, eliminating culture along with other 'non-rational' accounts. Culture survived as an object of study in certain areas of the social sciences, notably anthropology (Geertz 1973). The influence of anthropology on the other social sciences, however, was limited until recent years by its tendency to concentrate on what were once known as 'primitive societies', places untouched by modernity, in which pre-modern, non-instrumental and irrational beliefs could survive. A few European places, such as the Basque Country, could be added to this list and attracted disproportionate attention from anthropologists. The historians of the French *Annales* school may not often have explicitly invoked culture, but their work did examine the specificities of local societies and their continuities over time. French political geographers like Emmanuel Todd (1990) have traced continuities in behaviour among regions over long periods. Studies of Italian politics after the Second World War emphasized the persistence of subcultures based on the Catholic, Communist and lay poles and their dominance in particular parts of the country (Parisi and Pasquino 1985).

Within political science, cultural explanations have persisted in the political culture literature starting with the studies of Almond and Verba (1965, 1980), based on modern survey research about the attitudes of individuals and using these to account for political development and institutional performance. Specifically, as part of the 'political development' literature, their aim was to identify the prerequisites for liberal democracy by measuring the attitudes of the population. Their results and the methodology behind them attracted much criticism. The studies were said to be ethnocentric in taking the United States as the most advanced society and American values as universal ones. They used an essentially individualistic tool, the survey of individual citizens, to make inferences at the level of the society as a whole. They took states rather unproblematically as the relevant units of analysis, although they did examine the attitudes of social categories within them. Political culture studies have continued in the United States by scholars such as Ronald Inglehart (1988) but have been subject to much the same criticisms as the earlier work (Seligson 2002).

For the most part, however, social and political science during the post-war years sought to eliminate cultural explanations as part of the 'behaviouralist revolution'. This attitude stemmed from its universalist assumptions about human behaviour and action and the search for a science of politics and society that would be valid everywhere. It owed much to efforts to imitate the methods and approaches of the natural sciences with their universal validity and laws. There was also a normative element, in that cultural explanations, and the associated stereotypes, could be seen as a form of primordialism or even racism, giving sustenance to those who argued that colonial peoples could not equip themselves with the tools of liberal self-government or aspire to Western living standards. Progressives argued that, on the contrary, institutions and procedures are universally applicable and that social engineering can transform societies and lead them to modernity. Their convictions were only reinforced when conservatives embraced functionalist sociology derived from scholars such as Talcott Parsons, emphasizing the need for shared beliefs and values in order to maintain social order. Sections of the left even condemned Durkheim as the 'watchdog of the bourgeoisie' (Poggi 2000: 11). Political scientists, especially in the United States (Eatwell 1997),[1] were particularly reluctant to talk of the relevance of religion, perhaps because of their secular inclinations.

The aim of the dominant positivist social science was to explain matters using only universally applicable variables, so 'eliminating proper names' (Przeworski and Teune 1970). If societies differed it was because they were unevenly affected by these universal variables, for example industrial structure or levels of development, not because of anything inherent in the society itself. Cultural explanations were dismissed as tautological or redundant, or as mere attempts to redescribe differences that could better be accounted for in a more scientific way. Rational choice and methodological individualism, as they became dominant from the 1980s, provided even less space for culture, seeking links between the individual and the collective through game theory. New institutionalism was another way of linking the individual and the collective and the past with the present; but at least in its early forms, this too was informed by methodological individualism, with institutions imposing constraints and creating incentives for individual actors. It did seem, for a time, as though all the work being done by cultural explanations could be accomplished by other means. Like metaphysics before it, culture could retreat in the face of scientific advance.

The return of culture

Since the 1990s, there has been something of a rediscovery of culture. While in sociology this was known as the 'culturalist turn', political science has often used other labels so as not to arouse the criticisms received by the earlier approaches. There has been a widespread questioning of universalism and of the whole modernist paradigm with its assumptions about the convergence of societies on a single model. There has also been a change in the ethical status of universalism and particularism. In the 1960s those disputing theories of convergence were accused of being primordialists and essentialists, and of devaluing the ability of non-European peoples to develop and arrive at modernity. Now it is recognized that that vision of modernity itself was ethnocentric and the product less of genuine universalism than of the domination of American and European cultural values. The earlier assumptions have, to some degree, been reversed, with much of the political left now emphasizing diversity while large sections of the right insist on universalism and unity. This point was brought home forcefully in the controversy over Francis Fukuyama's (1992) *The End of History*, which explicitly proclaimed the universal triumph of the model of Western liberal capitalism as the culmination of history itself. There is a lively debate in normative theory on the idea of multiculturalism and the extent of diversity that might be possible or desirable in a democratic polity (see Bauböck, ch. 3). At the extremes, this flows into forms of post-modern analysis in which there are no grand narratives or historical progress at all, and sometimes into a form of moral relativism in which all cultural values are equal. It meets cultural studies, with their origins in literature and the emphasis on the subjective and the possibilities for multiple interpretations of the social sphere. I do not propose to follow that road here, but the idea that collective belief systems do influence behaviour has come again to influence even the more empirical forms of social science.

The rediscovery of culture has also been stimulated by criticisms of methodological individualism and rational choice. The latter has been accused of tautology in its assumption that people act in their individual self-interest. If self-interest merely refers to material benefit, the assumption is clearly wrong; if it encompasses everything that the individual values, the theory risks tautology (see Chwaszcza, ch. 8, and Pizzorno, ch. 9). Cultural approaches help us locate individuals in a social context in which their values, aspirations and associations are formed and in which their choices are given meaning. It also allows us to bring in emotional forms of action not easily explicable in the calculating language of rational choice. Indeed, if we take account of the varied sources of human behaviour, rational choice might be seen as merely one culturally determined form of action among others, itself in need of explanation. This exposes the assumption at the heart of much rational choice literature: that it is only collective action that needs to be explained, since the default position of human beings is individualism. Yet some of the profoundest thinkers of the Enlightenment (for example, Ferguson 1966) noted that the individual is itself a product of society, which evolved over time from essentially collective forms of action to individual-based ones, a problem that also concerned Durkheim.

There has been a certain retreat in the social sciences from grand explanations and universal theories towards more contextualized studies and limited comparisons. This is attributable to the failure of large-scale comparison often to say anything interesting or useful given the impossibility of controlling for all the variables at play. It also stems from a recognition that context itself is important and is complex, not reducible to a set of variables. Taken to the extreme, contextual forms of social and political analysis can end up as no more than a series of individual case studies, with the conclusion that they are all different. Properly done, however, comparison of whole cases can contribute to more general understanding (see della Porta, ch. 11, and Vennesson, ch. 12).

Earlier political culture studies were rightly criticized for assuming that cultural differences would correspond to the boundaries of sovereign states. This is part of a larger problem in the social sciences, the primacy of the 'nation-state' as the unit of analysis. Indeed, at one time, the state framework was so powerful that it was not even recognized, but served as the invisible container of social and political processes. Comparative politics was the study of different states, focusing usually on their different institutional configurations. Once again, there are normative assumptions, sometimes hidden and sometimes explicit, as in the dismissal of small and stateless nations and an assumption that large states represent universal values by liberals like John Stuart Mill (1972) and, more recently, Ralf Dahrendorf (1995, 2000).

Yet challenges to the state through global pressures, sub-state mobilization and the advance of the market have forced social scientists to recognize it as a partial and bounded social form often competing with other frameworks, including transnational regimes, sub-state regions, the markets and ethnic and identity-based communities. It is a historically contingent form, changing its boundaries, functions and status over time, and it is the propagator not just of universal values but of specific cultural norms, complemented and sometimes challenged by others. The legitimacy of the state and its extensions into civil society cannot be taken for granted but must be given explicit normative justification. As the state is demystified and seen as just one set of institutions among others, this has raised the question of how institutions operate and why people obey them.

The 'new institutionalism' covers a wide range of ideas and applications (March and Olsen 1984; Steinmo, Thelen and Longstreth 1992; Hall and Taylor 1996; Peters 2005; see Steinmo, ch. 7). At least three versions have been recognized. Rational choice institutionalism posits that institutions provide the incentives and disincentives to which rational actors respond in determining how to pursue their self-interest. So the individual knows his/her desires, but the institutions provide the mechanisms and mould the immediate choices on how to pursue those goals. Historical institutionalism explains continuity over time through 'path dependence', whereby decisions taken at one time constrain those taken at a later stage. Sociological institutionalism shows how the institutions in which an individual lives, through socialization and learning, shape the very values and desires of that individual.[2] It is thus a way of bringing culture back in, although its origins in post-war behaviourist social science and in organization theory mean that its proponents have often inherited the aversion to cultural approaches of their time and will often shun the very term 'culture'.

The debate on 'social capital' also takes us back to culture, while avoiding the term. This concept originated as yet another attempt to explain human co-operation, given the limitations of rational choice theory and its assumptions about individual self-interest (Coleman 1988). The social capital idea is that societies can generate norms and practices of trust and co-operation, which over time will strengthen each other by their positive results. It is a powerful idea but one that raises formidable problems in definition and operationalization. Too often, social capital has been defined not by what it is but by what it does (Portes 2001), a form of teleological explanation that reads backwards from effects to causes. Others identify social capital with associationalism and seek to measure it by counting the number of associations to which individuals belong. The problem here is that associations may be favourable to broad social co-operation or, on the contrary, mechanisms for veto points, rent-seeking and domination (Olson 1982; Portes 2001).

Diffuse reciprocity – that is, the willingness to act in the knowledge that the beneficiary will return the favour in due course, possibly through a chain of individuals – is important. So is the norm of trust – that is, the willingness to trust people one does not know personally. There is a broad agreement that, to address the problem of teleology, we must seek the origins of social capital not where it is manifested today but in some other area altogether. For example, norms and practices forged during an era of religious practice might then function as a means of sustaining social solidarity in a modern welfare society. This takes us ineluctably back into culture and the creation, sustenance and diffusion of norms over time.

These ideas have had a strong influence on the study of economic behaviour and development. This is surprising given the dominance of rational choice and individualist explanations in the science of economics and most portrayals of the market. Yet it has been known for a long time that capitalist markets do not work on competition alone, but on a balance of competition and co-operation. Institutional economics is an effort to break away from the neoclassical paradigm and focus on the importance of institutions in shaping economic decision-making. It bears a close resemblance to the neoinstitutionalism that later came to sociology and political science. There was an early reluctance to resort to culture as an explanation and a tendency to stick to a form of rational choice institutionalism. More recent work by Douglass North, however, adopts a richer and more normatively informed concept of institutions, and does not shy away from culture, defined as the 'intergenerational transfer of norms, values, and ideas' (2005: 50).

Capitalism itself can be explained only partly by rational self-interest, since it depends on capitalists accumulating wealth well beyond their own capacity to consume. Weber and later Tawney looked to a transcendental explanation, in the role of Protestantism in fostering the desire for signs of worldly wealth and in breaking down Catholic norms against entrepreneurship. The assumption that Catholicism is an obstacle to economic growth has been widely abandoned and recent works even show how it has promoted development (Berthet and Pallard 1997); but these serve merely to reinforce the link between religious beliefs forged for one purpose, and mundane matters of earthly wealth, through the forging of beliefs, norms and practices that carry over from one to another. There is now a literature on varieties of capitalism, which shows that there is not just one form of capitalist market order but variations. Again, these are usually explained by reference to institutional frameworks and historical path dependence, with the term 'culture' avoided; but norms and values do also feature.

Institutions and social capital have featured heavily in the new literature on local and regional economic development (Bagnasco and Trigilia 1983; Storper 1997; Cooke and Morgan 1998; Scott 1998; Crouch, Le Galès, Trigilia *et al.* 2001). These build on the findings that relative success and failure of regions and localities can no longer be explained by traditional factor endowments, access to raw materials and markets. Rather, the social construction of the locality or region, and the way in which firms, governments and other social entities are organized, better explains their fortunes. This picks up on an earlier insight by Alfred Marshall on industrial districts in late nineteenth-century Britain. After showing how firms in these districts were able to exploit economies of agglomeration and specialization, he added that these objective factors were not all and that there was 'something in the air'. Since the 1970s, attention has been paid again to industrial districts by scholars both in North America and in Europe. All emphasize the importance of local factors and the social construction of these districts, diffuse reciprocity and widespread trust. Some, notably the US-based authors, stress the role of institutions and incentives in creating systems of mutual dependence, while others (especially in Italy), drawing on organizational sociology, show how mutual learning takes place and individual and collective rationalities are bridged. This is the 'transaction costs' approach based in rational choice theory. Others go more directly to norms, values and traditions.

More contentiously, some scholars have sought to go beyond economic development in positing social capital as the basis for a whole model of local society. Putnam (1993) presents a rather simplified version of the argument in order to explain the relative success of the regions of Italy.[3] He introduces the expanded term 'civicness' as a composite covering economic entrepreneurialism, civic responsibility and democratic maturity, and seeks to measure it in a variety of ways. The book is written in the language of the new institutionalism, but the result largely repeats the stereotypical vision of Italy produced earlier by Banfield (1958). Amin (1999: 373) has argued that certain regions show 'public sector efficiency in the provision of services; civic autonomy and initiative in all areas of social and economic life; a culture of reciprocity and trust which facilitates the economics of association; containment of the high costs of social breakdown and conflict; and potential for economic innovation and creativity based on social confidence and capability'. Others have been more cautious, arguing only that at the regional level there may be a new synthesis between economic development and social solidarity (Cooke and Morgan 1998; Keating, Loughlin and Deschouwer 2003).

Putnam and his followers risk falling into the same trap as the previous generation of political culture studies, reasoning from individual directly to collective behaviour. Normative arguments often lie just below the surface, since it seems that the ideology of social capital or civicness offers an alternative both to the unbridled markets of neoliberals and to the statist traditions of the left, while not lapsing into the politically incorrect realms of culture. This gives it a huge appeal to politicians of the 'third way' tendency. It also represents an instance of the 'double hermeneutic' (see della Porta and Keating, ch. 2) whereby academic ideas get adopted by political actors and then refracted back to researchers.

Policy studies have similarly rediscovered norms and shared-values process. At one time, the policy process was studied as a goal-oriented activity, often with discrete stages, from defining the problem, through policy formulation, to implementation. Later this gave way to approaches emphasizing the different goals and strategies of the multiple actors at the various stages, often from a rational choice perspective, based on individuals' self-interest. More recently, there has been a return of ideas and of shared understandings and meanings that bind people in policy communities, 'advocacy coalitions' (Sabatier and Jenkins-Smith 1999) or 'epistemic communities'. Again, these writers shy away from the term 'culture', but what they are talking about often seems rather close to anthropologists' use of the term.

Another example of culture concerns nationalism and ethnicity. For a time after the Second World War, little was written about nationalism, which was seen as a legacy of the past, thankfully being transcended. Even the post-colonial societies, it was thought, would merely use nationalism as a mechanism for self-government before moving on. Nationalist revivals in industrial societies and the persistence of ethnic divisions in post-colonial societies from the 1970s provoked a new wave of literature. Most of these authors saw nationalism, not as a hangover from a pre-modern era but as a product of modernity itself (Anderson 1983; Gellner 1991). Condemning primordial approaches and insisting on the construction of the nation, they tended to downplay cultural factors and emphasize economic and social change. Yet, while sometimes convincing in showing how modernity had created the idea of the nation, they rarely succeeded in explaining why *particular* nations had emerged. Critics argued that there must be some underlying substratum of identity on which social modernization worked in different ways. The concept of ethnicity also made a strong comeback in the context of a revival of identity politics. Modern scholarship has shown that it is a malleable idea, with ethnic identities being made, remade and negotiated constantly. They cannot be understood or defined by purely objective criteria but rather by self-consciousness and common references. This takes us away from the old racial conceptions of ethnicity towards a more cultural one.[4]

It is not only ethnicity and nationalism that have been framed in a cultural way. In the early 1960s, E. P. Thompson's (1980) *Making of the English Working Class* broke with Marxist orthodoxy according to which social classes were the outcome of objective relationships to the means of production. For Thompson, the working class was formed in specific places according to its own traditions, practices and norms. More recently, there has been controversy over whether underachievement among certain groups may be connected to a culture of failure or 'dependency', transmitted across generations. Proponents argue that such an understanding points to the need for more detailed social intervention and shows the limits of the market as a mechanism for social inclusion. Critics complain that it is a form of 'blaming the victim' and diverting attention away from structural problems and public policies.

Bringing culture back in

Newer approaches to the cultural factor in the social sciences seek to avoid the reductionism and essentialism of the past, in which behavioural traits and customs were rooted in particular societies, largely immutable and distinct from rational behaviour. Instead, culture is taken as a complex of influences that shape the conditions for rational action, explain the workings of institutions and sustain social practices across time, but which are themselves mutable and amenable to human action. It has several components.

The first is as a means of defining the reference group, whether this be an ethnicity, a social class or a social or political movement. Identity has come to new prominence in social science, as the old categories of modern or industrial society seem to lose their power. In its worst form, this becomes a form of primordialism or essentialism, in which individuals are credited with ascriptive (that is, not chosen by themselves) identities which guide and explain behaviour. The terms 'culture' and 'identity' are often used in a confusing manner, overlapping in some cases, coinciding in others. There is a tendency in some writings to treat identity as a master-category so that ethnicity and gender determine behaviour as class supposedly did in the past. Sometimes, identities are presented as based on objective factors like income and wealth (for social class), sex (in the case of gender) or primordial traits (for ethnicity).

More sophisticated approaches see social and political identities as constructed, contested, open to change and often ambivalent. Individuals may have more than one identity, often corresponding to different social roles – say, as a parent, a member of a national group, a member of a class – but even competing as influences within a single role, as when people have more than one ethnic identity available. Identity in this sense is forged by socialization into a culture, which consists of an elaborate series of codes, including shared knowledge and interpretations, allowing members of the group to reinforce their self-identity and to recognize each other. Some cultural differences may be large and denote different lifestyles and social values, but this is not necessary for them to work as group markers. Rather, a sense of group solidarity and belonging is built on mechanisms of inclusion and exclusion. Subtle codes and signs are important in societies in which the differences among members of the groups are not otherwise apparent and where differences in substantive values might be insignificant. In Northern Ireland, there is an elaborate procedure known as 'guessing' whereby two individuals, in a first encounter, can each work out to which community the other belongs. Accents within many languages give clues as to regional and class origins and are used to display or disguise group affiliation.

A second element of culture is as a framework for interpretation and constructing visions of the world. Human society is highly complex and individuals are faced with a variety of stimuli and experiences, of which they have to make sense using limited cognitive faculties. They therefore need to select, to link ideas and to interpret. The scientific endeavour has historically been to establish one set of meanings and interpretation of the physical world, and positivist social science has since the nineteenth century had similar ambitions. Yet, unlike physical objects, human beings make their own interpretations of themselves, their situation and other humans, and social scientists in turn need to interpret the interpretations. An obvious example is religious beliefs, which contain their own cosmologies, including visions of both the physical and spiritual worlds not reducible to instrumental calculation. At the individual and interpersonal levels, there is a need for shared meanings of symbols and gestures, as Geertz (1973) illustrates with his example of winking, formally a mere physical contraction of the eyelid but imbued with deep significance according to the culture (see Kratochwil, ch. 5).

A third element concerns the value put on particular actions and attitudes. Here cultural approaches may complement rational choice ones (Lane and Ersson 2005). If rational choice analysis assumes that people will maximize their own utility function, cultural analysis helps explain what that utility function is. The pursuit of wealth may be an aim, but few would claim that this is the sole motivation of human behaviour, and wealth itself may be valued for different reasons. For some, it allows a high level of personal consumption and material comfort; for others, it gives social prestige; others again see wealth as a means of power. Some cultures place a premium on honour, interpreted in various ways. Some social norms value individualism while others give a higher status to community. Since the 1980s the 'post-materialism' literature has shown how many people in affluent societies are emphasizing non-material issues such as quality of life, liberty or culture (Inglehart 1990).

None of these three elements implies that societies are homogeneous and monolithic or unchanging over time. Societal cultures are almost always contested as valuations of behaviour and achievement evolve, and it is this very quality that leads to their more explicit articulation.[5] Interpretations of the world shift and are never more than partially shared. Definitions of group membership are contested at the boundary, which is where much of the most interesting work on culture is done, and groups are born and die. Individuals normally belong to more than one cultural milieu, receiving multiple and often conflicting signals. Cultural communities are rarely sealed but overlap and link at many points. So one may be a Catholic by religion, a member of a left-wing political subculture and a Basque, all of which are politically relevant but which do not always point in the same direction. It is precisely this form of contestation and debate that allows evolution and change so that any society will contain within it the seeds of its own transformation.

Cultural approaches emphasize symbols and their uses. These may be rituals, flags, names or songs, which signal belonging to a group and defence of its boundaries and implicit meanings. It is tempting to dismiss the resulting politics as 'mere' symbolism, an irrational attachment to things of no intrinsic value. Yet what matters is not the symbols but what they symbolize, as a shorthand for shared interpretations, membership boundaries and values. In the United States, the national flag is given such an exalted status that Congress regularly debates the desirability of a constitutional amendment to ban its desecration. Nations will often have symbolic places taken as representative of whole people. Many movements, including labour movements, religious communities and nationalists have traditions of marching, celebrating values and reinforcing group membership through a shared activity without immediate instrumental value.

A big role is played by myth, an often misunderstood term. Myths are beliefs whose effect is quite independent of their truth or falsehood. Typically they will have a kernel of fact embellished with layers of interpretation so as to create a common story of the group, its identity and its values. These stories and their genesis and transmission are an important object of study in themselves. Cultures also have their own historiographies and traditions serving again not as objective accounts of the past, but as legitimating devices for the dominant interpretation, group definition and value set.

Culture is essentially a collective concept, applicable to social groups, consisting of shared meanings and interpretations and enabling us to get beyond explanations of social processes that are the mere aggregate of individuals' actions or, worse, statements about individual psychology. On the other hand, it is a mistake to see it as something inherent in a collectivity, which then impinges on the individual, with the direction of influence being one way. Such an approach is rightly criticized by those sceptical of cultural explanations as reifying the community, giving it an identity and volition of its own, and making the individual the passive recipient of community influence. Rather than being an objective force bearing down from the outside or a purely subjective phenomenon existing only in the imagination of the individual, culture should be located in the inter-subjective domain, that of social exchange and the construction of shared meanings (Ross 1997). It links the individual and the collective levels of consciousness and action by socializing individuals in common meanings, while individuals in turn help to reshape it. It is not separate from behaviour and social structure, but part of them (Geertz 1973).

The extent to which social and political cultures can be invented and manipulated by elites is a difficult question, only answerable by empirical research; but there is at least a margin available for political action. There may, in addition, be critical times and junctures at which it is possible for another set of leaders to impose their own interpretation on the past and present and create a new vision for the society. This may happen at the time of revolutions, of crisis or of rapid social change in which people are open to new stories to explain their predicament. For example, the French Revolution opened the way for radical new doctrines, germinating for some time, to gain the public stage and forge new collective myths and forms of identity. In that case, victory for the new way of thinking about the state and nation was not achieved until after another hundred years of struggle; but this in turn helped solidify a republican culture and tradition, which powerfully affects French self-images today. Germany and Japan, following the trauma of total defeat, abandoned militaristic self-images for pacifist ones. Other countries (probably most countries) have more than one national image that can be invoked by leaders according to need.

These are sometimes referred to as national traditions, implying a continuity of belief and practice over time. Again, the extent to which this is manipulable is disputed. Hobsbawm (1983) has popularized the idea of the 'invention of tradition', that national identities (which he sees as essentially modern) can be buttressed by ceremonies and rituals that are purportedly ancient but actually recent. The thesis is debatable, especially in its assumption that, in contrast with the inventions, we can discover an objective historical reality. Nonetheless, the debate reintroduced into the study of history and other social sciences the question of how cultural symbols are produced, how they serve to underpin identities and beliefs, and how they adapt to changing circumstances. The study of history always involves selection and interpretation, presenting an analytical narrative with meaning. This is something often neglected in path-dependence theories in social science, in which past events, assumed to be knowable and known, are shown to influence the present. If we take historical interpretation seriously, however, we need to look not only at the past and its influence on the present, but also at how the past is used and reinterpreted in the light of present concerns. So not only the study of history, but also the study of historiography and they way it changes over time becomes important. Summing up, culture is neither primordial nor manipulated but closely tied to action itself (Delanty 1999).

Studying culture

One reason for so many social scientists avoiding the concept of culture has been the difficulty of operationalizing it. It is difficult to isolate cultural factors from other influences and too often the temptation is to explain as much as

possible using other factors, leaving culture as the residual to explain everything else. Yet culture is what gives meaning to other factors in social explanation. For example, the valued good of high social status may take very
different forms in different cultures, be it material wealth, educational
achievement, titled rank or land. Social class is a crucial variable in electoral
behaviour in most societies, but its indicators vary. Often it is associated with
material wealth, but other elements may be present as well, varying from one
society to another, with accent, manners, lineage, land ownership, education
and professional status all featuring. The nation may be available for political
exploitation, but the meaning of nationalism will differ from one case to
another, variously associated with aggression, racism, tolerance, democracy
and dictatorship. Yet if we cannot isolate it from other factors, we should also
avoid the opposite error, of treating it as a catch-all device that tries to explain
everything and succeeds in explaining nothing. This is not a reason for abandoning the concept, merely for treating it with care.

Another difficulty is the unit of analysis. If culture is an essentially social or
inter-subjective concept, then we need to identify the group and its members.
In the past, there was a tendency to identify cultures with nation-states. Yet
this is merely to reify one social unit, itself the product of power politics and
often contested by movements asserting other relevant units of identity,
belonging and common values. Just as past scholars made abusive generalizations about national character and their incompatibilities, so excessive generalizations are now made about global phenomena. The most notorious is
perhaps Samuel Huntington's (1996) thesis about the clash of civilizations, a
new set of cultural boundaries superseding old divisions in world politics.
This generalizes about units that are internally extremely diverse and under-
plays commonalities on other dimensions of culture and politics. It is also
easily manipulated. Thus in his earlier work, Huntington includes Mexico
and South America in the Christian/Western area, while in the later one
(Huntington 2004) he invents a new civilizational boundary between the
United States and Latin America.[6]

The appropriate unit of analysis must depend on the research question so
that if, for example, we are interested in class culture, we will look at social
classes. Yet determining their extent is always problematic, since cultures often
have contested boundaries or fade into others. One approach focuses on the
core, those individuals who are most clearly encompassed by a culture and
who may be assumed to possess its traits to the greatest extent. Another looks
at the boundary, where cultural norms may be most explicitly articulated in
contrast to neighbouring ones. It is well documented, for example, that

nationalist leaders often come from the marginal parts of the group in question, or have experienced periods of exile in other cultures.

There are several methods for exploring beliefs, identities and common values. These depend on (i) how we conceptualize culture; (ii) the macro–micro link; and (iii) whether we are most oriented to a social science that seeks to explain or to understand (see della Porta and Keating, ch. 2). The most obvious research instrument is a survey. This typically (i) conceptualizes culture as beliefs and attitudes; (ii) locates it at the individual level; and (iii) is based on the empirical logic of cause and explanation, with culture as the independent variable (Lane and Ersson 2005). So individuals are asked questions about their own identity, their values, and trust in other people in general and other groups in particular. This is the basis of the civic culture research mentioned above, and of the work on post-materialism by Inglehart (1998). Such surveys have uncovered much useful information about values and orientations and their persistence and change. They have highlighted the importance of ideas and socialization as opposed to mere interests, in shaping social and political action. The main problem with surveys, however, is the difficulty of making inferences from one level of analysis to another (Seligson 2002). Survey instruments are directed at individuals, taken out of their social context and then often generalized to the level of society. Yet culture, as we have noted, is essentially an intersubjective category, about the relations among individuals in particular situations. A societal culture is more than the aggregate of individual attitudes on issues and is both transmitted and recreated in social interaction in specific contexts.

This is no mere technical quibble, since we may get different results if we look at culture at the micro or the macro level. For example, studies have shown that political values across Europe have exhibited strong signs of convergence (Chauvel 1995), but local and regional differences in political behaviour have, if anything, increased as parties are able to synthesize policy positions in different ways and reinforce local and historical cultural references. Some survey work has sought to probe this by comparing individual-level attitudes with respondents' views of their own cultural group as a whole. Catalans individually see themselves as traditional and family-oriented, but when asked for their image of Catalonia they stress the publicly proclaimed qualities of entrepreneurialism and modernism (Keating, Loughlin and Deschouwer 2003). Other research has explored the differences between individual attitudes and stereotypes based on the view of one's own or another community as a whole (Sangrador García 1996). It again shows that the collective image of the group is not merely an aggregation of individual attitudes but must be appreciated at the macro level as well.

A second approach is the ethnological one, in which the researcher immerses him/herself in the society to comprehend the meanings that actors themselves give to their behaviour (see Bray, ch. 15). This approach, associated with anthropology, has been used increasingly to study modern social and political structures. It is based on the idea that culture is (i) to be defined broadly as identity, interpretation and values (see above); (ii) inter-subjective (both individual and collective); and (iii) open to interpretation rather than usable in causal explanation. Abélès' (1989) study of the politics in the region of Burgundy started not from the institutions of state and local government but from the behaviour and logic of individuals. His findings confirmed much of the political science literature on central–local power networks in France but gave new insight into the concept of *notoriété*, a form of social and political status that individuals build up and use to accumulate influence across various domains.

Exploring culture in this way allows us to see it as a series of reference points, which actors use to construct systems of action or policies. This is not to say that actors can simply invent new cultural references or bend any reference to any purpose; rather that symbols, memories and shared norms can be arranged to different purposes. This allows us a new take on the problem posed by studies of culture and development, from Almond and Verba to Putnam, which have reasoned directly from culture (independent variable) to development (dependent variable). By introducing actors and initiative it also helps avoid the fatalism of assuming that societies with the 'wrong' culture are doomed to failure. The study of development and change in local and national societies provides many illustrations. In places that are doing badly, actors often resort to cultural stereotypes such as traditionalism, collectivism, lack of entrepreneurial spirit or a tendency to collusive behaviour by social groups. Successful societies have their own self-congratulatory stories about common identity, cultural cohesion, social capital and co-operation (Keating, Loughlin and Deschouwer 2003). What is striking is that the components of these stories are very often the same, merely given a positive or negative interpretation. Since the 1990s, Ireland has succeeded in transforming its image, along with its economy, so that traditional music and even the Irish pub have gone from being symbols of quaint backwardness to the ultimate in post-modern cosmopolitanism. There were, of course, elements of truth in both descriptions, but one succeeded in conquering the public domain and establishing a shared narrative about the society. The legacy and implications of both

Christianity and Islam are contested in modern politics, with multiple streams within both, each with its own historic reference points. Both conservatives and modernizers can find material and justification in the tradition. Nationalism has proved a more resilient force than many modernists anticipated, not because people have inherent national identities, but because it provides a powerful set of symbols for redefining and closing political communities, where political entrepreneurs wish to do so and the conditions are propitious.

This shows the need for deep investigation and knowledge of the culture in order to show how these stories are generated and reproduced. In this way, we can move beyond a descriptive account of beliefs and towards an explanation of the logic of collective and individual action in the society or polity in question, if not to the strict causal logic demanded by positivist social science. The most promising approaches have been comparison of cases, in which constructions of meaning and the creation of belief systems can be compared directly to explore patterns of similarity and difference.

Combining cultural and other approaches

Culture is not a master narrative, an encompassing explanation of social and political behaviour. In the narrower meaning, it has been constructed as an independent variable governing outcomes. In the broader sense, it is a medium, a means of communication and a link among other factors. For this reason, it can be combined with institutional analysis; indeed, the sociological version of new institutionalism, as suggested earlier, comes very close to cultural explanation. It is not incompatible with forms of rational choice, with culture used to explain how peoples' preferences and motivations are formed in the first place.[7] Indeed, it has been suggested that cultural and rational choice explanations may be compatible at a deeper level, as cultural norms may be seen as historically learned responses to collective action problems (Kiser and Bauldry 2005). The concept of tradition can also inform historical explanations (and complement historical institutionalism) by showing how beliefs are transmitted, adapted and reinvented over time. Going back to Weber, we can explore how cultural values and institutional structures can interact and mutually reinforce each other without either one being determinant on its own (Lichbach 1997). Further insight into the complexity of culture can be gained through triangulation and combining different methods (Ross 1997). Thus surveys can tell us a lot about popular attitudes, while ethnographic work may be needed to explore their meaning. Debating the importance of institutions versus culture in shaping social behaviour then comes to resemble the debate between nature (genetic influences) and nurture (environment) in explaining the behaviour of individuals. Formerly divided fiercely on these rival views, scientists now tend to the view that these are not independent, discrete variables but are in constant interaction.

NOTES

1　Despite the United States being the least secularized of Western societies.

2　Héritier (ch. 4) writes of 'institutionalist explanations based on social norms'.

3　For a comprehensive set of criticisms, see the special issue of *Politics and Society* 24 (1) (1996).

4　Although racists have now also shifted their ground, claiming disingenuously that they do not object to other groups for what they are but because of their culture.

5　A good example is provided by Giner, Flaquer, Busquet *et al.* (1996), who show how the conflicting elements within Catalan culture go to make up the whole.

6　Again, there is a normative agenda. The book is not merely an account of cultural differences but a plea for cultural homogeneity within the state: 'I believe that America can do that and that Americans should recommit themselves to the Anglo-Protestant culture, traditions, and values' (Huntington 2004: vii).

7　As long as we do not assume that motives only count if they conform to a valid causal logic (Ross 1997). Saying that people make sacrifices to the gods to get better weather can be a good account of motivation, but is hardly part of a complete chain of causal explanation.

7 Historical institutionalism

Sven Steinmo

Historical institutionalism is neither a particular theory nor a specific method. It is best understood as an *approach* to studying politics and social change. This approach is distinguished from other social science approaches by its attention to real-world empirical questions, its historical orientation and its attention to the ways in which institutions structure and shape behaviour and outcomes. Although the term 'historical institutionalism' was not coined until the early 1990s,[1] the approach is far from new. Many of the most interesting and important studies of politics – from Karl Polanyi's classic *Great Transformations*, to Theda Skocpol's *States and Social Revolutions* and Philippe Schmitter's *Still a Century of Corporatism?* – would clearly be categorized as historical institutionalist were they written today.[2]

The best way to explain historical institutionalism (HI) is to situate this approach in a historical and comparative context, showing where the approach originated and how it is different from other approaches in the social sciences. In short, what follows is an HI account of historical institutionalism. The chapter concludes with a discussion of the implications of this approach for our understanding of political and social science as 'science'.

Origins

Institutional theory is as old as the study of politics. Plato and Aristotle to Locke, Hobbes and James Madison long ago understood the importance of political institutions for structuring political behaviour. Plato's *Republic* is a comparison of different forms of government in which he tries to understand how institutions shape political behaviour. Aristotle's *Politics* continues the

This chapter grew out of a series of conversations with Ellen Immergut and Bo Rothstein. Their contributions are found throughout this text, although all errors remain mine. I would also like to thank John Campbell, Carl Dahlstrom, Peter Mair, Mark Thatcher and Kathleen Thelen for insightful and very helpful comments on an early draft.

study of political institutions: he specifically examined institutional structures because he believed they shaped political incentives and normative values. Although rarely credited as the political theorists they clearly were, the founders of the American republic were interested in precisely the same sets of questions. Madison's 'science of politics' is a study of how different institutional arrangements will encourage and/or discourage different types of political action.

As the social sciences started to emerge as a modern academic discipline in the late nineteenth and early twentieth century, these classical traditions had a great impact (Almond 1996). Both in Europe and in the United States, students of politics were specifically concerned with the relationship between constitutional design and political (and even moral) behaviour. Indeed, much of what could be called early political science was about how to design perfect constitutions. This was an era of massive political and social upheaval when scholars were sometimes even invited to design institutions that could help build better societies. Perhaps the most famous case (and worst disaster) was Weimar Germany. After the defeat of the Kaiser, constitutional architects attempted to design what they believed to be the world's most perfect democracy. This historic occasion provided a nearly unique opportunity to apply 'political science' to the real world. The new German Republic, it was firmly believed, would be a model democracy that others would soon emulate. Unfortunately, things did not quite work out that way.

The failure of Weimar democracy led to increased disaffection with institutional analysis. This disaffection grew to scepticism – if not hostility – in the post-war years. While prior to the war one could imagine that democracy could be built with proper institutions, as we moved past the middle of the century such an argument became impossible to sustain. As the great European empires broke down, they often attempted to leave behind what they thought were the best practices and institutions in their former colonies. Sadly, however, finely designed democratic institutions fell to dictatorship, autocracy and even chaos, throughout the developing world. No matter what kinds of institutions were constructed, virtually all failed to produce the kinds of political behaviour necessary for democratic society to function.[3]

Increasingly, social scientists came to believe that institutions were mostly the vessels in which politics took place; what mattered was what filled the vessels. Given this understanding, both political science and sociology departments moved in two distinct directions. On the one hand, many believed that to be scientific, social science needed to be more theoretical. At the same time, others held that the study of politics and society should be broken down into constituent variables that could be measured, examined and analysed independently. In the process, institutions mostly fell out of the analysis.

It is important to remember that social science was growing within a broader political and historical context. In the post-World War II years, the physical sciences were advancing rapidly and there was no small amount of 'physics envy' in the social sciences.[4] To be taken seriously, it was sometimes thought that social science needed to be a 'real' science. Many believed that *real* science must follow *the* scientific method. If social science was to be a science, these reformers argued, it, too, must build predictive theories that are falsifiable and testable. Mark Blyth quotes Karl Lowenstein, who wrote in the *American Social Science Review* in 1944 that 'to overcome past errors comparative politics would have to become "a conscious instrument of social engineering" because the discipline ha[d] a mission to fulfil in imparting our experience to other nations . . . integrating scientifically their institutions into a universal pattern of government' (cited in Blyth 2006: 493).

After all, the problems of poverty, inequality, injustice, war and underdevelopment are just as important as anything studied by 'real' scientists. What scientists do, in this naïve view, is analyse their part of the physical world, produce hypotheses about how certain features work, and test these hypotheses with repeated experiments. In this account of 'real' science, scientists follow a methodology in which they dissect a complex phenomenon into its constituent parts and analyse these parts separately and independently. The goal is to analyse and understand the most basic units and processes and discover the laws that govern them. The fundamental Cartesian principle is that the world – and everything in it – is governed by basic laws. If we can understand these laws, we can understand and ultimately control the world we live in. This paradigm of science led from Newton's first observation of a falling apple, to more basic understandings of gravitational force, to a more general understanding of how and why the earth circles the sun, and eventually to the ability to send ships into outer space and to walk on the moon.

In its attempt to be more scientific (particularly in America, with the lure of funding from institutions such as the National Science Foundation), the cutting edge of social science moved away from historical analysis and 'thick description'. First, there was significant pressure to be more rigorous and quantitative. In the eyes of many, too much of the previous work had simply been historical and descriptive. History could be interesting, but it did not lend itself to easily testable and falsifiable propositions. It was not science.[5] Social science, the 'behaviouralist' thought, needed to move away from the particulars and treat cases as sets of values on variables. It was also important that social science restrict itself to factors that could be measured, counted and then compared and analysed. This meant that we should study *behaviours* that are measurable (such as social or economic position, attitudes or votes) and not *institutions* – which, almost by definition, are unique. Certainly, the behaviouralist agreed, social science was an infant science. The models were crude, the methods rough and the data pathetically incomplete; but all this was once true of physics and chemistry as well.

Surely, the new political scientist argued, the human world is governed by laws of behaviour and action – just as the physical world. If so, then the job of the social scientist is to discover these basic laws so that we, too, can predict, ultimately manage and even positively shape the world in which we live. Questions like 'Why do some countries or people benefit from high levels of democracy, growth and development while others are mired in vicious cycles of poverty, dictatorship and violence?' are big and complex. But if we deconstruct the processes and mechanisms of politics, just as chemists deconstruct the complex phenomena underlying disease, one day we may be able to build a better world – they thought.

The behaviouralists thus saw their role in the scientific process much as the chemist might. In order to understand the larger world around us, we first must break that world down into its constituent parts and try to understand those parts independently of each other. One day, they seemed to believe, we might have a 'Periodic Table of Politics'.

On the other hand, for the grand theorists – whether Marxist, structural functionalist, systems theorist, modernization theorist, or rational choice theorist – the key issue was to understand the basic processes and mechanisms motivating politics across nations, cultures and history. All countries throughout history faced the perennial, basic problems (Parsons and Smelser 1956); the scientist should focus on these great forces, not on the details and institutions. Institutions were either functional solutions to social problems or simple arenas where political battles took place. In either case, the specific construction of the arenas as such were not considered an important variable for determining the battles' outcomes (March and Olsen 1989; Steinmo, Thelen and Longstreth 1992)

It is useful to think of these grand theorists as the 'physicists' of politics. Their main goal was not practical; instead, their ambitions were grander as they focused their efforts on social science's search for the Holy Grail: The Laws of Politics.[6] For example, Adam Przeworski and Henry Teune wrote in their influential *Logic of Comparative Social Inquiry*, 'The pivotal assumption of this analysis is that social science research . . . should and can lead to general statements about social phenomena. This assumption implies that human behaviour can be explained in terms of general laws established by observation' (Przeworski and Teune 1970: 4). Whereas the behaviouralists sought out a Periodic Table of Politics, the grand theorists searched for a 'Theory of Everything'.

Studying the real world

Thus, by the 1960s and 1970s, social science's cutting edges had moved in quite distinct directions: the largely atheoretical micro-analyses of political behaviour on the one hand; and the macro- (and remarkably non-empirical) theorizing of Marxism, functionalism, systems theory and rational choice on the other. Although the work of the grand theorists and their behaviouralist brethren often did not intersect, a political alliance developed in many social science departments. These developments were most obvious in public universities in the United States in which significant shares of institutional funding came from scientific granting organizations.[7] Because the levels of government funding for scientific research in universities were significantly lower in most European countries, there was less pressure to adopt hard-science norms and practices to help fund social science programmes. Mobility between countries and even between universities within particular countries was also far more limited in Europe than in the USA. Consequently, new notions of science were adopted more slowly, as established professors in politics and sociology had fewer incentives to model themselves on the hard sciences.

Many political scientists, however, continued to be interested in studying politics and history. Indeed, it is sometimes said that historical institutionalism harkens back to a kind of social science that dominated over fifty years ago. From some quarters this is meant as an insult (HI is simply out of date); for others it suggests the recognition that many of the classics in political science and sociology were engaged in a kind of scientific inquiry that historical institutionalists would find familiar today. Max Weber, Stein Rokkan, David Truman, Karl Polanyi, Alexander Gershenkron, E. E. Schattschneider or Hugh Heclo would be identified as HI scholars if they were writing today, for they were specifically interested in explaining real-world outcomes, using history as an analytic tool, *and* they were strongly interested in the ways in which institutions shaped political outcomes.

Without necessarily denying the goal of social science *qua* science, many continued to be interested in the *meso*-level analysis and middle-range theory (see Mair, ch. 10). Disappointed with grand theory and bored or simply uninterested in the technical approach of behaviouralism, many political scientists continued to be interested in real-world *outcomes*. It was here that historical institutionalism was born. Political scientists, some believe, should actually try to explain important real-world events. When they began to ask questions like 'Why do real-world outcomes vary in the ways that they do?', institutions kept popping into their analyses. Most famously, Theda Skocpol wanted to explain the sources and patterns of the great revolutions (Skocpol 1979). But rather than *assume* that class structure or elite power would explain different patterns, she did the hard work of examining actual revolutions and placing them in their comparative and historical contexts. Eventually, Skocpol realized that the structure of state institutions in the pre-revolutionary period had enormous consequences for revolutionary outcomes. In hindsight, this may seem obvious, but at the time it was a revelation to many (especially American) social scientists that the state mattered.[8]

Skocpol was far from the only social scientist interested in explaining important real-world events, but there can be little doubt that her ideas had an important influence on the generation of young scholars who came after her. In the late 1970s and early 1980s there was a concomitant move in comparative politics research, in which students began to compare real-world cases rather than 'variables' (della Porta, ch. 11, and Vennesson, ch. 12). Once again, it may seem strange from today's vantage, but at the time, comparative politics was largely made up of detailed studies of particular countries, unions, movements or political parties. Anyone who studied a country other than his or her own apparently was a comparativist.

One of the most important volumes in this regard was Peter Katzenstein's (1978) *Between Power and Plenty*. This work also came out of a project in which a group of individual scholars were asked to analyse how and why different countries responded to the economic dislocations and hardships created by the oil price shocks of the early 1970s. This was a remarkable book precisely because it offered such careful and focused comparisons (by country experts). Once again, the structure of state institutions quickly came into the analyses of almost all of these scholars.

Historical *Institutionalism*

Not all political scientists or sociologists who use historical methods and who engage in case studies are *institutionalists*. Institutionalists are scholars who place special emphasis on the role institutions play in structuring behaviour. What are institutions? The most common definition for institutions is: rules.

Some students in this tradition focus on formal rules and organizations (Streeck and Thelen 2005), while others address informal rules and norms (Hall 1989; Marcussen 2000). Whether we mean formal institutions or informal rules and norms, they are important for politics because they shape who participates in a given decision and, simultaneously, their strategic behaviour.

Some examples are illustrative. Ellen Immergut's analysis of the politics of health care policy asked a straightforward question. Why do some countries develop comprehensive national health care systems while others have decentralized and fragmented insurance programmes? After analysing the political histories of several European countries, she observed that the structure of each country's political institutions offered different interest groups veto points[9] which had to be negotiated around. Looking more deeply into the specific cases, she came to see that the institutions not only provided obstacles to particular policy choices, but also ultimately structured the menu of choices available in different regimes (Immergut 1992). These different outcomes were *not* the products of different basic goals or aims put forth by particular parties or interest groups – but interest groups and parties did have to pursue different political strategies in different countries owing to the different political/institutional configurations established by the individual constitutions. In other words, she found that she could not explain the variation in policy outcomes without explaining the ways in which national political institutions structured both *who* participated in health insurance policies and the '*rules of the game*' in which they participated. The rules (especially differential access and availability of veto points) enabled different political strategies in different countries and ultimately shaped the different policy outcomes.

Similarly, Steinmo was interested in understanding why some countries have much larger welfare states than others do. His initial hypothesis was that political culture and/or public preferences would explain the major differences. But as he looked closer at the actual development of modern welfare states, he found that variation in attitudes could not explain how and why countries developed such wide variance. The evidence showed that citizens liked public spending; citizens in all countries wanted (and continue to want) *increases* in public spending on all of the most important and expensive arenas of public effort. The biggest constraint on these broad and common preferences, it seemed, was financial. Thus, he chose to examine the developments of national revenue systems. If the desire for public spending is constant, perhaps the fear of or resistance to taxes varied. Once again, attitudes and even political culture seemed of little analytic value. Neither of these variables made sense of the fact that countries like Sweden taxed the poor and working class much more heavily than the wealthy and the capitalist class. Even more curiously, the United States turned out to have a *more progressive* tax system than even Sweden. Detailed historical analysis of several cases brought this author to the conclusion that the very different political institutions through which public and elite preferences were translated into policy had enormous effects on the structure of actual tax policy outcomes. It was the structure of Swedish corporatist decision-making institutions – versus America's fragmented pluralist institutions – that best explained why specific tax policy choices were taken over time. These specific choices added up to hugely different revenue systems and consequentially different abilities to fund popular programmes like health care, education and labour market policies (Steinmo 1993).

We could continue with many other similar examples.[10] For example, in an effort to understand why some countries have higher levels of unionization than others, Bo Rothstein found that the particular structure of national unemployment insurance institutions was a hugely important mobilizing and organizing tool for unions in some countries but not in others. Countries employing the Ghent unemployment insurance system had far larger union movements than countries that did not (Rothstein 1992). Victoria Hattam wanted to explain the weakness of the labour movement in America and found that the structure of American parties and electoral institutions provided disincentives for union organizers to take a political strategy. Thus this important feature of American Exceptionalism was not a product of America's unique political culture, but instead a product of her uniquely fragmented political institutions (Hattam 1993).

It should be clear that three things distinguish these analyses so far. First, the scholars were not motivated by the desire to press an argument or push a methodology. Second, they were motivated by the desire to answer real-world empirical questions. Finally, they found *through empirical investigation* that institutional structures had profound effects on shaping political strategies, outcomes and, ultimately, political preferences.

Three institutionalisms

There are at least three types of institutional analysis in the social sciences today: rational choice, sociological institutionalism and historical institutionalism.[11] I will not attempt to rehash the debates among these forms other than to identify what I think is the key difference between historical institutionalists and the rest. First, there is considerable *agreement* among institutionalists in that they all see institutions as rules that structure behaviour. Where they differ is over their understanding of the nature of the beings whose actions or behaviour is being structured. The rational choice school argues that human beings are rational individualists who calculate the costs and benefits in the choices they face. Rational choice institutionalists think institutions are important quite simply because they frame the individual's strategic behaviour. They believe that people follow rules because humans are strategic actors who want to maximize their personal or individual gain.[12] We co-operate because we get more with co-operation than without it. We follow rules because we individually do better when we do so.

Sociological institutionalists, in contrast, see human beings as fundamentally social beings. In this view, humans are neither as self-interested nor as 'rational' as rational choice scholarship would have it (March and Olsen 1989), but are 'satisficers' who act habitually. For sociologists, institutions frame the very way in which people see their world and are not just rules within which they try to work. Rather than following rules to maximize their self-interest, humans are thought by sociological institutionalists generally to follow a 'logic of appropriateness' – meaning that rather than asking themselves 'What do I get out of X?', people first ask themselves 'What *should* I do? What is appropriate?' In this view, the important institutions (rules) are social norms that govern everyday life and social interaction.[13]

Historical institutionalists stand between these two views: human beings are *both* norm-abiding rule followers *and* self-interested rational actors. How one behaves depends on the individual, on the context and on the rules. While this statement may seem rather obvious, it has huge implications for how we should study politics. If all three of these variables (individuals, context and rules) are important in choice situations, then there can be no *a priori* way of knowing what one should study when trying to explain political outcomes. A historical institutionalist *does not believe* that humans are simple rule followers *or* that they are simply strategic actors who use rules to maximize their interests. A historical institutionalist can even be rather agnostic to these issues. What the HI scholar wants to know is why a certain choice was made and/or why a certain outcome occurred. Most likely, any significant political outcome is best understood as a product of both rule following and interest maximizing. How do you know which is the more important (self-interested, altruistic/collective or simply habitual) behaviour? The historical institutionalist would go to the historical record (also known as evidence) and try to find out.

Taking *history* seriously

These insights have important implications, both for what we study and for how we study it. Historical institutionalists study history because they believe it matters, not merely to increase the reference points for analysis (as is done in time-series analysis). There are at least three important ways in which history matters. First, political events happen within a historical context, which has a direct consequence for the decisions or events. An early example of this is the seminal work of Alexander Gershenkron, who argued that *when* a country industrializes necessarily affects *how* it industrializes. He shows us why late-comers cannot go through the same long trial-and-error process followed by early developers.[14] In other words, the process of industrialization is essentially different for late developers than for early developers. This is a huge insight that is easily missed in large-scale quantitative, cross-national comparisons, which very often pool data across continents and time periods and treat the time/place as inconsequential (or assume that it will 'wash out' of the analysis).

The second reason history matters is that actors or agents can learn from experience. Historical institutionalists understand that behaviour, attitudes and strategic choices take place inside particular social, political, economic and even cultural contexts. Rather than treating all political action as if fundamentally the same irrespective of time, place or context, historical institutionalists explicitly and intentionally attempt to situate their variables in the appropriate context. Thus, by deepening and enriching their understanding of the historical moment and the actors within it, they are able to offer more accurate explanations for the specific events that they explore than had they treated their variables outside the temporal dimension.

E. E. Schattschneider's early work on tariff policy showed how political choices made at time A have important consequences for time B. In this work he famously argued that 'new policies create new politics'.[15] Following Schattschneider, Paul Pierson has shown in several important works how and why policy choices at one point in time affect choices at subsequent points in time.[16] Similarly, Esping-Andersen pointed out in his seminal *Three Worlds of Welfare Capitalism* how, given the fact that we live in modern welfare states with unemployment insurance, health insurance, pension programmes and the like, 'Our personal life is structured by the welfare state and so is the entire political economy' (Esping-Andersen 1990: 141). The existence of the welfare state is a fact of modern political life that itself *shapes* politics, expectations and policy in the countries that have developed it.

Finally, again as Pierson has shown, expectations are also moulded by the past. While some might point to America's adventure in Iraq as a simple product of power politics and/or the demand for oil, a historical institutionalist would more likely look to the patterns of past wars for an understanding of why this country reacted in the way it did to the 9/11 bombings. Certainly they were mistaken, but there should be little doubt that America's past successes in Germany and Japan – to say nothing of their perceived victory over Communism at century's end – led policy-makers in the Administration to believe that they could assert American power and bring successful capitalism and democracy to a former dictatorship.[17]

In sum, for historical institutionalists, *history is not a chain of independent events*. There is more than the temporal dimension implied in this basic point. Taking history seriously ultimately means that the scholar is sceptical of the very notion that variables are independent of one another. Instead, acknowledging the importance of history suggests an explicit awareness that important variables can and often do shape one another. Historical institutionalists, more than political scientists in some other traditions, are explicitly interested in these interactive effects on the interdependence of multiple causal variables.

The historical institutionalist is something like the environmental biologist who believes that in order to understand the specific fate of a particular organism or behaviour, she must explicitly examine that organism in the ecology or context in which it lives. This implies a different scientific ontology than that commonly found in the hard sciences of physics and chemistry. At the root of evolutionary biology is the assumption that the objects of analysis – living organisms – are fundamentally different from inanimate matter. While objects in the physical world often adhere to constant 'laws' of nature, biological organisms often defy attempts to reduce them to their essential components because of their complexity. Thus, as eminent evolutionary biologist Ernst Mayr points out, the development of biology as a science has required an investigation of 'additional principles' that apply only to living organisms. He argues: 'This required a restructuring of the conceptual world of science that was far more fundamental than anyone had imagined at the time' (Mayr 2004: 26).

Historical institutionalism represents something like this ontological move in social science. In order to understand historically specific events and long-term political outcomes, one cannot strictly apply methods and epistemologies drawn from the study of invariant variables that have fixed relationships across space and time. This, of courses, does not mean that it is not science – unless one's definition of science excluded biology as well; rather, it implies that the scientific methods applied should fit the subject being studied.

Agendas

In recent years, two important intellectual agendas have emerged within institutionalist scholarship. The first is an attempt to understand better the mechanisms of institutional change; the second is an effort to comprehend the role of ideas in politics and history. I will discuss each separately and then argue that these issues are best dealt with when considered together.

It has become commonplace to argue that until recently most institutionalist literature had no fully theorized explanation for *change*. Indeed, the expectation for most institutionalists is that change will be difficult. There are several reasons for this. First, any given institution (whether a formal institution or a norm) is embedded within a larger set of institutions. Changing one set of rules can and often does have implications for others; therefore, there is likely to be significant resistance to change on the part of those who are advantaged in the broader context. Second, human beings form expectations around a given set of rules/institutions. Changing the rules can have long-term effects that may be difficult or impossible to predict. In this case, many would prefer simply to continue with the rules they currently have – even if they are not necessarily optimal. Third, institutions can become locked in because people invest in learning the rules. Changing rules can invoke significant up-front costs and be resisted by those who do not want to bear any new costs. Finally, because institutions affect behaviour, over time they can also shape preferences. Human beings may come to prefer a given institutional arrangement because it is what they are used to.

Given all these sources for stability, how can we explain change? Until recently, the dominant explanation has been 'punctuated equilibrium' (see Thelen and Steinmo 1992). The basic idea here is that institutions remain essentially stable (at equilibrium) until they are faced with an external (exogenous) shock. Increasingly, however, many historical institutionalists have come to criticize this logic, arguing that relying on exogenous shocks gives human beings no agency. There is something basically flawed, they argue, with the idea that political and institutional change is purely a product of fate.

Recently a number of scholars have pressed this agenda, with considerable success. Kathleen Thelen and Wolfgang Streeck brought together a group of younger scholars and asked each to explore the ways in which different political institutions are adapting or evolving in the context of global competitive pressures and demographic changes.[18] Through careful historically grounded analyses, these authors were able to identify a set of common patterns of institutional change. Thus they explore common types of institutional change. Unfortunately, Thelen and Streeck do not really offer an explanation for, or theory of, institutional change. Instead they explore various patterns of institutional change.[19]

To explain institutional change, one needs to bring 'ideas' into institutional analysis. If you are not a political scientist, you might be surprised to find that ideas play virtually no role in much current social science analysis. Marxism, rational choice and pluralism alike all assume that interests are the driving forces of politics, and that ideas are either justifications or simply 'noise'. While traditional behaviouralists have no *a priori* reason to argue that ideas are irrelevant to politics, it is clear that ideas are difficult to measure and quantify and are therefore left out of these analyses for practical reasons. Historical institutionalists, however, are not wedded to a particular grand theory or to a specific methodology; consequentially, 'ideas' have come to take a central place in their analyses.[20]

Peter Hall famously wrote about the power of economic ideas in his analysis of the growth of Keynesian economic thought, exploring how and why specific ideas about economic management came to dominate so many countries at roughly the same historical epoch (Hall 1989). Hall demonstrates how these ideas, once embedded, had framing effects and consequently became something like basic templates upon which other political decisions were made. Taking Hall's analysis as a starting point, Mark Blyth went on to explore the rise and fall of Keynesianism in the United States and Sweden, with the specific intent of understanding *both* how ideas develop and influence people *and* how they can be used as weapons in political struggles (Blyth 2002). In other works, Blyth has forcefully argued that the concept of interest itself makes no sense without appreciating how individuals understand their interests (see also Kratochwil, ch. 5 and Pizzorno, ch. 9). In other words, ideas are at the very root of political behaviour.[21]

In my view, much of the most interesting work in the historical institutionalist tradition today is found precisely amongst those who are trying to better understand the ways in which ideas, values and beliefs affect history and politics *and* who are specifically applying these insights to understanding institutional change more broadly (McNamara 1998; Marcussen 2000; Lieberman 2002; Katznelson and Weingast 2005). For these scholars, institutional change is the product of changes in ideas held by actors. I mean 'ideas' here in the specific sense that ideas are *creative solutions to collective action problems*. For example, when we normally say 'I have an idea!', we are in effect saying we have a solution to a problem. Seen in this way, institutional change comes about when powerful actors have the will and ability to change institutions in favour of new ideas. A group or collective may agree that a particular idea is a 'good idea' if they agree that there is a problem that needs solving, *and* they agree that this idea might actually solve the problem. Seen in this way, ideas are not 'irrational', but instead are best understood as creative adaptations that can be evaluated both on rational and emotive grounds.[22]

To illustrate these points, let us consider the example of basic welfare state institutions of the twentieth century (unemployment insurance, public pensions or banking regulations). First, it should be obvious that initially these proposals were simply untested ideas (creative problem solutions) whose promise was to help solve some of the social and economic problems created by the mid-twentieth century capitalist economy (economic dislocation, unemployment, increased poverty). As the economically vulnerable in society gained more and more power through the ballot box in Western democracies, and as the economic failures of unregulated capitalism became increasingly apparent, elites' ideas changed. The economic experiences of the 1920s and 1930s led many to see these issues as real problems. Additionally, the performance of the governments in World War II (economic management, regulation of production and quite simply the fighting/winning of the greatest war in history) led many to believe that governments could and would do a good job managing new tasks. Over time, then, there was widespread agreement that capitalism could and should be regulated and that government had an appropriate role in managing the economy and distributing the wealth generated in that economy. The specific tax, welfare and regulatory policies that were implemented over the following thirty or forty years cannot be understood as anything less than ideas which were eventually put into practice (institutionalized).

But, of course, modern democratic capitalism did not stand still (there was no equilibrium). Along with rising standards of living and increased equality, expectations grew as well. Moreover, political leaders kept promising things they were less and less able to deliver. Especially after the oil shocks of the early 1970s and the stagflation that followed, people increasingly came to believe that governments regulated too heavily, taxed some citizens unfairly, and in general were less capable than they promised to be.[23] Neoliberal ideas grew in popularity in the later decades of the twentieth century because more and more people (especially the rich and powerful) came to share the belief that 'government was not the answer, but the problem' to quote Ronald Reagan's famous phrase. Neoliberal pro-market policies became increasingly persuasive because an increasing number of people (elites and average citizens as well) were persuaded by the logic of the neoliberal argument; they accepted the problem definition and then came to agree to the problem solution. It is important to understand that there was no 'proof' that neoliberal policies would address these problems. The new policies (tax cuts, programme reductions and pro-market re-regulation) were simply 'ideas' that promised to dampen inflationary tendencies of the Keynesian era, put more money into the hands of capitalists who could reinvest, and constrain 'wasteful' government spending. Once again, those who believed these were good 'ideas' shared a sense of the problems facing capitalist democracies and believed that the neoliberal policy solutions would help solve these problems.

To be sure, both the establishment of welfare state institutions and neoliberal policies could be seen as being in the economic interest of the elites who promoted them. But to see it this way assumes that we have an objective and precise understanding of the ways in which the modern economy actually works and that there is an objective and easily knowable way of understanding an actor's 'self-interest'. One can argue that we have neither. First, the modern capitalist economy is far more complex and contingent than even the most sophisticated mathematical tools can hope to model accurately and precisely. Second, the very foundation of an individual's (or a group's) interest is fundamentally rooted in their beliefs (about how the world works), their values (what constitutes good outcomes) and how best to achieve these outcomes (problem solutions).

Consider the following question: did the tax cuts of the 1980s stimulate growth and increase government revenue as was promised, or did they simply create the largest budget deficits in history? The answer to this question depends on who you ask. If, for example, you ask an economist who believes in neoliberal economic theory (with or without a Nobel Prize), she will almost certainly tell you that the tax cuts worked and that the economy grew in the 1990s because of the tax cuts (she could also provide you a massive econometric model to show you this as well). If you asked an economist who does not believe in neoliberal economics (with or without a Nobel Prize) she would just as convincingly argue that the tax cuts did not work as promised and that it took the tax increases of the 1990s to get the economy back on track and back into balance. She too could provide a massively complex mathematical model to 'prove' her argument. Which economist you choose to believe is up to you. But the key point here is that even if economists cannot agree at the most basic level on the effects of economic rules or institutions in the past, then surely we have to understand that prospective policy ideas are even more a leap of faith. Second, if we cannot know the effects of past ideas, how can we rationally calculate our self-interest for future policy ideas?

Bringing ideas into our understanding of institutional change, then, brings agents back into institutional analysis. One could argue that a key weakness of institutionalism in the past has been that actors could be simple hostages of the institutions that they inhabit. Integrating ideas into the analysis addresses this problem by making institutions both a constraining/incentivizing force and the object of political contestation.

Bringing ideas specifically into institutional analysis thus allows for a better understanding of institutional evolution. A small, but growing group of historical institutionalists are in fact moving in this direction specifically attempting to bring evolutionary theories and ideas to the study of institutional change.[24] It is outside the scope of this chapter to expand on these theories, but the basic argument is to see institutions, ideas and the environment in a co-evolutionary process. This perspective sees history and politics as dynamic processes that are constantly evolving, rather than seeing history as a process lurching from one equilibrium to another. The evolutionary approach, moreover, sees outcomes as contingent and non-predictable rather than linear and predictable. Finally, the evolutionary approach specifically explores power relations and integrates agency into the analysis rather than seeing actors as prisoners of the institutions they inhabit.

Political and social 'science'

At the heart of many of the deepest and most difficult battles within social science is a fundamental struggle over the meaning of science. For many, science is the search for systematic regularities and generalizable laws. In this view, one studies the empirical world only because it offers the evidence that can be used to build and test theory. Particular cases or specific events may be interesting – just as a good novel is interesting – but the goal of social science is not to understand any particular event; it is to build theories that can be used to explain many (or even all) events. For these scholars, understanding real outcomes is not the most important point; creating, elaborating, refining a theory of politics is (Weingast 1996). Morris Fiorina describes his scientific orientation in the following way: '[We are] not as interested in a comprehensive understanding of some real institution or historical phenomenon, so much as in a deeper understanding of some theoretical principle or logic . . . [F]or most PTI scholars, breadth trumps depth; understanding 90 per cent of the variance in one case is not as significant an achievement as understanding 10 per cent of each of nine cases, especially if the cases vary across time and place' (Fiorina 1995: 110–11).

This reveals precisely the difference between historical institutionalists and their more 'rationalist' institutionalist brethren. Historical institutionalists *are* interested in the specific cases. Being able to explain 10 per cent of the variance in nine cases is probably no better than a semi-educated guess, and not particularly useful or interesting. If we could explain the important events (why revolutions happen, why some countries have large welfare states, why labour is so weak in some countries), I expect that most HI scholars would be happy with even less than 90 per cent.

Historical institutionalists (both political scientists and sociologists) are sceptical of the grand ambitions of social science – at least when understood as Newtonian physics. For most of these scholars, the goals are more proximate and the ideal theory should be less grand. The HI scholar is primarily interested in *explanation* – not prediction (see della Porta and Keating, ch. 2, for this distinction). Though it is rarely explicitly stated, a basic assumption of this view of social science is that meaningful prediction is impossible. For HI scholars, predictions can only be proximate and predictions, *not* because we lack the tools, models, datasets or computing power, but rather because of contingency, and the complex interaction of *inter*dependent variables over time. In history, the very objects of our study (institutions and human beings) change, adapt and are affected by history itself. Prediction and the related conception of science imply a linear analysis of variables that can be distinguished from one another and which react to one another in predictable ways (see Héritier, ch. 4). For many social scientists, such analysis denies the realities of the world in which we live.[25] In this view, the study of politics is not, and cannot be, like physics, because what we study and what we are interested in explaining are not inanimate objects to which absolute, invariant and fixed laws apply. Studying history with methods and models derived from physics is like studying poetry with algebra.

As several have pointed out, HI scholars tend to be interested in important and relatively rare events. A research programme motivated by an interest in real-world puzzles and rare events has advantages and disadvantages over a programme motivated by a desire to find general laws of history or politics. It is well known that some methodologists outside this tradition question the very validity of the HI approach because it tends towards 'selecting on the dependent variable'. To be sure, a research strategy that specifically focuses on important cases and big puzzles could potentially suffer from the obvious dangers of selection bias. This is an important criticism worth considering here. Does the very nature of the kinds of questions in which HI scholars are interested undermine the scientific credibility of their work?

First, as Pierson and Skocpol (2006) point out, we must think of social science scholars as a 'multi-generational research community' that results in a 'powerful accumulation of results, including falsifications as well as substantiated arguments'. Each new study contributes to our fund of knowledge about historical events; it retests and re-examines the analyses that went before. Second, as Dietrich Rueschemeyer argues, case studies can do more than generate theoretical ideas. They can test theoretical propositions, and they can offer persuasive causal explanations (Rueschemeyer 2003: 318). Noting the persistent scepticism towards historical case study work, Rueschemeyer goes on to argue, correctly, that it rests on the mistaken idea that a single case marks a single observation. Good historical analysis that is analytically oriented engages the case at multiple points, thereby confronting explanatory propositions with multiple data points (see Vennesson, ch. 12 for an elaboration of these ideas).

It is also important to remember that this research strategy has several methodological advantages. As noted above, HI scholars are interested in the ways in which history itself shapes outcomes. Thus, they specifically and self-consciously examine patterns over time. By extending the time frame, first, one expands the number of observations and thus helps to deal with the small-N problem noted above. But historical process tracing also allows the scholar to test for the arrow of causality in a way in which simple correlation analysis cannot. Finally, process tracing is an instrument that helps the researcher to be sensitive to the temporal boundaries, or period effects, with respect to the specific causal claims being forwarded (see Vennesson, ch. 12). If history matters, then looking at processes over time allows the researcher to place particular events in a particular time – without at the same time missing the overarching patterns. It is these patterns, after all, which are very likely to offer the most compelling and interesting dependent variables. Historical institutionalists, in other words, look at the forests as well as the trees (Pierson and Skocpol 2006).

Of course, there are also serious dangers in *not* looking at the big historically interesting puzzles – because they are too rare, or they are not randomly distributed or, most fundamentally, because these big events have an impact upon all subsequent events. Without historical accounts, important outcomes will go unobserved, causal relationships will be incorrectly inferred and, finally, significant hypotheses may never even be noticed, even less tested. Jim Mahoney (2000b), who surveyed several decades of scholarship and research on democratic and authoritarian regimes, concluded: 'If one were to strike all comparative historical research from the record, most of what we currently know about the causes of democracy and authoritarianism would be lost'. Indeed, if we were to follow strictly the logic of inquiry promoted by King, Keohane and Verba (1994), then Reinhard Bendix's *Nation Building and Citizenship*, Barrington Moore's *Social Origins of Dictatorship and Democracy*, Samuel Huntington's *Political Order in Changing Societies* and Theda Skocpol's *States and Social Revolutions* – to name just a few classics – could not have been written.[26]

Conclusion

It may be sadly true that much of 'political science' has moved away from asking important questions about the real world. It is certainly true that many political scientists believe we should ignore analyses that cannot be 'falsified' and eschew variables that cannot be quantified. Theirs is a political science that treats politics and history as if it grows in a Petri dish and can be measured in centimetres or kilos.

The historical institutionalist does not accept that political science *must* be so narrow. To be sure, many interesting things can be learned from formal, behavioural and, certainly, experimental approaches to the study of politics. But to take history out of our 'equations', institutions out of our models, and real people out of our analyses would leave us with an impoverished pseudo-science. Not everyone who agrees with this statement would call herself a historical institutionalist. But if you think history and ideas matter, institutions structure actors' choices but are subject to change by actors themselves, and real people make decisions that not always efficient or purely self-interested, then you probably are a historical institutionalist.

NOTES

1 The term came out of a small workshop held in Boulder, Colorado in January 1989. Participants included Douglas Ashford, Colleen Dunlavy, Peter Hall, Ellen Immergut, Peter Katzenstein, Desmond King, Frank Longstreth, Jonas Pontusson, Bo Rothstein, Theda Skocpol, Sven Steinmo, Kathleen Thelen, George Tsebilis and Margaret Weir. *Structuring Politics: Historical Institutionalism in Comparative Politics* (Steinmo, Thelen and Longstreth 1992) grew out of this workshop.

2 Some other examples of social science analysis written before this phrase came into usage but which would clearly be defined as 'historical institutionalist' today include Wilson (1891), Polanyi (1944), Selznick (1949), Truman (1951), Rustow (1955), Eckstein (1960), McConnell (1966), Polsby (1968), Eisenstadt and Rokkan (1973), Schmitter (1974), Tilly and Ardant (1975), Zysman (1977), Katzenstein (1978), Dodd and Richard (1979), Skocpol (1979), Huntington (1982), Rothstein (1982), Skowronek (1982), Esping-Anderson and Korpi (1983), Skocpol and Ikenberry (1983), Katznelson and Weir (1985), Gourevitch (1986), Skocpol and Amenta (1986) and Rokkan *et al.* (1988).

3 For a similar analysis, see Blyth (2006).

4 Indeed, it was in the immediate post-war years that many departments of government and/or politics changed their names to 'political science'.

5 Indeed, the emphasis in much of the historical descriptive work up to that point had been to explain the exceptional character of the particular historical epoch, country, region or revolution under study.

6 For a fascinating and thoughtful exposition of these views, see Wallerstein (2001).

7 Deans and department chairs understood that Institutional Cost Recovery (ICR) moneys could contribute substantially to university and departmental budgets. Thus, foundations such as the National Science Foundation (which were driven by hard-science norms) contributed to the shift.

8 It is worth noting here that this fact seemed obvious to most Europeans and scarcely came as a revelation.

9 George Tsebilis is often incorrectly credited with introducing the idea of veto points.

10 Amazon.com (accessed February 2007) lists 794 books when one searches for the specific phrase 'historical insitutionalism'. 'The New Institutionalism' brings up 1,679 books.

11 For a thorough discussion of these three types, see Peter Hall and Rosemary Taylor's (1996) excellent analysis.

12 I refer here to the standard rational choice (RC) school. Certainly, there are many RC scholars who have relaxed these assumptions considerably. To be frank, the more they do so, the more they sound like historical institutionalists. See Weingast (1996), Bates, Greif, Levi *et al.* (1998) and Ostrom (1998).

13 Still, these distinctions are difficult to sustain. For example, the widely known 'sociological institutionalist' text edited by Paul DiMaggio and Walter Powell, *The New Institutionalism in Organizational Analysis*, is explicitly interested in power and coercion as important variables for framing political behaviour, along with norm-building and pattern development (DiMaggio and Powell 1991). I thank John Campbell for pointing this out to me.

14 An example outside politics may prove illustrative. Many of us recognize that firstborn children have a very different developmental experience than second (or later) children. Not only are the parents more experienced after the first child, they are also taking care of more than one child at a time. Finally, and equally importantly, subsequent children grow up in a home where there are older siblings – something the first child, by definition, cannot do.

15 Cited in Pierson (1993: 595).

16 See, for example, Pierson (1993, 2000, 2004).

17 Just as certainly, the failure of the Iraq experience will shape American foreign policy for decades to come.

18 See also John Campbell's (2004) *Institutional Change and Globalization*.

19 The five models of institutional change identified by Thelen and Streeck are (a) 'displacement' – where one institution displaces another, (b) 'layering' – when an institution adopts new functions on top of older functions, (c) 'drift' – when the environment in which an institution exists changes, but the institution does not adapt in stepwise fashion (see also Jacob Hacker's chapter in Thelen and Streeck's volume), (d) 'conversion' – where institutions take on new functions, goals or purposes, and (e) 'exhaustion' – meaning institutional breakdown and failure.

20 To be sure, not all historical institutionalists are specifically concerned with the role or power of political ideas, but many are; see Campbell (2002).

21 See Blyth (1997, 2003), see also Marcussen (2000), Pasotti and Rothstein (2002) and Steinmo (2003).

22 There has been an unfortunate and unnecessary tendency to pit 'ideational' analysis against 'rational' choice in a way that appears to argue that one bases decisions *either* on ideas *or* on rational calculations. This is an absurd distinction.

23 Interestingly, there was significant variation in this regard. Quite obviously, some governments were more capable of delivering on their promises efficiently and fairly than others (compare, for example, Sweden and the United States). The best explanation for these variations is, of course, differing institutional structures (see Steinmo 1993).

24 For recent work pointing in these directions, see North (2006) and Lewis and Steinmo (2007).

25 For example, in basic statistical analysis it is common to tell students that they must watch for multicollinearity and take care only to examine questions in which the multiple variables in an equation can be separately identified. This is not because this is the way the real world works, but because unless one takes these precautions the statistical inferences drawn will be methodologically invalid. The problem, of course, is that the method we use can too easily define the questions we ask.

26 This obvious fact was pointed out to me by Jeffrey Kopstein.

8 Game theory

Christine Chwaszcza

Introduction

Game theory is a branch of so-called Bayesian[1] rational choice theory (RCT). It has two distinct forms of application:

(i) explaining individuals' behaviour in social settings by their motives and reasons;

(ii) as an abstract model for the analysis of social structure, within the paradigm of methodological individualism (MI).

Game theory is explanatorily useful only to the extent that it models individuals' motives and reasons appropriately. Modelling, by contrast, aims not at replicating the world, but at artificially isolating features in order to study their potential or dynamics.[2] An explanatory approach fails if it cannot explain observable real-life behaviour. An abstract model, by contrast, can be a very fruitful analytical tool exactly when it fails if it is precise enough to tell us *why* it fails, and how the model can be enriched, changed or modified. Insights achieved from abstract modelling do not themselves explain phenomena but can be used in the development of explanatory hypotheses or even concept-formation; but these hypotheses then have to be tested independently.

The first section of this chapter clarifies the basic concepts and assumptions of RCT: rational choice, preference, expected utility and the structure of modern utility theory. The subsequent section turns to game theory proper and remarks on its relationship to the broader concept of RCT. For that purpose, we introduce two concepts of 'equilibrium' – the von Neumann–Morgenstern equilibrium and Nash's concept of equilibrium; and two of the best-studied types of game – the so-called prisoners' dilemma (PD), and a variety of co-ordination games. It is argued that game theory is best employed in the social sciences as an analytical tool. Turning to the more recent development of iterated and evolutionary games, the final section shows how the failure to model co-operation and co-ordination has contributed to a better understanding of those problems.

Bayesian framework of rational choice: basic concepts and assumptions

Game theory is a model for rational decision-making in situations of social interaction. Social interaction, here, is to be understood in Max Weber's sense: as action that involves two or more intentional actors, and that is guided by mutual expectations about how the other person(s) will behave. To the extent that intentional action is guided by reasons and/or rational deliberation, game theory provides a model for an ideal type of reasoning about what to do. In that sense it is not a model for action or behaviour proper, but for *reasoning*.

Originally, game theory was developed as one of three branches of the broader rational choice paradigm: decision theory, social choice theory and game theory.[3] The core idea is a refinement of the everyday concept of means–end reasoning (i.e. that the best means should be chosen to achieve a given end) into a calculus of decision-making that integrates *probabilistic* reasoning (Savage 1954). That refinement was made possible by the development of modern utility theory (MUT). Although game theory is not as closely tied to MUT as other branches of the rational choice paradigm, it was originally developed within that framework by von Neumann and Morgenstern (1944).

MUT was originally developed in applied mathematics for decisions in non-interactive situations characterized by risk. More simply, this means how a single individual would decide, faced with a range of choices whose consequences cannot be predicted with certainty because they depend on other events.

The intuitive idea that motivates modern utility theory is quite commonsensical. In order for a choice among alternative courses of action to be rational, it obviously ought not be guided by wishful thinking: choosing the course of action that yields your most preferred consequences, if everything goes well. Yet prudence – even in an ordinary sense – requires that we consider not only the desirability of each consequence, but also the likelihood of its occurrence, given the presence of external events. The basic idea of RCT says that one should choose the course of action that maximizes one's *expected utility*, that is, the overall sum of all positive and negative consequences of a course of action, weighed with the probability of their occurrence.

Given that probability estimates are commonly given in numerical terms, weighing the desirability of a consequence with the probability of its occurrence is informative only if desirability, too, can be expressed in numerical terms – or, more precisely, if 'desirabilities' can be measured along a cardinal scale that also provides information about how much one consequence is desired over another. These cardinal measures are usually called 'utilities'; modern utility theory defines the (formal) conditions under which it is possible to assign numerical values to desirabilities, thereby constructing utility measures.

The first step is to define the relevant properties of the problem. As an axiomatic theory, RCT is strictly defined by the terms and conditions specified in its axiomatic foundations. No concept or assumption not defined in the axioms, nor derivable from them, can be expressed within the theory. Given that decisions are only required where alternatives are open, a decision situation is defined by (i) the set of all feasible options, and (ii) the set of all possible events that might influence the consequences (outcomes) of one's action, where it is assumed that consequences can be specified for all possible combinations and evaluated by the deciding agent by means of pairwise comparisons.

These pairwise comparisons represent the preferences of an agent, that is, a relationship between two alternatives, A and B, such that one is ranked above the other. The concept is taken to be primitive and is not meant to represent some specific evaluative attitudes, such as egoistic, altruistic or hedonistic values, or a specific ideal of the good life. Most commonly, preferences of agents are considered to be empirically given, or to be given by the assumptions of the model. In economics this is often maximization of profits or monetary payoffs, but it need not be.

It is assumed that an agent can rank all possible consequences according to their desirability, that is, ordinally from best to worst. If that ordering fulfils certain requirements of consistency, it can be proved that there exists a mathematical function to rank preferences over consequences in a cardinal ordering. That function is commonly called a utility function. In modern utility theory, the definitional set is given by the ordinal ordering of preferences over consequences, while the set of values is the set of rational numbers. The two most important consistency requirements are completeness (that is, all pairs of alternatives can be ranked) and transitivity (that is, if I prefer A over B and B over C, then I must prefer A over C); further requirements concern mathematical properties and the applicability of rules of probability calculus.[4]

Given a cardinal ordering and the assignment of numerical measures, it is now possible to weigh the utility of each consequence with the probability of its occurrence, and to determine the expected utility for each course of action in a way that allows for a meaningful comparison of all alternatives open to an agent. We can now define the expected utility of each course of action as the sum of the utility of each of its possible consequences weighted by the probability of its occurrence. We can then select the one course of action with the highest expected utility.

Maximizing expected utility is the criterion recommended for rational choice in *decision theory* (we will qualify this for game theory below). The rational choice concept of *rationality* is primarily defined by the consistency requirements that must be met in order to construct a utility function. The criterion of maximizing expected utility is an extension of the common-sense concept of means–ends rationality for decision-making under risk. The contribution of decision theory for the clarification of means-end rationality consists in the specification of the conditions that must be fulfilled to reason or act in accordance with that criterion.

Accordingly, the model of reasoning in RCT must be characterized as a *logical* model of reasoning. It is definitely not a *psychological* account, but a formal account that specifies the ideal conditions under which a specific account of reasoning, maximization of expected utility, yields well-defined solutions.

It will not be necessary to go into the details of the axioms to recognize that conditions in RCT are highly technical and quite demanding; obviously, people's everyday practice of probability reasoning rarely involves mathematical probability calculus. But even completeness (all pairs of consequences can be compared) and transitivity are far from trivial requirements if one considers complex situations where evaluations include multiple perspectives and dimensions (Kahneman and Tversky 1981).

This causes no worries for mathematicians or economists. They seek a formal presentation of how to construct a utility function that suffices as a (mathematically) meaningful interpretation of such a function. They are interested neither in utilities – or preferences – *per se* nor in real-life decision-making.

Yet the technical nature of the conditions of consistency and the construction of a utility function required by the model do not necessarily meet the expectations and requirements of social scientists, who are interested in explaining the behaviour of persons in real-life situations. Average persons do not engage in probability estimates that would meet the standards of mathematical probability calculus (Allais 1953). Also the very idea that persons ought to aim at maximization of expected utility was criticized as too demanding by Simon (1982), who suggested a more modest model of imperfect instrumental rationality that aimed at a level of 'satisficing' rather than maximization. The first wave of critical objections to MUT was not that the concept of rationality employed was too narrow, but that it was too demanding.

The second point to emphasize is that the implicit account of evaluation employed in MUT is purely *consequentialist* – that is to say, outcome-oriented – and instrumental. Consequentialism seems to be an innocent assumption within the context of means-end reasoning, and when decisions are not considered to affect other persons. But it comes with two important implications:

(i)   It implies that preferences are neutral as to moral or social descriptions of alternative courses of action – for example, whether an action conforms to social or moral norms or violates them;

(ii)   Consequentialism is *strictly forward-looking*.[5] Notoriously, consequentialism cannot provide rational explanations for actions that are reactions to events in the past – such as actions of other persons or past commitments and promises – or are derived from norms, based on habits, and so on (Hollis and Sugden 1993; Nida-Ruemlin 1993; Zintl 2001).[6]

Non-consequentialist aspects are often decisive in the processes of reasoning and decision-making for real-life persons, but given the way in which the axiomatic theory is structured, these aspects cannot be integrated into the framework without major changes. Some theorists say, 'that's fine', because they do not consider means-end reasoning to be the only form of practical rationality, but simply one among others. Others are not concerned because they think these other aspects are irrational. But consequentialism then implies serious constraints on the general applicability of the model. It fits only specific types of choice, namely those where consequences are the unique – or at least the most important – aspects of evaluation.

These two points seem to be the most important shortcomings of rational choice theory in the social sciences. Whereas probabilistic reasoning plays a lesser role in game theory, the logic of consequentialism is the same.

Rationality in interaction: the search for equilibria

Game theory is connected to modern utility theory through the assumption that agents choose a course of action they expect will have the best consequences given the alternatives available. It recognizes, however, that straightforward maximization of expected utility is not a rational option in situations that are characterized by social interaction.

The criterion for rational choice in game theory is to aim at an *equilibrium point*. There exist different concepts of equilibrium points, not all of them identical to the maximization of expected utility. Yet all of them are strictly consequentialist. Game theory concerns rational decision-making in situations where the consequences of one's course of action are partly determined by one's own decision, and partly by the decisions of the persons with whom one interacts.

The challenge of social interaction arises because agents must base their choices on mutual expectations about how the other will decide. Since the second person's decision depends upon what she thinks the first person will choose, the first person has to base her choice on the expectation of how the second person will react to what she thinks will be the choice of the first person, and so on.

The mutual dependency of choices raises the threat that agents end up in an infinite regress or circular expectations about expectations. There is no way in which agents can make a choice that deserves to be called rational – as opposed to arbitrary – unless they can identify a rational stopping point at which the reflection about mutual expectations can end. The challenge for rationality here is not one of *maximization*, but of *stability*: to arrive at a choice to which one can stick even if the other person knows how one is going to decide. This is the problem which the concept of equilibrium answers.

Aiming at an equilibrium point can coincide with choosing an action that maximizes one's subjective preference satisfaction, but it need not. The so-called minimax theorem[7] proved by John von Neumann and Oskar Morgenstern, which originally started game theory, says that all two-person constant-sum games have an equilibrium point that guarantees the players a maximal minimum payoff and minimal maximum loss, respectively, if mixed strategies are accepted.

Constant-sum games are by definition characterized so that the gain of one person equals the loss of the other – the game is *strictly conflictive*. A mixed strategy is given by a probability distribution over all the (pure) strategies available to an agent. It selects the strategy to be acted upon by using, for example, a random device for deciding among the available courses of action. If, for example, an agent can do either X or Y and has the mixed strategy of choosing X with a probability of 2/3 and Y with a probability of 1/3, he might throw a die and perform X if 1, 2, 3 or 4 is obtained, and perform Y if 5 or 6 shows. In principle, each possible probability distribution over the set of available strategies is a mixed strategy. Rational actors are supposed to choose a mixed strategy that minimizes losses or maximizes gains. Unfortunately, the minimax theorem turns out to have a rather restricted scope.

The minimax theorem proves that for all two-person constant-sum games, there exists at least one combination of mixed strategies for the players such that if the same game were played a sufficiently high number of times, playing the mixed strategy would minimize the maximal loss and maximize the minimal gain of the players; and if there exists more than one such combination of mixed strategies, all resulting equilibria would be equivalent. The assumption, of course, is not that the game will in fact be repeated a high number of times, but that one should chose as if that would be the case, even though the game is played only once.

The concept of rationality employed in the minimax theorem is a variation of Laplace's principle of insufficient reason: if one does not have a good reason for thinking that one belief is more likely to be true than another, one should regard each as equally likely to be true. (See Neurath (1913) for a similar maxim of practical reasoning.)

Such reasoning is unlikely to be accepted as a rational method of deliberation outside academic classrooms. Even more mathematically minded theorists seem to have some doubts, if only because situations of strict conflict – as modelled by two-person constant-sum games – do not occur very frequently. Most situations of social interaction are so-called *mixed-motive games* – that is, situations where the gains of one player do not equal the losses of another, because, for instance, both can win or lose. Alternatives to the von Neumann–Morgenstern equilibrium of mixed strategies exist, and they are not only much easier to determine, but much less psychologically demanding. The concept of equilibrium that is most widely accepted in game theory is Nash's concept,[8] which says that one should choose the best counter-strategy to what one expects the other person(s)' choice will be. Note that the concept of Nash equilibrium is defined relative to the actual choice of one's co-player.

Nash's concept of an equilibrium point has the significant advantage of offering a rational criterion that can be applied even to games where only an ordinal ranking of preferences over outcomes is given. As the prisoners' dilemma shows, however, Nash equilibria do not necessarily select the course of action that maximizes preference satisfaction of the agents.

Game 1: Prisoners' dilemma (PD)
Two suspects are taken into custody and separated. The district attorney is certain that they are guilty of a specific crime, but he does not have adequate evidence to convict them at a trial. He points out to each prisoner that each has two alternatives: to confess to the crime the police are sure they have done, or not to confess. If they both do not confess, then the district attorney states he will book them on some very minor

Table 8.1. Game 1: Prisoners' dilemma (1)

Peter, Paul	Not confess (Co-operate (C))	Confess (Defect (D))
Not confess (Co-operate (C))	3, 3	1, 4
Confess (Defect (D))	4, 1	2, 2

Note: Here and in the following $4 > 3 > 2 > 1$ always.

> trumped-up charge such as petty larceny and illegal possession of a weapon, and they will both receive minor punishments; if they both confess they will be prosecuted, but he will recommend less than the most severe sentence; but if one confesses and the other does not, the confessor will receive the lenient treatment for turning state's evidence whereas the latter will get 'the book' slapped at him (Hargreaves Heap, Hollis, Lyons *et al.* 1992: 99).

The payoffs obtained by each of the two prisoners, Peter and Paul, are shown in Table 8.1.

An alternative standard presentation (here showing the consequences for Peter) is displayed in Table 8.2.

As can easily be seen, each agent would be better off if both chose C rather than D because (C, C) > (D, D) for each of them. At the same time, each risks unilateral disadvantage if he or she commits him/herself to choose C, because the outcome (C, D) is worse than any other option. Since game theory – like modern utility theory – is strictly consequentialist, each agent must expect that the other's evaluation of the feasible courses of action is exclusively based on the consequences they will experience in the given situation. Neither of them, therefore, can expect that anybody would choose C if he expects the other to choose C, because (D, C) > (C, C) for each of them. Consequently, each knows that the choice of C is not rational for either of them under any circumstances, which makes D the dominant strategy[9] and (D, D) the unique equilibrium point of the game.

A common reaction to the dilemma is that it models a problem for egoists or persons tempted by self-interest. That reaction, however, rests on a misunderstanding, because the dilemma results from the structural properties of the game, not from any supposed theory of motivation. The structure of the game as given in the payoffs represents the preferences of the agents. It therefore does not make sense to ask whether altruists would 'prefer' C over D or (C, C) over (D, C), because *if* altruism versus egoism has any role to play in the evaluation, it is already reflected in the ranking of alternatives.

Table 8.2. Game 1: Prisoners' dilemma (2)

Peter, Paul	Co-operate (C)	Defect (D)
Co-operate (C)	R = reward	S = sucker
Defect (D)	T = temptation	P = punishment

A more sensible question to ask would be: can the prisoners' dilemma situation *occur* among non-selfish agents? That question, of course, is primarily an empirical one. To the extent that we consider real-life agents to be characterized by a mixed motivational structure that includes altruistic as well as selfish attitudes, the answer seems to be 'yes'. Such agents would resemble the average human being we know, and it seems that such agents find themselves in situations that structurally resemble the prisoners' dilemma. If not the two-person prisoners' dilemma, then at least the *N*-person prisoners' dilemma – also referred to as the 'Tragedy of the commons' (Hardin 1968) – seems to represent a rather common structural situation of social life.

> *Tragedy of the commons*
> The commons is a pasture open to all herdsmen of a village. Each herdsman can keep some of his cattle on the commons, the rest on his own land, and each herdsman can increase his herd by increasing the number of cattle sent to the commons. If each herdsman does so, the commons will be overgrazed.

This example has been applied to many real-life situations that require collective action or concern the provision and maintenance of public goods (see, for example, Olson 1971; Taylor 1987; Ostrom 1990)

Interestingly, real-life agents often do not end up at the Pareto-suboptimal equilibrium point, but actually co-operate – not only in daily life, but also in experimental settings (Rapoport and Chammah 1965).

Another assumption about what goes wrong in the model identifies consequentialism as the problem. An intuitive answer to why co-operation is successful in real-life environments is the existence of (coercive) institutions and (moral) norms or practices, such as promises or contracts that support and facilitate co-operation and overcome the constraints of rational individualism. This institutional solution, however, can only be integrated into the theoretical framework if its establishment and maintenance can be shown to be an equilibrium. (This question played an important role in the development of iterated and evolutionary games, which will be considered in a later section.)

In the simple one-shot game (Game 1), it can be easily shown that reference to attitudes of norm-obedience is unconvincing because of the consequentialist structure of the basic model. Assume that Paul *promises* Peter to choose C. Would that give Peter a 'reason' – compatible with the assumptions of modern utility theory – to choose C likewise? The answer of rational choice theorists is no. There are two reasons why not, a simple one and a more sophisticated one. The simple answer is that given Paul's promise, Peter would be tempted to exploit him – which, of course, can be foreseen by Paul and gives him an incentive to break his promise in the first place, which can be foreseen by Peter who consequently does not trust Paul's promise. Although both would be better off if they had the institution of promising, neither has a rational incentive to comply with it. The structure of the prisoners' dilemma repeats itself on the level of compliance (or enforcement) of institutions.

The more complicated answer points to the problem that consequentialism leaves no space for reasons or motives that derive from commitments (obligations) made in the past – such as a promise. Although such commitments are reciprocally advantageous, they cannot be introduced into the model because of the consequentialist structure of evaluation. An alternative path to take is to introduce more complex strategies such as 'co-operate with other co-operator', 'defect when meeting a defector'; but that changes the structure of the game: the PD becomes a *co-ordination game* (see Game 5 below).

The limits of consequentialism are most obvious in settings of social interaction, but can be equally observed in rational choice analysis of the political decisions of individuals. Consider, for example, Downs' (1957) economic theory of democracy. According to Zintl (2001) it provides an analytical test for assessing the limits and scope of conceptualizations of democracy as elite competition for votes – or, as one might say more generally, the *Homo economicus* model. Downs' ideal economic model of democracy analyses voting behaviour as utility-maximizing and party behaviour as competition for votes in order to maximize positions for party members. The assumption, famously, leads directly to the *voter's paradox* – the conclusion that voting is irrational. Given the minimal influence of each single vote, the costs of casting one's vote outweigh the potential gain to be received from it. Therefore, utility-maximizers should abstain. Although the ideal theory articulates only a foil against which Downs develops hypotheses about the role and significance of *prima facie* irrational attitudes (such as adherence to ideologies), neither the ideal nor the non-ideal model offers an escape from the voter's paradox. Although it is not obvious what follows, it definitely indicates the limits not

Table 8.3. Game 2: Traffic

Ann, Rosalind	Drive on the left-hand side	Drive on the right-hand side
Drive on the left-hand side	2, 2	0, 0
Drive on the right-hand side	0, 0	2, 2

Table 8.4. Game 3: Social trap

Jules, Jim	Meeting at the restaurant (A)	Meeting at the library (B)
Meeting at the restaurant (A)	2, 2	0, 0
Meeting at the library (B)	0, 0	1, 1

only of utility-maximization, but more generally of *consequentialist* reasoning within the explanation of socio-political behaviour.[10]

A second and different problem of identifying rational choice with the pursuit of equilibrium points is that in many types of game, more than one equilibrium exists; game theory does not indicate which one to choose. Such situations are commonly called *co-ordination problems* and are usually taken to model self-enforcing conventions (Lewis 1969). A standard co-ordination game is the following:

> *Game 2: Traffic*
> Two drivers, Ann and Rosalind, can drive either on the right-hand or on the left-hand side. Neither has a specific preference for one side over the other, but both prefer to drive on the same side of the road in order to avoid collisions.

The payoffs for this game are shown in Table 8.3. Game theory does not offer a well-defined solution for the problem, because neither Ann nor Rosalind has a basis for deciding independently on which side of the road to drive.

More intensely studied are co-ordination problems with several unequivalent equilibria, such as the following:

> *Game 3: Social trap*
> Two persons, Jules and Jim, plan to meet. Two meeting points are possible, the restaurant and the library, and both prefer to meet at the restaurant.

Game 3 (Table 8.4) has two Nash equilibria in (A, A) and (B, B) with (A, A) > (B, B) for each agent. As Hollis and Sugden (1993) show, however, neither agent has reason to choose A because that would be 'rational' only if

Table 8.5. Game 4: Battle of the sexes

Harry, Sally	Meet at the boxing match	Meet at the ballet
Meet at the boxing match	4, 3	2, 2
Meet at the ballet	1, 1	4, 3

he or she could expect the other also to choose A, and vice versa; but understood as the best counter-strategy to the other agent's choice, (B, B) is as rational a choice as (A, A). The concept of Nash equilibrium gives no reason to prefer one over the other. Intuitively, one would like to say that rational agents naturally choose the equilibrium that is better for all participants. But such a move is not part of the concept of Nash equilibrium, defined as the best counter-strategy to the other player's *actual* choice. In addition, such a move would be of limited help in co-ordination problems such as game 4 (see below and Table 8.5), where the two equilibria yield (4, 3) and (3, 4), favouring Harry in one case and Sally in the other.[11] It could therefore not replace the concept of Nash equilibrium, but would just define an additional concept and thereby repeat the co-ordination problem on a higher level, since it is only rational to adopt such a concept of rational choice if the other person does likewise.[12]

> *Game 4: Battle of the sexes*
> Harry and Sally have the overriding aim of spending the evening together, but Harry wants them to go to a boxing match, whereas Sally prefers that they see the ballet, each according to his or her personal preference for entertainment. They have no possibility to communicate their meeting point, but mutually know their preferences.

The intricacy of co-ordination problems has been extensively discussed by Schelling (1960) in *The Strategy of Conflict*, which included experimental settings with real persons. In the light of the empirical results, Schelling concluded that some equilibria somehow 'stand out' in the sense that they seem to 'have a special meaning' that made participants of the experiments select them. Schelling introduced the term *salience* to characterize the quality of standing out. But he also explicitly stated that salience cannot be adequately expressed within the theoretical framework of rational choice theory because it seems to presuppose a shared semantic practice. The point is far from trivial. Schelling implied that game theory is discontinuous with the Bayesian framework of rational choice theory (Schelling 1960; Spohn 1982).

Other theorists go even further, raising the question of whether the relevance of a shared semantic practice defies the project of methodological individualism (MI), one of the major assumptions of interest in game theory, because *salience* implies a form of holism – a 'common understanding' or 'meaning holism' (Hollis and Sugden 1993). Although meaning holism is a basic and fundamental prerequisite for any form of communication and reasonable interaction, it does not support any specific social ontology. It seems, therefore, insufficient to decide the debate between proponents of MI and holism; but it definitely increases the burden of arguments on the MI side.

'Too bad for the theory!' one might say. And so it may be if one expects game theory and rational choice to provide a straightforward explanatory approach for rational behaviour. The fact that game theory advises choosing the suboptimal equilibrium in situations of the prisoners' dilemma type has indeed been widely celebrated as a self-defeating result of the rational choice concept of rationality. The limits of rational choice detected in co-ordination problems, however, must be considered even more devastating in their implication that the notion of rational choice is ill-defined – that is to say, it does not provide a unique solution – for a rather significant number of games. As Hollis and Sugden (1993) remark, game theory, thus far, has failed to give us an adequate account of how two persons who meet each other in a narrow corridor should choose what to do.[13]

Taking stock

To return to the beginning: a judgement about the usefulness of game theory and rational choice theory in general depends not only on the *explanatory capacity* of the theory, but on the *use that is made of it*. Failures can be very instructive, if they allow for a precise diagnosis and theoretical improvement that goes beyond commonsensical objection or mere dogmatic opposition. They are most instructive when used for analytical purposes.

We can now come back to the possible uses and applications of game theory in the social sciences. The attractiveness of game theory for social theorists derives from a variety of motivations. The three most common seem to be the following:

(i) To the extent that rational choice theory was considered to provide an explanatory approach, one point of attraction seems to have been the expectation that it offers an alternative to behaviourism by opening up the 'black box' of the human mind (Monroe 2001). To the extent that causal explanations of agency are considered to require indications about (regular) psychological mechanisms (Hedstrom and Swedberg 1998), accounts of decision-making and reasoning are obviously attractive (see Héritier, ch. 4).

As a model of a specific account of reasoning, however, game theory competes with other approaches that also aim at explaining human behaviour by motives and reasons but endorse different accounts of 'practical rationality,' 'practical deliberation' or 'reasons for action'. The economic account of means-end rationality and the model of *Homo economicus* have sometimes been used unmodified as an ideal type for explanatory purposes[14] in both political science and sociology. More often, however, they are treated as ideal types and used as a device for the development of alternative and more realistic accounts for behavioural explanations.[15] Their results have also been transformed in explanatory accounts of institutional development and change as in Scharpf (1993), Aoki (2001), Congleton and Swedenborg (2006) and Héritier (2007). Evolutionary game theory, however, partly departs from the commitment to methodological individualism (MI).

(ii) On a more abstract level, game theory was welcomed as an agency-oriented approach by proponents of *methodological individualism* as an alternative to structuralist and functionalist approaches in social sciences. As Osborne and Rubinstein (1994: 1) remark, the models of game theory provide 'highly abstract representations of classes of real-life situations'. These models have been widely used for the analysis of the structure and the dynamic development of macro-phenomena such as institutions, norms and conventions in sociology (Coleman 1990), and in political theory in both its analytical and normative branches, especially social contract theory (Ullmann-Margalit 1977; Axelrod 1984; Taylor 1987; Bicchieri 2006). Since their attractiveness lies in their abstractness, these studies usually work with purely formal models.

(iii) Given its precise axiomatic foundations, the rational choice paradigm was appreciated as a path for the development of '*positive* (political) theory' – or rather *theorizing* – in the social sciences. Its success as a methodology obviously depends on the extent to which game theory allows us to derive explanatory models and hypotheses that are not only falsifiable, but also have the advantage of indicating rather precisely *where* and *why* they go wrong (Riker and Ordeshook 1973; Riker 1997). Although the precise axiomatic foundations of the rational choice paradigm do not entirely exclude controversial interpretations of the shortcomings of its models, it has indeed turned out to offer a fruitful method for the continuous development of research questions and – together with the development of statistics and computerized modelling – also improved models.[16]

In both political science and sociology, game theory has mainly been used as an analytical tool for theory-building, not as a straightforward account for explanation of individual behaviour or specific events.[17] As Zintl (2001) observes, there are two major areas of application in political science. The first is the analysis of institutional and social structures at a level where the motives or reasons of the individuals who constitute them are irrelevant – for instance, because the phenomena under consideration are macro-phenomena constituted by the actions of large numbers of persons with many different attitudes or reasons. Examples are phenomena such as general norms, social conventions or traditional practices – or in the analysis of social or institutional settings, where individual motives can be considered to be determined by structural aspects of the environment in which persons interact.

The second and most promising application of game theory, however, is on the level of conceptualization, the exposition of the problem or puzzles that one wants to study, and the construction of explanatory hypotheses. Zintl (2001) calls such applications 'sophisticated', contrasting them with straightforward endorsement of *Homo economicus* as a model for behavioural explanation, which he calls 'naïve'.

A classical example of the sophisticated application of game theory to explain political behaviour is probably Riker's *Theory of Political Coalitions* (1962). Starting from the assumption that the formation of minimal coalitions is the ideal rational choice for parties that try to optimize positions for their members, the frequency of non-minimal coalitions has set a research puzzle for more focused investigation of motives and incentives in coalition-building.

The major field of application for game theory, however, has been the analysis of institutions. Since no single article can give a satisfying picture of the scope of applications, and since studies in game theory are driven by problems, not by applications, the remainder of the chapter will focus on the most important analytical developments connected to prisoners' dilemma games.[18]

The final judgement on the usefulness of game theory, of course, will have to be made by the reader. But in order to provide some guidance, the final section will outline some of the more recent developments of game theory.

The use of game-theoretic models for analytical purposes

The prisoners' dilemma game is probably the most widely studied model in game theory, exactly because its game-theoretic solution is counterintuitive. Interestingly, although real-life situations seem to fit the structure of the prisoners' dilemma, co-operation is rather common in real life. One important reason seems to be that in real life, decision-making is facilitated by the existence of social and cognitive resources that support co-operation in PD cases.

The attempt to get a clearer picture of what those resources are has driven further analytical development.

The expectation is that to the extent that models can be modified, changed and revised, their study will reveal the conditions that must be satisfied for certain solutions to be possible or stable. The interest that drives the research is not so much the desire to make the model approximate reality – or to make reality compatible with the model – but rather the development of hypothetical scenarios that clarify the dynamics, structures and conditions of the stability or instability of certain forms of social structures. The more variations we get, the more information we receive. If, for example, the original model of single-shot game theory is developed into models of meta-games, iterated games and evolutionary games, the primary insight we can get from those variations concerns the conditions that facilitate or hinder the development of certain social structures, understood as patterns of individual behaviour.

In the remainder of this chapter, I will point to three results and further developments in game theory connected to the discussion of PD and co-ordination games:[19] the norm approach, which involves the transformation of the PD game into the so-called 'assurance' game (AG), also called the 'stag hunt' game; an interesting result from iterated PD games concerning group size; and some tools used in evolutionary game theory (EGT).

Norm-oriented reasons and the challenge of reciprocity

The first criticism of RCT has often taken the following form: its failure to offer an account of co-operative behaviour consistent with the basic assumptions of modern utility theory must be due to a bias in favour of egoism. Once we assume that personal preferences present not only egoistic concerns, but social – or moral – attitudes, the structure of interaction characterized by the PD does not occur. Instead, rational agents are confronted with a problem of reciprocity: the choice is not simply one between (a) to co-operate and (b) to defect, but between strategies or maxims for behaviour such as (a') co-operate with persons who are also willing to co-operate, and (b') defect if you encounter a person who is herself a defector. Such maxims can be called meta-strategies. A game that models the new interpretation is the so-called 'stag hunt' game (Table 8.6), named after a famous passage in Rousseau.

> Game 5: The stag hunt
> Two hunters can either jointly hunt a stag (an adult deer and a rather large meal) or individually hunt a rabbit (tasty, but substantially less

Table 8.6. Game 5: Stag hunt (assurance)

Peter, Paul	Stag hunt (C')	Rabbit hunt (D')
Stag hunt (C')	3, 3	0, 2
Rabbit hunt (D')	2, 0	1, 1

filling). Hunting stags is quite challenging and requires mutual co-operation. If either hunts a stag alone, the chance of success is minimal. Hunting stags is collectively most beneficial but requires a lot of trust among the hunters. It is a co-ordination game with two equilibria at (C', C') and (D', D'), reciprocal co-operation (C', C') being Pareto-superior.

Co-ordination games are no less theoretically problematic than PD games. Rational actors have no incentive to co-operate with rabbit hunters, and given the fact that stag-hunting results in an equilibrium only if one stag-hunter meets another, the stag hunt game has no obvious solution in the terms of RCT. The problem of reciprocal co-operation as posed by the stag hunt game consists in (a) identifying co-operators and defectors, and (b) co-ordinating co-operators so that they interact with each other.

Unfortunately, neither problem can be solved with the theoretical resources offered by classical game theory. Nevertheless, the criticism moved the discussion a significant step forward. It made clear that the prisoners' dilemma is less a problem of egoistic motivation that can be overcome by making persons more moral, than a *cognitive* one.

Iterated games – the challenge of free-riding

Another attempt to overcome the dilemma of the PD developed from the consideration that gains from repeated co-operation outweigh continuous mutual defection, and can even compensate for sporadic exploitation if reciprocal co-operation occurs frequently enough. This attempt remains within the consequentialist (outcome-oriented) structure of the broader rational choice paradigm, but it enriched the model by introducing a future orientation by through allowing for iteration and learning from experience. The latter development was made possible by (a) developing iterated games and (b) programming strategies that based decision-making on information about the outcomes of the previous round. Famously, Axelrod organized computer-based round-robin tournaments for PD games that were run with strategies sent in by the professional and non-professional publics. The tournaments modelled interaction between strategies for the iterated PD game, not between agents, and conducted iterated rounds of bilateral encounters. Some of these strategies were exploitative, some were co-operative, and the winning one – 'tit for tat' – played a strategy of reciprocity: 'tit for tat' always co-operates in the first move and then plays the strategy that was chosen by its partner in the previous round.

The interest in iterated games and evolutionary games concerns not so much questions of choice or strategic logic, but the conditions under which certain results or strategies can be achieved or expected to be stable. Accordingly, the attraction of the study of these games consists in identifying relevant parameters and modifying them in order to study their effects.

Axelrod (1984) summarizes a few general results. The tournament revealed that the success of co-operative strategies depends heavily upon their strategic environment; also, there is no single equilibrium, and several equilibria are possible. Although unconditional defection is always an equilibrium, co-operative equilibria can also occur under certain conditions, but only when co-operation is conditional on being reciprocated and when defection is punished. Unconditional co-operation encourages exploitative strategies. The strategy that received the highest average payoff, tit for tat, has been derived from empirical experiments conducted by Rapoport and Chammah (1965).

Although Axelrod summarized the results of his tournament optimistically as 'evolution of cooperation among egoists', his results are rather limited because the tournament consisted of repeated and aggregated bilateral encounters of each strategy with every other strategy over several rounds. The much more interesting case for the study of co-operative structures, and/or *general* social norms of co-operation, would have to be a genuinely *N*-person variation of the prisoners' dilemma game that is commonly used for modelling the provision of public goods (Hardin 1985; Taylor 1987).

The striking difference between the two-person case and the *N*-person case is that the payoffs are completely determined by the interaction between the two strategies in the first case, whereas in the second case they depend also on the degree of co-operation of those players with whom one does not interact.[20] This difference in the structure generates a serious free-rider problem in the iterated game and actually an incentive to boycott co-operation. Such games were construed and analysed by Taylor (1987), who found that the selection of a co-operative equilibrium in iterated *N*-person PD games is not excluded, but that the conditions under which it can occur are so strict that it is highly unlikely that they will ever be realized in practice.

As a side effect, Axelrod and Taylor's study of iterated PD games sheds light on an assumption that has been held by quite a number of sociological theorists, namely, that group size can make a difference and that duals, bilateral relations, follow a quite different dynamic from multilateral forms of interaction. Generally, the problem that game theory cannot isolate clear-cut equilibrium solutions for all games has resurfaced in the study of iterated games.

Evolutionary games – the instability of co-operation

Evolutionary game theory (EGT) studies the conditions under which pre-programmed strategies can become stable patterns of behaviour. EGT is primarily interested in the frequency of specific strategies within a population searching over time for dynamic equilibria. That allows one to analyse also the mutual influence or dependency that holds between individuals and the social environment. EGT has developed an impressive range of variations for both strategies and the construction of different social environments. Evolutionary simulations, for example, have used strategies that are capable of 'learning' or 'signalling'; others vary 'environmental' settings such as spatial locations of strategies, i.e. isolated or in clusters, and forms of encounter, which range from random combinations over the construction of 'neighbourhoods' to mechanisms for selecting partners.

Most interesting for the social sciences are two apparent motivations for the study of EGT: (i) the hope that it provides a better understanding of agency and the development of rationality in social (strategic) interaction; and (ii) the hope of arriving at a better understanding of the role of collective agencies (institutions) and the efficiency of spontaneous versus constructed orders.[21]

An important step towards evolutionary models was taken by the biologists Maynard Smith and Price (1973), who developed the concept of an *evolutionarily stable strategy* (ESS). Maynard Smith and Price were interested in the dynamics of selection of behavioural patterns within groups of individuals. The puzzle they addressed concerns the robustness of behavioural patterns against individuals or groups of invaders. A 'hawk–dove' game, which structurally resembles the chicken game (see note 11), is used in order to specify the conditions under which a population of doves can survive the invasion of hawks, and vice versa. For that purpose, an evolutionarily stable strategy is characterized by two properties that are familiar from the concept of a Nash equilibrium: (i) it is the best response to itself, and (ii) it is the best response to any other strategy in the environment.

The concept of ESS was also used by Axelrod (1984) for an evolutionary simulation of PD situations, which supported the result already achieved in iterated games: that (unconditional) co-operation is not an evolutionarily stable strategy. Although unconditional defection is always an ESS, conditional co-operation (following the logic of tit for tat) can also be stable in specific environments.

Another tool used in evolutionary modelling is so-called replicator dynamics. Replicator dynamics model strategy change in iterated games by changing the frequency of strategies within a given population in the following way: a strategy that does better than average increases in frequency at the expense of strategies that do worse than average.[22] The main interest in those studies again concerns the effect of the modifications of parameters, which is difficult to summarize. Two general results from the study of replicator dynamics in various games (chicken, hawk–dove, PD, stag hunt), however, seem to be as follows:

(i)   Whereas equilibria for ESS are always also Nash-equilibria, there can exist equilibria in replicator dynamics that are not Nash-equilibria (Taylor and Jonker 1978).

(ii)   Under certain conditions, replicator dynamics result in co-operative equilibria.

The latter point is especially strong in models that study reciprocal co-operation, such as the stag hunt game. A quite accessible presentation of the results of increasingly rich modulations of the stag hunt game is offered by Skyrms (2004), who also discusses their relevance for social science.

Paying tribute to the importance of contingencies in biological evolution, some models introduce random mutation (also called noise) in order to study the influence of contingent disturbances for dynamic equilibria. Equilibria that are resistant to small perturbations (noise) are often called asymptotically stable.

The results from evolutionary game theory show clearly that both the enrichment of cognitive resources (learning, signalling) and spatial closeness increase the likelihood of stable reciprocal co-operation. So far, it seems that the results do not indicate that institutional orders provide better mechanisms for equilibrium selection than do spontaneous orders, or vice versa.

A warning might, however, be appropriate. All strategies used in evolutionary game theory are algorithms that can model the behaviour of human beings as well as of bacteria or robots; that includes mechanisms of 'learning', which so far have been varieties of learning by reinforcement or imitation. Nevertheless, the EGT approach represents an agency-oriented approach, because social structures are perceived as being constituted by individuals' patterns of behaviour. Regarding the agent–structure debate and the MI paradigm, however, the results of EGT seem strongly to support the thesis that a mutual dependency between individual strategies and social environment exists, and that structures not only constrain individual behaviour, but also provide motives for agency (Hargreaves Heap and Varoufakis 2004: 264).

With EGT, in fact, we leave the paradigm of Bayesian RCT behind us. For evolutionary game theory does not model the choices of agents, but the success of different strategies for choice under varying circumstances by using algorithms. Algorithms, obviously, are quite different from agents, not only because of the lack of psychological properties, but also because they are in a sense deterministic. They are pre-programmed, even if they can learn. Thus, the later stages of dynamic evolutionary models are far removed from the original model of modern utility theory. Although it might be an open question whether algorithms that determine the behaviour of bacteria will provide us with insights into patterns of human behaviour, which can neither be affirmed nor excluded *a priori*, such algorithms provide an illustrative example of how theory development can proceed.

For further theoretical studies, however, one result seems especially crucial. Evolutionary games strongly indicate that the basic assumptions of the rational choice concept of rational agency have to be revised. If the social environment provides not only constraints, but also reasons for agency, basic assumptions of Bayesian rational choice theory have to be changed. As Hargreaves Heap and Varoufakis (2004: 264) conclude: 'The learning model, directed as it is instrumentally to payoffs, may be more realistic but it is not enough to lead unambiguously to some equilibrium outcome. Instead, if we are to explain actual outcomes, individuals must be socially and historically located in a way that they are not in the instrumental model. "Social" means quite simply that *individuals have to be studied within the context of social relations within which they live and which generate specific norms*.' (See Keating, ch. 6, and Steinmo, ch. 7.)

At the present stage, it is not easy to assess whether and what the social scientist can learn from EGT. But it certainly will reshape the scholarly debate, if not about human agency, then about Bayesian RCT.

NOTES

1 This chapter will not consider non-Bayesian approaches.

2 The distinction between the two applications is sometimes blurred because individual motives and reasons are often considered to be given by assumption, or to be irrelevant because the objects of study are large-N-person settings, or taken to be determined by the properties of the social setting under investigation.

3 For a comprehensive selection of major contributions to all branches of RCT, see Allingham

(2006). Public choice theory can be considered to articulate a game-theoretic alternative to social choice theory (Buchanan and Tullock 1965; Mueller 1989).

4 For reasons of space, these conditions cannot be specified here. The most accessible presentation is still Luce and Raiffa (1957: ch. 2).

5 It is, however, neither necessarily amoral nor egoistic; utilitarianism is consequentialist too.

6 The view has been held that positive and negative evaluations of the course of action can be integrated if we consider 'psychological costs' that accompany the performance of a specific course of action, such as buying rather than stealing. The preference over owning a good if ownership is brought about by theft, and the preference over owning it if ownership is brought about by legal transfer from another person, need not be the same. Such a move is certainly possible in principle, but against the logical spirit of the model.

7 The minimax theorem is, as the name says, a theoretical proposition that can be proved. It should not be confused with the so-called minimax criterion for decision-making under uncertainty; for further clarification, see Luce and Raiffa (1957) or any other coursebook for decision and game theory.

8 An excellent and updated introduction to game theory is Hargreaves Heap, Hollis, Lyons *et al.* (1992).

9 A dominant strategy is a strategy that has better consequences than any other strategy available for all possible courses of events or strategies chosen by another agent.

10 For criticism and further development, see for example, Tsebelis (1990) and Brennan and Hamlin (2000).

11 The so-called 'chicken' game, which has been widely used as a model for threatening, is an even more intricate co-ordination problem: 'Two adolescents, Dean and Brando, decide to resolve a dispute by riding towards each other down the middle of a road. The first to turn away loses. If both continue straight ahead, they will crash and risk serious injury' (Hargreaves Heap, Hollis, Lyons *et al.* 1992: 106). The payoffs are shown in the following table.

Dean, Brando	Hold straight	Give way
Hold straight	0, 0	4, 1
Give way	1, 4	2, 2

12 For an exhaustive discussion, see Hollis and Sugden (1993).

13 For a solid and informed discussion of shortcomings of the rational choice concept of rationality, see Green and Shapiro (1994) and Friedman (1996).

14 For a general critique, see Sen (1977).

15 See Simon's account of 'bounded rationality' (Simon 1982) and Elster's studies on irrationality, preference change and the 'subversion of rationality' (Elster 1979, 1983, 2000). For applications of game theory in sociology, cf. Abel (1991), part III.

16 Some of the advanced models in evolutionary game theory even seem to come as close to experimental settings as non-natural sciences can be expected to come (Skyrms 2004).

17 An exception is bargaining theory, which seems to constitute a practice of interaction fit for the application of economic models if – or as long as – the questions at stake can be considered not to be exceptional. But obviously, bargaining is guided not only by logical strategies of choice, but also by psychological aspects; the more important the latter is considered

to be, the less reliable rational choice models become. For analysis and applications of game theory to problems of bargaining and negotiation, see for example, Brams (1990), Brams and Taylor (1996) and Raiffa and Richardson and Metcalfe (2002). For a criticism of the psychological shortfalls of rational choice theory, see Mercer (2005).

18 It has to said, though, that this development was also supported by the improvement of computer technologies.

19 A fourth development, psychological games, goes beyond the scope of the present chapter; interested readers are referred to Hargreaves Heap and Varoufakis (2004: ch. 7).

20 One might think of the problem of building a dam to protect a small island against a flood. If the dam can be built in time by eighteen persons, and there are twenty-five persons living on the island, then seven of them can refrain from co-operating without defying the co-operative gains of the other eighteen.

21 A more theory-immanent interest, of course, concerned the problem of selection of equilibrium points.

22 The standard model was developed by P. Taylor and Jonker (1978). An easily accessible presentation is given in Hargreaves Heap and Varoufakis (2004: ch. 6); for a more formal presentation, see Weibull (1995).

Rationality and recognition

Alessandro Pizzorno

Shylock: You'll ask me, why I rather chose to have
A weight of carrion flesh than to receive
Three thousand ducats: I'll not answer that:
But, say, it is my humour: is it answered?
(William Shakespeare, *The Merchant of Venice*)

Introduction

A central problem in the social sciences concerns the relationship between the individual and larger social aggregates (see della Porta and Keating, ch. 1). One influential approach is based on methodological individualism, allied with the assumption that individuals are motivated by a rational assessment of their own self-interest; larger social processes are merely the sum of individual actions. Some of the difficulties of this approach are addressed by Christine Chwaszcza (ch. 8), who shows how even self-regarding individuals must consider the actions of other people.

A different approach is the one that could be considered the classical sociological approach (from Durkheim to Lazarfeld and Merton), pre-dating the introduction of methodological individualism. What follows is a redescription of such an approach taking into consideration the necessity of answering certain positions advanced by rational choice theory.

In discussing some important contributions in classical sociology this chapter will advance the general position that sociality is based not on the social action of an actor maximising utility (or self-interest) but on a relation between actors attributing to each other a social name, or social identity. In other words, the object of a social science is the constitution of social positions, and the way they are formed by the reciprocal recognition during the encounters of social actors.

To confront this position with the alternative position of rational choice theory, a terminological clarification seems necessary regarding the different meanings of 'rationality'. This notion was introduced relatively recently in the social sciences, in response to two principal developments. The first was the failure of logical positivism to consolidate a view of the social sciences based on causal explanation, thus requiring the development of an alternative type of explanation. This was found in the view that an action could be sufficiently explained by referring to its *reasons*. Why did X perform action P? Because he had reasons to do it. To have *reasons to do something* is a very different view of a social action from being *caused to do something*. When mention of reasons is considered a sufficient replacement for causes in explaining action, I shall use the notion of *subjective rationality*.

The second development was the increasing influence of microeconomics on theory construction. Von Mises, writing in 1949, thought 'that the transition [in economic science] from the classical theory of value to the subjective theory of value [i.e. introducing the principle of marginal utility] . . . is much more than merely a theory of the "economic side" of human behavior and man's striving for commodities. It is the science of every kind of human action.' In Von Mises' interpretation the rationality of human action, understood as preference-fulfilling choice, is an *a priori* truth; it has to be accepted as a premise, not submitted to empirical verification. In research practice, an observer can only judge the rationality of a certain action if he knows the intention of the agent. But since the observer has no way to know empirically what the intentions of the agent are, he either has to assume that the agent's intentions are the same as those he, the observer, would express in similar circumstances, or that when one observes an action one presumes to possess the special gift of penetrating the mind of the actor.

A typical difficulty in applying subjective rationality arises in cases of weakness of the will (*akrasia*), when (to use the pithy description from Davidson's *Problems of Rationality* (2004: 18)), 'the agent knows what he is doing, knows that it is not for the best, and knows why'. How do we sort out, in this case, the true intention? Similar difficulties arise with behaviour concerning rituals. How should we understand the action of going to Mass? As fulfilling the preference to go to Mass? Not very enlightening. As a means to a further end? Who could say which end?

A more relevant shortcoming of using subjective rationality in analysing social action is the impossibility of explaining the production of public goods, and therefore the existence of collective action, as the game of the prisoners' dilemma illustrates (see Chwaszcza, ch. 8). From this, it follows that we should consider irrational (or leave as unexplainable) types of behaviour that we normally consider rational – such as voting, going to religious ceremonies, giving money to worthy causes, or other actions that cannot be easily classified as being in the agent's best interest – at least not without falling into logical circularity.

An alternative way of conceiving rationality is to link it, not to the intention of the subject of an action, but to how an action is received and interpreted in the culture (or merely the cultural situation) where it takes place. This definition of rationality is the one usually adopted in the social sciences. According to the legal philosopher Neil MacCormick (2007: 11), 'an elaborate set of patterns for human conduct is taken to be binding on all persons within the ordered domain, and order prevails among the persons addressed to the extent that they succeed in matching their conduct to the stipulated pattern. The possibility of orderliness arising out of conformity to such patterns depends obviously, on the set of patterns amounting to a *rationally intelligible totality*' (emphasis added). In other words, behaviour is rational when it corresponds to a 'pattern of orderliness', as defined by the participants within a given situation. It is my contention that the whole sociological tradition (including Weber) implicitly used this conception of 'rationality' in their analysis, at least prior to the penetration of microeconomics and the subjective theory of action.

This point emerges clearly if one describes the process of research in the following realistic way. An event takes place that a group of people (let us call it 'the audience'), given the existing theory in their possession, is unable to understand. An observer entrusted with analysing the event should seek to describe how the event has been *received* by its participants; how it has been understood; which consequences it has provoked; and with which other practices it is connected. Having performed this task, the observer brings his analysis back to the original audience so that it may modify its ideas of rationality in order to include them in their explanation of the event.

This research procedure recognizes that we must develop theories able to embed individual action within interpersonal or cultural premises, thereby illustrating the impact of the participation of other people (let us call them *circles of recognition*) on the development of individual action (see Keating, ch. 6, and Bray, ch. 15). With this in mind, I shall try to reanalyse a series of authors who, explicitly or implicitly, used this model of social action. The first thinkers to whom I shall refer, Adam Smith and Jean-Jacques Rousseau, look at first sight to belong to different schools of thought. They show, however, unexpected similarities.

Smith and Rousseau: the other as a spectator

At first sight it may appear strange that the first modern thinker to highlight the importance of judgement by others in forming motivations for individual action was Adam Smith, founder of modern economics, the discipline that is mistakenly considered to have introduced the idea of *Homo economicus*. Yet a crucial argument within Adam Smith's work is that human beings do *not* act primarily to satisfy their personal needs, but rather to obtain favourable judgement by their peers. This idea emerged out of the Scottish Enlightenment, as Hutcheson had already affirmed that the search for moral approval from others was 'an innate basic feeling' common to human beings. Smith then formulated a system of 'moral sentiment' based on the concept of the 'impartial spectator', whose judgement the agent would bear in mind when making his choices. One effect would be the acquisition of a strengthened capacity for 'self-command' – defined by Smith in microeconomic terms as the capacity of a person to give greater importance to future gains than to present ones.[1] This influences the organization of individual behaviour through time, so that we are able to judge our actions only if we can see them through the eyes of others; anticipate their judgement; and behave in order to obtain praise and avoid criticism. Praise will inevitably raise our self-esteem, while criticism will inevitably lower it. Smith concludes that only when persons act in society can they find the mirrors with which to judge themselves.

However, Smith failed to explain a phenomenon that can be characterized as 'general rejection of heteronomy', whereby it is seen as normal that a person abhors the idea that her actions are guided by the views and judgements of others. True, this objection is implicitly considered by Smith: he states that the observer who guides and judges our actions must be an *impartial* one, hence not the daily spectators whose eyes are upon us at every moment of the day. We should see this abstract and impartial figure as the source of judgement of our actions, as a true super-ego that we can imagine emitting cogent judgements on our virtues or lack thereof. Yet, there is a difference from the Freudian super-ego, which is imagined as being located within ourselves and thus unlikely to invalidate our aspirations for autonomy. The Smithian super-ego is instead located outside of ourselves, in the view of others, thus potentially weakening our claim to autonomy.

In order to overcome our anxiety at our lack of autonomy, we need to divide the 'others' whose judgement could influence us into two categories. The first is the 'primary socializers', present more or less from the beginning of our development (such as parents, teachers, classmates), and not of our choosing. The second category is the 'secondary socializers', individuals (real or imagined) whom we encounter during the course of our lives, and who may (or may not) be of our choosing. These secondary socializers crowd around the primary ones, making the judgement of the latter less extraneous to our self, so that we feel able to formulate a personal ideology through which to convince ourselves that we are truly autonomous. We then protect this imagined autonomy, expelling the notion of external influence and assuming that we are the sole authors of our choices. This leads us to believe that we are *being ourselves.*

Jean-Jacques Rousseau seems to interpret the views of others in a less Olympian manner: 'If men see me differently to myself, what do I care? Is the essence of my being contained in their glances?' (Rousseau 1959: 985). Yet the relationship of Rousseau to the 'others' was considerably more complex. Why else would he have needed to write 'Rousseau judged by Jean-Jacques', an untriumphant defence against the glances of others, which Rousseau experienced as an obsessive persecution that followed him into his daily life and ruined his capacity for being sociable? In this way, Rousseau sought to construct his own self, which he developed into an 'immortal' concept. Yet in doing so, he was interacting with the few people present in the salons where he read his work,[2] and whose judgement weighed heavily on his behaviour ('The essence of my being is in their glances', he complained); it was outside this audience that he aimed at a different recognition that would allow him to deflect the malicious views of his enemies, who had made it so difficult for him to be himself. Instead, he had in mind a historical audience composed of *real* glances. Yet, having theorized that the presence of others transforms the legitimate *amour de soi* into an *amour propre*, Rousseau himself caved in to that small but important audience of enemy-friends, thus weakening his self-esteem.[3]

Uncertainty on the judgement that others give to our actions, and contradictions in the autonomy of our choices, are not easily reconcilable states of affairs. The ancients conceived of interpersonal relations in which the judgement of others was not influential in our choices, while virtue was the principle that defined our autonomy. The tension between the desire to be ourselves and the need for recognition from others is confirmed by a number of moralists (from Seneca to Schopenhauer) who preached that people *ought* to behave without concern for the judgement of others, and that *doing the right thing* should be sufficient compensation. Yet when these moralistic positions are placed under the lens of the social sciences, which do *not* have the objective of evaluating how people *should* behave but must seek ways to understand how moral judgements affect individual behaviour, what answers can be provided? Perhaps no more than highlighting the personal motivations of the moralists. Or perhaps raising the veil on the presumptions of the self-righteous, who find themselves in the right only because they are unable to see reality without veils.

This modest but important feat is all that the social sciences can and should do in support of the moral order.

Hegel: interpersonal relations as the structure of subjectivity

The question of recognition was present implicitly in the work of Hobbes, yet we must attribute to Hegel the modern use of the metaphor of 'recognition'. He developed this idea in his early writings as a result of his discussions with Hoelderlin in Tübingen (Pinkard 2000: 170–1) which he later included in his concept of *Sittlichkeit* (Honneth 1992).

Hegel's dialectic of the master and the servant (DMS) has been used in very different ways. While relinquishing any attempt to interpret literally *what Hegel really said* in his *Phenomenology*, we can recall this metaphor in order to reconstruct the notion of recognition, formulating it in terms that can be useful for the empirical social sciences.

What I propose in order to clarify the notion of 'recognition' is a simplified DMS model, describing the following situation: A and B are two people who meet. Both are motivated by their vital desires but realize that these will only appear legitimate when, entering into a relationship, the other recognizes their desire not only as an animal instinct, but as a legitimate human will. A and B both know that in doing so there is a risk, given that both have a principle that cannot be ceded, namely the preservation of their selves (this is what Hobbes calls 'self-preservation' and Rousseau calls '*l'amour de soi*'). Yet both know that this love of self, should A and B remain isolated, will not be enough for their self-preservation, as only a relationship with another can provide this certainty. They are therefore prepared to give themselves to each other but *not completely*, as the condition of self-preservation requires that they do not sacrifice their lives. They have understood that to attain autonomy they must be recognized as such by the other, yet paradoxically they can achieve this only if they show to the other that they do not need his recognition. The winner (or Master) is the one who demonstrates the ability to live without the other, while at the same time accepting the crucial importance of being recognised.

References to recognition in sociological thinking

While the political thought of German Romanticism and Scottish anti-contractualism laid the basis for overcoming the subjectivist orthodoxy, different paths emerged within sociological theory that sought to counter subjectivism. To that end, I shall refer here to the classic distinction between Durkheim and Weber, in which the former is viewed as the leading exponent of a holistic theory of social reality and the latter is presented as a supporter of methodological individualism. This section will explore whether this characterization is accurate.

Max Weber

On the basis of explicit declarations by Weber, it seems that his individualism does not harbour doubts. Weber reiterates that only individual actions, those attributable to subjective intentions, are comprehensible to the observer. Yet according to him, the actions of an individual cannot be considered *social* if they are directed towards inanimate objects. To become social, there must be a plurality of actors guided by the anticipation of the meaning that others will attribute to their actions.[4] If somebody cuts wood for the purposes of exercise, this cannot be considered a social action; if they cut wood to give to a friend in order to keep him/her warm at night, this is a social action. In a similar vein, religiosity is not social when it is concerned merely with contemplation or solitary prayer. For a social action to be rational, it is crucial not only that it express the intention of the agent but also that it create an expectation of comprehension from subjects other than the agent.

The idea that an action can be considered rational only if accepted as such by those involved, and therefore that rationality is linked to *reception* as well as intention, is not explicitly proposed by Weber. Yet it should not escape our attention that Weber's conception of rationality is not microeconomic or individualistic, and that his theory of action is not merely a decision theory. Weber insisted on the centrality of individual actions in constructing social institutions, albeit within the limits outlined above; yet, when he developed historical interpretations or sought to explain the results of his research, Weber abandoned the subjectivistic focus. Actors are described not as individuals free of every socialization, acting only according to individual utility, but as members of a community into which they have been socialized and from which they receive the values and social functions that structure their choices. For example, in the passage from one system to another (as in the emergence of capitalism), Weber highlights only the involvement of collective actors who act based on their social and institutional positions (Poggi 1983: 37).

Furthermore, the concept of religion is only considered relevant when shared by a group whose members take into account the behaviour of others practising the same faith, thus displaying a common identity. Examples abound where Weber displays strong contradictions between his declarations on methodological individualism and his interpretation of historical events. One of these is his explanation for the diffusion of the Mithraic cult throughout the Roman Empire between the second and fourth centuries AD.[5] Weber adopts the following reasoning. In Imperial Rome, the importance of the bureaucracy and the army (both presented as *collective* entities) was such that it inspired a strong feeling of religiosity among its members. Weber assumes here that the nature of the religion the bureaucrats and soldiers prefer would be similar to the structures in which they operated daily (which cannot by the way be taken for granted), attributing the success of the Mithraic cult to a monotheistic hierarchy that generates a feeling of religious solidarity similar to the *esprit de corps* of the army or bureaucracy. Not only is Weber's explanation of this phenomenon far from a micro-sociological one – as might be expected from someone inspired by an individualistic methodology that seeks to open the 'black box' of human intention – but it also represents a form of *vulgar collectivism* (to adopt a Marxist expression). With regard to the specific analysis of the Mithraic cult, we should note that:

1 Not all soldiers and public officials joined the Mithraic cult, so those who did must have had a reason other than their public position.

2 Although the notion that a daily hierarchical experience may lead to a preference for hierarchical religious faith cannot be excluded *a priori*, it would also be easy to argue the opposite, namely that someone living under a tightly disciplined daily environment would seek mystical detachment in their religious faith.

3 To organize a religious movement, people must meet, communicate, develop a common identity and manifest this in lasting social ties, thereafter making recognition of their common faith the basis for their actions. In this sense, a religious movement is characterized by many common collective constraints, rather than by a series of individual intentions.

In the social sciences we should seek to transcend the analysis of the 'black box' of individual intentions and their contestable rationality, instead reconstructing the rationality that is expressed through the process of interaction and attribution of identities that allow people to recognize themselves in new guises. If Weber refrains from developing an analysis of such processes, it is probably because of his individualistic preconceptions. Indeed, the actor he considers is embedded in at least two normative constraints: the socialization of military functions and the norms that make possible the access to a religious movement.

Emil Durkheim

Turning to Durkheim, how can we distinguish his perspective from that of Weber? The methodology of his research on suicide is founded on the following reasoning: social institutions (religious, familial, territorial, urban–rural) are distinguishable from each other by their level of anomie, that is, the extent of the normative pressures they exert on the individual. In several passages Durkheim refers to the 'social forces' that act on the individual. It is this concept of social forces (sometimes referred to as 'collective conscience'), characterizable as a trans-subjective reality tied to the actions of the individual, which led many observers to the conclusion that Durkheim views the actions of the individual as totally conditioned by society. Yet if we look beyond this metaphor, the concept of 'social force' is actually rather vague and is not crucial to the explanations Durkheim employs.

Let us look at how Durkheim formulates the results of his research on suicide. The suicide rate among Catholics is lower than among Protestants. This occurs because Catholicism is a religion that promotes a rituality compelling the individual to have durable relations with others, leading to the sharing of a common identity. In other words, the real explanatory variable for Durkheim is the level of *moral density*, which measures the intensity of significant interpersonal relations within a given community. Another finding is that the suicide rate is lower among married people than singles. Here again, this is because Durkheim attributes a greater moral density to married people. The suicide rate is lower among women with children than among childless women, again because married women live within a context of greater moral density. Finally, Durkheim notes that suicide is lower during war than during peace, and considerable evidence suggests that moral density (in the form of co-operation, solidarity or reciprocal aid) is also higher during war. Yet, what is moral density if not the intensity and durability of social situations, through which people meet and thus recognize the existence of a common identity?

Durkheim also highlights another correlation to explain variations in the suicide rate, which at first glance suggests a theory different from that of moral density. He finds that the rate of suicide is closely related to the economic cycle, increasing not only during recessions (as could be expected) but also during the early phases of recovery (which is counterintuitive). How can this be explained? By observing that during recessions there is an increase in bankruptcies and failures, while during a recovery there is a rise in expectations which will be followed by disappointment for some. This will in turn lead to more suicides. In this explanation, moral density is not presented as an independent variable, and everything seems to occur within the mind of the isolated individual. Yet if we analyse this situation more closely, we may note that what is at stake here is the relationship of an individual's present self with its future self. It is as if lack of moral density prevents the unity of these two selves of a person, the one that chooses in the present and the one that will judge in the future. In this case the former is failed by the latter and hence loses the willingness to continue living.

What emerges from this comparison is a strong convergence in the analysis of the two founders of modern sociology, both of whom seek to overcome the eternally repeated dichotomy between individual and society. Both highlight processes of socialization as being those instances where different roles merge and contrast, recognize and reject, attract and repel, and implicitly or explicitly form *enduring and comprehensible forms of sociality*.

The contemporary theorist who has come closest to a theory of recognition is probably Habermas. Reconstructing the positions of the classical sociologists, in particular assigning a crucial role to Herbert Mead, Habermas develops the idea of communicative action as something antinomical to instrumental action, yet subsuming the latter. However, the normative centrality of linguistic communication, based on dialogue that inevitably aims towards consensus, makes it difficult for Habermas to include within his analysis those situations where recognition is not oriented towards understanding in the double sense, meaning both comprehension and implicit agreement, that he understands this term (*Verstandigung* in German). If, instead, we define situations of recognition as merely the 'reciprocal attribution of identity' and thus the building-blocks of every form of sociality (even conflictual), recognition will then reflect the presence of actors (incomplete actors, according to the Hegelian metaphor, if not recognized by others) in a system of relations, which may be either co-operative or conflictual. A macrosociological example for the formation of such systems of recognition is the system of the European nation-state, which emerged through a process that culminated symbolically (if not conclusively) in the Peace of Westphalia. We should note that this was the result of two processes that implied the recognition of the nation-state as sovereign, that is, a subject of rationally understandable action: vertical recognition of the state authority by the local nobility; and horizontal recognition of the inviolable sovereignty of an individual state by other states in an international system. This attempt to achieve reciprocal recognition through a specific type of political union was the outcome of agreements and conflicts, which disrupted or stabilized this system, yet generally preserved the principle of reciprocal recognition.

Concluding remarks

The following conclusions can be drawn from this chapter.

The development of the social theory of action away from subjectivistic premises has introduced an interpersonal dimension that has transformed the unitary choosing subject into a plurality of role-performing actors. Further, introducing an intertemporal dimension has allowed us to consider the choices of our present selves as actions that could be assumed to be judged by our future selves. The fact that our future selves tend to converge with the selves lastingly recognized by a circle of recognition protects us from value uncertainty. Convergence, indeed, is most effective when the subject acts within circles of other individuals who will keep recognizing his choices with the same value they had when they were initially made.

The activity of judging that the subject performs when engaged in inter-personal encounters refers to two distinct functions. The first is to reach a judgement of affinity with the other person, allowing us to come out from what Rousseau and Hobbes describe as our state of nature (or isolation). The second function is instead to furnish us with moral criteria for judging our own choices and actions. Judgements of affinity and moral judgement tend generally, but not always, to coincide.

The concept of reception, as opposed to intention, has been introduced in order to define as rational that action that the participants accept as receivable in their culture. Not the external observer, but the participants in a social action (the circles of recognition) are the judges of its rationality.

The idea of the audience (or public) therefore becomes central. It represents the entity that first poses the research question and then operates with its results so that transforming the original theory should force their under-standing. Consequently, the judgement of rationality takes place at two suc-cessive levels: that of the participating actors, whose judgement is local and necessarily relative, relying on relations between participants acting within a defined context; and the subsequent judgement of the audience, which seeks to advance a more universal notion of rationality. This will be comprehensive, but also temporary, as it will always be exposed to new theories that emerge each time the audience obtains new information.

Our achievement of these (meta-)theoretical aims appears to justify the use of elementary responses to explain situations which, from the approach of rational choice theory, are merely considered enigmas. Rational choice theory tends to view individual action as being consistent only in seeking to maximize gains. Yet in doing so, such theory ignores two essential points. First, that participants and observers alike give meaning to an event only when they consider it a component of some durable social process. Second, that the self-interest of an individual cannot be considered as a reality that precedes and motivates the action. It is instead the outcome of a process whose full content is not known by the subject, and hence by the non-knowledgeable observer when the actor engages in social action. Self-interest, as defined by the actor as well by the observer, represents the outcome of the action rather than its premises.

NOTES

1 We should note that in preferring a lower present gain in favour of a greater future gain, the actor does not maximize her gains in the interval, thus failing to maximize her overall gains. Smith does not address this problem in his analysis.

2 Rousseau read part of the *Confessions* manuscript in several sittings (1771–2), to both nobility (including the prince of Sweden) and Parisian intellectuals (Rousseau 1959: 1611).

3 On other roles that the concept of 'recognition' plays in the work of Rousseau, see Carnevali (2004).

4 It should be noted that according to this definition it is not entirely clear whether some classic research, like that of Durkheim on suicide, can be considered sociological. For a rigorous analysis of weaknesses and contradictions in the Weberian notion of social action, see Gilbert (1989: 24–55).

5 I selected this example from many others because it has been used in recent texts (in particular by Boudon) as an example of Weberian methodological individualism, whereas I argue that this example actually demonstrates the opposite.

Part II

Research design

10 Concepts and concept formation

Peter Mair

Most political and social science research, whether explicitly or implicitly, is comparative research. That is, most research is concerned with findings which are directly compared across countries or cases, or which can be tested against theories and inferences derived from such a comparison of countries and cases. Comparison also involves explanation, in that one of the principal reasons that we invoke comparisons is to explain how ostensibly different factors have led to similar outcomes, or how ostensibly similar situations have led to different outcomes. Why, for example, does turnout in national elections fall below 50 per cent in two countries as diverse as the United States and Switzerland (Franklin 2004)? And why has a far-right populist party, the Vlaams Belang, enjoyed substantial electoral success in the Flemish-speaking region of Belgium, while the equivalent party, the Front National, has failed miserably in the French-speaking region (Coffé 2005)?

The first, and in many ways most important lesson in developing and understanding these comparisons is to know whether like is being compared to like. Are the objects being compared – national electoral contests, far-right populist parties – similar to one another? Are they the same thing, or perhaps even functional equivalents? Or are they so different that any comparison between them is likely to prove meaningless? In England, when like cannot be compared to like, and hence when the objects involved are strikingly different, people tend to speak of chalk and cheese. This is indeed a difficult comparison, since on almost any of the key properties of the two objects – taste, capacity and so on – it is impossible to substitute one for the other. Think of chalk sandwiches, or using cheese to write on blackboards. In the Netherlands, the most striking differences are treated as being analogous to apples and pears. Here the contrast does not seem so sharp. Both are sweet seasonal fruits,

I am grateful to Jørgen Møller, Cas Mudde and Karin Tilmans for many useful suggestions when preparing this chapter, and to Rainer Bauböck, Christine Chwaszcza and the two editors for comments on an earlier version. The usual disclaimer applies.

ripening at more or less the same time and playing a similar role in our diet. Each is good to eat with cheese (but not with chalk), and we are often equivocal when having to choose between them. In other words, the distance between apples and pears is a lot more limited than that between chalk and cheese. In Sartori's (1970) terms, as we shall see later, you scarcely have to climb up the ladder of abstraction before you find a concept which embraces both apples and pears, whereas you have to climb almost to the very top of that ladder before you find a concept that is general enough to embrace both chalk and cheese.

In this chapter, I will focus on the crucial stage in the research process in which initial ideas and hypotheses are translated into an operational research design and into real research practice: the stage at which the concepts are defined. I will work mainly with Sartori's classic rules of concept formation, and with reference to his so-called ladder of abstraction. In brief, Sartori assigned concepts among three levels – high, medium and low – in which the degree of generality or abstraction of the concept is related to the range of cases which it covers. The more abstract the concept, the wider the range of cases; the more concrete the concept, the narrower the range of cases. This is fairly self-evident. What comes next is often less easily accepted, however, at least in research practice: when we move from a narrower to a wider range of cases, it follows that we have to make our concepts more abstract – we have to lighten them in order that they may travel farther. If we fail to do this, we run the risk of what Sartori calls 'concept stretching', that is, we end up stretching the original concept beyond sensible limits in order to accommodate or fit the new range of cases. Equally, when we wish to move from a more wide-ranging to a more limited comparison, it is often worthwhile to weigh our concepts more heavily and to concretize them more fully. By following Sartori's rules of concept formation, we therefore learn where we are standing on the ladder of abstraction, and when it is necessary to go up and when to go down.

Having outlined these various rules, I will then go on to offer examples from recent research in comparative politics of how concepts travel and of how they are sometimes stretched. From these examples we will learn that getting the concepts right is difficult, but also essential. Since Sartori's approach is sometimes difficult and demanding, we will also look at some of the alternatives, focusing in particular on Collier and Mahon's (1993) valuable adaptation of Wittgenstein's notions of family resemblance, as well as their discussion of so-called 'radial' concepts.[1]

The 'what-is' question

The first point that Sartori makes is very clear: when we begin our research, we should always specify and define our concepts. For Sartori (1984: 74), a concept can be defined as 'the basic unit of thinking', such that 'we have a concept of A (or of A-ness) when we are able to distinguish A from whatever is not-A'. Sometimes we specify our concepts based on observations, which is when we deal with empirical concepts; sometimes we specify them on a more abstract basis, which is when we deal with theoretical concepts. Sartori instances 'structure' as an example of a theoretical concept in this sense (1984: 84), whereas 'legislature' would be an example of an empirical concept. Either way, however, whether empirical or theoretical, our concepts are always shaped and rendered meaningful by theory (see also Kratchowil, ch. 5).

As noted, we should begin our research by addressing the 'what-is' question; only later, if at all, do we address the 'how-much' question. That is, we need to know what we are going to measure and compare before we begin with the measurement and the comparison. This logic applies to both dependent and independent variables in any theoretical model. Building from the classic approach to qualitative analysis developed by Lazarsfeld and Barton (1951; see also below), Sartori (1970: 1038–40) argues that quantification, or measurement, or comparison, must come *after* the stage of concept formation, and hence that the logic of 'more-and-less' must come after that of 'either-or'.

For example, if a researcher wishes to account for the varying degrees of corporatism in the West European polities, a research theme that was particularly important in the late 1970s and 1980s, then she must first define what is understood by the term 'corporatism', which is the dependent variable here. If a more contemporary researcher wishes to explain the impact of varying levels of Europeanization in different policy sectors in Europe, then she must first make clear what is entailed by the concept of Europeanization, the independent variable here. If a researcher wishes to investigate the impact of Europeanization on corporatism and related forms of interest intermediation (as does Falkner 2000, for example), then she needs to have a clear conceptual understanding of both the dependent and the independent variables. In other words, the first task of any researcher is to specify the nature of the objects of their research, and hence to define the primary concepts with which she is concerned. This seems self-evident.

But although self-evident, it is not always easy in practice. One of the reasons that the debates on corporatism raged so fervently in the 1970s and 1980s was because scholars operated with different definitions and understandings of the concept itself (Molina and Rhodes 2002); and one of the reasons why scholars today find such difficulty in agreeing about the impact of Europeanization is because they operate with very different versions of what it entails (Featherstone 2003). It is of course possible to proceed without a clear definition of the object of research, and hence to avoid seeking a clear initial answer to the question 'What is it that I am researching?'. But although this approach may avoid the difficulty of concept formation and definition at the beginning of the project, it can often lead to more acute problems being confronted during the course of the research, or even at the end. Moreover, the lack of a clear or even workable conceptual definition at the beginning of the project often makes it more difficult to explain to others what precisely the research involves. For this reason as well, it is best to begin by trying to answer the 'what-is' question, and this is also one of the main purposes of conceptualization.

Sometimes there are no easy answers, and no clear definitions seem possible, in the sense that there is not even a single specific property or attribute that can be incontestably associated with the concept (Gallie 1956; see also below). Sometimes, indeed, it is easier to say what the concept is not, rather than what it is. This is what Sartori (1970: 1042) refers to as 'negative identification', where the concept is defined by negation. It may be difficult to specify the nature of the Saudi Arabian regime, for example, but we do know that it is not a democracy.

Alternatively, if no precise definition is forthcoming, or if there is a conflict between alternative definitions, then a clearer sense of the meaning of the initial concept can be derived by asking: 'Of what is this an instance?'. Is the concept with the disputed definition a subcategory of a more clearly defined and more generally applicable concept? And if so, which one? For example, while the meaning and definition of Europeanization might be widely disputed, there are at least two broader concepts of which it is possibly an instance: 'globalization' (itself a disputed term), on the one hand, and 'nationalization', on the other. At the same time, there is a clear theoretical difference between regarding it as an instance or subcategory of globalization and regarding it as an instance of nationalization or state-building; for this reason the broader concept to which one is linking must also be chosen carefully and with a view to the theory with which one is working. Globalization usually refers to the dissolution of state and other boundaries across the world, whereas nationalization refers to the building of boundaries and the creation of new divides. In the one case, we can hope to understand what Europeanization entails by harking back to the literature and concepts dealing with empire or the pre-Westphalian order; in the other, we need to look to the literature and concepts dealing with nation-building and state formation (compare, for example, Bartolini 2006 and Zielonka 2006).

To query whether the object of research, and hence the concept, is an instance of something else is in any case a useful step in developing an effective research strategy. It is also perhaps a more evident starting point for case studies than for case comparisons (see della Porta, ch. 11, and Vennesson, ch. 12). When comparing multiple cases, it is particularly important to know whether the object of study – say, corporatism – is the same or functionally equivalent across the different cases. In this sense, the 'what-is' question should clearly receive priority. In single-case studies, on the other hand, a better understanding can sometimes be achieved by focusing on the question 'Of what is this an instance?'. By querying whether the policy change she was researching was an instance of depoliticization, for example, Paola Mattei (2007) could bring useful fresh insights to bear on her study of welfare reforms in Italy and could frame her research in a fashion that connected to wider questions being addressed in Italy as well as further afield. In short, knowing what it is that one is researching, or knowing what it is an instance of, is a crucial first step in any research design. We begin by getting the concepts right.

But where do we get these concepts? In some cases, as Gerring (1999) outlines, we start with real-world phenomena, and then we seek to define these in more or less precise terms. For example, we might be taken with the notion of 'delegation', which is a phenomenon of increasing relevance in advanced post-industrial democracies (Thatcher and Stone Sweet 2002; Strøm, Müller and Bergman 2003), and then we try to specify what delegation is, what it is not, and how it fits within the wider understanding of new forms of governance. Alternatively, we might be drawn to a concept because of the frequency of its use in popular discourse, such as in the case of Tony Blair's notion of the 'Third Way' or his advocacy of 'joined-up government', and we might wish to explore the relevance of these ideas to contemporary political strategies and policy-making. A concept might also emerge from theoretical discussions, such as the concept of 'governance' itself (Peters 2000; Goetz 2008), and we might wish to specify its properties and explore its relationship with more traditional notions of government. This also applies to the process by which we seek to define a phenomenon as an instance of something else, since the higher-level category we choose can be drawn from a number of different alternatives. Sometimes, of course, these different sources may offer different versions of what appears to be the same concept, and this can be a source of confusion. In ethnographic research in particular (see Bray, ch. 15), but also in comparative social research more generally, it is therefore important to distinguish between the observer/scholar's version of a concept and that of the actors who are being studied.

Classes and comparisons

The second point emphasized by Sartori, which follows from this, but which is also more contested, is that 'more and less' comparisons should only be conducted within the same *classes* or categories: 'quantification enters the scene after, and only after, having formed the concept' (1970: 1038). In other words, the concept is defined and classified qualitatively, by language and theory, and quantification or measurement takes place within the terms of reference or class specified by the concept.

This is the principle of *per genus et differentiam*, whereby each object can be defined by its *genus* – the class of objects to which it belongs – and by its *differentiam* – the particular attributes that make it different from all the other objects in the same class. This mode of classification is known as a taxonomy. In practice, this means, for example, that we have to define what corporatism is before accounting for its development, just as we have to know what Europeanization is before trying to explain its impact. If I am writing a paper for a conference or a learned journal in which I discuss the recent research findings on Europeanization and then propose a new interpretation or set of findings myself, my concept of Europeanization has to be shared or at least accepted by my peers. Otherwise, they will simply claim that I am talking about something else entirely and disregard my paper.[2] That said – and I will come back to this later – the meanings do not need to be shared in their entirety, and indeed a lot of progress in research is made by refining and respecifying concepts that otherwise might not seem to prove contentious.

Classifications have two important characteristics (see Lazarsfeld and Barton 1951). First, each class in the classification should be *exclusive*. That is, the same item or phenomenon cannot belong to more than one class. Second, the classification should be *exhaustive*. No one item or phenomenon can be left out of the classification on the grounds that it does not fit any of the classes. In a classification of forms of cabinet government in modern Europe, for example, we can make a distinction between majority single-party governments, majority coalition governments, minority single-party governments and minority coalitions. No one government can belong to more than one of these categories, in the sense that each is exclusive, and no government should fall outside the four categories, in the sense that together they offer an exhaustive listing. If it were possible to find a government that matches none of these definitions, then an additional category would have to be created.

When two or more classifications are combined, whereby the categories move from being uni-dimensional to being two- or multidimensional, the result is a *typology* – and again, the same rules apply as with classifications: the types must be both exclusive and exhaustive. Each item must belong to only one type, and no item must be incapable of being included. Moreover, with typologies, as with classifications, it is essential to know the answer to the 'what-is' question; that is, it is necessary in any typology or classification to know to what the particular types and classes refer. Classes and types need labels. A very good example is the typology of democracies elaborated by Arend Lijphart almost forty years ago, a typology that he established by combining a classification of political cultures with a classification of forms of elite behaviour (Lijphart 1968). The labels were very clear in this instance: Lijphart was distinguishing types of democracy, and he was classifying forms of elite behaviour and forms of political culture. It should also be noted that in building typologies we are moving from simple classification towards explanation (see Héritier, ch. 4). Lijphart classifies both elite behaviour and political culture in order to establish his typology of democratic regimes, and in so doing he also advances an explanation for the differing types of regime that he examines. Following his reasoning, we can argue that consociational democracies differ from centrifugal democracies *because of* the different pattern of elite behaviour.[3]

But while the rules of classification and typologizing are generally accepted in the social sciences, Sartori's argument that one must only measure or compare *within* classes has often been contested or even ignored. For DeFelice (1980), for example, to paraphrase the title of his paper, this is 'common nonsense'. Citing Sartori's 1970 paper, as well as an earlier argument by Kalleberg (1966), DeFelice argues that this approach prescribes 'procedures that are in fact . . . dysfunctional for a general science of politics' (1980: 120), since they prevent universal or semi-universal comparisons. If like can only be compared with like, he argues, and if we can only measure differences of degree within specific classes or kinds – *per genus et differentiam* – then we are limited in the range of our comparisons. To follow these rules means that the political culture of non-democracies cannot be compared to that of democracies, for example, and hence the goals and progress of political science inquiry are unnecessarily curtailed. Jackman (1985: 167–9) voices a similar criticism. Even if objects differ from one another, he argues, they still can be compared, and this means that concept formation does not have to stand prior to measurement or comparison. Moreover, he views some concepts as being

Table 10.1. Sartori's ladder of abstraction

Levels of abstraction	Major comparative scope and purpose	Logical properties of concept
High-level categories Universal conceptualizations	*Global theory.* Cross-area comparisons among heterogeneous contexts	Maximal extension, minimal intension
Medium-level categories General conceptualizations and taxonomies	*Middle-range theory.* Intra-area comparisons among relatively homogeneous contexts	Extension and intension in balance
Low-level categories Configurative conceptualizations	*Narrow-gauge theory.* Country-by-country analysis	Minimal extension, maximal intension

Source: Sartori (1970: 1044).

'inherently continuous' and having no upper or lower boundaries, which means that they must be specified quantitatively rather than qualitatively. In these cases, we find out what we are researching by asking 'how much?' instead of 'what is?', and hence we deal with concepts that are defined in terms of 'more-and-less' rather than 'either-or'. As examples, he suggests concepts such as 'national wealth' or 'cultural pluralism'.

Neither criticism is very convincing. In DeFelice's case, to suggest that the range of comparison is narrowed by *per genus et differentiam* is to misunderstand the notion that these concepts stand in a hierarchical order, in which two different classes at one level become part of a single larger class at a higher level. Sartori elaborates on this notion quite precisely with reference to his 'ladder of abstraction', and we shall come to this shortly (see Table 10.1). For now, it is important to emphasize that comparison across classes – such as, for example, occurs when democracies are compared to non-democracies – is also perfectly possible within Sartori's approach, and can be effected simply by moving up the conceptual hierarchy to a more abstract and more widely encompassing category. Democracies may be compared with one another at a given level of abstraction; non-democracies may also be compared with one another at a given level of abstraction; and democracies may be compared to non-democracies once we invoke concepts that operate at a higher level of abstraction and that embrace both forms of government. One such concept is 'regime', of which both democracies and non-democracies are instances. DeFelice is correct when he argues that the range of comparison is narrowed at any given level of conceptual abstraction and classification, but not when he suggests that the range is narrowed *per se*. On the contrary, more universal comparisons can always be effected by adopting a more abstract and inclusive notion that is higher up in the conceptual hierarchy.

Jackman's criticisms are also unconvincing. To say that some concepts are inherently continuous is to confuse the nature of the concept, on the one hand, with its measurement, on the other. 'National wealth' may have values that run from 0 to N, but it must also be a definable concept, for if we do not know what national wealth *is*, then it seems pointless to try to measure it. Jackman is also concerned that some concepts, so-called *umbrella concepts*, may be multi-dimensional. These are concepts 'that carry too much baggage to be reducible to a single unidimensional variable', and include examples such as political culture, democratic stability and political institutionalism (Jackman 1985: 169). But while each of these concepts certainly has a number of different attributes, it is not at all clear that they resist clear definition or specification. Indeed, if anything, to ask the 'what-is' question of any of these particular concepts, and hence to seek to situate them within a hierarchy of other categories and subcategories, is likely to reduce their inherent ambiguities. Is democratic stability a form of political stability that is democratic, or is it a form of democracy that is stable? Is political culture a subcategory of culture more generally defined, or is it simply an aggregate of individual-level political attitudes and political behaviour? To be sure, concepts are sometimes difficult to define and to specify, and there may be different dimensions that are difficult to untangle, but the research effort can be badly undermined if any attempt at definition and specification is written off from the beginning. Indeed, complex phenomena and so-called umbrella or multidimensional concepts are those that are especially in need of clear definitions, since it is often these concepts in particular that are the source of the greatest scholarly confusion.[4]

One such umbrella concept that has frequently been debated back and forth among scholars of social and electoral behaviour is that of 'cleavage'. In the analysis developed by Bartolini and Mair (1990: 212–49; see also Bartolini 2000: 15–24; Mair 2006), it has been argued that a cleavage has three distinct components, and that in this sense we are dealing with a multidimensional concept. The first of these elements is the social division that distinguishes among groups of citizens based on status, religion, ethnicity, and so on, and that lies at the basis of every cleavage. The second element is the sense of collective identity, with the groups on which the cleavage is based being conscious of their shared identity as Catholics, workers, farmers, or whatever. The third element is the organizational expression of the cleavage, which might be realized through a trade union, a church, a party or some other medium. Each of these three elements is an essential component of what may be defined as a cleavage. Elsewhere in the literature, by contrast, the three different elements are sometimes used to define three different types of cleavage, such that scholars speak of separate and distinct 'political', 'social' and 'value' cleavages. In fact, this simply leads to conceptual confusion, for it is impossible to distinguish a so-called 'political cleavage' from a conventional political conflict or divide, and it is equally impossible to distinguish a so-called 'social cleavage' from the notion of social stratification. In neither case, then, is any added value offered by the concept of cleavage (see Bartolini and Mair 1990: 211–20). When the concept of cleavage is defined as referring to phenomena in which the three components of social reality, identity and organization are combined, on the other hand, we have a concept that relates to the fundamental divides that have shaped the parties and the party systems of contemporary Europe (see Lipset and Rokkan 1967). In this case, then, accepting the multidimensionality of the concept actually pins it down more precisely and helps to avoid confusion.

The ladder of abstraction

Sartori's third key point deals with the ladder of abstraction, or what Collier and Mahon (1993) later referred to as the ladder of generality (Table 10.1). Concepts that are defined by a large number of properties, and which thereby have a more limited range of applications, are located towards the bottom of the ladder. Concepts that are defined by just one or two properties, and hence which are very abstract and have a very wide range of applications, are located at the top of the ladder. This also refers to the hierarchy of concepts and categories discussed above. Thus, for example, 'regime' is a more abstract category with fewer properties than either 'democracy' or 'non-democracy', and hence sits above (and thereby also embraces) the latter two concepts on the ladder of abstraction. One way of conceiving the differences between the upper and lower levels of the ladder of abstraction is to think of a concept as being like a hot-air balloon. If you want to be higher, and hence get a view of even greater swathes of countryside, you have to have a lighter basket – in conceptual terms, you throw out certain properties and become more abstract. If you want to be lower, and look more closely at something on the ground, you need a heavier basket and, by implication, you have more properties.

Most importantly, the ladder of abstraction can also be seen in matrix form, whereby there is a trade-off between the number of cases to be researched and the number of properties or attributes belonging to each case. The more cases, the fewer the properties of each that can be looked at, and hence the more abstract the concept; the fewer cases, the more properties, and hence the more concrete the concept. Drawing from logic, Sartori uses the terms 'extension' and 'intension' to refer to these dimensions of the concept, and hence also to the matrix. The extension of a concept refers to the range of cases it covers, or its *denotation*; the intension of a concept refers to the number of attributes or properties that it has, or its *connotation*.

A good example of how the different levels (or rungs) on the ladder of abstraction function in practice is offered by the concept 'political party'. At the top of the ladder, and in its most abstract form, we get the minimal definition of party – that specified elsewhere by Sartori (1976: 63) – as 'any political group identified by an official label that presents at elections, and is capable of placing through elections (free or unfree), candidates for public office'. This is about as minimal as one can get, and would thus embrace even the sketchiest parties in almost any conceivable polity, democratic or not. In other words, the definition is minimal, abstract – just one property or attribute – and with a hugely wide-ranging cross-national and cross-systemic application. It has a minimal intension and hence a maximal extension and is mainly employed to distinguish between political parties (groups that are engaged in nominating candidates for public office) and interest groups (which are not so engaged).[5] Further down the ladder, the definitions of the subcategories of party acquire more properties and apply less generally – they become more intensive and less extensive. Further down, for example, we find the mass party, a particular type or class of party characterized by a mass and relatively homogeneous membership, a hierarchic organization that continues to function between elections, a collective leadership that is accountable to the membership, and so on. This is a subcategory of the political party at the top of the ladder, but with a much more demanding definition and set of properties and hence with a much more limited application – for example, it might be suggested that this was a type of party that was relatively common only in Western Europe in the 1950s and 1960s (Scarrow 2000). Finally, towards the very bottom of the ladder we might find many more specific models of party, including, for example, what Hopkin and Paolucci (1999) have identified as the 'business firm model' of party, a particular type of party that was electorally unstable, politically incoherent, was intent on serving particularistic interests, and was observed through one example in Spain in the late 1970s and another in Italy in the 1990s. In other words, this is quite a heavily specified concept with limited application. It has quite a maximal intension and a relatively small extension.

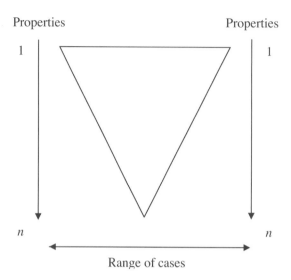

Range of cases

Fig. 10.1   The trade-off between cases and properties

This trade-off between cases and properties can be conceived in terms of an inverted pyramid (see Figure 10.1), in which the range of cases, spanning left to right on the horizontal axis, progressively narrows as the number of properties (indicated on the vertical axis) grows. By the end, that is, at the apex of the inverted pyramid, there is going to be just one case and a maximum number of attributes; at the base of the inverted pyramid there is a host of cases, but just one or two attributes.

It is when we get away from the extremes, however, and when we work in the middle layers, that we find the most interesting concepts – in both the empirical and theoretical sense. At the top of the ladder, where the concept enjoys just a minimal definition, and where extension is maximized, there is not much that can be said beyond what is intended to delimit the scope of inquiry in theoretical terms. At the bottom of the ladder, where intension is at its maximum and the extension is relatively limited, discussion and analysis can often prove descriptive and quite atheoretical, although work at this level can be important in identifying concepts that can later be 'lightened' and hence applied more widely. At the middle level of the ladder, by contrast, where the concepts have a medium extension and a medium intension and can travel across a reasonably wide range of cases, theory-building and analysis in the social sciences is often at its most interesting and challenging (the *locus classicus* is Merton 1968).

One good example of the value of the middle level also comes from the literature on parties and concerns a discussion about the role of parties in the then new post-Communist democracies. In a provocative essay looking back at the experience of the first decade of democracy in east central Europe, Philippe Schmitter (2001) argues that, for a variety of reasons, political parties were largely incapable of performing their basic functions within these new democracies, and hence that they risked proving largely irrelevant to the future course of post-Communist politics. Political parties may have played a leading role in consolidating democracy in earlier waves of transition, he argued, 'but they will not necessarily do so in the present or the future' (Schmitter 2001: 72).

At one level, this argument was clearly untenable. As was argued elsewhere in the same volume (Bartolini and Mair 2001: 331), Schmitter was holding up to the light a particular definition of party – a concept of party – that was based on the classic mass party of the 1950s and 1960s, and showing how this sort of party was scarcely to be found in contemporary post-Communist politics. It was on this basis that he argued that parties were irrelevant. Against this, of course, came the obvious retort that while these sorts of mass parties were unlikely to prove relevant in post-Communist democratic consolidation, other sorts of parties might well play an important role, including parties that could be defined in less demanding terms. In other words, even if the traditional mass party discussed by Schmitter could be deemed irrelevant, other types of party should not be so easily dismissed. Indeed, taking Sartori's minimal definition as our guide, it can be argued that every democracy, new or old, will always contain some sorts of parties.

At another level, however, it was Schmitter's argument that was the more interesting. To stay at the very top of the ladder of abstraction and to conclude, on the basis of the minimal definition of party, that parties will always be present, is correct in itself, but it offers little of theoretical (as opposed to definitional) interest. To say that there will never be parties of the mass type, on the other hand, and to work within the middle range of the ladder, is to make an interesting theoretical argument about the conditions for the emergence and success of such parties, and their role as intermediaries in the contemporary political order. In this case, then, as is often true of analyses at the middle level, the questions that can be asked are more fruitful than those posed at the top or at the bottom of the ladder.

Finally, the ladder of abstraction is also relevant to the question of the multidimensionality of concepts, particularly insofar as this relates to work on the *history of concepts* and their changes of meaning over time (Hampsher-Monk, Tilmans and van Vree 1998; see also above). For Terence Ball (2002), for example, one of the most prominent political theorists working in this field, one of the key differences between the work of empirical social scientists and that of political theorists like himself is that the former tend to treat concepts as if they have just one meaning whereas the latter treat concepts as having many meanings, depending on the time and place of their expression. If we follow Sartori's approach, however, it seems that there need be no serious problem here. That is, we can suggest that the same concept can have one meaning, when it is at the top of the ladder of abstraction, *and* many meanings, when we have climbed down that ladder of abstraction. The real question is not how many meanings there are, but rather knowing where on the ladder we stand.

Every concept must have a core or minimal definition, which is shared by all users of the concept. Otherwise, we end up with a situation which Ball defines as analogous to the Hobbesian state of nature, where 'each individual is a monad, radically disconnected from all other individuals insofar as each speaks, as it were, a private language of his own devising. Because the concepts comprising these individual languages cannot be translated or otherwise understood, each speaker is perforce a stranger and an enemy to every other' (Ball 2002: 24). But at the same time, this minimal definition can be expanded – the container can be filled with additional properties – and then different meanings are developed, each appropriate to a particular time and place. One very good example of this can be seen in the development of the meaning of the Dutch concept of *burgher*, or citizen, which has been transformed in a number of ways since it was first used in the sixteenth century (Tilmans 2004). In the case of *burgher*, there is both *one* meaning, which would be located at the top of the ladder of abstraction, and *many* meanings, the meanings that develop as we descend the ladder, add additional properties, and take account of the ways *burgher* has been given meaning by different people through the centuries. What must be avoided, however, is the notion that the concept can enjoy *any* meaning whatsoever. When we can have any meaning at all, then a concept can mean whatever anybody wants it to mean, and this is precisely when we enter the chaotic situation of which Ball warned.

Despite Ball's concerns, therefore, there is no necessary conflict between one meaning and many meanings. Every concept should have both, with either 'one' or 'many' being brought into play depending on where on the ladder of abstraction we are located. Rather, the conflict is between working with either 'one' or 'many' meanings, on the one hand, versus working with 'any' meaning, on the other. Moreover, unless we can agree on the 'one', core, or minimal – most abstract – meaning, then we can never properly appreciate why the 'many' meanings also arise, and we can also never properly compare these many meanings with one another. Without first understanding what 'citizen', or 'nation' or 'state' or whatever means – the core meaning – we can never fully understand how and why one particular meaning of 'citizen', 'nation' or 'state' differs from yet another particular meaning. In other words, we must start with the 'one' meaning, at the top of the ladder of abstraction, and then climb down to the 'many' meanings, at the lower levels, and in particular contexts. And we must make sure not to fall off the ladder entirely and end up in a situation where 'any' meaning becomes acceptable.[6]

Learning from the ladder of abstraction

Three lessons in particular can be drawn from Sartori's ladder of abstraction. First, as discussed above, comparison across classes can always be affected by going up the ladder of abstraction. Democracies can be compared to democracies at one level, and can then be compared to non-democracies within the terms of reference of a higher-level and hence more abstract concept such as regime. In this sense, the concerns of DeFelice (1980) and Jackman (1985) that comparison is hindered by the need for concept formation to come prior to quantification seem relatively groundless. The problem is solved by moving up the ladder (see also O'Kane 1993).

Second, concepts can be seen as 'data containers', which include a number of different attributes or properties. In presenting what is one of the most useful practical guides to concept formation, Gerring (1999: 357–8) suggests that concepts have three distinct aspects: (a) the events or phenomena that are to be defined, that is, the extension; (b) the properties or attributes that define these phenomena, that is, the intension; and (c) the label that covers both intension and extension. 'Concept formation is a triangular operation', he adds, and 'good concepts attain a proper alignment between *a, b* and *c*' (Gerring 1999: 358).[7] As the concept is changed, and made more abstract, the properties are reduced in number; as it is made more concrete, the number of properties increases. In both cases, of course, the label also needs to change. To move from the notion of the political party to the mass party and then on to the business firm model of party is therefore to add an ever greater number of attributes or properties.

In his extensive analysis of concepts and concept formation in the social sciences, Goertz (2006: 5–7) treats these properties as constituting the 'secondary level' of the concept, with the indicators chosen to measure the properties constituting the 'third level'. In the case of Hadenius' (1992) treatment of democracy, for example, which Goertz takes as one of his illustrations, 'democracy' itself is what he calls the *basic level* concept – the core concept, as it were; the two properties of democracy that are identified at the *secondary level* are 'elections' and 'political freedoms'; and the various indicators or data sources at the *third level* which are then used to measure or operationalize these properties are 'suffrage', 'elected offices' and 'meaningful elections', on the one hand, and 'freedom of organization', 'freedom of expression' and 'freedom from coercion', on the other. This offers a very useful complement to Sartori's approach, since it emphasizes that we not only need to define concepts and identify their properties, but we also need to identify them in a way that will facilitate the selection of indicators that can be operationalized and measured.

Third, when we want to widen the range of application of a particular concept, it is necessary to make it more abstract, or lighter, by dropping one or more of its properties. This is a crucial lesson. Movement on the ladder is up and down rather than traversal. To take a concept that is applicable in a given range of cases and then extend it at the same level and *with the same properties* to a broader range of cases is to *stretch* the concept, and this is problematic. It is therefore advisable to make the concept more abstract by dropping particular properties or attributes and thereby to widen its scope. Concepts can travel, of course, and in comparative political and social research they must travel; but, like hot-air balloons, they need to be lightened before they can be moved very far.

Other approaches to concept formation

Sartori's approach to concept formation has been described by Collier and Mahon (1993: 845) as the 'classical' approach, in which the relationship among concepts is seen 'in terms of a taxonomic hierarchy, with each category [or concept] having clear boundaries and defining properties shared by all members'. Collier and Mahon argue that not all concepts easily fit this approach, however. Sometimes it is difficult to establish precisely what is meant by a particular concept, or precisely what its properties are; and sometimes concepts do not appear to stand in a clear hierarchy to one another, particularly in terms of the ladder of abstraction, in that some concepts at a lower level of generality appear to have fewer properties than those at a higher level of generality. In other words, intension and extension do not always vary inversely.

In the case of the concept of 'democracy', for example, particularly given the variety of forms democracy has taken since the explosion of Third Wave transitions in the 1990s, it is very difficult to establish a clear hierarchy of definitions and categories. Sartori's ladder of abstraction begins with a minimum definition, including the *necessary and sufficient* conditions that are employed to define the concept in question. But identifying this level in the case of 'democracy' is very problematic. If one says that democracy involves multiparty elections, and that this is the minimum definitional property as it was usually taken to be prior to the fall of the Berlin Wall in 1989, then the category 'democracies' will also end up by including systems in which basic rights and freedoms are denied to many citizens. These are the so-called 'illiberal' or 'electoral' democracies that have been analysed by scholars such as Diamond, O'Donnell and Zakaria.[8] If, on the other hand, we define 'democracies' as being characterized by the guarantee of rights and freedoms, and disregard electoral processes because they are sometimes discredited, we miss a hugely important element in any democratic process: the right of voters to sack their governments. And finally, if we demand both criteria as a minimal condition for democracy and thereby begin to approximate to the dimensions of contestation and participation used by Dahl (1971) in developing his concept of *polyarchy*, then we end up with relatively few regimes that can be considered effective democracies or liberal democracies, and, moreover, we lose our hierarchy, since clearly 'electoral democracies' (defined as liberal democracies with inadequate guarantees for individual rights and freedoms) cannot be regarded as a subcategory of liberal democracy. In the definition of democracy, then, we struggle to find a working starting point.

One solution to this problem, proposed by Collier and Mahon (1993: 848–52), borrows from cognitive science and involves the adoption of so-called *radial categories*. This is, in fact, a very complex way of developing concepts and is not easy to adapt to real-world situations. In brief, radial categories begin with a single primary category, which is equivalent to an ideal type[9] in that it contains all possible defining attributes of the concept. In the case of democracy, which is one of the examples offered by Collier and Mahon, the primary category includes the main attributes associated with democracy in general, even though in practice not all might be found together in any real-world case: effective political participation, limitation on state power, and a commitment to emphasizing social and economic equality. Each of the series of secondary categories that are then applied to real-world cases takes a single core-defining feature of the primary (ideal-type) category, and combines it with one *or* other (or none) of the other possible attributes. Thus, if we regard effective political participation as a core-defining feature of democracy – as being necessary but not sufficient to define democracy – then the secondary real-world categories are participatory democracy, which takes this element on its own; liberal democracy, which takes this element in combination with the limitation on state power; and popular democracy, which takes this element in combination with the pursuit of equality (Collier and Mahon 1993: 850).

An alternative solution to a somewhat different problem posed by the classical approach is Wittgenstein's notion of *family resemblance categories*, an approach that is borrowed from linguistic theory (Collier and Mahon 1993: 846–8) and that is intended to solve the problem of dealing with objects that are clearly linked or associated with one another, much as family members are linked genetically, but where none is characterized by *all* of the relevant set of attributes. In other words, there is no single core that is shared by each object, and hence they would not be part of the same class in Sartori's sense of the term. Let us assume, for example, that there are six cases, and a total of six attributes, that each of the cases has five of the attributes, and that no two cases have the same set of five. These cases can be compared, it seems, since they all appear to be part of the same family of cases, but they do not belong to the same class. The conceptual category that defined them, and that set the boundaries on what could or could not be included, would not have a 'necessary *and* sufficient' definition.

As Goertz (2006: 74–5) clearly shows, the family resemblance approach to concept formation turns Sartori's argument about the extension and intension of a concept on its head. Sartori's ladder of abstraction and his classical approach to concept formation relies explicitly on the necessary and sufficient condition, such that as the number of properties (the intension) increases – in a logical process of AND, AND, AND – the range of cases covered (the extension) necessarily declines (see Figure 10.1 above). In the case of family resemblances, on the other hand, the defining properties are 'necessary *or* sufficient', and hence the greater the number of properties – added in a logical process as OR, OR, OR – the greater is the range of cases.

In sum, to follow the family resemblance approach is to find that more attributes mean more cases rather than fewer cases, and hence that intension and extension vary together rather than inversely. The problem we then confront is establishing where this process should stop. From a comparative social science perspective, the end point is reached when we have both a universe of cases and a universe of properties, and hence when we have the complete elimination of variation. This clearly cannot work, and hence the conceptual boundaries have to be established at a much earlier stage. Since the number of cases we are observing serves to define the properties that are collectively shared by the cases, it is difficult to find a rule that works for inclusion and exclusion. As in the film *Wedding Crashers*, anybody or anything can be claimed to have some family connection to those at the centre of the action, and hence boundaries, like wedding invitations, ultimately lose their utility.

Conclusion

Some fifty years ago, W. B. Gallie (1956) famously introduced the notion of 'essentially contested concepts'. These were concepts whose operational meaning had been subject to continuous debate and dispute, and which would probably always remain without a firm and fast definition. Among the examples of such concepts proffered by Gallie were art, religion, science, democracy and social justice, while others have typically added power, law and leadership to that original list. What marks these concepts out is not that they have two or three competing meanings, but rather that they have one quite abstract meaning that is accepted by most users, while the application of this meaning is regularly contested. We all know what art is in the abstract, but we argue whether certain objects may be classified as art; we all know – more or less – what democracy is, but we disagree as to whether certain polities may be defined as democratic. Indeed, it might even be suggested that the reason the social sciences are marked by such a large number of these essentially contested concepts is because of their inherently normative character, with the application of terms such as justice and morality, or fairness, legitimacy, authority and terrorism, to real-world situations being inevitably subject to challenge and revision.[10] As Ball (2002: 21) has suggested, 'the history of political thought is in large part the history of conceptual contestation and change'.

But even when we accept that the particular application of a concept might be challenged, this does not mean that we should accept a free-for-all in which every scholar can use whatever definition she likes, and hence in which communication and cumulation fall by the wayside. We still need common ground if we work within a scholarly discipline – otherwise, quite literally, there is no scholarly discipline – and hence we also need to develop and justify coherent definitions of our concepts and to defend these definitions against potential challenges. As noted above, we always need to begin our research with the 'what-is' question, and we always need to be ready to defend our answer to that question against any alternative answer that might be proffered elsewhere in the discipline.

This should not be taken to mean that we have to offer concepts with immutable definitions, however, which would be the other extreme. Research in practice requires more pragmatism and flexibility than that, and hence individual research projects will often tailor the meaning of a concept in order to improve operationalization and measurement. As Collier and Adcock (1999: 546) suggest, 'scholars should be cautious in claiming to have come up with a definitive interpretation of a concept's meaning. It is more productive to establish an interpretation that is justified at least in part by its suitability to their immediate research goals and to the specific research tradition within which they are working.' But, we can add, this should always operate within a reasonable range. To be too tight in one's definition may well put research-ability at risk; but to be too pragmatic and too flexible is to risk stretching the concept too far. Concepts also require a core meaning, and in extending that meaning for practical research purposes, or in qualifying it, the steps involved need to be carefully argued and specified. Meanings and applications may vary, but they must be explained and justified. This is where opinion ends and comparative social science begins.

NOTES

1 The Collier and Mahon (1993) article is one of the first in a series of key publications discussing concepts and concept formation that have recently been published, including Collier and Levitsky (1997), Collier and Adcock (1999), Gerring (1999), Adcock (2005) and Goertz (2006). These offer a much more extensive and nuanced treatment of the themes discussed in this chapter.

2 This also relates to what Gunnar Sjöblom has identified as the 'cumulation' problem in political – and social – science: see Sjöblom (1977) and Anckar (1997).

3 For a very extensive and successful application of typological analysis to the variations in post-Communist regimes, see Møller (2007a).

4 This is clearly the case with the concept of political culture: see, for example, the assessment by Formisano (2001) as well as Keating (ch. 6).

5 This also means that groups that are incapable of placing candidates through elections – former parties that are now outlawed, or opposition groups in non-democratic regimes – should also not be considered as parties, but rather as 'groups', 'movements', or whatever.

6 As in Lewis Carroll's *Through the Looking Glass:* ' "When I use a word," Humpty Dumpty said, in a rather scornful tone, "it means just what I choose it to mean, neither more nor less." '

7 Gerring's argument here also carries an intriguing echo of Roland Barthes' (1972: 111–17) tri-dimensional treatment of semiology and myth, in which the signifier and the signified are combined through the sign (the concept). This particular echo is also relevant in another sense, since Barthes points out that while the sign can have many potential meanings, once tied to a particular signifier and signified its meaning becomes fixed. Similarly, once a concept is associated with a particular set of properties, its meaning becomes fixed and should not be stretched to refer to other meanings. At the same time, however, in different

contexts the signifier combines with a different signified and hence a sign which takes on a different meaning. See also Sartori (1984).

8 See Møller (2007b); see also the overview in Mair (2008).

9 On ideal types, see Goertz (2006: 82–8).

10 I am grateful to Rainer Bauböck for highlighting this argument.

11 Comparative analysis: case-oriented versus variable-oriented research

Donatella della Porta

Comparative analysis holds a central place in social science research. There is a well-established view in the social sciences that it should be based on variables (see Héritier, ch. 4, and Schmitter, ch. 14). Yet much research – especially in political science, but also in some branches of sociology – is case-oriented: that is, it aims at rich descriptions of a few instances of a certain phenomenon. This chapter argues that both approaches are legitimate. Variable-oriented studies mainly aim at establishing generalized relationships between variables, while case-oriented research seeks to understand complex units. Some people would argue that case-based comparisons follow a different logic of research, while others insist that the rules are essentially the same.

The chapter starts by introducing the debate on comparative analysis, distinguishing the experimental, statistical and 'comparative' methods. We then single out two main strategies of research, presenting their origins in the methodological reflections by Durkheim and Weber, and focusing on the assumptions that are linked to the variable-oriented and case-oriented approaches, respectively. Advantages and disadvantages of each will be discussed on the basis of illustrations from social science works on democratization, political violence and political participation, looking at examples of large-N statistical research designs and contrasting them with small-N comparisons, especially in the tradition of historical sociology. The chapter also discusses recent attempts to bridge the gap between the two approaches, in particular with qualitative comparative analysis (QCA) and recent reflections on the case-oriented strategy. Conditions that might influence the choice of one logic or the other include environmental conditions (such as stages in a research cycle or types of data available) and researchers' epistemological preferences as to approach and methodological skills. We then look at strategies

I am grateful to Marco Giugni, Michael Keating, Leonardo Morlino, Philippe Schmitter, Pascal Vennesson and Claudius Wagemann for helpful comments on previous versions of this chapter.

for comparative analysis, addressing some of the main methodological choices: the relevant unit of analysis; the number of cases; the trade-off between most-similar and most-different designs; and ways in which to address the time dimension.

One or two logics: the debate on comparative politics

Comparative analysis

In sociology and political science, there has been a strong tendency to consider all social sciences as following one and the same logic (see della Porta and Keating, chs. 1 and 2; King, Keohane and Verba 1994). Validity depends on following a set of rules of scientific inference, whose purpose is attempting to infer beyond the immediate data to something broader that is not directly observed.[1] If we accept this, the differences among research projects will refer to the matrix of data: large-N (statistical) research designs cover many cases, while small-N (comparative) studies only a few. From this perspective, larger-N projects are considered stronger in providing valid and significant inferences. In the 1970s, in sociology and political science, this position was supported by the influential works of Neil Smelser and Arendt Lijphart, both dealing with comparative analysis.

Comparative analysis responds to this need for broadening the territorial scope and depth of political information (Lasswell 1968). It has often been understood as that branch of political science concerned with comparing nations (Verba 1991). Yet, the debate on the comparative approach has played an important role in the more general methodological discussion across the social sciences.

The field of comparative politics boomed in the 1960s, in line with the acknowledgement of an 'accelerated interdependence of the world arena' (Lasswell 1968: 3). Comparative political scientists extended their range of interest from Western democracies to second- and third-world countries, shifting their concerns from formal institutions to the political process. At first, theories of development dominated the field, with a strong emphasis on global comparison and the normative aim of bringing Western-style economic and political development to underdeveloped countries. The Vietnam War brought to light the dramatic effects of such interventions, justified with the purpose of helping developing countries. In the 1970s, assumptions about a unique pattern of development in political and economic life based on

Western experience were criticized, and the developmental approach was attacked for its 'Cold War origins and overtones' (Wiarda 1991: 21). With the renewal of attention to cross-national comparison in the 1980s, the hopes for global theories were abandoned, together with the developmental approach, leaving space for various *middle-range theories* (that is, those that are meant to hold only for specific societies) in various subfields of the discipline. Comparative politics has indeed been described as aiming at developing concepts and generalizations at a middle level, between what is always true for all societies and what is true of only one society at a single point in time (Bendix 1963: 532).

Reflection on the specificity of the comparative approach remained central, however. It was defined at the outset as one of the scientific methods available to control hypotheses on the relations between two or more variables, keeping constant (or parametrizing) all potentially disturbing elements. The empirical control of hypotheses requires a distinction between conditions treated as *parameters* (which are assumed, or made not to vary) and causal conditions treated as *operative variables* which, in a specific investigation, are instead allowed (or made) to vary in order to assess their influence (Smelser 1976). Three main approaches exist within comparative analysis: the experimental method, the statistical method and the comparative method; all perform, with declining strengths, the task of converting most of the variables into parameters in order to isolate the effects of the remaining variables. There is, as so often in the social sciences, a certain terminological confusion here. Sometimes the term 'comparative method' is used to cover all three approaches; elsewhere, it is restricted to one of them. For clarity, we will use the umbrella term 'comparative analysis' to cover all three, and 'comparative method' for the third of them.[2]

In the *experimental* method, conversion of variables into parameters is achieved in the creation of data. In an artificial setting, we control the effect of any changes in the values of an operative variable on the values of the other operational variables, by keeping all other potential influences stable. In an experimental situation (as used in the natural sciences and some social sciences, notably psychology), it is possible to allow for changes only in the variable on which we focus our attention by, typically, taking two identical groups and introducing a stimulus in only one of them. All of the differences between the two groups may thus be attributed to that one stimulus. In this sense, the method is very strong, offering robust criteria to choose between rival theories (Lijphart 1971). Unfortunately, only a limited number of social phenomena may be investigated via experiments.

The *statistical* method – based on mathematical elaboration of empirically relevant data (Lijphart 1971; see also Franklin, ch. 13) – approximates the experimental method by intervening after the data are created. It is already weaker than the experimental method as a means of making inferences, insofar as parametrization is obtained via the mathematical elaboration of empirical evidence (Smelser 1976: 157), typically by creating subsamples in which potentially disturbing variables are kept constant. Although the statistical method is weaker than the experimental method, it still provides good tests for eliminating rival theories. The main problem of the statistical method is the need for large samples: the higher the number of variables that potentially 'disturb' the measuring of a correlation coefficient, the larger the number of cases needed in order to build subsamples large enough to be statistically significant. This is not only very expensive, but also often impossible because of the limited number of homogeneous macro-units endowed with particular characteristics.

The term *comparative method* is used, rather confusingly, for an approach within comparative analysis that provides an alternative to the statistical method. When the number of cases is too low for statistical manipulation, the investigator approximates it 'though without the same degree of confidence – by systematic comparative illustration' (Smelser 1976: 157). The comparative method supplements with *logical reasoning* the lack of a sufficient number of cases for systematic tests via partial correlations. For scholars like Smelser and Lijphart, the logic of the comparative method is identical to that of the other methods, 'in that it attempts to develop explanations by the systematic manipulation of parameters and operative variables' (Smelser 1976: 158). Like the other methods, it aims at establishing general, empirical relations between two variables and controlling them by keeping all other variables constant (Lijphart 1971). In this sense, the comparative method adopts the same logic as the statistical method, adapting it to those situations in which we deal with complex phenomena without the large number of cases necessary for a statistical analysis: the famous situations of 'many variables, small N' (Lijphart 1971: 686). Timothy McKeown (2004) suggests that the belief that there is a single quantitative logic to all empirical social scientific research reflects the idea that all empirical research faces the same problems of causal inference as quantitative research does. This implies assumptions such as the existence of a clear distinction between the formation and the testing of hypotheses, the search for simplicity (if not parsimony) in theory, and the pre-allocation of each case within a class of cases. In a variable-oriented research design, the lower the number of cases, the fewer should be the explanatory variables, since degree-of-freedom problems would make the research design indeterminate.

The logic is, however, the same: 'the comparative method resembles the statistical method in all respects except one. The crucial difference is that the number of cases it deals with is too small to permit systematic control by means of partial correlation' (Lijphart 1971: 684). Conversely, '[a]s soon as the number of units becomes large enough to permit the use of statistical techniques, the line between the two is crossed' (Smelser 1976: 161).

Dealing with a small number of cases – usually between two and twenty – the comparative method is a preferred strategy for political and social scientists when they investigate institutions or other macropolitical phenomena. In fact, the comparative method is considered the only choice for controlling hypotheses that apply to large units that are too few for statistical analysis. Although in this approach the quality of control of the relationship between variables is low, it is often the *only* scientific method available for the study of macrodimensional, interdimensional and institutional processes (Eisenstadt 1968).

Case-oriented versus variable-oriented: diverse tools, shared standards?

This assimilation of statistical and comparative methods into 'one and the same logic' did not, however, remain unchallenged. Some scholars, while agreeing on the search for shared standards, warned about the need to keep in mind the methodological implications of the use of diverse tools (Brady and Collier 2004).

Indeed, the divide between those analysing a large number of cases on a few characteristics and those studying a few cases in depth (that is, looking at a large number of dimensions, usually within a historical perspective) has been growing with the specialization of the social sciences. Given this plurality of approaches, the insistence on a single logic by King, Keohane and Verba (1994) has been criticized for ignoring the differences among the many objectives social scientists might pursue on the basis of their ontological beliefs about 'the extent to which different "truths" are accessible to human observers, the level of abstraction at which "truths" are to be formulated, and the extent to which these "truths" can be generalized across contexts' (Sil 2004: 314; see also della Porta and Keating, ch. 2).[3]

Yet in many research designs, the choice of the comparative method is not just a second-best one imposed by the availability of data; rather, it is justified by its capacity to go beyond descriptive statistical measures, towards an in-depth understanding of historical processes and individual motivations. Ragin and Zaret (1983) suggested two decades ago that there are *two* different logics in comparative politics (or social sciences in general), often addressed

Table 11.1. Durkheim versus Weber: the 'logics'

	Durkheim	Weber
Aim at . . .	Generalization: search for trans-historical, permanent causes (different from historical contingencies)	Complexity: search for limited generalizations about historical divergence and concrete knowledge about specific processes
Relying upon (Mill's) mode of . . .	Concomitant variation as logic of analysis	Methods of agreement and differences
Instrument of analysis is . . .	Statistical correlation, regression	Narrative
Understanding explanation as . . .	Explanation as functional proposition about patterns of relations among abstract variables; singling out (external) causes	Explanation as genetic (combinatory) understanding of historical diversity; singling out (internal) reasons
Through the construction of . . .	Social species (discrete types of society) – as intermediate between the confused multitude of societies and the single although ideal concept of humanity	Ideal types (hypothetical models developed as aids for explanations: enable generalization about historical divergence)

by contrasting Durkheim's and Weber's research approaches. I suggest in the following that it is indeed useful to rehearse the debate, not to challenge the need for *shared standards*, but in consideration of the specificity of *diverse tools* when prescribing methodological standards. The differing research 'logics' linked to Durkheim and Weber have been compared on various dimensions (Table 11.1; see also della Porta and Keating, ch. 2).

First of all, many scholars have pointed at the *different aims* present in a scientific enterprise. In statistical comparison, we aim at building law-like propositions. For Durkheim, sociology as a science must favour generalizations over details: 'Sociological explanation consists exclusively in establishing relationships of causality, that a phenomenon must be joined to its cause, or, on the contrary, a cause to its useful effects' (Durkheim 1982: 147).[4] As we are going to see in what follows, survey-based research on political participation is aimed at singling out the average effects of some variables (such as level of education, or interest in politics) upon the use of different forms of collective action. As Mahoney and Goertz (2006) recently put it, in this logic of research the aim is to estimate the average effects of independent variables, that is to investigate the 'effects-of-causes'. In historical comparison, *à la* Weber, the aim is the in-depth understanding of a context (or the searches for the 'causes-of-effects', *ibid.*). The case-oriented strategy focuses upon a relatively small number of cases, analysed with attention to each case as an interpretable whole (Ragin 2000: 22), seeking to understand a complex unity rather than establish relationships between variables. Studies oriented at understanding the reasons for the strength of, say, the Italian Communist Party or nationalist political violence in Ireland are illustrations of this type of approach.

A related issue is the *logical tools* used for the explanation. Referring to John Stuart Mill's work (1843), methodologists have observed that the variable-oriented and case-oriented approaches use different logical 'canons'. While statistical analyses are based on the search for *concomitant variations* (that is, looking at whether independent and dependent variables vary together, with regression as the main instrument for measuring causal inference), comparative analyses use the methods of similarities and differences. In the Durkheimian approach, concomitant variation is considered 'the supreme instrument for sociological research' (Durkheim 1982: 153). Statistical techniques based on a probabilistic logic allow for generalizations, even when the explanation is not valid for each single case. According to the method of *agreement*, if two or more instances of a phenomenon under investigation have only one of several possible causal circumstances in common, the cause of the phenomenon is the one circumstance that is present in all the analysed instances (Ragin 1987: 36). In this sense, we proceed by looking for invariant patterns, eliminating as potential causes all variables on which the units have different values. Mill's method of *difference* assumes that when two or more cases have different values on a certain phenomenon we want to explain, we have to look for the one circumstance on which they differ. Although the determinism of the search for necessary causes has been criticized as unrealistic for the social sciences (Lieberson 1994), the search for necessary conditions has been considered of substantive relevance for social theory (Goertz 2003). Focusing on a small-*N*, case-oriented comparison usually points at similarities and differences through dense *narratives*, with a large number of characteristics being taken into account, often together with their interaction within long-lasting processes.

There is also, however, a deeper difference between variable-oriented and case-oriented research, and this refers to the very concept of *explanation*. Neil

Smelser (1976: 204) admits the differences in the 'modes of comprehension' with an 'idiographic–nomothetic dilemma'. When looking at aggregated cases, the researcher is typically interested in the variables that affect one another causally. When focusing on individual cases, however, she might aim at an understanding of a complex unit, by grasping the relations among its constituent parts. He or she is not looking for a causal explanation, but rather, in Smelser's words, 'the operation may be more akin to an "appreciative" or "esthetic" act, an effort to understand the principles by which the parts consistently fit together'. While Smelser seemed to consider the second type of knowledge as somewhat residual, more balanced assessments developed later on. Recently, Ferejohn (2004: 150) has distinguished external, more or less causal explanations, and internal, or deliberative, explanations. *External* explanations present agents doing things because of some configuration of causal influence, while *internal* explanation identifies reasons for an action. Thus, 'An action is explained internally as an outcome of a deliberative process in which the agent is assumed to act for reason . . . To "explain" in this sense is to "justify"'' (Ferejohn 2004: 152; see also Pizzorno, ch. 9).[5] Statistical analysis on large-N cases of typical instances of political violence try to assess the contextual conditions that facilitate their development. Recently, analysis of the distribution of car burnings (as indicators of the intensity of urban riots) per municipality has been oriented to explain the French urban riots in autumn 2005 on the basis of some characteristics of the areas in which riots were more prevalent (that is, more cars were burned). In this way, characteristics such as spatial segregation, the level of poverty or rates of unemployment have been identified as causes for rioting (Lagrange and Oberti 2006). In a different perspective, ethnographic research has identified the motive of the rioters, that is the justification of their actions, in the development injustice frames (Auyero 2007).

Various *heuristic devices* are developed for working towards these different aims. In Durkheim's work, inductive reasoning on empirical data aims at reconstructing the different social species – which he locates between 'the confused multitude of historical society and the unique, although ideal, concept of humanity' (Durkheim 1982: 109). The properties of a social species influence the course of the social phenomena developing within them, since 'the causes of social phenomena are internal to the society' (*ibid.*: 114). The search for permanent causes implies a focus upon explanations that point at patterns of relations among abstract variables that are trans-historical in nature (*ibid.*: 739). Since concomitant variation is usually oriented to the search for permanent causes (Ragin and Zaret 1983: 737), there is no space for plural causation: an effect cannot have different causes in different contexts.

In this approach, understanding the recourse to political violence in given systems would imply, for instance, finding the correlation coefficients of various indicators of potential contextual preconditions (such as the degree of democratization and per capita income) with indicators of the spread of political violence (such as the number of people wounded/killed in political events or for political reasons and the amount of material damage during protest events).

In a case-oriented approach, by contrast, an in-depth knowledge of a small number of cases provides the basis for generalizations that are temporarily limited to the cases studied and whose wider relevance should be controlled through further research. Macro-units (such as countries) are therefore considered as unique and complex social configurations (Skocpol and Somers 1980), even though concepts are built that transcend the validity of individual cases (see Goldthorpe 2000: ch. 3). In qualitative, historical comparison based on a case strategy, explanations are genetic (i.e. based upon the reconstruction of the origins of a certain event), and generalizations are historically concrete (Ragin and Zaret 1983: 740). Theorization and generalization, in this tradition, are provided not by statistical regularities but by *ideal types*. These are abstract models, with an internal logic, against which real, complex cases can be measured. An ideal type, Weber (1949: 90) explains, 'is no "hypothesis" but it offers guidance to the construction of hypotheses. It is not a description of the reality but it aims to give unambiguous means of expression to such a description'; it is an 'idea', a 'unified ideal construct', 'abstracted out of certain features' and keeping the 'essential features' (*ibid.*: 91). This analytical construct is 'ideal' in the sense that it allows singling out relationships which 'our imagination accepts as plausibly motivated and "objectively possible"' (*ibid.*: 91–2). It is oriented to facilitate the empirical analysis, without reflecting either an ethical imperative, or a historical reality. As Ragin and Zaret (1983: 731–2) noted, ideal types enable limited generalization about historical divergence, pointing to different patterns of process and structure in history. Such generalizations go beyond the uniqueness of historical events, although without approaching the degree of generality of natural scientific laws.

In this approach, understanding political violence would imply in-depth description of the contexts in which violence developed, locating the specific process of evolution of violent political actors in their broader environment. The existence of several different paths to the same outcome is largely accepted and anticipated; for instance, similar degrees of political violence in different countries or times might well be produced by different causes (or combinations of causes). The presence of unemployment could be very important to explaining violence in some historical contexts, as it is combined with other elements (for instance, presence of armed militia); but it may be totally irrelevant in others.

Summarizing, we can distinguish a case-oriented approach from a variable-oriented one on the basis of different concepts of 'understanding': related either to generalizable knowledge of relations among variables (aiming at generalization), or to dense knowledge of cases. Some comparativists use case-oriented strategies in order to understand or interpret specific cases because of their intrinsic value; many, however, also have a causal-analytic purpose (Ragin 1987). A valuable feature of the case-oriented approach is the development of an extensive dialogue between the researcher's ideas and the data in an examination of each case as a complex set of relationships, which allows causal complexity to be addressed.

As I will argue in what follows (see Table 11.2), these differences affect the research design. In particular, the characteristic of comparison as a method that respects the historical specificity of the units under analysis is contrasted with the sort of 'anonymity' of the cases belonging to a statistical sample. Variable-based projects tend to follow (or mimic) statistical rules: a high N is considered as preferable; in particular, the logic of variable-based research design implies that with a small number of cases, we can cope with only a small number of variables. Explanation is understood as measuring the different variables' contributions to causing a certain phenomenon (how the dependent variable covaries with each independent variable). The assumption of homogeneity of the units of analysis (see Héritier, ch. 4) is made at the beginning of the research. Here, 'generality is given precedence over complexity', and therefore 'the wider the population, the better' (Ragin 1987: 54). Time is used mainly for increasing the number of cases by building subunits, through periodization or as points of observation within longitudinal studies.

In contrast, case-based logic tends to explore diversity (and deviant cases) by thick description of one or a small number of cases, often contrasted on several dimensions. This means that a few cases are analysed based on a large number of characteristics. Explanations are narrative accounts with limited interest in generalization. The degree to which the cases selected do belong to the same category, and therefore are comparable, is assessed in the course of the research itself (Ragin 1994). The method is not very sensitive to the frequency distribution, and a single case can cast doubt on a cause–effect relationship established on the basis of many observations (Ragin 1987). Time is especially useful here in order to build narratives of processes.

Table 11.2. Research design in variable-based versus case-based comparisons

	Variable-based	Case-based
Cases as	Anonymous (transformed into variables)	Names with capitals (complex units)
Concepts	Predetermined and operationalized	Constructed during the research
Independence of cases	Assumes cases that are independent from each other	Addresses systematic process analysis
Number of cases	Increase N whenever possible	Keep N low
Number of variables	Reduce the number of variables in order to avoid undetermined research design (degrees of freedom problem)	Increase number of variables in order to make the description thicker (full accounts; case knowledge)
Case selection	Tend to select randomly or on the independent variable	Tend to select paradigmatic cases
Diversity as . . .	Parametrization – search for generalization in area studies or subsystem research project	Understanding through differences – exploring diversity
Use of time	Periodization	Processes and temporal sequences; eventful temporality

We shall discuss these elements in more detail in what follows.

Definition of case and case selection

All of these differences in the research logics (or tools) must be taken into account when dealing with the steps of a research design, an important one being the selection of cases.

What is a case?

First of all, the process of defining cases (*casing*) is different. In variable-oriented research, the homogeneity of the units of analysis is stated at the very beginning, when defining the population of cases, considered as empirically given (Ragin 2000). In case-oriented research, cases tend not to be determined at the beginning of a research project – instead, 'they often coalesce in the course of the research though a systematic dialogue of ideas and evidence' (Ragin 2004: 127). In this process of casing, singling out the degree of homogeneity of the cases (by answering the question 'What is this a case of?') is part and parcel of the research process, which often ends with the construction of types and the allocation of cases to them.

This difference is linked with the different function and timing of conceptualization (see Mair, ch. 10, and Kratochwil, ch. 5): concepts are predefined and then operationalized at the onset of the research in a variable-oriented design; and constructed (in their sociological meaning) in the course of the research in a case-oriented design. Additionally, it reflects differences in the consideration of the unit of analysis: in variable-oriented approaches, statistical procedures decompose the original cases into values on variables, while in case-oriented approaches they maintain their unitary character; that is, even when variables are mentioned, the single cases are still approached as complex units (Corbetta 2003: 18; see also della Porta and Keating, ch. 1). In variable-oriented approaches, the cases become anonymous; in case-oriented ones, they are complex units, given capitalized labels.

The number of cases

The two 'logics' also have different implications for the *number of cases*. As noted, comparison by variable tends to privilege large N: 'because the comparative method must be considered the weaker method, it is usually advisable to shift to the statistical method if sufficient cases are available for investigation' (Lijphart 1975: 165). In a similar vein, Giovanni Sartori (1971: 8, emphasis added) agrees that 'comparison is a control method of generalizations, previsions or laws in the form of "if . . . then", that may be used in *cases in which stronger methods are not available*'.

The issue of the number of cases is dealt with in variable-oriented research designs by some specific rules oriented to address the issue of the degree of freedom (see Franklin, ch. 13). The number of cases should vary according to the number of variables included in a research design: the larger the number, the more likely that regression coefficients are statistically significant. Indeterminate research designs – with a smaller number of cases than required by the number of operational variables – are defined as designs from which 'virtually nothing can be learned about the causal hypotheses', since the researcher has 'more inferences to make than implications observed' (King, Keohane and Verba 1994: 118–19). An increase in the number of variables would require an increase in the number of cases or, if this is not feasible, a refocusing of the study on the effects of particular explanatory variables rather than on the causes of a particular set of effects.

Within this approach, case studies are considered useful mainly for the falsification of hypotheses or their specification through the analysis of *deviant* cases. In Lijphart's (1975) view, case study stands apart from other methods in that it cannot produce empirical generalizations, nor be used to test hypotheses.[6] The case study is 'a system for questioning, not for answering' (Stretton 1969: 247), and its context-dependent, idiographic knowledge is considered less useful for social sciences than the general knowledge derived from large-N, variable-oriented studies.

Case-oriented researchers, on the other hand, oppose the suggestion that increasing the number of cases produces 'better-determined' research designs. They stress, first of all, the methodological losses involved, especially in cross-national comparison, with increasing the N. First, an increase in the number of cases normally brings about an increase in the number of *third variables* – that is, of variables external to the hypothesis we want to control – thus reducing the reliability of our inference or imposing a further increase in N (on this point, see Morlino 1990: 387–8). Especially in cross-national research projects, including new countries augments the problem of concept-stretching (Munck 2004; Mair, ch. 10) as well as of the reliability and comparability of measures and indicators used to translate national experiences into comparable operational categories (Mair 1996). Working with many countries or long historical periods, in a field in which few reliable and comparative 'hard data' are available, increases the risk of building on insufficiently deep knowledge of each single country. More generally, some scepticism has been voiced about the ability, even in large-N, non-experimental research designs, to have enough observations to adjudicate among rival explanations. In this sense, the differences between experimental designs and statistical ones have been noted – so much so that some have found it 'problematic to suggest that any observational study can ever be "determinate"' (Collier, Brady and Seawright 2004b: 236). While experiments are indeed capable of keeping additional variables constant, causation can only be inferred in observational studies if the researcher imposes 'several restrictive assumptions, which may be difficult to test or even to defend' (Collier, Seawright and Munck 2004: 48). Indeterminacy can also derive from multicollinearity, where two or more independent variables move together.

Some scholars emphasize the contribution of interpretative work, and of other qualitative approaches, to goals that a regression-oriented framework addresses less successfully – including concept formation and fine-grained description (Brady and Collier 2004; Collier, Seawright and Munck 2004). Case-oriented studies are said to be stronger in these two tasks, as well as in research programmes oriented towards understanding the cognitive protocols that capture the actors' definition of the situation (McKeown 2004: 153). They are also considered particularly effective in identifying causal processes and therefore in developing theories. So 'seen in this light, the test of a hypothesis – the central theoretical activity from the standpoint of conventional quantitative research – is but one phase in a long, involved process of making sense of new phenomena' (McKeown 2004: 167).

Recent debates on case studies and small-*N* comparison have challenged the idea that – as Dietrich Rueschemeyer (2003: 305) put it – exploring the impact of a large number of relevant factors and conditions in only a few cases does not help in learning anything that is theoretically relevant. Case studies are praised for their detailed knowledge of processes (at different moments, or 'data points' in Rueschemeyer's definition), considered as particularly useful for the discovery of social mechanisms (see Héritier, ch. 4). In this sense, a case study goes beyond a single observation, and confronting analytical propositions with many data points can be useful not only for theory building but also for theory testing.[7]

The selection of cases

The choice of number of cases is linked with that of the case selection. In variable-oriented designs, methods of sample selection are usually constrained by statistical rules. Random samples (or stratified ones) are preferred when the main aim is to randomize unwanted sources of variation (Smelser 1976: 211). As King, Keohane and Verba stated, 'if we have to abandon randomness, *as it is usually the case in political science research*, we must do it with caution' (1994: 124, emphasis added). So they accept that random sampling is only one of the possible ways of selecting cases, with some obvious advantages but difficult preconditions of applicability. Not only in qualitative research, but also in much quantitative research, random selection might not be feasible because the universe of cases is not clearly specified. Even when feasible, it is not always the best strategy, given the risk of missing important cases. In these situations, they suggest selecting observations that would ensure variation in the explanatory variable and the control variables. King, Keohane and

Verba, in fact, follow a long tradition of insisting that we should never sample on the dependent variable. It may be tempting, in this way, to search for observations that fit our theory, but selecting only cases with the same value (or a limited range of values) on the dependent variable would prevent us making any causal (statistical) inference about the relationships between the dependent and independent variables. This is because cases with different values on the dependent variable could, for all we know, be correlated with the same independent variable. For example, we could take a group of cities that had experienced riots and find that they all had high levels of unemployment. Yet it is possible that other cities, which had not experienced riots and which we therefore did not consider, also had high unemployment; hence unemployment cannot be the critical variable.

Case-oriented research follows a different strategy of case selection. Selection of cases for small-N research is, in this perspective, not to be evaluated on the basis of the classical rules oriented to avoiding selection biases in statistical (especially regression) analysis. In particular, selecting on the dependent variable is a quite common and legitimate practice. Case-oriented researchers may intentionally select cases that differ relatively little from each other with respect to the outcome under investigation (Ragin 2004), focusing in particular on positive cases, that is cases where a phenomenon (such as revolution) is present. There are analytic gains to be derived from an in-depth analysis of positive cases of a phenomenon like revolution, especially when little is known about it (Collier, Seawright and Munck 2004: 48), or from the higher capacity to evaluate the impact of a main causal variable by focusing on cases with high scores on both the dependent and the independent variables (Collier, Mahoney and Seawright 2004: 102). Typically, research on peasant revolts or revolutions or anti-WTO riots focuses on cases in which those phenomena developed, without taking into account the entire range of variation in outcome. In contrast to variable-oriented analysis, the selection of cases in case-oriented research requires an appreciation of their relevance for a specific set of hypotheses. Additionally, some cases are considered as more substantially important and non-conforming cases are evaluated in detail. So, a theory of revolutions that is unable to account for the 1789 revolution in France would be highly problematic.

For research following both strategies, criteria for case selection have been suggested. Smelser (1976: 174) has listed five criteria that may guide our choices: units of analysis 'must be [1] appropriate to the kind of theoretical problem posed by the investigator . . . [2] relevant to the phenomenon being studied . . . [3] empirically invariant with respect to their classificatory criterion . . . [4] reflect the degree of availability of data referring to this unit . . .' and '[5] decisions to select and classify units of analysis should be based on standardized and repeatable procedures'. All selection of cases implies, however, trade-offs among what Gerring (2001) called:

- *plenitude*, referring to the number of cases: the larger the number of cases used to posit a causal relation, the higher the confidence in the results; additionally, large samples help in specifying propositions;
- *boundedness*, referring to the range of generalizability and therefore the inclusion of relevant cases, but also the exclusion of irrelevant ones (*ibid.*: 172);
- *comparability*, referring to the similarity among cases on some relevant dimensions;[8]
- *independence*, referring to the autonomy of units: if a unit is strictly linked to another, one risks studying the same unit twice;
- *representativeness*, referring to the capacity of the sample to reflect the properties of the entire population;
- *variation*, referring to the range of values registered on relevant variables;
- *analytical utility*, with reference to the theory to test, or the scientific approach chosen;
- *replicability*, referring to the possibility of replicating the study.

Even with these specifications, comparative social science remains a wide field with many strategies of comparison, and scholars' preferences on the number of cases have varied over time. In the 1960s, large-scale comparisons were at the core of an increasing attention to comparative politics. After the 1970s, there was a resurgence of comparisons of a small number of countries, often analysed over long periods (Collier 1990). Growing attention to interpretative social sciences stressed the relevance of 'thick descriptions' of few cases (Geertz 1973).[9] In the early 1990s, much of the work aimed at a limited generalizability, with middle-range or even lower-level theories for which the specificities of the historical context played a crucial role (Mair 1996). More recently, the preferred number of cases has increased again, under external pressures such as the development of new statistical methodologies for multicase comparison and the enlargement of the European Union.

An intermediate strategy is offered by Charles Ragin (1987, 1994, 2000), in his *qualitative comparative analysis*. Based upon Boolean algebra, this relies upon medium-N comparison based upon analysis of similarities and differences in a search for necessary and sufficient conditions. It compares *configurations of causes* – that is, the effects of the contemporaneous presence/absence of a combination of factors, not of the presence or absence of each of them. Although still following a deterministic logic, it allows for multiple causation through the analysis of several different combinations of causes.

Especially within neoinstitutional approaches, historical sociology or international relations, the use of case studies continues, however, to be considered as a main strategy in order to address complex historical phenomena (see Vennesson, ch.12, and Steinmo, ch. 7).

Similar versus different cases

Preferences vary, not only on the number of cases, but also on the right balance of similarities/differences among them. Two different strategies have been identified: the so-called *most-similar systems* design, in which we compare similar cases, and the *most-different systems* design, where we compare dissimilar ones.

Working with *similar systems* (for example, similar countries) facilitates the *ceteris paribus* rule – that is, it reduces the number of 'disturbing' variables to be kept under control. For Lijphart (1975), cases for comparative analysis should be selected in such a way as to maximize the variance of the independent variables but minimize the variance of the control variables. Within a most-similar systems design, we assume that factors common to the countries sampled are irrelevant in explaining some observed differences, focusing instead on the variables that are different. If we want to explain why left-wing terrorism spread in the 1970s in Italy, but not in France, we would mention neither the presence of a Communist party nor of a pluralistic system of industrial relations, since these were present in both.

In many fields of sociology and political science, cross-national comparisons often address countries belonging to a common geographical area (such as southern Europe or eastern Europe) and sharing historical traditions, cultural traits or economic development. The advantage is that many variables are 'parametrized': if we have more or less the same degree of economic development, similar culture and the like, we can consider these characteristics as constant and check for the influence of other factors. In area studies, the relative similarity of situations enables an appreciation of the marginal difference and its causes (Dogan and Pelassy 1990: 134).

A disadvantage, however, is that, in comparing similar systems, we cannot go beyond so-called middle-range theories – theories that apply only in a restricted area. An additional problem is that comparison of similar cases still leaves open a risk of overdetermination (Przeworski and Teune 1970), where many variables may intervene, and we cannot control for their influence. The contexts of the compared situations are never similar enough to permit considering as null the influence of the environment; accordingly, the researcher will never be able to exclude from her conclusions the contextual variables that she could not keep constant (Dogan and Passy 1990).

By *maximizing the differences* among the cases, we may instead generalize beyond a restricted area, although at the cost of an increase in the number of independent variables to be kept under control. As Przeworski and Teune (1970: 35) have suggested, in the most-different systems design, the choice is in fact to sample *different* countries in order to 'identify those independent variables, observed within systems, that do not violate the assumption of the homogeneity of the total population'. A *most-different systems* design allows for checking if a correlation holds true no matter in which country. This type of analysis focuses on a lower level than the systemic one – most often at the level of individual actors (Przeworski and Teune 1970). This relies on the assumption that individuals will act the same way faced with the same stimulus; hence researchers look for general statements that are universally true.[10] The research strategy that may produce them is based on random samples of the world population, regardless of the social systems to which individuals, groups or subsystems belong. So social science theories should aim not at explaining phenomena as accurately as possible in their specific historical circumstances, but rather at explaining phenomena wherever and whenever they occur (Przeworski and Teune 1970).

In privileging variables referring to individual over systemic variables, Przeworski and Teune (1970: 7) admit that social science based on this kind of assumption, would be 'a priori a-historical'. So research on individual political participation has sampled individuals from different countries with the aim of finding common patterns – for instance, the research of Verba, Nie and Kim (1978) on the impact of social inequalities on political participation in seven countries of the 'first', 'second' and 'third' worlds. Recent research with large numbers of countries searches for a common explanation of individual behaviour beyond historical specificities in different countries (Norris 2002). In their *Dynamics of Contention*, Doug McAdam, Sidney Tarrow and Charles Tilly (2001) apply a most-different strategy design to paired comparisons, not to look for correlation between variables, but to identify common mechanisms. The analysis of 'most-different' countries and historical periods aims to depart from the common foundational tradition by using paired comparisons 'not to maximize resemblance or even to pinpoint differences among whole countries, but to discover whether similar mechanisms and processes drive changes in divergent periods, places and regimes' (McAdam, Tarrow and Tilly 2001: 82).

Useful for investigating some micro-dynamics of participation, the most-different systems design does have shortcomings. The most ambitious projects, aiming at explaining phenomena worldwide, risk ending up with hypotheses that explain little. As past attempts have indicated, the hope for global theories is likely to be frustrated. For instance, the search to explain development once and for all brought explanations that were too big for accurate empirical work (Verba 1991). Similarly, the relative deprivation theory, based on macro-comparison of large numbers of countries (Gurr 1971), was strongly criticized when in-depth case studies indicated that grievances are always present in a society, but they are mobilizable only when resources are available for the aggrieved groups (Oberschall 1973).

The definition of most-similar and most-different systems designs refers to the units of analysis, but it also has implications for the type of knowledge we seek. Very often, the most-different design is used to obtain generalizable results – that is, to look for historically invariant correlations. The most-similar design often looks to other countries for confirmation of a hypothesis developed in a single country. However, we may have other choices. Differences among dissimilar countries may be used to contrast contexts; or differences among similar countries may aim at specifying hypotheses. In historical sociology, macrohistorical analysis has been, and continues to be, pursued in different ways: looking for single or multiple forms of a phenomenon, or trying to explain one or all cases (Tilly 1984). Among the studies that privilege the search for a single form, *individualizing* comparisons deal with each case as unique, while *universalizing* comparisons identify common properties among all instances of a phenomenon (*ibid.*). Other studies identify multiple forms of a phenomenon, either to explain, in an *encompassing* way, a single instance, or to *find variations* among all cases. As Tilly admits, empirical research usually simultaneously involves different types of comparison, mixing the ideal types; but there is often an implicit or explicit preference for one design or the other. Alternatively, however, most-different systems can be chosen in order to explore deviant or paradigmatic cases. In this sense, good cases are not the most typical, but the most telling, because they help to clarify theoretical problems. In particular, qualitative analysts often select cases where the outcomes of interest occur (positive cases). This strategy, often criticized as selecting on the dependent variable, has been defended as particularly useful for singling out different paths to certain outcomes (Mahoney and Goertz 2006). Additionally, the selection of 'positive cases' can be considered as a choice oriented to finding necessary causes of some phenomena, especially rare ones such as revolutions. In this sense, it is linked to the definition of the population more than to that of a 'dependent variable'.

Besides the individual preferences of the researcher, the various research designs tend to follow a certain order in the accumulation of knowledge of a certain phenomenon. Skocpol and Somers (1980) suggested a 'research cycle' in which the comparative method is oriented towards: (a) *macro-causal analysis*, in which historical cases are compared for the purpose of making causal inferences about macro-level structures and processes; (b) *parallel demonstration* of theories, applying old theories to new cases; and (c) *contrast of contexts*, looking instead to 'bring out the unique feature of each particular case' included in the research. According to Skocpol and Somers (1980: 196), the three logics are complementary for the accumulation of knowledge:

Parallel comparative history tends to call forth Contrast-oriented arguments when the need develops to set limits to the scope or claims of an overly generalized social-scientific theory. Contrast-oriented comparative history may give rise to Macro-analytic arguments when juxtapositions of historical trajectories begin to suggest testable causal hypotheses. Finally, too, Macro-analytic comparative history can create a demand for the kind of general theorizing that precedes the construction of a Parallel comparative analysis.

Time and history in comparative politics

The definition of the units of analysis and the selection of cases also involve another strategic choice: the use of time. The historical approach is particularly relevant for case-oriented research designs that are by definition context-bound. Long-term processes are particularly important for 'internal' interpretation (what is usually called *verstehen* rather than *erklären*). Variable-oriented analysis is less in need of historical depth, aiming at general knowledge. However, especially in the field of comparative politics, the variable-oriented approach also has a particular interest in the use of time, especially in the form of periodizations that allow for the multiplication of (sub)units of analysis; so the same country in different time periods could be treated as a set of distinct cases. This has received less attention in the social sciences (Bartolini 1993: 131).

References to history do not automatically make for a *diachronic* research design – that is, for a matrix of data that involves collection for at least two points in time. For instance, Theda Skocpol's classic work on revolutions

(1979) refers to Mill's methods of agreement and differences, but without introducing time as a variable. According to Stefano Bartolini (1993: 135), hers is an example of a research design based upon the observation of cross-case *synchronic* variance: 'history is present in the unquestionable "historicity" of events located in the remote past; but there is no time in the scheme, no variance along the temporal dimension in the variables which are considered, and therefore there is no method that is specifically historical'.

Bartolini calls for a use of time through research designs that are *explicitly diachronic* – that is, based on the collection of data at several points in history. Very often, case studies analyse the development of some characteristics, in a single unit, over a certain time span; comparison is then developed between periods. Allowing for the parametrization of many variables and an in-depth historical knowledge, the *cross-time comparison within a single unit* offers many advantages for hypothesis building. Historical analyses of a single country are useful in the development of hypotheses in new fields, insofar as they are able to keep under control – or at least, have knowledge about – a vast range of independent variables that may intervene to 'disturb' the control of a hypothesis. On the basis of an in-depth analysis of a single country, as well as by taking into account the timing of some events, historical case studies may help in developing new hypotheses (see Vennesson, ch. 12).

What is true in a certain country (with a peculiar culture, social structure, model of economic development, and especially configuration of all the different variables), however, is not necessarily true in others. *Cross-national diachronic studies* tend to reach higher levels of generalization and to specify the hypotheses developed in historical case studies that aim at comparing the case of country A at time X with that of country B at times Y and Z. Within a variable-oriented strategy, while increasing the number of countries has the disadvantage of increasing the number of variables to be kept under control, expanding the time span reduces that risk, allowing an in-depth historical knowledge of the cases under analysis (though hampering the assumption of independence between cases).

The use of diachronic research designs is especially common when we expect relevant changes in some dimensions between time t and time $t + n$. In this sense, we treat time as a variable. This is done, for instance, in research on developmental processes involving an interest in steps or thresholds, crisis and transition phases, or trends and sequences. Time is central in grand theories of development, which often assume a teleological scheme 'in which the description of some "primitive" stage enables a number of factors of development to be identified, which then point to some future direction' (Bartolini

1993: 143). In Rokkan's (1970) research, the *timing* of the different processes of nation building and industrialization influenced the evolution of the main social cleavages that survive today. Similarly, Robert Dahl (1971) pointed at the different outcomes related to the precedence given in democratization processes to extending the number of rights to contestation/opposition versus the number of people who enjoy those rights. The timing of the various phases, steps and thresholds involved in the pattern of political modernization is particularly illuminating for understanding democratization in various countries. These analyses tend to share some of what historical sociologist William H. Sewell (1996) calls *teleological temporality*, which explains events through abstract transhistorical processes 'from less to more' (say, urbanization or industrialization), and *experimental temporality*, which compares different historical paths (for example, revolution versus non-revolution, democracy versus non-democracy).

Referring to Skocpol's work, Mahoney has focused attention on a strategy to assess causal inference, which he calls *narrative*, in contrast with the nominal and ordinal approaches. While the nominal strategy (using nominal variables) relies upon Mill's logic of similarities and differences and is therefore deterministic, and the ordinal strategy allows for (probabilistic) analyses of concomitant variation, the narrative strategy addresses phenomena such as revolutions as 'the product of unique, temporally ordered and sequentially unfolding events that occur within cases' (Mahoney 1999: 1164). In the narrative strategy, 'one criterion for judging a causal argument rests with the ability of an analyst to meaningfully assemble specific information concerning the histories of cases into coherent processes' (*ibid.*: 1168). In this sense, it allows one to control, at a disaggregated level, whether the posited causal mechanisms plausibly link explanatory variables with a specific outcome.

While the first two strategies are useful in producing parsimonious theories by eliminating variables, the narrative method scores better on in-depth idiographic knowledge. For instance, if we want to explain why terrorism develops in some countries and not in others, we might proceed by sampling cases in which terrorism was present and others in which it was not, contrasting them on the basis of a nominal logic. If we trust statistics on terrorist events, we might instead measure the presence of terrorism in different countries and rank them in an ordinal way. However, these data are usually static: they allow us to eliminate variables that are not necessary causes or have low or statistically insignificant correlation coefficients, but not to look at the processes through which terrorism develops. This could be done instead through an in-depth narrative of one or a few cases in which terrorism developed, with attention paid to tracing back the temporal evolution of the various steps of radicalization (della Porta 1995; see also Vennesson, ch. 12).

Sewell (1996) reflects on another way of dealing with time: using the notion of *eventful temporality* for research that recognizes the power of events in history. Events are defined as a 'relatively rare subclass of happenings that *significantly transform structure*'; and an eventful conception of temporality takes into account the transformation of structures by events. Events produce historical changes mainly by 'transforming the very cultural categories that shape and constrain human action. Because the causalities that operate in social relations depend at least in part on the contents and relations of cultural categories, events have the power to transform social causality' (Sewell 1996: 263). Attention to 'eventful temporality' reflects the assumption that conjuncture and strategic action make transformative events possible. The conception of an 'eventful sociology' implies social processes that 'are inherently contingent, discontinuous, and open-ended . . . "Structures" are constructed by social action and "society" or "social formation" or "social systems" are continuously shaped and re-shaped by the creativity and stubbornness of their human creators' (Sewell 1996: 272). Such events as the seizure of the Bastille or, less dramatically, the 'Battles of Seattle' (during the contestation of the Millennium Round of the World Trade Organization) not only have a transformative impact on the lives of those who took part in them, but their symbolic relevance spreads to those not directly involved, changing routines and disrupting institutions (see Steinmo, ch. 7, and Keating, ch. 6).

For both diachronic case studies and diachronic cross-national comparisons, *periodization* is a delicate step, since in order to identify temporal variance it is first necessary to define the temporal units which determine such variance (Bartolini 1993). While spatial units are often easy to single out, as they are defined by geopolitical borders, temporal units are not. In fact, temporal variance is assessed by the observations of different time points (separated by more or less regular intervals) or of the general character of *periods* that follow one another. In order to understand how a variable has changed over time, we have to choose significant points in time – that is, to define a time 1, time 2, and so on. Various periodizations may appear as legitimate: what we need is a periodization that is significant according to our theoretical model. It must take into account the main changes in the dependent variable, but it cannot overlook the evolution of the other operative variables.[11] Already in a single-country design, the need to take into account variables that vary with a different timing may imply difficult choices between different periodizations. In cross-national designs, we have to deal with the additional problem of finding comparable periodizations in various countries: similar phases may well develop in different historical periods.

Some projects locate research within a historical perspective, recognizing the value of the long time span, or *longue durée*, with its attention to structures as 'coherent and fairly fixed series of relationships between realities and social masses' (Braudel 1980: 31). The field of historical sociology has been particularly sensitive to this issue. Charles Tilly's research (1986) on the change in the repertoires of collective action in the evolution of the nation-states, covering many centuries of French history, is an example of this type.

Conclusion

We have reviewed two main types of social science comparative analysis and various elaborations of these. One type focuses on large numbers of cases, regularities in behaviour and universal patterns. The other concentrates on context, complexity and difference. Some scholars argue that these follow two different logics, as outlined in Chapter 2 of this volume. Others insist that there is a single logic and that both must follow the same basic rules, albeit using different techniques and materials. The response will be obviously related to the (still vague) conceptualization of 'logic': Henry E. Brady and David Collier (2004) have recently underlined in the very title of their edited volume that *social inquiry* must follow *shared standards* while allowing for *diverse tools*. However, the discussion is still open in the social sciences regarding which should be the 'shared standards' and how much the presence of 'diverse tools' affects the various steps of a research design. In this chapter, we have suggested that many choices in the research design, such as those that refer to conceptualization, case selection and the very conception of explanation and inference, are indeed influenced by the (more or less ontological) preferences for a focus either on cases or on variable-oriented design. This does not, however, have an effect on the standards of empirical research, which must be kept high in both logics.

NOTES

1 For a similar conception of inference as the basis of the sociological enterprise, see Goldthorpe (2000, especially ch. 3).

2 Similarly, 'comparative politics' is used in different ways. Sometimes it refers to the study of countries one by one; sometimes it involves an insistence on the thematic and cross-national

study of insitutions and behaviour; while at other times it refers to the use of a variable-oriented approach.

3 Scholars also disagree on the capacity of statistical methods to match the experimental design through mathematical manipulation of the data.

4 Criticizing John Stuart Mill, Durkheim (1982: 148) states that his 'alleged axiom of a plurality of causes is a negation of the principle of causality'.

5 Internal explanations have also been called teleological (understandable on the basis of goals); external ones are causal (or mechanistic).

6 In this understanding, 'a case is an entity on which only one basic observation is made, and in which the dependent and independent variables do not change during the period of observation' (Lijphart 1975).

7 Critics have countered the accusation that case studies are biased towards verification, stressing instead their importance for the falsification of (non-probabilistic) hypotheses (Rueschemeyer 2003).

8 Units are usually considered homogeneous when they respond in similar ways to similar stimuli (Gerring 2001: 176).

9 This trend was also helped by statistical techniques that are better suited to the analysis of comparative politics (with small N) because they reduce the impact of deviant cases and allow for simulations that artificially increase the number of cases (Collier 1990: 495).

10 'If all relevant factors were known, then the same multivariate statement would yield a deterministic explanation regardless of time and place' (Przeworski and Teune 1970: 7).

11 Periodization can be deductive, derived from theoretical assumptions, or inductive, based on empirical observations.

Case studies and process tracing: theories and practices

Pascal Vennesson

Pascal Vennesson

Introduction

A significant part of what we know about the social and political world comes from case studies. Case studies famously contributed, for instance, to uncovering the tendency towards oligarchy in political parties, the inner working of the exercise of power in democracies, the dynamics of international crises, the logics of authority and control in organizations, the interplay between values and institutions in the Indian caste system, the sources of success and failure of deterrence, and the causes of social revolutions (Michels 1911; Dahl 1961; Crozier 1964; Dumont 1970; Allison 1971; George and Smoke 1974; Skocpol 1979). Beyond these classical and influential works, the case study research tradition remains popular as researchers explore the political development of imperial Germany in comparative perspective, the causes and characteristics of nuclear accidents, the 1986 Challenger launch disaster, the evolution of institutions, the role of reputational claims in foreign policy decision-making or the genesis of the welfare state (Esping-Andersen 1990; Sagan 1993; Mercer 1996; Vaughan 1996; Berman 2001; Thelen 2004; for more examples, see Feagin, Orum and Sjoberg 1991; George and Bennett 2005: 287–325; Gerring 2007: 2–5). In international relations, case studies have made a central contribution to both the international security and the international political economy subfields (Snyder 1989; Kacowicz 2004; Odell 2004).

What is a case study and what purpose does it serve? From an epistemological point of view, what is the place, and contribution, of case study research?

For their insightful comments and suggestions on an earlier version, I thank Zoe Bray, Donatella della Porta, Mikael Eriksson, Jörg Friedrichs, Dorith Geva, Michael Keating, Thomas Lindemann, Christine Reh and Thomas Teichler, as well as the participants in the seminar 'Approaches in Social Sciences' at the European University Institute, 3–4 May 2007.

How can case studies be performed empirically, especially using process tracing, a research procedure intended to explore the processes by which initial conditions are translated into outcomes? This chapter answers these questions and adds to the existing discussions of case study research in two ways. First, it addresses the persistent difficulty of practitioners of case study research to articulate their epistemological and methodological contributions, compared to other approaches, especially quantitative ones (Gerring 2007: 5–8). Even the classic work of Eckstein, for example, heralded as a keystone in the renaissance of qualitative methods, was rather restrictive and only favourable to certain types of case study (Eckstein 1975; 1992: 118). I argue that the social scientific contributions of case studies remain underappreciated, not because of the case study approach itself, but because the common epistemological framework of discussion usually focuses on data collection and testing. To get a fuller sense of the social scientific contributions of case studies, researchers would benefit from incorporating the epistemological conception of Gaston Bachelard, which treats the different elements of research, from conceptualization to investigation, as inseparable (Bachelard 1938, 1949).

Second, this chapter explores the ways in which case studies are performed empirically, in particular through the use of process tracing, a procedure designed to identify processes linking a set of initial conditions to a particular outcome. Process tracing is an important, perhaps indispensable, element of case study research (George and Smoke 1974, 1979; George and McKeown 1985). Yet, the most recent and systematic formulation of process tracing by George and Bennett is cast in a positivist perspective well-suited for certain kinds of case study, but less adapted for others (George and Bennett 2005: 205–32). Process tracing can be fruitfully used in both positivist and inter-pretivist research designs, allowing researchers to combine a positivist and an interpretive outlook in case study research. However, process tracing is also fraught with pitfalls and has limits. I discuss these limits and provide sugges-tions to overcome the main obstacles. In sum, this chapter belongs to the growing body of work that seeks to explore the interrelations between the-oretical issues and the actual experiences of case study research (Davis 2005; George and Bennett 2005; Trachtenberg 2006; Gerring 2007). While this chapter is relevant for both single cases and comparisons of a small number of cases (commonly between one and ten), I concentrate on within-case analysis, where the researcher examines multiple features of each case to assess causal and constitutive relations between factors (the comparative research strategies are presented by della Porta, ch. 11; on within-case analysis: Mahoney 2000a: 409–17; George and Bennett 2005: 18).

My argument proceeds in three steps. I begin by defining the notion of case study and highlighting the main characteristics and purpose of case study research. Based on Gaston Bachelard's epistemology, I then propose a framework to identify, and get a better sense of, the social scientific contributions of case studies. Finally, I turn to the empirical practice, especially the different ways to envision and conduct process tracing. I also identify some limits of process tracing and suggest ways to overcome them.

Case study: what is it? What for?

What is a case study?

Since the pioneering work of Frédéric Le Play at the end of the nineteenth century and the Chicago school of sociology in the 1920s and 1930s, case studies have been ubiquitous. However, their importance and influence have waxed and waned, and their meaning and characteristics have changed as well (Platt 1992a, 1992b). Within each discipline in different countries, and even within subfields (for example, in foreign policy studies, comparative politics, public administration or political sociology), one can trace the cyclical alternation of enthusiasm and disappointment with case study research. Case studies are diverse in their objectives, characteristics and results. Their contributions to social scientific knowledge, their role in theory building, their empirical added value, and the ways in which they are conducted are regularly debated (della, Porta, ch. 11).

As soon as one ventures beyond a limited core, researchers' preferences differ on key characteristics of case studies: the ideal number of cases, the nature and richness of the data collected, the ways in which the data can, and should, be collected, the logic of generalization, the role of inductive and deductive approaches, the importance of time span and historical depth, the access to actors and their perceptions, the units of analysis, the connection with fieldwork, and participant observation. These theoretical and methodological debates are shaped both by the partially autonomous logic of each discipline, and by deep-seated, but often overlooked, national intellectual traditions (Galtung 1981). These discussions are also influenced by the transnational diffusion of ideas that often come from the United States, stemming from the evolution of social science disciplines in that country (Monroe 2005).

While virtually everyone claims to seize the epistemological middle ground, the conceptions of case studies range from the most positivist (King, Keohane and Verba 1994; Maoz 2002) to the most interpretivist (Burawoy 1998; Passeron and Revel 2005), with a set of intermediate positions (Ragin and Becker 1992; McKeown 1999; Brady and Collier 2004; George and Bennett 2005; Gerring 2007). Not only are there different conceptions of what case studies are and should be, but there are also troubling discrepancies between case study theorizing and case study practices (Platt 1992b; Rogowski 1995).

The ordinary meanings and usages and the history of the word 'case' provide a useful starting point to getting a better grasp of its social scientific meanings and their evolutions. The word 'case', derived from the Latin *casus*, means an occurrence, something that happens, usually with an unfavourable connotation: an accident, a misfortune. It belongs to the legal vocabulary to designate a scandal or a lawsuit, and pedagogically in law and business to designate a learning method. The word 'case' also belongs to the religious vocabulary and refers to a particular, and embarrassing, moral problem which raises a difficult ethical debate (casuistry) (Jansen and Toulmin 1988; Passeron and Revel 2005). Finally, 'case' is also used in mathematics (limit case) and in medicine, where it designates the state and the history of a patient. These common meanings point us to some key characteristics of the ways in which 'case' is used in social sciences. On the one hand, the case appears as an unusual and specific challenge to established descriptions or reasoning. A case is therefore disconcerting: it provokes reflection and points to the need for an adjustment of a theoretical framework (Platt 1992: 24; Passeron and Revel 2005: 10, 16). On the other hand, the case requires a solution, its meaning defined in relation to theoretical frameworks and, however unique, it can be put in relation to other cases (Bradshaw and Wallace 1991; Abbott 1992: 53–82; Passeron and Revel 2005: 10–11). In sum, confronted with the case, the challenge is to acknowledge and uncover its specific meaning, while extracting generalizable knowledge actually or potentially related to other cases.

A case is a phenomenon, or an event, chosen, conceptualized and analysed empirically as a manifestation of a broader class of phenomena or events (on definitions: Eckstein 1975: 85; Jervis 1990; Ragin 1992: 1–17; King, Keohane and Verba 1994: 51–3; 1995; Yin 1994; George and Bennett 2005: 17–19). A case study is a research strategy based on the in-depth empirical investigation of one, or a small number, of phenomena in order to explore the configuration of each case, and to elucidate features of a larger class of (similar) phenomena, by developing and evaluating theoretical explanations (Ragin 2000: 64–87). Four points related to these definitions can be emphasized. First, the case is not just a unit of analysis or an observation, understood as a piece of data. It is not a data category, but a theoretical category (Ragin 1992: 1; Hall

2003: 396–7). Second, the case is not *a priori* spatially delimited. The delimitation of the case, spatial and otherwise, is the product of the theoretical conceptualization used by the researcher. These boundaries are by no means obvious or to be assumed: they result from theoretical choices (Rueschemeyer 2003: 320). Third, the phenomenon under study does not have to be contemporary; it can be from the past. Fourth, in case study research, data can be collected in various ways, and it can be both qualitative and quantitative.

Varieties of case studies

What purpose do case studies serve? Case studies come in different shapes and forms, and they can serve a variety of purposes, often simultaneously (Lijphart 1971; Eckstein 1975; Levy 2002). Researchers use case studies to develop and evaluate theories, as well as to formulate hypotheses or explain particular phenomena by using theories and causal mechanisms (Bennett 2004: 21). Furthermore, some works can be defined as case studies although their authors do not explicitly describe them as such (Allen 1965; Dore 1973). Case studies are also combined with other methods like statistical analysis and computer simulation, for example (Voss 1993; Biddle 2004). I identify four main types of case study, each corresponding to a different purpose (for different typologies: Lijphart 1971; Eckstein 1975; Levy 2002; Bennett 2004: 21–2; George and Bennett 2005: 74–6).

First, the descriptive case study (configurative-idiographic) is a systematic description of the phenomena with no explicit theoretical intention. It is common to label this kind of research as simply suggestive and to dismiss its social scientific contribution. It is true that the notion of a descriptive case study does not sit easily with our definition, which implies a theoretical framing. Still, while the work of many historians and anthropologists might lack an explicit theoretical framework, that does not mean that a theory is altogether absent. Furthermore, in any type of case study there is an unavoidable descriptive dimension. Case studies sometimes explore subjects about which little is previously known or phenomena in need of an interpretation that sheds new light on known data, and their descriptive aspect is invaluable.

Second, the interpretive case study (disciplined configurative) uses theoretical frameworks to provide an explanation of particular cases, which can lead as well to an evaluation and refinement of theories. Third, the hypothesis-generating and refining case study (heuristic) seeks to generate new hypotheses inductively and/or to refine existing hypotheses. The researcher can clarify the meaning of certain variables and the validity of empirical indicators, suggest alternative causal mechanisms and identify overlooked interaction effects. A deviant case is especially useful to generate new hypotheses and/or to adjust theoretical propositions. Fourth, theory-evaluating case studies are used to assess whether existing theories account for the processes and outcomes of selected cases.

The social scientific contributions of case studies

Bachelard's applied rationalism and case study research

How can practitioners of case study research better articulate what they are doing, epistemologically and methodologically speaking? What are the specific social scientific contributions of case study research? Borrowing from Gaston Bachelard's epistemology of science, I suggest one way to highlight as a coherent whole the different social scientific dimensions of case study research. This connection between the case study method and Bachelard's epistemology is needed for two reasons. First, the epistemological categories that we use, explicitly or implicitly, affect the ways in which we evaluate the social scientific contributions of research strategies and methodologies, including case studies. I bring a different epistemological tradition to bear in debates about case studies that have been predominantly shaped by the analytic tradition in the philosophy of science, embodied in the work of Popper, Kuhn and Lakatos for instance (Davis 2005; George and Bennett 2005: 127–49). While not limited to case study research, Bachelard's epistemology helps us to get a fuller and more coherent perspective on its contributions.

Second, Bachelard's epistemology is useful because it treats as inseparable the different dimensions of scientific practices and does not focus on one taken in isolation. It is not that the usual focus on data collection, theory testing and causal inference is wrong, but it is important to keep in mind that this is only one aspect of a social scientific investigation. These operations depend on other epistemological acts that should be evaluated as a whole and not separately. Yet, in an intellectual context dominated by a conception of epistemology that focuses on data collection and theory testing, it is difficult to find the categories, and reasons, that give their full epistemological meaning and value to the other epistemological acts. When we adjust the epistemological framework, it becomes clearer that case study research is not just a casual idea generator, and that it is not limited to theory development.

The French philosopher of science Gaston Bachelard (1884–1962) probed the epistemological implications of the transformation of scientific practices in chemistry, biology and physics, especially relativity theory and quantum physics (Bachelard 1934, 1938, 1949, 1971). He examined scientific thought, not so much in the static form of scientific theories, but by emphasizing the dynamic process of the experimental and theoretical practices of science (Tiles 1984: 9). His main concern was the creation, revision and rejection of scientific theories. Closely linking philosophy of science and history of science, he sought to reconstruct the philosophy implicit in the practice of scientists and to identify what he called their applied rationalism (Tiles 1984; Gayon and Wunenburger 2000; Wunenburger 2003; for an application of Bachelard's epistemology to the social sciences: Bourdieu, Chamboredon and Passeron 1968).

The central point of Bachelard's applied rationalism is that the different epistemological acts at the core of scientists' practice cannot be separated from one another. A data collection is only as good as the theoretical construct that it tests; in turn, the value of this theoretical construct depends on its capacity to break with common sense and to provoke a genuine epistemological rupture. Thus, on the one hand, Bachelard rejects the empiricist approach that focuses on the observational aspects of scientific activity, notably testing and data collection, in order to generalize the findings. On the other, he rejects the idealist conception, which ignores instrumented experiment altogether and recognizes no demand for systematic empirical testing of theories (Tiles 1984: 52–3). In short, for Bachelard a scientific fact is conquered, constructed and observed (*conquis, construit, constaté*; Bourdieu Chamboredon and Passeron 1968: 24, 81; Kratochwil, ch. 5).

On this basis, I argue that case studies should be conceived as contributing to each of these three epistemological acts, and not to one or the other in isolation. First, as a research strategy, case studies imply a break with the immediate experience that is highlighted by the question: 'What is this a case of?'. Researchers are not passive; they engage in 'casing', and in so doing they hope to overcome the epistemological obstacles that stem from conventional categorizations. Second, case studies are shaped by an explicit effort of theory construction. Third, case studies are not based only on assumptions about actors' goals and preferences. An in-depth empirical investigation using different types of data-gathering methods and procedures, like process tracing, is a key component of case study research.

Epistemological rupture, conceptualization and observation in case study research

'Casing' corresponds to Bachelard's first epistemological act: the rupture with conventional wisdom. Cases are not waiting out there to be studied. The process through which researchers delimit, define and describe cases contributes to carving an aspect of reality that is different from the ways in which the phenomenon, or the event, is taken for granted. Researchers make something into a case: they are 'casing' (Ragin 1992: 218). Casing takes place at various stages during the research, but especially at the beginning and at the end. A case study does not presuppose a relatively bounded phenomenon, nor is it based on the need to select such a phenomenon. The boundaries of the phenomenon are defined by the investigator. Quite often the process of 'casing' leads the researcher to define units of analysis in a way that is different from conventions, legal, bureaucratic or otherwise (Ragin 1992: 218–21). Thinking in terms of case means rendering problematic the relations between ideas and evidence. While it is possible to choose conventional casing to simplify some problematic relationships between theory and data, this choice is itself an aspect of the conceptualization. It can be a useful starting point, but in the course of the investigation the researcher can build categories and time frames and uncover new relations. If so, 'casing' becomes a way to break with conventional images of the social and political world.

The case is the product of a preliminary, and then of an ongoing, effort to define the object of study. The type of population under study is not given; it is a working hypothesis that is revised in the course of the research (Ragin 2000: 14, 43–63). In short, 'casing' implies a critical reflection on the conventional boundaries and commonly accepted categories of social and political phenomena. Furthermore, when we ask 'What is this a case of?', we are constructing a representation of the experience, or of the observation (Davis 2005: 81). The researcher is breaking with a commonsensical representation of a historical process, and she is conceptualizing a problem. The epistemological rupture and the conceptualization go together. The case is defined and constructed by a theoretical approach that provides a framework of hypotheses to probe the various aspects of the empirical data.

The theoretical framework that underlies case study research corresponds to Bachelard's second epistemological act: theory construction. Case study research implies a theoretical intention translated in a new vocabulary. A purely historical description differs from a social science approach to a case, converting historical information into a suitable analytical vocabulary that can be applied to other cases (George 1979; George and McKeown 1985; Walton 1992). The empirical analysis is based on this theoretical intention, which helps to define both the hypotheses and the data needed. It is also in this conceptualization that comparisons, ideal types and typologies play a role. This theoretical construction is not confined to the beginning of the investigation. The researcher revises his main concepts because he is learning from the cases that he has decided to examine (Ragin 2000: 31–2). In sum, the definition of the empirical category and the clarification of the relevant theoretical concepts are an element of the theoretical and empirical contributions of case study research, quite apart from the data generated, the interpretive insights and the capacity to evaluate theories empirically.

Process tracing is one possible way to translate into practice Bachelard's third epistemological act, the empirical observation. In their empirical inquiry, researchers use, and often combine, cross-case comparisons and within-case observations and methods. For within-case analysis, several options are available: congruence method, process tracing, and typological theory, which integrate comparative and within-case analysis (Elman 2005; George and Bennett 2005: 179, 181–204, 235; see also Mahoney 2000). Initially formulated by Alexander George, the notion of process tracing became increasingly widespread in case study research (George 1979; George and Bennett 2005: 205–6). George argued that a research strategy was needed to assess whether the correlations among variables discovered using statistical methods were causal or not (George 1979: 46). Process tracing is: 'a procedure for identifying steps in a causal process leading to the outcome of a given dependent variable of a particular case in a particular historical context' (George and Bennett 2005: 176; Steinmo, ch. 7; on the epistemological implications of a focus on sequences of actions, Favre 2005). Several notions like analytical narratives as used in a rational choice perspective (Bates, Greif, Levi *et al.* 1998; Rodrick 2003), or systematic process analysis (Hall 2003; see also Heritier, ch. 4) are close, if not virtually identical, to the notion of process tracing. Using process tracing, the researcher assesses a theory by identifying the causal chain(s) that link the independent and dependent variables. Her goal is to uncover the relations between possible causes and observed outcomes. This procedure can be used in theory testing as well as in theory development.

Because the notion of process tracing is by now widespread in political science, scholars have used it in a variety of ways: to discover a causal mechanism and show that a posited underlying mechanism connecting causal and dependent variables exists; to demonstrate the conjunction and the temporal sequence of variables; to increase the number of observable implications that a theory predicts; or to operationalize variables, measuring independent and dependent variables, by looking at the decision-making process to search for relevant evidence (Elman 1996: 17–18). How process tracing can be put to work and contribute to both positivist and interpretivist research designs is the question to which I now turn.

Bridging positivist and interpretivist approaches to process tracing

Process tracing in action

In *Case Studies and Theory Development in the Social Sciences*, George and Bennett, building on George's previous work (1979) as well as his collaborative contributions (George and Smoke 1974; George and McKeown 1985), give a systematic and comprehensive account of process tracing. Their reformulation is important because, until then, the notion was presented in a dispersed fashion. Now, the most common conceptions of process tracing are more standardized than the original formulation, and they emphasize the identification of a causal mechanism that connects independent and dependent variables (Mahoney 2000: 412–15; Bennett and Elman 2006: 459). The emphasis is on causality, deduction and causal mechanisms. However, something has been lost in the more recent formulations of process tracing. This is unfortunate, since process tracing can make an important contribution to both a positivist and an interpretivist empirical approach to case study research (Adler 2002: 109; Kacowitz 2004: 108–11; Davis 2005: 176–7; see also Dessler 1999; Finnemore 2003; Checkel 2006). Political phenomena have clock-like (regular, orderly, predictable), cloud-like (irregular, disorderly, unpredictable) and interacting (creative, adaptive, problem-solving) characteristics; process tracing can help to uncover all three of them (Almond and Genco 1977; Jervis 1997). Process tracing also provides an opportunity to combine positivist and interpretivist approaches in the making of a case study (Lin 1998: 166–9), allowing the researcher to explore both the causal 'what' and the causal 'how'.

In a positivist perspective, the main goal of process tracing is to establish and evaluate the link (or the absence of a link) between different factors (see Héritier, ch. 4). Through the use of histories, archival documents, interview transcripts and other sources, the investigator examines whether the causal process of the theory that he is using can be observed in the sequence and values of the intervening variables (Mahoney 2003; George and Bennett 2005: 6). Thus, the researcher can check whether the indicators used to measure the dependent and independent variables have been well chosen, including whether they resonate with the actors' beliefs and representations. He also examines critically the reliability of the data and its representativeness, in order to evaluate the relative importance of plausible causal factors. The researcher's focus is on learning whether a particular factor can be traced and linked to another.

In an interpretivist perspective, process tracing allows the researcher to look for the ways in which this link manifests itself and the context in which it happens. The focus is not only on what happened, but also on how it happened. It becomes possible to use process tracing to examine the reasons that actors give for their actions and behaviour and to investigate the relations between beliefs and behaviour (Jervis 2006). Process tracing is a fundamental element of empirical case study research because it provides a way to learn and to evaluate empirically the preferences and perceptions of actors, their purposes, their goals, their values and their specification of the situations that face them. Process tracing helps the researcher to uncover, directly and indirectly, what actors want, know and compute (Simon 1985: 295).

Confronted with the problem of the variety and complexity of human perceptions, preferences and motivations, two types of solutions are available (Simon 1985, 1986, 1995; Frieden 1999: 53–66; Scharpf 2006). One option is to make assumptions about actors' preferences and perceptions. The researcher relies on common-sense intuition or deductive reasoning and makes a judgement call on their plausible or reasonable character (Simon 1985: 297). Hence, there is no point in process tracing. The other option is to acknowledge that preferences and perceptions are empirical questions that only a painstaking empirical investigation can uncover (Simon 1985: 298, 300). From this perspective, it is not enough to add theoretical assumptions about the shape of the utility function, about the actor's expectations or about their attention to their environment. In social sciences, these assumptions must be submitted to a careful empirical test.

By using process tracing in this way, a connection that appears as only plausible, or *ad hoc*, can be integrated in a broader framework with a more consistent overall logic. This richer account appears coherent with the actors' frames of reference, even if it might appear less coherent outside of this framework. One of the strengths of process tracing is to help the researcher to flesh out causal mechanisms. For example, previous work experience is a significant factor in some people's exit from welfare in the United States (Lin 1998: 165). This previous experience is linked to employability. But how? Many plausible mechanisms can be embedded in the relation between previous work experience and the probability of exiting welfare. As Lin explains, previous work experience might signal to employers that one already has some relevant training or knowledge of the workplace. They might also see this experience as a sign of the employee's motivation. Alternatively, while employers might not care at all about work experience in and of itself, it may still matter because it is linked to something else that they see as important: recommendations from past employers. And there might be other possibilities that simply have not been identified in advance. To know which of those plausible mechanisms is at work, process tracing is invaluable. It might reveal that the causal mechanism that was assumed at the onset does not fit the empirical observations. This new knowledge would then feed back into theory development, showing the inductive potential of process tracing.

For some types of case studies, devoted to the study of norms, for example, uncovering the reasons that actors give for their actions is a key aspect of the empirical investigation (Amenta 1991: 179–80; Davis 2005: 179). The challenge is similar when researchers seek to uncover the kinds of problems that actors are trying to solve, and how they conceive solutions, their assumptions about their professional activities and their efforts to explain why their actions are reasonable and sensible. For example, this is what Lynn Eden did when she explained why and how, in the US Air Force, the 'blast damage frame', centring on damage from high-explosive conventional bombs, came to dominate the 'fire damage frame', emphasizing damage from incendiary bombs, in the understanding of the impact of nuclear weapons (Eden 2004; see also Evangelista 1999; Homer-Dixon 1999). Hence, process tracing helps the researcher to reconstitute the actors' beliefs and perspectives and to regroup them in a limited number of categories, keeping in mind the evaluation of broader theoretical arguments.

Process tracing based on intensive, open-ended interviewing, participant observation and document analysis helps to understand the meaning and role of established regularities, and can help to suggest ways to uncover previously unknown relations between factors. In the original formulation of process tracing, George was aware of this need to combine both perspectives. Process tracing, he explained, involved both reconstructing the ways in which the actors characterized the situation, and developing a theory of action (George and McKeown 1985: 35). Furthermore, the process that is uncovered does not have to be only causal, it can be constitutive as well – that is, accounting for the property of the phenomenon by reference to its structures and allowing the researcher to explain its conditions of possibility (Davis 2005: 175, 176). In his original formulation, George talked not only about a causal mechanism, but also of an intervening process, a causal nexus (George 1979: 46). Finally, it has become common to refer to the inductive use of process tracing in theory development. But in the original formulation, the resort to induction was broader. George underlined that to translate the historians' terms (or the actors' terms) and to evaluate the variance in the values of independent, intervening and dependent variables was a delicate operation. The loss of information and simplification could undermine the theory's validity and its usefulness. Consequently, the variance in each variable could be described inductively to check whether, and to what extent, a particular variable varies in different cases (George 1979: 47). Process tracing can be used to assess the relative impact of certain variables, but also to get a better sense of the actors' perceptions.

Is process tracing different from telling a story, however? There are different varieties of process tracing; some are close to a detailed narrative – similar to the type of narrative commonly found in the work of historians and anthropologists – while others rely more on broad causal explanations (Bennett and George 2001). In general, process tracing differs from a pure narrative in three ways (see also Flyvbjerg 2006: 237–41). First, process tracing is focused. It deals selectively with only certain aspects of the phenomenon. Hence, the investigator is aware that some information is lost along with some of the unique characteristics of the phenomenon. Second, process tracing is structured in the sense that the investigator is developing an analytical explanation based on a theoretical framework identified in the research design (these are the characteristics of the comparison, but they apply to process tracing as well: George 1979: 61). Third, the goal of process tracing is ultimately to provide a narrative explanation of a causal path that leads to a specific outcome.

Combining a positivist and an interpretivist perspective in process tracing is a stimulating opportunity, both theoretically and empirically. But it is important for policy reasons as well. Since the beginning of the twentieth century, case study research has had an important policy component. In their classic account of deterrence in American foreign policy, George and Smoke made an explicit link between theory and policy in international relations (1974: 616–42). Recognizing both dimensions of process tracing helps the transition from the recognition of causal patterns towards the discovery of solutions. For example, a correlation between variables might be significant but not subject to manipulation by policy-makers. No matter how well identified the cause–effect link, a policy needs the support and co-operation of stakeholders to be implemented in order to avoid unintended consequences and to facilitate implementation (Lin 1998: 168). Evaluating the material benefits or costs of a policy for a population means that the frames of reference to identify costs and benefits are themselves identified and known.

Finally, case study research, together with process tracing, can help to improve and refine the analogical reasoning of practitioners (May 1973; Neustadt and May 1986; George 1993).

In sum, a positivist perspective of process tracing helps to identify the existence of causal relations, to go beyond correlation and evaluate causality empirically (Dessler 1991). However, the positivist approach to process tracing faces difficulties in explaining how the mechanism implied in the causal relation actually works. The interpretivist perspective of process tracing leads to a detailed examination of the causal mechanism and explains how specific variables interact. This perspective, however, faces difficulties in weighting the relative importance of different factors.

Challenges and limits in case study research and process tracing

Process tracing as such is no guarantee that one will successfully conduct an empirical investigation. Case study research in general and process tracing in particular face four main challenges: the reliance on pre-existing theories; the assumption that each case can be treated autonomously and that the cases are distinct from one another; the need for empirical data; and the pitfalls of cognitive biases (see also Collier and Mahoney 2006; Checkel 2006: 367–9). While these limits are not all specific to case study and process tracing, they are particularly relevant in this type of research. The first limit regards theories. In case study research, the case selection, the comparison, the within-case analysis and the empirical investigation are all theory-dependent. Case study research and process tracing presuppose the existence of theoretical frameworks. These frameworks are supposed to guide the researcher in his approach, as in his empirical work. But time and again, case study specialists recognize that either those theoretical frameworks are lacking, or they are ill-suited, leaving the researcher vulnerable to an ethnocentric bias or forced to use an ill-adapted theory. When a theory does exist, it is often insufficiently specified and rarely tailored to the problem at hand. There can be elements of theories, dispersed or available in a primitive formulation, but they have to be rethought and redesigned. In such situations, which are fairly common, researchers are engaged in theory development and their contribution to case study and to process tracing remains significant.

Since at times there are not off-the-shelf theories ready to be evaluated – or the situation is uneven depending on subfields and research areas – it implies that most of those who do case studies are quasi-systematically engaged in theory development. Furthermore, the line between theory development and theory evaluation is often blurred. Many researchers want to do both: to contribute to the development of a theory, but also to propose a preliminary evaluation. Indeed, this is exactly what George and Smoke did in *Deterrence in American Foreign Policy* (1974; see also Vaughan 1992). It might be prudent to label this kind of work 'theory development', but the label is misleading, since the researcher is also evaluating theories. In sum, case study research and process tracing are heavily dependent on the existence of middle-range theories that provide a set of hypotheses – sometimes even broad guidelines rather than clearly formulated hypotheses, which serve as a guide for the conduct of the research. Yet, in many situations, researchers should keep in mind that they will have to contribute to this theoretical endeavour themselves. Off-the-shelf theories are likely to be either lacking completely, or inadequate to the task.

The second challenge has to do with the autonomy of each case. At the root of case study research is the assumption that cases, however defined by the researcher, are autonomous instances of something. They are distinct from one another and can be treated as separate units of analysis. However, some major social and political trends, like the European Union or the growing interconnectedness of the international system, for example, seem to put this assumption in question. Cases are often deeply connected to one another, even embedded in one another, and the task of the researcher becomes accounting for both the distinctive and the common dimensions of the cases.

The third challenge is related to empirical sources and their treatment. Case studies are dependent on the existence and accessibility of empirical sources. Process tracing can only work if a sufficiently high level of accuracy, and reliability, can be reached on specific processes and events. This is not a given, particularly for topics that involve confidentiality and secrecy, like a foreign policy decision or a counterterrorism policy. One can only highlight the importance of the diversity of empirical sources, and the need to allow sufficient time and resources in the research process for the collection and treatment of empirical data. It is also at this point that the knowledge and practice of various investigation techniques – content analysis, participant observation, interviews, statistical methods, and so on – become significant (see Bray, ch. 15; Checkel 2006: 366–7).

The fourth challenge – common to any type of social science research – has to do with cognitive biases, which can alter the researcher's reasoning and skew his results (Tetlock 2005). Three biases, in particular, are worth mentioning regarding case study research and process tracing. First, the confirmation bias: in the course of process tracing, the researcher might seek information that confirms her beliefs and gloss over what could contradict them (George and Bennett 2005: 217). This bias can affect the ways in which the researcher plans to collect information, what she pays attention to, what she reports and does not report. Second, the results of process tracing might be consistent with too many theories. It then becomes difficult to assess whether alternative explanations are complementary or if some are just spurious (Njolstad 1990). Third, negative evidence might be ignored. Since positive evidence is more striking and vivid than its absence, in tracing the process, the researcher overlooks the things that do not happen.

Regarding the confirmation bias, the best strategy is an explicit effort to consider alternative hypotheses that could lead to the outcome in question through the process of interest. Focusing on other theories and hypotheses can help, as well as on counterfactuals, which can be a powerful tool to challenge our pre-existing theories (Weber 1996: 270; Davis 2005: 168–75, and more generally Tetlock and Belkin 1996). The key question here is: 'What else can it be?' To answer, the researcher might use insights mentioned in the literature, in the memoirs of participants, or in interviews, for example. To probe the argument, the comparative analysis of process tracing can be useful as well. Perhaps the factors that the researcher considers to have generated the expected consequences were present in cases in which the consequences did not happen.

Regarding the overdetermination problem, the aim is to find ways to reduce the number of explanations. Some evidence consistent with the researcher's interpretation can be coherent with other interpretations as well. There are several suggestions for dealing with such a situation: clarify potential conflict of interpretations about the evidence; clarify whether competing explanations address different aspects of a case; compare various cases; and identify the scope conditions for explanations of a case (Njolstad 1990).

Finally, regarding negative evidence, case study research and process tracing can be useful in helping to identify situations in which a specified behaviour does not occur, or in which evidence is absent. This is significant if an important proposition or argument implies that some type of evidence should be present. One way to evaluate a proposition is to ask what events should occur and what evidence should be observable if this argument or explanation is correct (Jervis 2006: 26). In-depth case studies can uncover non-events and their characteristics, for example in the relations between democracy and peace, or in deterrence success (Maoz 2002: 457).

In sum, researchers doing case studies and using process tracing should think about the answers to the following questions (George and Bennett 2005: 105–6): how can I show my readers that I did not impose my favoured theory as the explanation? Do I consider alternative theories, and is this explicit? How do I explain that the cases that I selected constitute an easy, or a tough, test for the theory? Do case findings really support the theory in question? How do my readers know? Do the findings support other theories as well? Is it a problem and, if so, how do I deal with it?

Conclusion: Problem-solving and case studies

When he met political scientist Richard Neustadt at the White House, former Secretary of State Dean Acheson famously grumbled: 'I know your theory, you think Presidents should be warned. You're wrong. Presidents should be given confidence' (quoted in Steinbruner 1974: 332). Similarly, researchers should be given confidence in the epistemological and methodological contributions of case study research. Confidence does not mean that anything goes, nor that overconfidence is warranted, however (Rueschemeyer 2003). Just like any other research strategy, case studies have limits and can be done well or poorly. Researchers should be aware of the theoretical and methodological assumptions embedded in the very idea of doing a case study, and make full use of this methodology.

This examination of case study research and process tracing confirmed the discrepancies between case study theorizing and case study practices. When practitioners attempt to codify their epistemological and methodological practice, in order to make sense of it and/or to teach it, they often seem to lose something of the creativity, ingenuity and flexibility that was the trademark of their practice. Finally, as in any epistemological and methodological discussion, we should not confuse ends and means. Problems and problem-solving are the core of social science research. Methods are important, and they should help researchers in various ways. Ultimately, however, they cannot substitute for a 'passionate curiosity about a great problem, the sort of curiosity that compels the mind to travel anywhere and by any means, to re-make itself if necessary, in order *to find out*' (Mills 1959: 105).

13 Quantitative analysis

Mark Franklin

Quantification is one way of employing the scientific method to discover things about the world. In the social sciences we are trying to discover things about the social world, but the approach we use can still be regarded as scientific. The scientific approach attempts to abstract from the nuances and details of a story the salient features that can be built up into a theoretical statement (or statements) expected to hold true of any situation that can be defined in terms of the same abstractions. If such a theoretical statement does not hold true in some specific situation, this is presumed to be either because the theory was wrong or because it was not sufficiently elaborated. Elaborating social theories to bring in additional features of the world, found necessary for a full explanation, is an important feature of the scientific approach; but for elaboration to progress very far we need to employ quantitative analysis, as this chapter will try to show.

The transition from case studies to quantitative analysis is largely a matter of the number of cases. If you have one case, no causal inferences can be made. If you have two cases, you can rule out something as a necessary condition for something else. If you have three cases you can rule out two things, or you can start to make quantitative statements (for example, something might be found to pertain two-thirds of the time). As soon as you start saying things like 'this happens two-thirds of the time' you are doing quantitative analysis. But in order to make such statements you need to be able to abstract general features that are common to many cases, which tends to require a more elaborate theoretical basis for a quantitative study than for a case study. You also need a fairly large number of cases.

Exactly what constitutes 'fairly large' in the above statement is not at all clear, and in practice there is a large area of overlap in which one researcher would talk of a 'multiple case study' while another would talk of a 'small-N study' (the letter N in the quantitative tradition stands for 'number of cases'; as soon as you see cases referred to in that way, you know you are reading something written in the quantitative tradition).

Table 13.1. Governance and social networks

	Multiple social networks going back to C12	Lack of social networks even today
High-quality democratic governance	Northern Italy	
Poor governance		Southern Italy

Source: Adapted from Putnam (1993).

Table 13.2. Governance and social networks (after additional studies)

	Multiple social networks going back to C12	Lack of social networks even today
High-quality democratic governance	2	0
Poor governance	1	3

So whether you do case studies or quantitative studies depends, over a large area of overlap, on what tradition you are working in rather than on what you are doing. Consider an example from Robert Putnam's (1993) study of democracy in Italy (Table 13.1). This rather famous example[1] was called into question only a few years later by a Harvard PhD thesis that looked at French regions and found a case of poor governance even where there were long-standing social networks. What to do? One possibility would be to conduct additional studies in the hope of discovering that either the French or the Italian findings were happenstansical – so unusual as to be not worth worrying about. One might, after a lot of work, come up with Table 13.2, where two cases of high-quality governance and three cases of poor governance match Putnam's findings, while the exception found in the just-mentioned thesis earlier turns out to be the only one.

That seems pretty definitive: Putnam's findings hold true far more often than not. Moreover, we can express the findings in terms of a condition that appears to be necessary for good governance (no examples of high-quality governance in Table 13.2 occur without it), even if that condition is not sufficient to ensure good governance.

It would, of course, be far more interesting to discover *why* the exception occurred, which would mean using the additional cases to see whether some other condition accounted for the exception. If we could find a magic ingredient (call it entrepreneurship) that accounted for the difference, we could make Table 13.3. This more elaborate test lets us see that there are actually two conditions, both of which must be present for high-quality democratic

Table 13.3. Entrepreneurship and networks

	Entrepreneurship		No entrepreneurship	
	Networks	Lack of networks	Networks	Lack of networks
High-quality governance	2	0	0	0
Poor governance	0	1	1	2

Table 13.4. Territorial policy communities

	Multiple social networks			
	Yes		No	
Political entrepreneurship	Brittany	✓	Languedoc	✗
	Tuscany	✓		
Lack of entrepreneurship	Aquitaine	✗	Provence	✗
			Liguria	✗

Source: Smyrl 1997.

governance: the one found necessary by Putnam, and an additional condition he knew nothing about, which appears to be responsible for the exceptional French case. The additional condition turns out to be a second necessary condition for high-quality governance; entrepreneurship without multiple networks does not yield high-quality governance any more than do multiple networks without entrepreneurship.

Let me put the actual names of the regions concerned into a simpler table where the two conditioning variables determine where each region appears in the table, and the quality of governance in each region is indicated by a tick or a cross (Table 13.4). Even though both tables let us use the same logic of inference, Table 13.4 is the sort one would expect to see in a multiple case study, whereas Table 13.3 is the sort one would expect to see in a quantitative analysis. (In Table 13.4 I use the terminology of the author of the thesis.)

Of course, with only six cases, it is hard to be sure that one has exhausted the possibilities. Additional exceptions may lurk around the next corner, and additional conditions might need to be taken into account. But it is pretty obvious that to discover more one would need a great many additional cases, and with a great many additional cases the format used in Table 13.3 becomes more useful than that in Table 13.4. If we had dozens of names in Table 13.4 instead of only six, the information would not be very useful if presented in that format. With more than about ten cases, it becomes helpful to use numbers to summarize what you have learned, trading off specificity for generality. But with small-N studies, what you can say with numbers is still quite limited. From this perspective, the next important watershed comes with the transition to 'large-N studies', where you can bring to bear the full power of what is called 'multivariate analysis'. Again, there is no fixed boundary. Small-N studies shade into large-N studies at somewhere between 30 and 300 cases, with progressively more powerful analyses being possible as N increases.

So what can be done with small-N studies that cannot be done with case studies, and what can be done with large-N studies but not with small-N studies? Essentially we can say that, as the number of cases goes up, so the researcher is better able to:

(a) specify the conditions under which causal effects are felt (how widespread they are);

(b) specify the nature of the causal effects (how strong they are);

(c) specify how likely it is that the effects are real rather than happenstansical (how significant they are).

The vocabulary of quantitative research

The distinctions I have just made (among widespread, strong and significant causal effects) brings us to the main difficulty involved in quantitative analysis. To be able to talk quantitatively, one has to be able to make distinctions that to most people do not come naturally. Many of these distinctions, and the words used to make them, sound rather arbitrary. In ordinary English, the distinctions among strong, widespread and significant are not obvious. All appear to be variants on the word 'important'. That is true, but, as with the (perhaps apocryphal) fifty different words that the Inuit have for 'snow', distinctions that appear unimportant from some points of view can seem very important from other points of view.

In brief, a presumed causal effect is strong if it appears to have extensive effects. It is widespread if it occurs in many different circumstances and situations, and it is significant if it is unlikely to be spurious or happenstansical. When talking about accidents we use much the same vocabulary, distinguishing between a freak accident that probably will never happen again and one that is significant because it is part of a predictable pattern. But even a significant accident might have small or restricted consequences. Alternatively, its consequences could be major and/or widespread.

There is quite a lot of vocabulary to be learned in order to be able to talk sensibly about quantitative social research findings, or to make sense of the literature that uses this vocabulary. In the rest of this chapter, I will go through some of the more important words concerned. Clearly, learning to do quantitative social research involves somewhat more than just learning the vocabulary. There are some corresponding skills, but I have always found that the vocabulary confuses people, rather than the skills. You may find it helpful to take a sheet of paper and write down the words in quotation marks that follow, to have a crib sheet to use as you move forward.

Sources of quantitative information

Quantitative information can be collected in exactly the same way as any other information: by means of interviews (in the quantitative tradition these are generally called 'surveys') or by looking it up in compendia of various kinds (or on the Internet). Although there is no logical reason why this should always be true, surveys generally involve 'sampling' (we select a subgroup to interview because there are too many individuals for us to interview them all), whereas information that we look up is generally exhaustive (we can obtain data for the whole 'universe' of cases that interest us). It is important to know whether information was gathered from a sample rather than from a universe, because samples are subject to error when we try to generalize beyond the sample. This, of course, is equally true for many case studies, where the possibility of an 'unrepresentative case' is synonymous with a 'bad sample'; but there are certain types of sample ('probability samples') for which it is possible to use statistical methods to generalize beyond the sample with a known probability that the generalization will be true. This is a very powerful feature of 'random samples' that is unavailable to those who select their cases in other ways; in the case study tradition it is, strictly speaking, impossible to say how indicative a case might be. Most surveys are based on random sampling. Although there are different types of random sample, which need to be distinguished in practice, such distinctions are beyond the scope of this introduction.

The dataset and data matrix

As soon as one starts talking about quantitative information, one is forced to start talking about data. Data (the word is plural – treating data as a collective noun is common but wrong) arise from standardized information. In this sense, a biographical compendium contains data, because the characteristics of each individual are presented in a standard form: gender, birthdate, schools attended, and so on. A dataset goes further in coding the standardized data, generally in numerical terms (e.g. 1=female, 2=male) and providing a dictionary or 'codebook' with which to interpret the codes. When organized in this way, the codebook is conceptually distinct from the 'data matrix', which is a table organized with different cases in different rows. Across the table are columns, each column containing a particular characteristic (such as gender, age, income, or party voted for). These are known as 'variables'. By looking at the intersection of a particular row with a particular column, one can read off the particular characteristic or 'value' associated with a particular case. Thus if turnout at a European Parliament election were to be the variable in the third column of the table (Table 13.5) and France were the case in the fourth row, then by looking across the fourth row to the third column one would find that French turnout was 60.7 per cent at that election.

Variables and levels of measurement

Talking about variables is complicated by the fact that there are different types of variable. Implicitly we have already mentioned two types: variables like gender, where the values ascribed are quite arbitrary, and variables like age, where the values ascribed have an intrinsic meaning (age is generally measured in years). In the case of a 'nominal' variable like gender, men could as easily be coded '1' and women '2' as the other way around – or the two possible values could be coded 'M' and 'F'. All we are doing with a nominal variable is distinguishing the characteristics that can apply to different cases in terms of that variable – the values we employ do no more than name the characteristics (hence 'nominal' from the Latin for 'name'). But with 'interval' variables like age, the intervals between the values are meaningful (a year or a dollar, or some other 'unit of measurement').

Two more levels of measurement are important to social science researchers. Variables can be 'ordinal' if the values have an order that is implied by their numeric values (5 is bigger than 4) even if there is no unit of measurement; and they can be 'dummy variables' if all they do is indicate the presence or absence of some characteristic (for example, 0=not British, 1=British). When the data come from a survey of individual people, the most common variables are nominal and ordinal, whereas the variables we really want in order to be able to conduct multivariate analyses (see below) are interval. A lot of time and

Table 13.5. European Election turnout (1)

Data matrix

Country	Electn	EPturnout	Natturnout	Yrsleft	Compuls	First
bri	1979	32.2	76	4	0	1
den	1979	47.8	86	0.36	0	1
bel	1979	90.4	95	2.4	1	1
fra	1979	60.7	83	2	0	1
ger	1979	65.7	91	1.3	0	1
gre	1981	82.2	82	0	1	1
ire	1979	63.6	76	2	0	1
ita	1979	84.9	91	4	1	1
lux	1979	88.9	89	0	1	1
net	1979	57.8	88	2	0	1
bri	1984	32.6	73	3	0	0
den	1984	52.4	88	3.2	0	0
bel	1984	92.2	95	1.3	1	0
fra	1984	56.7	71	1.7	0	0
ger	1984	56.8	89	2.6	0	0
gre	1984	82.2	82	0.96	1	0
ire	1984	47.6	73	2.7	0	0
ita	1984	83.4	89	3	1	0
lux	1984	88.8	89	0	1	0
net	1984	50.6	81	1.9	0	0
por	1984	72.4	73	0	0	1
spa	1984	68.9	70	2.4	0	1

Codebook

Variables	Meaning (and values)
Country	Three-character country ID
Electn	Date of election (year)[1]
EPturnout	Turnout at European Parliament election (per cent)
Natturnout	Turnout at previous national election (per cent)
Yrsleft	Years to next national election (years and parts of years)
Compuls	Compulsory voting at time of EP election (0=no; 1=yes)
First	First EP election held in country (0=no; 1=yes)

[1] Note that Greece, which held its first EP elections in 1981, is generally not distinguished from the 1979 election countries.

effort is expended by researchers in 'transforming' their data to overcome this problem. The solution generally adopted in political science research is to treat ordinal variables as interval (provided they have enough categories) and to recode nominal variables into their dummy counterparts, which can be regarded as honorary interval variables with a unit of measurement that is the

Table 13.6. Types of variable

Level of measurement	Example	Additional information contained
Interval variable[1]	43% Lab; 10% Lib Dem; 47% Con	Quantity (Con is 4% more than Lab)
Ordinal variable	1=Lab, 2=Lib Dem, 3=Con	Order (left–right relative location)
Nominal variable	1=Lab, 2=Con, 3=Lib Dem	Mutual exclusivity
Dummy variable	0=Not Labour; 1=Labour	n.a.

Note:
[1] Sometimes interval variables are further distinguished into those with a 'real zero point' which are called 'ratio scale' variables, but the distinction is not needed in the social sciences.

presence or absence of the attribute in question. This takes quite a lot of skill but, done properly, does not do violence to the data.[2]

In Table 13.6, not only do we see examples of different types of variables, but we also see a summary of the additional information needed to code a variable at a higher level than the level below it in the table; this is also the additional information imparted by such a coding. Dummy variables can be thought of as having the lowest level of information – the presence or absence of an attribute. Descriptions made in ordinary language generally consist of strings of attributes ('the man has blue eyes'). Talking of attributes enables us to string together different attributes of the same type ('the man has one blue eye and one green eye'). As soon as we move up to the nominal level, we assert that the attributes are mutually exclusive; one is allowed to vote only for a single political party, so a code of Conservative implies not Labour and not Liberal Democrat. By taking an additional step to the ordinal level, we introduce some additional concept that enables us to order the values – and also introduces the possibility of miscoding the variable according to this concept, as in the example in the table, where commentators argue about whether Labour and Liberal Democrat have recently swapped places in left–right terms.

Talking about variables requires us to make one further distinction, between variables we are trying to explain (dependent variables) and variables we are using in order to explain them (independent variables). In the example we used earlier, quality of democratic governance was the dependent variable because we were trying to answer the question 'What does the quality of governance depend on?'. Extensiveness of networks and the availability of entrepreneurial talent were independent variables because we were not (in that analysis) asking what they depended on. (Note that in some other piece of research one or other of those variables might very well be treated as dependent if, for example, we wanted to know what the availability of entrepreneurial talent depends on).

Units and levels of analysis

Qualitative as well as quantitative analysis can focus on many different types of entity. One may analyse countries, years, regions, cities, schools, people or events – and much more. The entities we analyse are referred to as the units of analysis, or cases. The number of cases is referred to by the symbol N, as already mentioned. Units of analysis can be distinguished by the level of analysis at which they fall: the national unit is at a higher level than the city unit, which in turn is at a higher level than the individual who lives in that city and country. In Table 13.6, the example given of an interval variable is of a variable measured at a higher level, not only of measurement but also of analysis. To be able to say that Labour received 43 per cent of the vote, one has to be talking about an aggregation of individuals (most likely all of those voting at a particular election in a particular country) rather than of a particular individual. Because higher levels of analysis so often involve information about multiple individuals, the data concerned are often referred to as 'aggregate data'. The other examples in the table are ambiguous as to level of analysis (they could refer to political parties as easily as to individuals), but it is likely that they are variables measured at the individual level of analysis.

Although it is possible to investigate research questions that involve units at different levels of analysis, it is important to be clear about how these units are related to each other. This is just as true in qualitative as in quantitative studies, but with large-N studies it is easier to become confused about the level of analysis of different components of the study. The most important thing to realize about the level of analysis is that the types of variable we find at different levels tend to be different. I already mentioned that with individual-level data we get very few interval variables; in order to find an example of an interval-level variable relating to parties, I had to move up to an aggregate level of analysis. In addition, individual-level data generally contain a huge amount of error or 'noise'. People make mistakes when answering survey questions or when filling in forms. People fail to understand the questions they are asked or the meaning of the answers that they give. Most important, there is always a disjunction between the person who designs the questions (and hence the coding scheme for those questions) and the person who answers them (thus implicitly providing the values that will be coded). For this reason the questions often fail to communicate exactly the meaning intended. All of this results in error. There is generally much less error in higher-level data because individual-level error is averaged out during the process of aggregation. We are also much more likely to find interval variables in aggregate data because the very act of aggregation yields variables that count the number (or proportion or percentage) of individuals in different categories or with different characteristics. The percentage voting Conservative (an aggregate phenomenon) is very definitely an interval variable, whereas the same variable at the individual level (voted Conservative) is a nominal variable, as we have already seen.

This might sound like a good reason to focus on aggregate rather than individual-level data, but there is a problem about deducing individual-level behaviour from aggregate-level data or vice versa. For instance, discovering that US states characterized by a high proportion of blacks in the population are states with a high proportion of illiteracy does not allow us to infer that blacks are more likely to be illiterate. In a famous article (Robinson 1950) it was found that in such states there was no difference between the literacy rates of whites and blacks. Both were less likely to be literate in states characterized by a high proportion of blacks. The error of inferring individual-level relationships from aggregate-level findings is called the 'ecological fallacy'. There is a corresponding 'individualistic fallacy' in inferring aggregate-level relationships from individual-level relationships. For example, the strong positive relationship found at the individual level between education and voting does not translate into a corresponding positive relationship at the national level. To the contrary, the two countries with among the best education systems on earth (the United States and Switzerland) have among the lowest rates of voter turnout (Franklin 2004).

So data need to be collected and analysed at the level of analysis appropriate to the research question that is being asked, and analysts should avoid making generalizations at a different level of analysis from the level of the data that gave rise to the findings. This requirement is an instance of a more general requirement, common to all types of investigation (quantitative or qualitative), of thinking carefully about how variables are measured and about the inferences that can be made from different types of variable used in different ways. Measurement error is always a threat to inference, whether in qualitative or quantitative work (see King, Keohane and Verba 1994).

Statistics

In order to talk about quantitative research findings, one needs to use statistics. Technically speaking, statistics are 'coefficients' that summarize things of interest about data. Statistics are also the procedures by which one arrives at such coefficients, generally referred to by those who do it as 'statistical analysis'. A percentage or an average is a statistical coefficient (generally referred to as a 'descriptive statistic' because it describes a body of data), but much more interesting to social scientists are coefficients that address the questions summarized earlier: How widespread? How strong? How significant? We will start with the last of these.

How significant?

'Significance' relates to the chances of being wrong when making some assertion. Statistical methods allow us to determine the chances of being wrong about conclusions reached from a random sample. By extension, most researchers apply these methods to any dataset for which there is no reason to doubt its representative nature. Questions of significance can be applied to what are called 'point estimates' (for example, statistics can tell us how likely it is that we are wrong if we estimate that the Democrats will win 53 per cent of the two-party vote at the next US presidential election); but much more interesting to social scientists are questions about the significance of a relationship between variables. If we take the example, used earlier, of the relationship between the extent of policy networks and the quality of governance, it would be worth knowing the chances that the relationships found by Putnam and Smyrl are significant ones – that is, that they are unlikely to be the result of happenstance and are thus likely to be found again and again as we look at other regions and countries.

Whether a relationship is significant depends on three things:
(1) the strength of the relationship;
(2) the number of cases investigated when establishing the relationship;
(3) the degree of certitude required before we are willing to accept a statement as true.

Starting with the last of these, if we require 100 per cent certitude (generally referred to as 'confidence'), it will follow that no relationship is significant. Virtually all social science statements are probabilistic by nature (whether discovered using quantitative or qualitative methods). The industry standard in the quantitative social sciences is to accept a statement as true if it is likely to be correct in 95 per cent of the instances to which it might be generalized, which is the same as saying that the statement will be false in 5 per cent of these instances – for which reason it is referred to as 'significance at the 0.05 level'.

Note that this is not a very stringent test. If 5 per cent of situations to which a finding might be generalized will fail to show the relationship concerned, this means that one in twenty situations will fail to show it. Equally, if we cannot establish a finding at the 0.05 level of significance, then there is still a one in twenty chance that the relationship in question is nevertheless real. If we want greater certitude, we need to conduct a more stringent test; for instance, requiring significance at the 0.01 level, which would imply being wrong only once in a hundred times when generalizing from the finding. But for this we need more cases, as will now be explained.

If we want to be able to assert that there is a relationship between the extensiveness of social or policy networks and the quality of democratic governance, the more cases we have investigated in arriving at that assertion, the better. If we examined every single relevant case and found that all of them showed the same relationship, we would be pretty confident about our assertion. With a proper random sample of cases, we can say how confident we are that all the unexamined cases would show the same relationship as that found among the cases that were investigated. Enough cases can render any relationship significant at any non-zero level of significance, so with enough cases the question of significance ceases to be very interesting; but in general, the more cases the better.

However, it is also important to realize that, even with a relatively small N, relationships can prove significant if they are strong enough, which is the third thing needed for significance (the first one as listed above). As should already be clear, it takes many cases to establish that a weak relationship is significant, while a very strong relationship can be established even with relatively few cases. In the unusual situation where we expect definitive relationships of the kind 'all X's are Y's' or 'no X is ever a Y', we only need enough cases to rule out measurement error. If we expect to find a less deterministic relationship (and most relationships in the social sciences are probabilistic rather than deterministic, as mentioned), then we need more cases in order to be confident of our findings.

How strong?

To determine how strong a relationship is, we must determine the amount of change in the dependent variable that is brought about by change(s) in the independent variable(s). A small change is much more likely to be happenstantical than a large change, but more importantly, a small change is not very interesting even if it were to prove significant. When talking about strengths

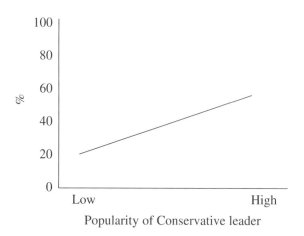

Fig. 13.1   Chances of a Conservative electoral victory

of relationships it helps to think of a graph that has the dependent variable arrayed up and down the vertical axis and an independent variable arrayed along the horizontal axis. For a given movement across the horizontal axis we can then read off the corresponding movement up the vertical axis, as shown in Figure 13.1.

In that graph, we see the chances of a Conservative victory increasing from only 20% to about 60% as the popularity of the Conservative leader increases from low to high. This corresponds to a 40% difference (60% – 20%, or an 'effect' of 0.4, since effects are generally expressed as proportions). One can think of the slope of the line in terms of the leverage it shows the independent variable having on the dependent variable. An almost flat line corresponds to very little leverage. A strongly sloping line corresponds to much more leverage. An effect of 0.4 gives quite a lot of leverage. By contrast, it is clear that an effect of only 0.04 (4%) would yield a line that was almost flat – a line with almost no leverage. A downward slope is also possible and would indicate a negative relationship: increasing values of the independent variable would correspond to decreasing values of the dependent variable.

The relationship shown in a table (such as those we used earlier) can easily be converted to a graph such as the one in Figure 13.1 by percentaging the table in the direction of the dependent variable. Thus, in Table 13.2 above (the first of those relating to Putnam's theory that contained any numbers), the dependent variable (quality of governance) runs down; so we percentage down and find that 67% of regions with extensive social networks (2 out of 3) see high-quality governance, whereas 0% of regions without extensive networks see high-quality governance. Subtracting, we find that social networks make a difference of $67 - 0 = 67\%$ to the quality of governance (i.e. social networks have an effect on governance of 0.67). That is a pretty strong effect on a scale that goes from 0 to 1 which, if turned into a graph, would show a slope even steeper than the one depicted in Figure 13.1. The steepness of the slope in this example corresponds to our intuition that a single exception to Putnam's asserted rule does not amount to much; but the small number of cases would preclude even so strong an effect from being statistically significant even if the cases had been chosen randomly.

Correlations between variables

At this point, we need to take a brief detour to talk about correlations. Rather than referring to the effect of one variable on another, when dealing with only two variables social scientists often talk about the 'correlation' between them, generally denoted by the symbol r (or sometimes R). R stands for 'relationship', and talking about relationships between variables does not require us to distinguish between dependent and independent variables. Two variables are related if their values tend to move together (taller people tend to be heavier so there is a relationship between height and weight). There is also said to be a relationship – a negative relationship – if two variables tend to move inversely (the thicker the clouds, the dimmer the daylight). If both variables are scaled between 0 and 1 (or, in general, both are measured on the same scale), then measures of correlation will take on approximately the same values as the effects we have been talking about. The effects of 0.4 and 0.67 to which we have referred would correspond to correlations of 0.4 and 0.67, or very nearly. Correlations are preferable for some purposes, however, because the value of a correlation coefficient does not depend on the scale of measurement of the variables concerned. If we were investigating the relationship between age in years and income in euros, the effect of age on income would certainly be far greater than 1.0 (a one-year increase in age would generally result in several hundred more euros in income) and would be hard to interpret, whereas the correlation coefficient would be somewhere in the range -1.0 to $+1.0$, just like the coefficients we have been discussing. Table 13.7 shows the approximate substantive meaning to be ascribed to correlation coefficients of different magnitudes when using individual-level and aggregate data (boundaries are not hard and fast and would be disputed by some analysts).

Table 13.7. Strength of correlation

Strength of correlation	Interpretation with individual-level data	Interpretation with aggregate data
r/R = 0.00–0.06	Trivial	Trivial
r/R = 0.07–0.19	Slight	Trivial
r/R = 0.20–0.34	Moderate	Slight
r/R = 0.35–0.49	Strong	Moderate
r/R = 0.50–0.65	Spectacular	Strong
r/R = 0.66–0.80	Highly spectacular	Very strong
r/R = 0.81–0.95	Suspect	Spectacular
r/R = 0.96–1.00	Very suspect	Suspect

Note: Interpretations apply to *r* for bivariate analysis, R^2 for multivariate analysis (see below).

As stated earlier, it is difficult to find strong relationships using individual-level data because those who design the question categories are generally not those who answer the questions, so that any number of misunderstandings can result. Also, individuals are frequently quite uncertain about how to answer even questions that they correctly understand, and often cannot be bothered to think carefully about their answers. This results in a great deal of error that is largely absent from aggregate data, or is averaged out when individual-level information is aggregated. Thus, we expect stronger correlations (and stronger effects) with aggregate data than with individual-level data. Indeed, individual-level correlations above 0.8 are so unusual as to generally suggest that something about the analysis was done wrongly, or something about the data is not quite right. Very often in such cases the analyst has employed two variables that are in reality different measures of the same thing, so that the finding is tautological. With aggregate data, correlations above 0.9 are quite attainable (though unusual), and only correlations above about 0.95 suggest the testing of tautological relationships.

How widespread?

The extent to which a relationship is widespread is a matter of the number of situations in which it is found. A relationship found only where there are extensive social networks is less widespread than one which is also found where social networks are absent. Establishing how widespread is a relationship requires the use of multiple independent variables in order to specify the different circumstances in which that relationship does or does not hold. In the Putnam example we started with, the relationship between networks and governance held only in the case where entrepreneurship was present, so this relationship proved not to be as widespread as originally supposed by Putnam. A relationship that holds only in certain circumstances is said to be subject to an 'interaction'. In this case there was an interaction between entrepreneurship and the extent of social networks, such that each had its effect only in the presence of the other. In order to test for interaction effects it is necessary to employ a great many independent variables, one for each of the circumstances in which an effect might or might not be found to hold true. But we need multiple independent variables for another reason as well, to which we now turn.

Multivariate analysis

So far, except when examining the Putnam thesis, we have been talking only about so-called 'bivariate' relationships: relationships that may be found when a single dependent variable is examined in relation to a single independent variable. It is unusual to be able to explain much about the world with bivariate relationships, partly because there is so much error in our data (especially in our individual-level data) – error that often needs to be measured and specified in order to correctly estimate the effects of the variables of interest.[3] More importantly, the social world is a complex place. All the circumstances that might affect how widespread a relationship is (as just explained) may also contribute to an explanation of the dependent variable of interest. When we bring additional independent variables to bear in this way we are said to be 'elaborating' our explanation, as mentioned in the opening paragraph of this chapter. Indeed, the need to take account of multiple simultaneous effects on a dependent variable occurs in practice more frequently than the need to take account of interaction effects. But as soon as we move beyond bivariate analysis we need new tools for thinking about relationships, and when we use such tools we are said to be performing 'multivariate analysis'.

Strictly speaking, the analysis we performed in Tables 13.3 and 13.4 were multivariate analyses because more than a single independent variable was involved. However, the tools we used (tables, percentages, percentage differences) were the tools of bivariate analysis. When we move to multivariate analysis proper we need to think of effects in terms of equations, and this is another step that many budding social scientists find quite daunting – unless it is explained to them that equations are perfectly straightforward tools that everyone uses implicitly every time they add up the charges they expect to incur on their next mobile phone bill.

A typical mobile phone bill has a total that is the result of taking a standing monthly charge and adding to it an amount for calls in excess of some maximum, perhaps an amount for roaming, perhaps an amount for taxes, and so on. The result is a sum that can be spelled out as an equation such as:

$$\text{Total due} = \text{standing charge} + \text{minutes}^*\text{charge}_{\text{per minute}}$$
$$+ \text{roaming}^*\text{charge}_{\text{per roaming minute}}$$

(perhaps with another component for taxes). In the equation, the plus sign signifies addition and the asterisk signifies multiplication. People find it fairly straightforward to multiply the number of minutes by the charge per minute and the number of roaming minutes by the charge per roaming minute and add those two products to the standing charge. What gives them trouble is when the words used in the above equation are replaced with symbols, as in the following:

$$Y = a + b_1 X_1 + b_2 X_2$$

Here the total due is replaced by the symbol Y, the standing charge by the symbol a, the number of excess minutes by the symbol X with a subscript of 1, and the number of roaming minutes by the symbol X with a subscript of 2. Each b is the charge per minute for the corresponding number of minutes (again with the appropriate subscript).

The use of symbols in place of words looks quite cumbersome but is actually very powerful. By convention we always use the symbol Y to stand for the dependent variable and X (with different subscripts) to stand for different independent variables. Each b measures the effect of the relevant X on the dependent variable. The symbol a is always used to denote a constant, which might be zero if, in an example such as the telephone bill, there was no standing charge. Evidently we can extend the equation with many more X's without running out of space on the line, and we can talk conceptually about what we are doing without having to use any specific examples of actual variables. In the Putnam example, we could write the equation that we were implicitly evaluating exactly as above, where Y stands for the quality of democratic governance, X_1 for the extent of social/political networks and X_2 for the availability of entrepreneurship. In practice, in this example the constant (a) term was implicitly zero because the quality of governance was so poor in the absence of the two necessary conditions.[4] Note that we cannot actually estimate the effects inherent in Table 13.2 without considerable gyrations. The only effect we calculated – the 0.67 effect of networks on quality in the case where entrepreneurship was available – is what is called a 'partial effect', an effect that applies only in a specified circumstance.

In order to calculate effects of independent variables on dependent variables in a multivariate analysis, several methods are available; but the most widely used is called 'regression analysis'.

Regression analysis

This type of analysis gets its name, in a most unlikely way, from the fact that it was developed by geneticists to study the way in which offspring who are taller or shorter than their parents tend themselves to have children whose height 'regresses towards the mean'. In this brief introduction there is no need for us to explain how the calculations are performed. All that is necessary is to know that, for any given dependent variable Y, regression analysis produces values for the constant a, and for each of the b's used in investigating the relationships concerned. The analyst must supply the data for Y and for each of the X's, which will generally be contained in a data matrix such as the one presented earlier. Using those same data, from Table 13.5, we can investigate whether the level of turnout at European Parliament elections for different countries is predictably related to turnout at each country's most recent national election together with the length of time until its next national elections, along with a correction for compulsory voting (countries with compulsory voting see much less drop-off in turnout at European Parliament elections than other countries do). The results can be expressed in this equation:

EPturnout = 24.7 + 0.30*Natturnout + 32.9*Compuls + 7.2*First

This equation would tell us that there is a floor to turnout at European Parliament elections of about 25%, to which can be added a small proportion (0.30) of the turnout at the previous national election, but with a correction that adds almost 33% in countries with compulsory voting, and another 7.2% in the case of the first European Parliament elections ever conducted in the country concerned.

Of course, extracting that information from the output of a statistical package is not totally straightforward. Table 13.8 reproduces a portion of that output from a typical software package – output giving rise to the equation above. The names of variables appear down the left-hand side (dependent variable at the top). The coefficients in the next column are those used in the

Table 13.8. European Election turnout (2)

EPturnout	Coeff.	s. e.	t	Prob
Natturnout	0.30	0.18	1.66	0.10
Compuls	32.90	3.30	9.95	0.00
First	7.16	2.90	2.47	0.02
(Constant)	24.67	14.02	1.76	0.08
Number of observations				64
$F(3, 60)$				66.38
Prob $> F$				0.00
R^2				0.77
Adjusted R^2				0.76

equation. Other coefficients are described later or are beyond the remit of this chapter, but the column headed Prob (sometimes Prob is abbreviated to P) gives the level of significance of each effect. The fact that the effect of Natturnout has a probability of 0.10 of being spurious tells us that European Parliament turnout is probably not in fact affected by turnout at the previous national election, so that this component of the equation should in practice be eliminated (and will be eliminated in Table 13.9, as our story proceeds).

The output from the regression program also tells us the R^2 associated with the analysis, among many other statistics. The R^2, not surprisingly, is the square of R (or r) – the coefficient often used to describe bivariate relationships that was discussed earlier. The value is squared in multivariate analysis partly because, with more independent variables, it is easier to achieve a high value of R. By squaring this coefficient, one arrives at a smaller coefficient more appropriate for use in multivariate analysis (a proportion of a proportion is a smaller proportion – for example, a half of a half is a quarter). To evaluate values of R^2, one can use Table 13.7 for interpreting different values of r. A spectacular individual-level multivariate finding is one that yields an R^2 above 0.5, whereas with aggregate data the R^2 would have to be above 0.8 to be spectacular, and so on. Table 13.8 also lists an adjusted R^2, which is the value generally reported.

In the remainder of this section, we will describe the analysis that followed from the discovery (illustrated in Table 13.8) that turnout at European Parliament (EP) elections was not significantly affected by turnout at the previous national election for each country. This finding came as quite a surprise, because EP elections are supposed to be secondary to *national* elections (Reif and Schmitt 1980), demonstrating features of the national situation rather than features pertaining to the EP election itself. Thus, although it is natural

Table 13.9. European Election turnout (3)

Independent variables	Model A b	Model A (s.e.)	Model B b	Model B (s.e.)	Model C b	Model C (s.e.)	Model D b	Model D (s.e.)
Natturnout	0.30	(0.18)						
Compuls	32.90	(3.30)**	36.22	(2.66)**	38.30	(2.98)**	38.62	(2.74)**
First	7.15	(2.90)*	8.30	(3.86)*	1.51	(5.38)		
First*NotCompuls					9.41	(6.34)	10.92	(3.31)**
(Constant)	24.67	(14.02)	47.80	(1.62)**	47.15	(1.66)**	47.14	(1.65)**
Adjusted R^2	0.76		0.75		0.75		0.76	
N	64		64		64		64	

Note: Dependent variable is EPturnout; $p =$ *0.05, **0.01.

to theorize that a primary determinant of EP election turnout is national election turnout, the relevant coefficient is not significant in Table 13.8.

Table 13.9 presents the findings of a series of different regression analyses (described as 'models' in the table), each one using slightly different independent variables, in order to step the reader through the findings that led to the rejection of the intuitively more appealing theory and the acceptance of a model (which might be quite surprising to some) that makes no use of national election turnout as an independent variable. The table is laid out in a fashion customary in contemporary journal articles, with the names of the independent variables down the left-hand column and then a pair of coefficients for each variable for each model. The first in each pair of coefficients for each model is the coefficient of primary interest – the b coefficient that might be taken from the output of a computer program (such as illustrated in Table 13.8) and transferred to an equation (such as the one presented earlier). The second coefficient in each pair is headed s.e. (which stands for 'standard error' – coefficients that can also be found in Table 13.8), which measures how much error there is in each b coefficient; sometimes the parenthesized standard error appears under its corresponding b coefficient. It is not important for the purposes of this chapter to understand these coefficients, but they are used to determine the level of significance of the effect (the Prob coefficients in Table 13.8), which in published tables that look like Table 13.9 are generally indicated by one or more stars following the coefficient. The critical question those coefficients answer is 'How much error is there in the b coefficient relative to its size?'; as the amount of error approaches or exceeds the size of the coefficient, so significance is reduced. In Table 13.9, coefficients are given one star to show that they are significant at the 0.05 level and two stars to show that they are significant at the 0.01 level, but other conventions are also seen.[5] The meaning ascribed to the stars is always given in a footnote to the table. When the data come from a random sample, we stand only a 1 in 100 chance of being mistaken when we assert that effects with two stars are real. In the last two rows, at the foot of each model, are presented the number of cases included in the analysis (N) and the R^2 associated with the analysis, which we have already described in connection with Table 13.8.

Based on this rather minimal introduction, we can proceed to explain why the intuitively more appealing notion (that turnout at EP elections would depend on turnout at national elections) was rejected in favour of an explanation that does not even mention national elections. Model A is the model already presented in Table 13.8, repeated for reference purposes. This is the theoretically expected model in which, however, national turnout proves not significant (no stars for the effect of 0.30). In Model B, we see what happens when we simply remove national turnout from the model. The other variables increase their effects a little, but the effect of first election is still significant only at the 0.05 level, and the variance explained (adjusted R^2) goes down a bit. Some thought suggests that perhaps we are misspecifying our first election variable, because theoretically the fact that there is something special about an election should not affect turnout in a country that already has compulsory voting. Specifying an appropriate interaction between first election and compulsory voting, in addition to first election, yields a model (Model C) in which neither of these variables proves significant, but the interaction effect is by far the stronger of the two effects. Since first election was significant when it was the only measure of the concept (in Model B), its failure to prove significant when accompanied by its new variant (in Model C) must be because the two variables are largely measuring the same thing (this is called 'multicollinearity'). There are several ways to deal with multicollinearity, but in this example we address it by simply eliminating the less powerful of the two alternative measures. The result is model D, where all effects are highly significant and variance explained is back up to where it was in Model A.[6] (For a detailed presentation of these ideas, see Franklin 2001.)

The way forward

There is much still to learn about quantitative analysis. In particular, there are a great many types of multivariate analysis, many of them designed for specialized research situations, with the choice among them being largely dictated by the nature of the data being analysed. For example, data in which the cases constitute different points in time require a whole set of specialized procedures, as do data measured at different levels of aggregation.

Nevertheless, regression analysis is something of an 'industry standard' for multivariate analysis. Being able to understand the coefficients presented in published research papers that derive from regression analysis (together with the vocabulary used to describe those coefficients and the analyses that give rise to them) will take budding social scientists a long way. Being able to 'do' regression analysis in their own research will help them to be critical consumers of such research findings. Such relatively straightforward skills will also cover a large majority of the situations they are liable to encounter in the world of quantitative research.

This chapter has also illustrated a feature of quantitative analysis that is frequently overlooked. It is often stated that the scientific method proceeds deductively by testing propositions derived from theories that originate elsewhere (see Héritier, ch. 4). More typical of scientific research (not just in the social sciences) is, however, the example given in the previous section of how our understanding of turnout in European Parliament elections was elaborated. Scientists do not use data only to test their theories. They also use data to revise their theories and/or arrive at new ones. Archimedes discovered his Principle by observing his bathwater overflow, and virtually every scientific discovery is based ultimately on observation. Sometimes the observations concerned are direct (as with Archimedes or Putnam) and sometimes they are indirect, based on analysis of data collected for other purposes, as in the example reported in Table 13.9. This very important distinction is referred to elsewhere in this volume.

A huge part of what we know about the world is based on data analysis, and this is especially true in the social sciences. In these disciplines, relationships are often so complex that many variables need to be observed and manipulated simultaneously in order to control for all the things going on in the world that are not of primary interest but that could contaminate our findings. Often, a clear view can only be obtained by means of quantitative analysis of the data. That clear view will generally be at a high level of abstraction but, even though abstract, it can help greatly in the understanding of specific developments in particular places: it can help those conducting case studies to decide what to focus on,[7] just as much as case studies can help quantitative researchers decide what to measure.

NOTES

1 Robert Putnam's *Making Democracy Work* established the concept of 'social capital' within the contemporary literature of political science (it originated in the work of sociologist James Coleman). Putnam himself developed it in his later book *Bowling Alone*, but the ideas in *Making Democracy Work* were also picked up by other political scientists so that social capital studies have become something of a growth industry in recent years.

2 The mutual exclusivity of nominal-level variables (see below) is not something we find very useful to know, so losing this information does not cost us much. Pretending there is a unit of measurement for an ordinal-level variable equally need cost us little in practice.

3 This can be thought of in terms of measuring the various contaminants that would otherwise threaten the reliability of quantitative findings. In some of the natural sciences, contamination can be ruled out by careful cleaning of scientific instruments. In the social sciences, contaminants must be measured and relevant indicators included in any analysis that hopes to arrive at correct (what econometricians call 'unbiased') results. Many of the variables included in multivariate analyses are of no interest on their own account but are included because they are known to affect the dependent variable, and to leave them out would result in 'omitted variable bias'. Measuring and including contamination can even substitute for the use of proper random samples if the sources of error are sufficiently extensively specified.

4 Actually, that might not be true. The need to specify a constant term in an equation draws attention to something missing from the common characterization of Putnam's findings. Presumably the quality of governance in southern Italy was not zero, and perhaps was different in different southern regions, pointing to the need to elaborate Putnam's theory. Sometimes trying to specify empirical findings numerically can throw into relief the fact that we have failed to ask some obvious questions about a case study. Equally, recourse to a case study can suggest the need for additional (or different) variables in a quantitative analysis. The two types of investigation should go hand-in-hand as each type can illuminate the other. Franklin (2004) uses both approaches in tandem in this way (see also note 7 below).

5 The ratio of each coefficient to its standard error is given in the column headed t in Table 13.8. This ratio determines the level of significance of each effect – the 'Prob' in Table 13.8 or the number of stars in Table 13.9.

6 Strictly speaking, an interaction term needs to be accompanied by both of the variables from which it is composed, and we would have retained the first election variable had the interaction term proved significant. But in small-N studies, this often is not feasible. We can justify eliminating one component of the interaction on the basis that the effect of the interaction goes up (from 9.41 in Model C to 10.92 in Model D) by the amount of the component that was eliminated (1.51). Technically, we prefer Model D for this reason rather than its higher variance explained. Model B (the alternative) does not account for both effects. (See Bramber, Clark and Golder, 2006.)

7 Those studying Switzerland never thought to consider that country's coalition arrangements as a source of turnout decline until a quantitative study (the Voter Turnout study mentioned in note 4) drew their attention to the likely importance of the so-called 'Golden Rule'.

14 The design of social and political research

Philippe Schmitter

Let us assume that you have an *idea* that has led you to identify a *topic* that you believe to be of sufficient importance and of feasible execution to conduct research on it. It may be a doctoral dissertation, or just a seminar exercise, but regardless of length and complexity no topic can 'research itself'. You will have to translate it – via a series of strategic choices – into a *project*. It is this process of translation from something problematic or puzzling into something on which you can gather valid data and about which you can make compelling inferences that constitutes your *research design*.

Granted, much social scientific research is not self-consciously designed – it is not subject to a deliberate and critical process of choosing its components and defending its overall configuration. In many areas of inquiry, the design is literally given along with the topic. So much research has already been conducted on it that adding yet another case or extending it to yet another time period does not seem to require a novel effort of translation. Indeed, the universal desire of all sciences to produce cumulative knowledge seems to militate against continuously challenging and changing the standard way of doing research. If you do propose a change in design – say, a reconceptualization of the topic, a revised instrument for measuring variation, a different way of selecting relevant cases, or a novel method of testing for association – you will risk confusing your reader-cum-critic. He or she may find it difficult to distinguish whether eventual differences in data or inference are 'really' due to the topic itself or 'merely' to your meddling with the established way of researching it.

Most young social scientists, however, will not be choosing topics whose research design is given. They will have to find or invent an apposite design – and they should be prepared to understand and defend the choices involved. Moreover, if their immediate or eventual intent is comparative – if they anticipate including more than one case or set of observations and drawing inferences across them – then their choice of design will be even more crucial. Making the right strategic choices will greatly enhance the value of the data

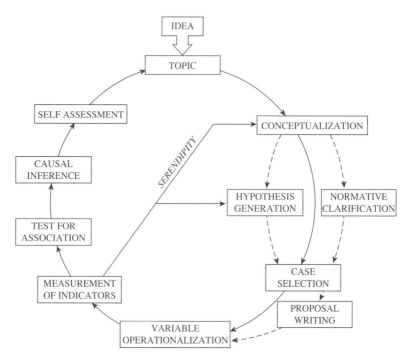

Fig. 14.1   The cycle of social and political research

they gather and the inferences they can draw from them; neglecting these choices or taking them for granted could result in idiosyncratic scraps of information and inferences rooted in exceptional circumstances that make no reliable or cumulative contribution to scientific knowledge.

Figure 14.1 is a schematic and idealized representation of the complete 'social and political research cycle'. Each of its boxes involves an important set of interrelated strategic choices, and its implication is that these should be made in the displayed sequence, beginning with an idea that defines a topic at 12 noon and proceeding clockwise until the researcher arrives at an evaluation of his or her findings that may or may not redefine the original topic at midnight. Inside the boxes lie a number of alternative courses of action. Choose among them wisely, and you will do better research. Ignore them or fail to grasp their significance, and you risk accepting serious fallacies at each stage.

The most important message to keep in mind while proceeding through the entire cycle is that there is no single best strategy or set of strategies for researching all topics. Everything depends on your point of departure, the initial substance you have decided to research. At the beginning of the cycle in Figure 14.1, the range of options tends to be most extensive – and, hence, most confusing. Interesting topics clamour for equal attention; different theories and concepts can seem equally compelling. As one proceeds clockwise, the successive choices are increasingly related to each other and the options become more limited. At some point, you may well adopt or fall into an 'established disciplinary routine'. You can save yourself a lot of time and worry by doing this but this will only benefit you if your topic and, especially, its conceptualization is sufficiently isomorphic with the original – that is, it conforms to the basic characteristics of the topic that has already been successfully researched by others. Applying even the best established and/or most fashionable design to the wrong topic can be a formula for disaster, especially when it comes to drawing inferences.

Very few researchers really enter Figure 14.1 at noon and leave at midnight. Most take shortcuts to get started in the process. Many social scientists begin their research careers already knowing on which case or cases they intend to work. Not infrequently, it happens to be the country from which they come or in which they are trained. So-called 'area specialists' usually have some prior personal commitment involving their knowledge of history, culture or language, and this tends to affect the topics they select. Others may have picked up some novel statistical technique or measurement device that they wish to show off – and they search about for an apposite topic to which to apply it. Perhaps the most common (and, in my view, pernicious) point of departure concerns theories or approaches that are currently fashionable in sociology or political science. Imbued with the conviction that only those espousing such a 'paradigm' will find eventual employment, young researchers are prepared to take up any topic – no matter how trivial or obscure – if only to demonstrate their fidelity to its assumptions and postulates.

Do not presume that, once in the cycle, you will have to go all the way around. As we shall see in the conclusion, there are many points of exit that will still permit you to make an original and significant contribution to knowledge.

Wherever you have really begun your research and whatever your motives for doing so, I recommend that you at least pretend that you are beginning at the top of Figure 14.1, if only to help you clarify *ex post* the design choices you should have taken deliberately or have already taken implicitly. Try to imagine that it all began with an idea about a substantive topic that is important to you and that only later did you place it in an explicitly conceptual context, elaborate specific hypotheses about its occurrence, choose the cases to study, and so forth.

Now, we can proceed to look sequentially into the 'little black boxes' in Figure 14.1. Attached to each of them the reader will also find a list of 'possibly optimizing' choices and 'potentially damaging' fallacies.

Choice of topic

No one can predict where and when ideas will appear. With some knowledge of the researcher's personal and professional background, however, it may be a bit easier to predict the conditions under which an idea becomes a topic – that is, when someone will attach sufficient importance to a given thought and place significant boundaries around it to make it worthy of investing his or her energy to explain how it came about or what its consequences might be. This highly personal effort at selection can be an important source of distortion throughout the rest of the design and, especially, when it comes to drawing inferences from whatever data distributions or associations are generated. The very fact that you care enough to select some topic probably means that you also value what it contributes or the effect that it has. However subliminal the thought may be, your values become embedded in the topic and can exert a persistent influence on your choices as you make your way around the rest of the research cycle. They may have an even greater impact when you decide to make a 'premature' exit from the cycle.

It is often the case that one is attracted to a topic because the society or polity also cares about it. Never is this more evident than when the subject matter is in crisis or in fashion. As social scientists, we are attracted to phenomena that call attention to themselves – whether they do so by creating further problems or by providing novel solutions. Which is another way of saying that our topics tend to be either failed experiences at the end of their useful existence or recent successes that have yet to reveal their complete impact. Rarely does one come across designs explicitly focused on explaining social or political phenomena that are mediocre or inconsequential.

Grosso modo, topics of research come in two guises: (1) *projections*, where the researcher is confident that the existing approach and methods are adequate and deserve to be applied to units or time periods that have not already been covered or with greater precision to cases that only seem to be exceptional; and (2) *puzzles*, where the researcher begins with the assumption that something is deficient in the way that the topic has been previously handled and that the units or time periods to be examined will demonstrate the existence of anomalies. Both projections and puzzles should be approached in the same 'critically rational' manner, but the perspective of the researcher differs. If the topic selected is regarded as a projection, he or she has the intent (at least, initially) of confirming established wisdom and will take more seriously the obligation to make a cumulative contribution to knowledge within a specific discipline or paradigm. The perspective when tackling a puzzle leads one to seize on anomalies that seem to expose deficiencies in how the topic has been conceptualized, measured or reported, and that is more likely to lead the researcher to alternative concepts and methods – frequently by drawing on other disciplines. Needless to say, both are capable of making valid contributions; both are needed by all social science disciplines.

Possibly optimizing choices

1 Choose a topic that you care enough about to be willing to spend the time to complete the project.
2 Choose a topic (and make an argument) that interests other social scientists (even those outside your field); the better it is, the more it will interest those working in adjacent fields and disciplines.
3 Specify the temporal, spatial and, if necessary, cultural boundaries of the topic in a way that makes the research feasible, but does not make it trivial or 'unique'.
4 Acknowledge your initial source of inspiration for the topic and your personal preference about its outcome, without apologizing for them.
5 Never justify your selection only on the grounds that it has been 'underexplored', and, especially, do not ignore, trivialize or dismiss what has already been written on the topic.
6 Try to reach as far back as possible in social and political theory to find grounds for the relevance of your topic and avoid being manipulated by academic fad and fashion.
7 By all means, listen to your advisor and your peers, but be absolutely certain that, regardless of who first suggested it, the topic 'belongs' to you.

Potentially damaging fallacies

1 'Fad-ism': Your topic (or method or theory) is being very much and very favourably discussed right now in your field, so that if you adopt it your work will be less criticized and you will be more likely to find a job.

2 'Wishful thinking': Your topic has already produced well-publicized and promising results for the society or polity; therefore, if you conduct research on it, your findings will be taken more seriously and favourably.

3 'Ambulance-chasing': Because the topic of your research is presently in crisis, you will have greater access to data and the public will be more interested in whatever you find out.

4 'Presentism': The assumption that whatever you find associated with some topic in the present must have been there in the past and will probably remain there in the future.

5 'Standing on the shoulders of the past giants': This might apparently allow you to see further and to avoid being distracted by the squabbles among contemporary pygmies – yet those giants might not have been looking at the same thing or in the same direction.

Conceptualization

Almost all substantive matters emerge 'pre-conceptualized' in the strict sense that they can only be recognized by the potential researcher and shared with others if they are expressed in some intelligible language. The idea may come initially as a shape or a colour or an emotion, but *words* are the indispensable way in which it acquires factual specificity and shared significance. The complication for research resides in the high probability that the words initially involved will be those of the social or political actors involved – which implies that their words could bear many different meanings and be attached to a wide range of contrasting assumptions.

Conceptualizing a topic involves translating the words that surround it in 'real-existing' societies or polities into *variables* (although see Della Porta, ch. 11, and Bray, ch. 15). These are not just fancy academic labels applied to a specific event or process. They should identify analogies, generic conditions that are shared by a distinctive set of events or processes and can take on different values over time – whether these are quantitatively or qualitatively observed. They acquire their peculiar status as causes or effects according to the way they are connected to other variables by theories. Once these variables have been assembled, whether from the same or varying theories, they constitute your provisional *argument* concerning the topic you have chosen to explain.

Which brings us to the 'Elephant-in-the-Room' that is so rarely mentioned but so frequently the source of confusion at each stage of designing research. Even the most elementary and frequently used concepts – such as class, status, gender, age, region and religiosity for explaining voting behaviour – derive their meanings from being inserted into a more comprehensive (and presumably coherent) matrix of concepts (see Kratochwil, ch. 5, and Mair, ch. 10). Their definitions may sound the same and, as we shall see later, operationalization of these variables may even be identical, but their role depends on prior assumptions and contingent relations that differ according to the theory, paradigm, approach or framework that is being applied. And no single piece of research can possibly specify what these are. If you tried to do this, there would be no time or space left for your analysis. In other words, all social and political research is part and parcel of 'the state of theory' prevailing at the moment it is conducted. No research can be conceptualized *ex novo* without reference to what has been produced already on that and related topics. This applies just as much to those who are trying to solve puzzles as to those who are 'merely' trying to make projections.

Choosing one's concepts is only the first step. Making them into variables means assigning a status to them, and this is where their embeddedness in theory most saliently enters into the research design. The most important task is to distinguish between those that are regarded as *operative* with regard to the chosen topic and those that are *inoperative*. The former are expected to play some discernible role in the explanation of outcomes – either as an *explicans* (that which does the explaining) or as an *explicandum* (that which is to be explained). The more elaborate the prior theory and, hence, the conceptualization derived from it, the more it may be possible to assign different statuses to the operative variables, for example, by distinguishing between primary and secondary ones (according to their explanatory power), direct and intervening ones (according to how near the effect is to the cause), continuous and episodic ones (according to how constant in time their effect is), and so forth. Needless to say, all these initially assigned roles can be inverted, especially where and when the objective is to explain a relatively long-term sequence of social or political processes. *Inoperatives* are variables that are present and can be expected to take on different values during the subject matter being researched, but whose effect is not expected to produce a discernible or significant difference. Of course, when it comes to making eventual inferences, allegedly inoperative variables may turn out to be an important potential source of spuriousness. Even *constants*, variables that were present but not thought to vary during the research period and, hence, *a priori* considered not capable of contributing to variation in the outcome, may gain eventually in importance – especially when it becomes evident that the impact of operative variables was contingent on slight modifications or even simple reinterpretations of such background factors. Hopefully, *irrelevant* variables – those whose variation cannot conceivably be logically or empirically associated with the topic under investigation – will remain that way.

Possibly optimizing choices

1   As much as possible, avoid references to specific persons, countries or cultures with 'upper-case' names by using only 'lower-case' variables to describe them and their prospective effects in your argument.
2   There is nothing wrong with using a 'hunch' as your starting point in con-ceptualization – the world surrounding most interesting topics is usually full of them – but try as soon as possible to identify the more generic theory in which this hunch is embedded, switch to its language, and explore its axioms or presumptions before going further.
3   Try to avoid 'multicollinearity' – clusters of variables that are closely asso-ciated with each other – and simplify by only using the dominant variable in such clusters or providing it with an ideal-type connotation that captures as precisely as possible the nature of the cluster.
4   Make as explicit as possible not only the operative but also the inoperative variables and the constants, those characteristics that do not vary, in your argument – and be prepared to change their status in the course of con-ducting the research.
5   When using classification systems (see Mair's chapter), make sure that the categories are both inclusive of all observations and exclusive in their assign-ment of every single observation – and that all of them are potentially rele-vant to explaining outcomes, including those that are vacant for the moment.
6   Specify as soon and as explicitly as possible the universe to which your con-ceptualization is intended to apply in both time and space.
7   Exercise caution when using concepts and variables across long periods of time or different cultural contexts, since their meaning to actors and, hence, their effect may change.
8   Strive for parsimony by eliminating double-dealing or superfluous vari-ables, but without resorting to excessive simplification. One way of doing this is to restate your argument several times and to make it more concise each time.

Potentially damaging fallacies

1   'Obscurantism': If you cloak your conceptualization in highly abstract terms or fit all of your observations into some complicated classification

scheme, no one will notice that all you are doing is describing what happened.

2 'Attribute-ism': The more definitional attributes or analogous properties you attach to a given concept, the more significant it is likely to be in explaining the outcomes you want to understand.

3 'Concept stretching': A concept used successfully to identify an analogy among events in one time and place must be equally valid when applied to other times or places.

4 'Isolation': Your preferred variable plays such an important role in explaining your topic that it can be conceptualized, measured and manipulated alone, without regard for the network of other variables surrounding it and the prior axioms upon which it rests.

5 'Novelty at any price': Because existing concepts are so embedded in (old) theories, by inventing and using novel ones, you will be credited with greater originality in your research.

6 'Arbitrariness': Since all concepts are basically arbitrary – a function of unpredictable practical uses and/or theoretical fashions – it will make no difference which ones you use, provided that your public and peers come to accept them.

7 'Consensual-ism': If everyone in your discipline is using some concept and seems to agree on its meaning, as well as its explanatory relevance, you should feel safe to do so.

Formation of hypotheses

Not all research designs involve the formation (or the testing) of explicit hypotheses. There exists a very broad range of social and political topics for which it is possible to conceptualize the variables that may contribute to an explication, but not to assign any sort of provisional 'if . . . then . . .' status to their relationships. For these topics, the apposite research logic is one of *discovery* and not of *proof.* The purpose is to improve one's conceptualization of a topic, probe its plausibility against a range of data and eventually generate hypotheses among its conclusions, but it would be premature to expect them as a pre-condition for conducting the research itself.

The determining factor is again that 'Elephant-in-the-Room', the prevailing state of theory on a given topic. Substantive matters that are of recent occurrence, that are only characteristic of a small number of cases, that incite strong emotions or political controversies, or that fall between different social science disciplines are obvious candidates for 'discovery' status. The potential researcher is reminded that this should not be taken as a sign of inferiority. Somewhere behind all social scientific research that today routinely follows the logic of proof, there must have been a glorious moment in the past when someone launched a voyage of discovery. Unfortunately, behind the facade of increased professionalism and standardization of techniques, this message has been suppressed. Only the most intrepid of young scholars will accept the challenge of trying to make sense out of alternative conceptualizations of the same topic; or piecing together potentially coherent and general arguments by 'process tracing' on the basis of specific cases; or admitting that, in instances of highly interdependent and complex social or political systems, it may never be possible to distinguish between independent and dependent variables, much less to express them in terms of a finite set of bivariate relationships.

Possibly optimizing choices

1 Ensure that the assumption of any 'if ... then ...' relationship is sufficiently precise that it specifies its 'micro-foundation', the functional dependence, structural mechanism or intentional logic that is supposed to connect its variables and, where possible, introduce an independent measure of its presence.

2 Do not assume *ex ante* that only individual human beings are capable of laying 'micro-foundations', when the 'real-existing', historical world is chock full of social and political units that have acquired the capacity to act collectively in ways that cannot be reduced to individual intentions and choices.

3 Ensure that the presumed cause is independent of the presumed effect, and not parallel or convergent manifestations of the same social or political process.

4 Where possible, specify explicitly the existence of intervening conditions or prevailing constants that must always be present for the hypothesized relation to produce its effect – even if these contextual factors do not vary during the research.

5 An ideal research situation can emerge when you find yourself in a 'two-ring circus' – when two rival versions of the same hypothesized relation are plausible and would explain diametrically different outcomes based on different theoretical assumptions.

6 Be prepared to recognize and deal with 'equifinalities', similar outcomes that are produced by different sequences or mechanisms, when they emerge, and therefore to test different sets or, better, 'strings' of hypotheses – not just isolated ones.

7   Remember that you always have three hypotheses to test, namely, the ones that suggest a positive or a negative relation, and the null hypothesis that no 'if . . . then . . . ' relationship exists. The latter should be regarded as the most probable in occurrence. Everything may be related to everything else in our complex environment, but not always in a predictable direction or to a significant degree.

8   Try *ex ante* when elaborating hypotheses to differentiate between variables that you think are 'necessary' (always likely to be present when the outcome is present), 'sufficient' (always and only present) and merely 'helpful' (sometimes present, sometimes not). Never assume that your set of variables is going to be both 'necessary and sufficient' and, therefore, make space for the inevitable 'error term'.

9   Since most research projects consist of 'clusters' and 'chains' of related hypotheses that contribute to explaining a selected outcome, it is often useful to draft a 'model' of these simultaneous and sequential relations using time and space as co-ordinates.

Potentially damaging fallacies

1   'Scientism': If your variables are not organized into hypotheses with clearly differentiated independent and dependent variables, your research will not be scientific.

2   'Fear of failure': If your hypothesis or hypotheses are disproved, you will have made no contribution to knowledge.

3   'Infinite regress': All hypotheses about variable relationships in the social sciences are preceded by a potentially infinite historical chain of causality and consequence, therefore, it makes no difference when you choose to break into that chain.

Selection of cases

For all but a few projects, the potential number of societies or polities affected by the chosen topic will exceed the researchers' capability for gathering data, testing for associations and drawing inferences. It is, therefore, normal that only some subset of these units will enter into your analysis. One of the most prominent of the strategic choices you will have to make involves the number and the identity of those to be included and the criteria you impose to select them. This can vary from one unit (the single case or person) to as many as are apposite (the universe of those affected); but there is a fairly inescapable trade-off between the quantity of variables that have been included in your initial conception of the topic and the number of units for which you will be able to gather data. Including more cases probably also means poorer quality data, more missing observations and greater problems of conceptual equivalence. Inversely, the more narrowly you have defined and operationalized those variables – that is, the lower they are on the ladder of abstraction – the less likely they are to be relevant in a wide range of cases.

Case selection may have its practical side when it comes to gathering data and, especially, making one's own detailed observations; but its real payoff is analytical. Manipulating the identity of cases provides most sociologists and political scientists with their closest equivalent to experimentation. It 'simulates' the introduction of control variables. By 'holding constant' across the sample such potentially relevant conditions as cultural identity, geographic location, level of development and temporal proximity, the researcher can at least pretend that variation in them is unlikely to have produced the outcome one is looking at. Granted that the controls can be somewhat approximate and that there still will remain many potential sources of 'contaminating' differentiation among units in the sample – still, this is the best design instrument that he or she has available. It should, therefore, be wielded with deliberation – and caution.

Strictly speaking, the researcher does not select individual cases but 'configurations of variables' that co-habit the same unit and may even co-vary in a unique or distinctive fashion within that unit. But one cannot analyse 'France' as such and compare it with, say, 'Spain' or 'Italy'. There are simply too many different (and potentially relevant) conditions within each of these countries with regard to almost any topic you choose to work on. This holds even when comparing micro-units within the same country, where the number of variables can be more reliably controlled because of common constraints at the nation-state level. So-called 'holistic' research is, therefore, largely an illusion in social and political research and, when tried, it usually amounts to little more than a detailed or 'thick' description of one case (or of parallel ones if more units are covered) (but see Bray, ch. 15, for a different view).

This is not to say that there are not significant differences between designs that are driven by the effort to isolate a small number of variables and test exclusively for their association with other variables across a larger number of units, and designs that begin with a large number of interrelated variables (often combined via ideal-type constructs) within one country and then seek to find significant and persistent connections across a few, carefully selected units of an allegedly comparable nature. But in either strategy, what you are usually comparing are variables – one or many, alone or in clusters – not units.

This brings us to the second aspect of case selection, which has long been taken for granted and yet has recently become of growing concern. For a unit of observation to be a valid case for analysis, it must possess identical or, at least, comparable degrees of freedom with regard to the topic under investigation. A design that drew inferences – descriptive or causal – from a sample of units composed of Brazilian municipalities, Mongolian provinces, Spanish *comunidades autónomas* and the permanent members of the United Nations Security Council about the efficacy of taxation systems would not attract much attention. Much as its author might (correctly) protest that this 'sample' embodies a 'most-different systems design', critics would (rightly) object that actors in these units did not have remotely equivalent powers to make or enforce their decisions on taxation.

The usual formula for getting around this problem was to select only units that were at the same level of aggregation and enjoyed the same formal status within the world social and political system. This presumably explains why so many comparative research projects have been based on nation-state units or, to a lesser degree, on relatively autonomous subnational units within federal or confederal systems. The *reductio ad absurdum* of this strategy has been reached with large-N comparisons containing all the members of the UN for which data can be obtained – despite the blatant fact that these so-called sovereign states have radically divergent capabilities for governing their respective populations or even satisfying their most elementary needs.

Since Donatella della Porta has contributed an entire chapter (ch. 11) to this volume that deals extensively with the issues involved in case selection, I have little more to add. I will, however, provide a pedagogic device that I have found useful in explaining to students what their options are at this point in the research cycle (Figure 14.2).

Where researchers are committed to producing scientific knowledge (defined here as causal inference), the preferred case selection strategy should usually be the experimental one, choosing the units of observation randomly and introducing some element of change in a subset of them while holding variation constant for the others. Unfortunately, most social and political scientists have to operate in 'real-existing' settings, where this is not possible. And even when they are permitted to engage in experimentation, the topics tend to be so trivial and the settings so artificial that projecting inferences based on such findings to more 'realistic' contexts is very hazardous.

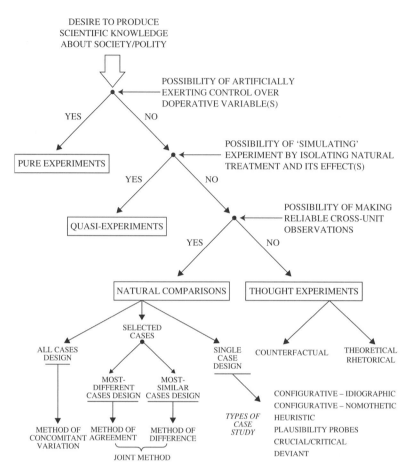

Fig. 14.2   A schematic for the selection of cases

Quasi-experiments may be second-best, but they offer some interesting advantages, with regard to both the efficiency of research and the credibility of inferences. The case-base can be as low as one, although it is better to repli-cate the quasi-experiment in several other settings, if possible, within the same time frame. They are, however, limited to real-world situations where the independent variable is highly discrete and temporally circumscribed and where data-gathering over a sufficient period of time has been consistent and reliable. Assessing the effect of a new public policy or the impact of some unexpected social or natural event tends to fit this narrow bill of particulars, but only if nothing else is happening to the unit or units at the same time. This is also a strategy of case selection that is especially vulnerable to diffusion or contagion effects, if the units involved know of each other's behaviour.

Most sociologists and political scientists will have to settle for the study of variations in their subject matter that appear 'naturally', whether within a single case or across different numbers of them. Della Porta (ch. 11) explores the implications of making these choices.

There are, I would add, a number of other alternative strategies that are not usually included in texts on research methods or design – presumably because their scientific status is dubious. They typically arise in contexts in which it is risky or impossible to observe and record the behaviour of 'real-existing' social or political units. All involve what Max Weber once called 'thought experiments'. The best-known goes under the rubric of *counter-factualism* and involves the researcher in an effort to imagine what would have happened to the topic if some condition, person, event or process had not been present. Usually, this focuses on a single country – for example, 'How would Germany have evolved politically if Hitler had not been "available" in the early 1930s?' It can also be applied to a sample or even to the universe of cases – for example, 'What would be today the level of international insecurity in Europe if the EU did not exist?' Or, 'How many people in the world would know how to speak English if the Americans had lost their Revolutionary War?' If this sounds 'exotic' and somewhat 'flaky', you should remember that every time that you invoke the famous and indispensable Latin phrase, *ceteris paribus*, before advancing a hypothesis, you are being a counterfactualist.

Moving even further from social scientific orthodoxy, one finds a vast number of seminar exercises, MA papers and PhD dissertations that are essentially rhetorical, theoretical or normative. These certainly deal with topics – often more important ones for 'real-existing' societies and polities than those chosen by empiricist-cum-positivists – but their purpose is to follow the development of concepts or discourses over time, or to examine the logical consistency of particular arguments, or to promote the ethical acceptance of specific forms of human behaviour. Such projects do indeed involve research. In a 'heuristic' and 'nomothetic' way they have influenced empirical inquiry. Just think of the impact of recent works by John Rawls, Jürgen Habermas and Jon Elster upon how even the most 'hardcore' empiricists select and conceptualize a wide range of topics (see Bauböck, ch. 3).

Possibly optimizing choices

1 If you are not trying to cover the entire universe, consider the possibility of selecting a sample of cases randomly and how that would affect your project.

2 As a rule, when randomization is excluded and you have to be purposively selective, choose your cases based on their relation to the independent variable or variables rather than the dependent variable or variables.

3 And when you make this choice, try to ensure that the cases chosen 'represent' as wide a range as possible of scores on those independent variables.

4 When your topic will not permit this, when you are motivated to research something precisely because it involves a compelling, arresting or extreme outcome and you therefore have to select on the dependent variable, remember this as a potential source of bias when it comes to drawing inferences.

5 Keep in mind that you do not have to use only one strategy of case selection and that so-called 'nested strategies', where you start with a large N of cases and relatively few crudely measured variables and, subsequently, shift to a small N with a much more detailed 'battery' of variables, can give you the advantages of both strategies when it comes to drawing inferences.

6 Always prefer the lowest level of spatial or functional aggregation that is compatible with the actor behaviour presumed by your conceptualization, since you can subsequently reassemble your research upwards – but not downwards – in scale.

7 No matter which or how many cases you initially select, some may prove to be 'decomposable', in that you may be able to generate additional cases by dividing up the initial ones, but only provided these subunits possess some and the same degree of autonomy.

8 Before selecting the number and identity of the cases for which you intend to gather data, make sure that you are aware of the criteria that you originally used for classifying your topic and ask first: 'What is this a case of?' Only after satisfying that demand will you know what units are 'eligible' for inclusion, and you can proceed to exclude some of them for good reason.

Potentially damaging fallacies

1 'Notoriety': Just because a particular case has been prominent in public discussion, it will be more interesting to research, and others will pay more attention to your research.

2 'Numbers': It is always advantageous to have a larger number of cases, even when, by adding them, you are compelled to attenuate their relation to the topic or to use less valid indicators.

3 'Cruciality': Because a given unit is an outlier according to your criteria of case selection, it will be a crucial case whose conformity or non-conformity provides a definitively significant test of causal association.

4 'The illusion of control': Selecting cases because they seem to share certain general cultural, locational or structural characteristics necessarily controls for their relevance – when it is still possible that minor or qualitative variations in 'controlled variables' could be affecting variation in what you are trying to explain.

5 'Contemporaneousness': In units chosen for comparison within the same time frame, the actors must have similar (or at least sufficient) awareness of the relevance of common variables and be capable of acting upon them simultaneously – when these units may be at different points in longer cycles or simply on different time schedules.

6 'Imitation': When actors in the selected units are acutely aware of having to deal with some topic within the same time frame, they will also be sensitive to what others are doing about it and will learn from each other's successes and failures – in fact they may be quite ignorant of what the others are doing.

Writing the proposal

This stage in the research cycle is 'optional', although highly desirable. Different graduate programmes place greatly different emphasis on the importance of defending a formal proposal. Some require it before allowing the candidate to 'go into the field'. My personal experience suggests that the greater the plurality of approaches or paradigms surrounding a given topic and present in a particular institution, the greater will be the emphasis on writing and defending your proposal. In scholastic contexts dominated by a single theoretical or disciplinary orientation, the effort may be eschewed completely. The reigning orthodoxy favours problems rather than puzzles and may even dictate in considerable detail how topics should be conceptualized and operationalized. At the extreme, there is no 'field' to go into, no specific cases to select and no measurement details to discuss. What matters at this stage is the normative or logical consistency of the 'argument', of one's conceptualization of the topic and how well it conforms to prevailing orthodoxy. The number and identity of cases are relatively unimportant, if not irrelevant, to the extent that both prior axioms and subsequent expectations are believed to be universal. The data can be simulated or assembled from the usual sources for illustrative purposes. The eventual inferences are usually predictable and in line with original expectations. The fellow members of your 'research club' will enthusiastically congratulate you on your cumulative contribution to knowledge. Practitioners of other disciplines and members of other clubs within your discipline will yawn and tell you that you have 'rediscovered the wheel' or produced something utterly trivial. In other words, there are costs as well as benefits in belonging to an established research tradition.

Another condition affecting the utility of proposal-writing is its potentially critical role in obtaining research funding. Where such support is assured or not subject to competitive pressures, the researcher may content him- or herself with a brief statement of intention. Otherwise, your ability to summarize coherently and justify convincingly the design choices that you have made up to this point could make all of the difference in determining whether you will be able to carry out your project at all. Although it is not frequently discussed openly, this 'commercial' aspect of proposal-writing can also be a source of distortion when the preferences of the sponsor come to be anticipated in the proposal itself and the researcher finds him- or herself pandering to them by modifying the topic, changing its conceptualization, restricting the range of hypotheses and even selecting different cases in an effort to please the prospective sponsor. More experienced researchers soon learn how to 'fine-tune' their proposals to get support from donors and then go on to follow the course of inquiry they think will lead to the most compelling inferences. Fortunately, national or supranational sponsors rarely control for conformity between proposals and the research actually performed. At most, they may be interested in whether or not the policy implications drawn from such research conform to their preferences.

The 'real' purpose of writing a proposal should be to give the researcher a chance to sit back and reflect critically on the strategic choices he or she has made – and to exchange these reflections with supervisors and peers before plunging into the inevitably messy and absorbing process of gathering data and trying to make sense out of them. There may be subsequent moments for self-criticism and changes – see the remarks below on the importance of *serendipity* – but writing and defending a proposal at this stage offers a unique opportunity to 'rewrite' and 'resubmit' before becoming irrevocably locked into a course of action.

Operationalization of variables

In principle, the conceptualization of variables should be carried out beforehand and without regard for how they will be converted into indicators and eventually measured. There is a good reason for this. What is of paramount theoretical importance is to specify clearly the condition or factor that is supposed to be present in order to produce some anticipated effect – alone or in conjunction with other variables. Having previously and independently conceptualized the projection or puzzle in such a fashion should provide a strong incentive subsequently to specify the observations that need to be made in order to verify the presence, magnitude, direction, or persistence of that variable. During the early stages of research, this means that you should adopt the attitude that all social and political variables can potentially be operationalized – and later be prepared to compromise when you start looking for indicators in the real world.

In practice, unfortunately, anticipations of such difficulties do tend to intrude and can even inhibit scholars from using concepts that are known to be 'impossible' to operationalize. Just think of such indispensable political properties as power, authority and legitimacy; or of such social ones as esteem, respect and trust. For none of them is there a standard and easily accessible set of measures. Even elaborate (and expensive) attempts to operationalize them based on 'reputational' criteria from public opinion surveys have been problematic. And criticisms of these efforts become more insistent the more such indicators are stretched across countries and over time.

Another way of putting this dilemma is that there are bound to be *trade-offs* that have to be made at this stage in the research cycle. The higher one's concepts are on the ladder of abstraction – and, presumably, the wider their prospective range of application – the more difficult it is going to be to make convincing observations about their presence in a specific case or set of cases. Increase the number of units in your study – either of persons or of organizations – and you are almost bound to run into problems with missing data and misleading indicators. Do not be afraid to make these trade-offs, but do so self-consciously. Tell your reader-cum-critic when you are settling for a less satisfactory indicator or a less specific level of observation. Be prepared when necessary even to eliminate cases, but also be sensitive to how this may distort your eventual capacity to draw inferences. Those research sites where operational requirements are most difficult to satisfy are usually places where social and political behaviour is the least 'normal' and their exclusion from the design will probably narrow the range of variation and reduce the eventual strength of association.

The theme that haunts all aspects of this stage of the research cycle is *validity*. Do the observations you propose to make accurately reflect and, hence, capture the meaning of the concepts you have chosen to bear the burden of explanation? No matter how accurate the observations, how comparable they are across units, how replicable they turn out to be when another scholar makes them, if they are not valid, your research will have broken down at one of its most vulnerable points. You may well have discovered something important and the associations revealed by your indicators might be incontrovertible, but you have not proved (or disproved) what you started out with. Your findings are irrelevant in the strictest sense. They have told you nothing about the topic you announced that you intended to work on – unless you are prepared to rely on serendipity (see below) and reconceptualize your entire project from its very origins.

Possibly optimizing choices

1 Pay close and critical attention to the correspondence between your initial concepts and their proposed indicators or assessments by comparing them to research by others on the same or related topics.
2 Be wary of variable specifications and of empirical indicators that have been applied routinely over time and across units to measure different concepts.
3 Make sure that the concept and its indicator(s) are applied to the same level of analysis and are as close as possible in level of abstraction.
4 When available, use alternative operationalizations and multiple potential indicators and, where necessary, rely on 'triangulation' among them to resolve disparities and to improve validity.
5 All things being equal (although they never are), you are better off using unobtrusive rather than obtrusive indicators, since the actors whose behaviour is being observed will have less of an opportunity to respond strategically, ethically or emotionally to your request for information.
6 Remember that there are various ways of assessing the validity of indicators, ranging from consensus among independent respondents to co-variation between different 'internal' measures and, least reliably, correlation with other hypothesized 'external' outcomes.

Potentially damaging fallacies

1 'Availability': This indicator exists and has been used successfully by others; therefore, it must be valid when applied to your topic.
2 'Operationalism': You decide to include in your analysis only variables for which you know that a valid (or consensually accepted) indicator already exists.
3 'Mimetism': 'X' got away with using data on this to indicate a concept similar to yours, even when drawing upon a different theory; therefore, you can safely use it for the same purpose.

4 'Ignorance of the uncertainty principle': If you operationalize a variable by intruding on the 'real-existing' world of your respondent, you can nonetheless ignore the possibility that his or her answer will be contaminated by prevailing norms of correctness or strategic calculations of interest, or that you will be creating rather than measuring variation.

Measurement

At this point in the cycle, your choices will be more or less dictated by the ones you have already made – whether you did so consciously in relation to the specificity of your problem or puzzle (as I hope was the case) or whether you settled into an established research tradition – whether quantitative or qualitative – and obediently followed its dictates. Moreover, there is a good reason why you should let yourself 'go with the flow' at this point. Using existing techniques of observation and indicators for variables not only saves you a lot of time and anxiety, but can also provide you with an element of internal 'quality control' – provided that the measures used are valid, that is they capture the characteristics of the variable that you are relying upon for an eventual explanation. When it occurs, successful replication of previous research is a very desirable result – and one that can be personally very reassuring. Should you decide to invent and apply a new indicator or, worse, battery of indicators – especially to measure some frequently used variable – you will have to make an especially strong effort at justification. Otherwise, you will run the risk at the inference stage of confounding the reader: 'Is this seemingly compelling finding really novel, or is it only due to some change in measurement?'

The discussion on measurement tends to be dominated by the distinction between quantitative and qualitative indicators – with a marked bias in favour of the former. There is no reason to be surprised by this, since most methods texts are written by quantifiers and they have convincing arguments in their favour. Numerical data are said to be more *reliable*, i.e. more likely to provide agreement among independent observers, more *accurate*, i.e. more likely to produce agreement across units, and more *useful*, i.e. more compatible with different ways of testing for association. Certainly, the social science disciplines have tended to assign greater 'scientific status' to quantitative than to qualitative research – and to reward its practitioners accordingly.

This is unfortunate for at least three good reasons: (1) it has encouraged researchers to attach numbers to variables when the validity of their connection with the designated concept was dubious; (2) it has resulted in the exploitation of standard numerical indicators whose multiple components are often theoretically disputable and whose weighted combinations are poorly understood by those who use them; and (3) it has discouraged the innovative use of more direct and imaginative techniques of observation – precisely to capture qualities inherent in complex and contingent relations. You can assign a number to anyone and anything; but nothing guarantees that the assignment will produce relevant information. If these qualities are differences in kind (nominal) rather than in magnitude (cardinal or ordinal), then – whatever the rule of their assignment – the number could well be a worthless piece of disinformation. What matters is how you have conceptualized your topic, not the allegedly superior virtues of one over another form of measurement.

Of all of the stages in the cycle, this is probably the one that is best suited for *serendipity*, for learning from the research process itself in ways that can feed back to your previous choices and lead you to introduce improvements in them before 'path dependence' has completely taken over. At last, you are back in touch with the 'real-existing' subjects/agents of your topic – having spent much time wandering around making abstract 'disciplinary' decisions. If you are lucky, they will talk to you directly about their intentions and perceptions, and they may even have some opinions about what you are asking them and intend to do with their answers. Even if your research relies exclusively on secondary or publicly available sources, there can be 'voices' in such documents that can speak in ways you have not anticipated. Of course, there will be a lot of sheer 'noise' generated by the data you are gathering, and that can be very confusing when juxtaposed to the relatively parsimonious approach you have been applying to the topic. Nevertheless, keep your eyes, ears and mind open for subtleties and surprises, and be amenable to introducing 'course corrections' – even some that go all the way back to the boundaries you initially placed around the topic or key aspects of your original argument.

Possibly optimizing choices

1 Routinely test for the reliability of indicators, if possible by using alternative sources of data and/or alternative persons to score the data.

2 If validity requirements can be satisfied, opt for quantitative over qualitative measurement, since the technical advantages are considerable and because you can more easily move from the former to the latter.

3 Always opt for the highest, most informative level of measurement possible (given the nature of the variable), since it will later be possible to shift to a

lower level. Cardinal data can always be made ordinal, and virtually anything can later be dichotomized or filed away in nominal categories – but you cannot move in the reverse direction.

4 Make your instructions – even if only for your own use – concerning the assignment of quantitative scores or qualitative labels as transparent and complete as possible so that the measurement operations can be replicated by you or someone else in the future.

5 Especially when working on the macro level of a complex society or polity, most variables will contain multiple components and be indicated by composite measures – which should obligate the researcher to devote concerted attention to how such 'scales' are aggregated.

6 Especially when gathering information over time about social or political processes, make sure to check that changes are not due to modifications of the instruments of observation rather than to changes in actual behaviour.

7 Many measurement devices are calibrated to pick up only relatively large-scale and consequential changes in variables, which means that they may systematically fail to capture more modest and gradual ones. Social and political 'revolutions' are always recognized; 'reforms' are more often underreported, until their effects have accumulated sufficiently to draw attention to them.

8 Try to estimate before actually gathering the data where the error sources are most likely to come from and how they will affect your findings. Worry less about random errors (they will attenuate possible associations) than about systematic ones (they will bias the direction of your findings).

9 Try to catch yourself before adjusting the data or correcting for errors in them in ways that make these data fit better the general expectations or specific hypotheses with which you started.

Potentially damaging fallacies

1 'Composite-ness': Many concepts are complex and multidimensional in nature and, therefore, can only be measured by similarly complex and multidimensional indicators – regardless of variation in their internal structures and, hence, the probability that identical scores will be assigned to quite different clusters of variation.

2 'Longevity': It is always better to use an indicator that has been around for some time, used in a variety of research settings, and can provide the researcher with a longer time perspective – despite the likelihood that

during this period the techniques for measurement will have changed and the meanings of items for actors may not be the same.

3 'Clarity': It is always preferable that each variable be given a specific and unambiguous score – even if the nature of its conceptualization and theoretical status is calculatedly 'fuzzy' or 'radial'.

4 'Reification': What you are measuring is identical to what you have conceptualized which, in turn, is identical to the way in which actors perceive 'it' – regardless of how much is lost in translation as the researcher moves from one realm to another.

Test for association

By now, the researcher may have momentarily lost almost all strategic control over his or her project and, at best, should consult one among many texts on methodology to discover which among all of the verbal or mathematical, symbolic or numerical, parametric or non-parametric, deterministic or probabilistic devices available for testing for association best fits the data that he or she has gathered.

Variables can be associated with each other in different ways. Typically, the social scientist will be interested in *direction*, or whether the fit is positive, negative or null; *strength*, or how much one variable affects another; and *significance*, or the likelihood that the fit could simply have been due to chance. Since his or her research will almost inevitably be 'historical', the *time, timing* and *sequence* of how they fit to each other should also be important – indeed, these chronological dimensions often provide the basic orientation to how one's findings are presented and defended.

The reason for this is that the most powerful means of testing for the fit among variables and, therefore, for presenting one's findings has long been to tell a believable story in chronological order. Perhaps, within some highly professionalized niches in sociology and political science, storytelling is no longer regarded as acceptable. The occupants of these niches – not infrequently, Americans or those trained in America – have forgotten that their disciplines are profoundly and irrevocably historical. What counts is not just what happens, but when it does and in relation to what else has already happened or is simultaneously happening. Moreover, the actors themselves are not just passive recipients of scores, but active and reflexive keepers of the score. They remember what they and their ancestors did in the past, and their preferences in the present are conditioned by this knowledge. In my opinion, no means of testing for such associations has yet been invented that can supplant or even surpass the chronological narrative in capturing these subtleties of time and timing, and in bringing simultaneously into focus the multitude of variables involved in the sheer complexity of most social and political phenomena. The narration of your findings can, no doubt, be considerably bolstered in credibility by inserting quantitative tests about specific associations into the basic narrative. Cross-tabulations, rank-orderings, regression equations, factor- or small-space analyses, even mathematical models, can often be helpful, but primarily when analysing topics that are heavily circumscribed in time and space and that can be separated into relative simple and repetitive components.

Even social and political scientists relying exclusively on quantitative data may find it occasionally useful to tell a plausible story that places the associations they calculate and the inferences they draw in some chronological order. Narration can also serve to fill in the gaps between cause and effect by providing a verbal description of the mechanisms involved – especially when mathematical formulae and formal models typically treat such exchanges as taking place within impenetrable 'black boxes' (see Héritier, ch. 4, and Vennesson, ch. 12). The findings of hard-core quantifiers often circulate only among small groups of *cognoscenti* and are incomprehensible to outsiders; but whenever sociologists or political scientists aspire to enlighten and influence wider publics, they will either have to learn how to narrate their findings or hire someone else to translate the esoteric results of their tests into more intelligible stories.

Possibly optimizing choices

1 Never forget the 'inter-ocular impact test' that consists in simply eyeballing the data – scatterplots are especially useful for this – and forming your own visual impression of what is going on among the variables and across the cases.

2 Always try to apply different tests of fit and only try the more demanding ones once you have experimented with simpler ones.

3 If possible (and it will be much more possible with quantitative designs), manipulate the number by eliminating one or two, and/or by dividing the sample into subsamples – say, by size or location – and do not be discouraged if this shakes up their fit, but try to discover what variables may have intervened to produce such different results.

4 Remember that most tests for association – quantitative for sure, qualitative for some – are exceedingly sensitive to extreme cases, so that you may be well advised to eliminate them in order to find out how persistent or

significant is the association among variables when only more 'normal' units are included in the analysis.

5 Remind yourself of the time dimension and test whether successive cross-sections through the data – say, at ten-year intervals – produce equally strong associations. If they do not, reflect on what intervening or contextual variables might be responsible for the new findings.

6 Your tests for association will be all the more convincing, the more effort you put into falsifying initial hypotheses, rather than merely seeming to verify them by grasping at all favourable distributions of data.

7 The treatment of 'deviant' cases that do not fit the general pattern of association is often taken as an indicator of how seriously the researcher accepts the task of falsification. Ignoring them (or transforming their scores) suggests that you are excessively concerned with verification; embrace them, exploit their contrariness and try to determine the extent to which they call into question the hypothesis and you will gain favour as a 'falsificationist'.

Potentially damaging fallacies

1 'Spuriousness': You have found a close association between two variables and you report this finding – without considering that if you were to introduce a third variable, it might explain variation in both of the original ones.

2 'Contingency': The associations you find are strong and significant, but only if and when certain, usually unspecified, contextual variables are present.

3 'Curve-fitting': Since there is always 'noise' and 'error' in the data, it is permissible to 'smooth' distributions by transforming the raw data or eliminating outliers and this will usually result in a more 'satisfactory' fit.

4 'Anachronism': Whatever are the associations that satisfy your test criteria and the time period covered by your research, the findings they generate will be valid whenever.

5 'Ad-hocracy': At some level of abstraction and measurement, each case can be uniquely identified and used to 'explain away' any and all observed deviations from the outcome predicted by those variables included in the study.

Causal inference

This is by far the most hazardous – and the most rewarding – of the stages in the research cycle. It is the one in which you will have the least disciplinary or academic guidance and, hence, the widest range of discretionary choices to make.

Many social researchers will have exited the process before arriving here. They will have made their accurate observations, published their empirical descriptions and gone home. Others will have stopped even earlier, before having gathered any data, and left satisfied that they have advanced further the plausibility of an argument or helped to specify the universe to which it can be applied. Some will have gone further and proffered tests – numerical and narrative – illustrating how frequently and strongly variables have been associated with each other. But they will have prudently refrained from trying to answer two further questions: (1) the retrospective one of *why* and *how* these variables combined to produce the outcome that was the topic of the research in the first place; and (2) the prospective one of *what* the consequences of this will be in the future and *when* these consequences will happen.

Consider, as an example, the current controversies over climate research. Do you think that if climatologists and other scientists had merely filed reports demonstrating that temperatures were rising across the planet and that various chemical substances have been accumulating in its atmosphere, there would have been much of a reaction? As far as I know, these facts were accepted by all as uncontroversial. It was only when these researchers correlated these indicators and drew the inference that increases in them masked a causal relation that could not be due to chance or fate that things became controversial. When they attributed primary causation to factors related to human intervention and, even more, when they began to advance threatening projections about what will happen in the future, then all hell broke loose!

Without even hinting that all social scientists have a responsibility for generating such controversy, they should feel a more modest responsibility for exploiting their data to the fullest extent possible; that almost inevitably commits them to drawing retrospective and (sometimes) prospective inferences. Just think back to the number of occasions when you have read a report on extensive and expensive research and still found yourself asking the 'why' and 'how' question at the end. This could be regarded as favourable by younger researchers, since it means that there is a very considerable amount of unexploited data out there just waiting for 'secondary analysis' at low cost. Nevertheless, it is lamentable when the scholars who initially chose the topic, conceptualized it, selected the cases and gathered the data do not go as far as they could in drawing 'grounded' inferences about the causality it might reveal. Manuals for sociology and political science are full of sage advice concerning the limits of doing this. Not infrequently, teachers of graduate courses and dissertation advisors will revel in providing the student with egregious examples of researchers who exceeded the confines of their data or ignored the contribution of other variables, and made what proved to be erroneous statements about causality or consequence.

The controversy that tends to dog most discussions about inference is *generalizability*. A cautious researcher who draws inferences from his or her findings that are restricted to the cases investigated and the time period covered is unlikely to face much criticism – or to generate much attention. Specialists on the topic will, no doubt, have something to say about the validity of indicators, the accuracy of measurements and the appropriateness of tests for association – but it is not until you dare to generalize across temporal, spatial or cultural contexts, until you trample on someone else's turf, that you will be seriously challenged. No one likes to be told that his or her topic can be differently explained by someone intervening from another theoretical or disciplinary perspective.

And there are good reasons for this. Although they may seem arbitrary or anachronistic (and some no doubt are), the lines of specialization built into different social science disciplines have served to enforce professional standards and preside over the accumulation of knowledge. Generalizations that are based on alternative conceptualizations and/or novel methods should be especially carefully scrutinized. Nevertheless, this is where the real scholarly excitement lies – this is where 'seminal' contributions are to be made – provided the researcher is well prepared to face his or her critics.

The strategy of case selection will play an especially significant role. Single-case studies are rarely a convincing basis for generalization – even the so-called 'crucial' ones. Large-*N* studies should be less objectionable, were it not for the fact that many of their cases are dubious in terms of their (alleged) common capacity to act and the probability that behind any associations found in the whole universe there are bound to be subsets of cases where the fit differs considerably – and may even reverse itself. Middle-size samples based on controlling for the 'usual suspects' (geographic location, development, size, religion, cultural area) by their very nature inhibit generalization, unless they are replicated for different samples. Indeed, replication can be a powerful weapon – and not just to the extent that other cases or periods produce the same direction, magnitude and significance of association. If you can show that a reliable pattern holds at different levels of aggregation within the same sample, you will have made the inference that it is more likely to hold elsewhere considerably more compelling.

The other critical factor will come from accusations of researcher bias, often alleged to be the product of the national or disciplinary context in which the researcher operates. It is only human to prefer to discover what you thought was there in the first place and, then, to extend that finding to other places about which you know less. Most often this can be attributed to a natural tendency to 'over-observe' what you expected to see and to 'under-observe' variation that you were less prepared to encounter. Along with this 'type I confirmation bias', one has to mention that type II errors also exist. In this instance, for some perverse reason, the researcher prefers to reject his or her original hypothesis and, thereby, underestimates the degree of association that actually exists. Whether the peculiarities of national cultures or academic disciplines have anything to do with either of these typical errors seems dubious to me, but there is no doubt that both exist.

The most secure way of guaranteeing enduring respect for the inferences you have drawn from your research – and of securing your place in the Pantheon of Notable Social Scientists – is to place them under the protection of a covering law. Such a law offers an explanation for a much broader range of social or political phenomena, for example the Darwinian 'Law of the Fittest'. It should be widely, if not universally, accepted by the Notables who have preceded you and, ideally, it should not be derived from the theory you started with. But do not worry if you do not make it to the Pantheon. Your contribution to knowledge can still be significant and your career as a social scientist still very rewarding.

Possibly optimizing choices

1 Add alternative explanatory variables suggested by other cases or experiences (if available without conducting an entirely new piece of research) to discover whether the original fit within your sample is maintained.

2 Probe your data by subtracting subsets of cases from the initial sample to see how robust the findings based on it were, especially when you think you are dealing with the entire universe but have reason to suspect 'regional' variations.

3 Be careful not to 'anchor' your inferences by relying too much on a single prominent association among variables at the expense of lesser (and less expected) ones.

4 When assembling a batch of inferences from a research project, do not privilege or attach greater significance to findings that were easier to document or closer to your own experience.

5 It will be risky, but try on the basis of your inferences from a given sample to predict what analogous behaviours have been in a different sample of

persons or places that you know nothing about; and (even more risky) to apply the inferences you have drawn to predicting the future performance of the units you have studied.

Potentially damaging fallacies

1 'Triumphalism': You have made a significant finding; therefore, your work is over – even though it could be the result of some variable you forgot to include and that may be very prominent in other cases or samples.

2 'Pago-Pago-ism': Whenever you think you have found something that applies everywhere, there will always be some place that you do not know (or have not even heard of) where the finding does not fit – and there will always be a scholar who knows the place and will inform you of your error.

3 'Exceptionalism': You chose to study a particular topic only in a particular country because you considered that the context was exceptional and, then, you turn around and claim that your findings are universal.

4 'Cross-level replicability': Associations among variables that have been found to be consistent in direction, strong in magnitude and significant at one level of analysis will replicate themselves at other – lower or higher – levels of aggregation within the same sample.

5 'Cognitive dissidence': If variables that simply 'should' not go together still seem to be associated, this must be due either to some unidentified measurement error or conceptual confusion, so that you are justified when drawing any inference by excluding the case or withdrawing the variable from your analysis.

6 'Temporal proximity': You choose to give greater prominence and to attach greater importance to associations of variables that have occurred more recently and to presume that earlier associations (or dissociations) should be 'discounted'.

Self-assessment

Once you have arrived at whatever stage in the research cycle you have chosen as your point of exit, your objective should be quite simple: make yourself into the best possible critic of your own work. Anticipate all of the potential objections at each of the previous stages. Where possible, return and enter appropriate corrections. Since this is often impossible, given the numerous and irreversible 'path dependencies' built into the research cycle, signal to your reader-cum-critic that you are aware of the defect and have tried your best not to be misled by it or to magnify its impact. Above all, remind yourself right from the start that no research is perfect and all researchers make mistakes. Inscribe above your desk (or on your screen saver) the Latin phrase *Errare est humanum* – 'to make mistakes is to be human'– and recognize that to be a human being studying human behaviour is to be doubly vulnerable to this maxim.

My overarching purpose in writing this chapter has been to help you to become your own best critic.

Conclusion

Social and political research is characterized by the diversity of its concepts, theories, designs – and logics. Only a few will work 'around the clock' in Figure 14.1 and conclude with empirically grounded inferences about causal relations among variables. Many will choose a topic for which this would be premature or inappropriate, given the existing state of his or her discipline or his or her purpose in selecting a particular topic. They may exit the cycle relatively early, sometime between 1 and 3 p.m. – hopefully, with an improved understanding of the generic relations involved and, possibly, with a more elaborate set of hypotheses for future research. Still others will be interested in drawing out the ethical and normative implications of these relationships, perhaps by exploring analogies with previous experiences or prior philosophic assumptions. In Figure 14.3, I have labelled this point of exit as the 'logic of discovery', the idea being that those who take it will have made their original contribution by discovering empirical or normative relationships previously ignored or distorted by existing wisdom. The chapters in this volume by Zoe Bray, Alessandro Pizzorno, Sven Steinmo and Rainer Bauböck should be especially useful to those who choose to leave the cycle at this point.

From 3 to 6 p.m. fewer social and political researchers will be leaving the cycle.[1] Their distinctive contribution will have been to identify the apposite universe surrounding the topics selected, to select cases that represent specified distributions of key variables and to have invented new ways of defining these variables and embedding them in more comprehensive theories. Most importantly, they will have carried further and in greater detail the existing conceptualization of the relationships surrounding their topic – hence, the notion that they have followed a 'logic of explication'. Donatella della Porta, Peter Mair, Christine Chwaszcza and Friedrich Kratochwil have

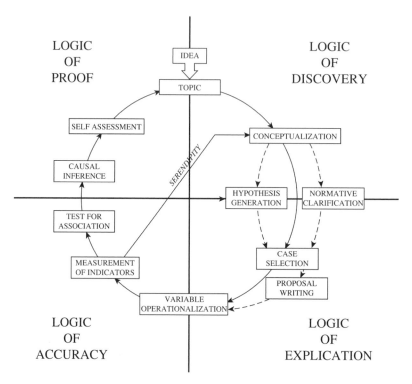

Fig. 14.3 The cycle of social and political research and its four logics

contributed chapters that should be of particular interest to them, but all of them presuppose that explication is not an end in itself, but only a necessary pre-condition for passing to the next stage which involves the specification of indicators and the gathering of data.

Many more social and political scientists will exit after 6 p.m. and before 9 p.m. They will have produced research that is fundamentally descriptive in nature. Here, the preoccupation is with the validity of their measurements and the accuracy of their observations. They will have gone into the field – even if it is in their own backyard – and generated new data about social and political phenomena. They are also most likely to have contributed to the development of better instruments of observation and more reliable indicators. Mark Franklin's chapter deals primarily with this 'logic of description'.

The chapter by Adrienne Héritier is the one that comes closest to tackling head-on the issues involved in the 'logic of proof', although virtually all of the authors touch at least peripherally on the very controversial objective of making empirically grounded inferences about causal relations in the political and social sciences. This may be where the ultimate payoff lies – and certainly where the highest disciplinary status is usually awarded – but only a select few make it to this stage in the cycle, and even their conclusions are always contingent upon eventual replication by other scholars.

The reader should not be discouraged by this. To do original research on a topic about which you care is an adventure. It can take you in different directions and end in different places. A lot will depend on your point of departure, but you will also be influenced at every turn by your professors and peers – not to mention the fads and fashions of your discipline. The most important thing is to be conscious and confident of the choices you will be making, and then to know when and where to exit from the cycle. Hopefully, this and the other chapters in this volume will help you to make the voyage easier and, ultimately, more rewarding.

NOTE

1 Unfortunately, many of them will be so-called ABDs (all but dissertations) who come up with a design for a previously conceptualized piece of research, could have written a proposal and may even have given some thought to operationalizing its variables, but never managed to actually find the time, resources or energy to gather the relevant data – much less to write them up.

15 Ethnographic approaches

Zoe Bray

Introduction

Once students in the social sciences have identified their personal research interest, they must find the most appropriate methodology. In this chapter, we explore a methodology central to the qualitative approach in the social sciences: that of ethnography. Its value lies in the flexible process by which it takes place, giving precedence to empirical findings over theoretical formulating. It is described as a naturalistic approach whose main data-gathering and analysing techniques consist of participant observation and open-ended interviewing. Ethnography is also a form of writing that encompasses a research philosophy central to the qualitative approach. Ethnography provides a valuable contribution to the social sciences that can be taken into account by researchers with differing quantitative and qualitative inclinations.

Vignette 1

In a small Spanish town, a group of women, accompanied by a few men and children, walk in silence along the main street, lined by local onlookers. As the evening gradually darkens, the lanterns they carry light up their colourful medieval-style garb. A researcher, also dressed in ceremonial clothes, walks alongside them as they approach a large concrete expanse. Gathered in this space, the members of the group stand in a wide circle surrounding a large heap of wood and bracken. An old woman steps forward from the group and sets fire to it. Soon, a big bonfire is blazing. The members of the group remain there for awhile, still holding their lanterns, before resuming their procession back through the town. The researcher, discreetly standing alongside the other members of the group, pays close attention to the event, listening to the words exchanged among the other participants and observing the serious expressions on their faces, dimly lit by the golden flames of their lanterns and the bonfire. Mentally, she makes a record of what she is witnessing. Later in the evening, in the privacy of her room, she writes it all down in her notebook.

Vignette 2

In a tidy apartment in an anonymous suburb of Mexico City, a researcher sips the coffee served by his hosts, a middle-aged couple who recently moved here from a rural part of the country. Taking a tape recorder from his bag, he places it on the table. After making sure that it is working, the researcher asks the wife to tell her life story, beginning however she wants. The wife is surprised and, a little disconcerted, asks 'Are you not going to ask me some *real* questions?!' The researcher replies that what he would like is to hear from her what *she* considers important and what is relevant to her life today in her new home. Glancing at her husband, the wife appears reassured and begins her story. As she talks, she gradually forgets that what she is saying is being recorded, and speak more freely. As the researcher listens, nodding encouragingly at the woman, he also takes mental notes of her non-verbal communication.

Vignette 3

Back in Europe, in a French provincial city, a group of strikers and union representatives are occupying a factory. Flags representing the ensigns of workers' unions from different countries are fluttering above the crowd. There is a sense of anticipation as people chat excitedly with each other in the various national languages. They are here to discuss the progress of negotiations with employers and to consider further consequences for the debate on workers' rights and policies of employment. As a woman wearing blue overalls appears at the door, the crowd hushes. Casually greeting bystanders in French and English, she walks to the other end of the room. Facing them and speaking now mainly in French, she briefs them on her discussions with the executive board as the representative of the factory workers' union. The board, she tells them, is only willing to compromise under certain conditions. Questions from the floor follow, with those expressed in languages other than French translated by a mustachioed man also in blue overalls, standing with a microphone in the corner of the room. A researcher, sitting amongst them, takes notes. As she listens to the discussion, she observes the interaction, body language, facial expressions and language choices. Later, the researcher will take a few of the participants aside and ask them in a group, and individually, to further explain some of their impressions on the meeting.

These vignettes describe the main data-gathering techniques of ethnographic research: participant observation and open-ended, discursive and semi-directed interviews. All are used in fieldwork, which is then written up and analysed as ethnography. Aimed at acquiring a deep knowledge of the social community and the individual, fieldwork typically entails adapting to a local area and culture, carrying out open-ended interviews, and spending time with members of the community. Knowledge is considered 'deep' when a subject is examined in the context of its complex connections.

While conventionally associated with anthropologists, ethnography may be useful for social scientists of other disciplines. Just as we challenge the mutually exclusive categorization of quantitative and qualitative approaches in the social sciences in the introduction to this book, we argue that other social and political scientists, however quantitative their research, may at some point find it useful to consider the ethnographic approach – at least as something useful to delve into at different points in their work and as a means to further elucidate or illustrate some aspects of their findings. In this chapter, we shall explain the classical research approach of an ethnographer. It is then up to the student to judge for herself how much to draw upon it (see also Tarrow 2004).

Ethnography lies at the heart of the social sciences because of its inherently holistic and naturalistic character. By an in-depth, holistic and naturalistic study, we mean the examination of a subject in its natural context. Whether it is the study of the macro-structures and processes that organize or affect society, such as race, ethnicity, gender and class stratification; institutions of a social, religious, political or commercial nature; or micro-processes such as interpersonal interactions and the socialization of individuals, ethnography has an important role to play. Social and political scientists are all concerned with the dynamics of interaction between people; with the multiple ways in which power is exerted, formally and informally, seen and unseen, direct and indirect; and with how these dynamics determine relations in the domains of culture, economics and politics. Ethnography provides an approach to recording and analysing data in a flexible fashion that can help in understanding the dynamics of the human social world that the researcher will encounter as she goes about her investigation (Campelli 1996).

In this chapter, we review what we mean by the ethnographic approach, explaining some of the features of its main data-gathering techniques: participant observation and open-ended interviews, including discursive and semi-directed interviews. Ethnography also includes the process of writing up the research. Inherent to it is a particular philosophical approach to research and the treatment of data.

What is ethnography?

Ethnography is at the heart of qualitative methods in the social sciences, in relation to the descriptive and interpretive approach. Qualitative research has come to be defined as involving findings reached in a manner other than by statistical procedures. As explained in the introductory chapter to this book, qualitative research is exploratory, while quantitative research is conclusive. Quantitative research addresses such questions as 'what, where and when'. Qualitative research, by contrast, investigates the 'why and how' of social action.

Within the 'why and how' mode of investigation, however, there are various techniques, many of which may be quantitative. The 'what, where and when' question may sometimes produce more complex or open-ended answers than expected. It is therefore misleading, as also indicated by della Porta and Keating (ch. 2), to present qualitative and quantitative research as mutually exclusive categories. Rather, they are complementary approaches that may employ interchangeably the techniques primarily associated with one or the other.

While methods are just ways of obtaining data, methodology is about how methods are used to resolve epistemological and theoretical issues. To attain a full understanding of a given system, research attention needs to be given to behaviour as well as to ideas, drawing on information of both a 'hard' and a 'soft' nature. A social subject is better understood when looked at from both a macro and a micro point of view, using quantitative and qualitative empirical data. A researcher looking at how the different social and economic backgrounds of children affect their professional future, for instance, may collect statistics covering a high number of children, graphing their parents' professions and income and their parents' and their own educational paths, as well as investigating in a systematic fashion their cultural and social activities and mobility. The researcher could also select a few particular children and, via participant observation and interviewing, explore the social dynamics in which these children move, as well as perhaps those of their parents. Via the second mode, the researcher will be able to provide a more contextualized understanding of the data collected through the former mode. Similarly, a researcher interested, for example, in the new possibilities of political participation offered by the Internet could count the number of websites deemed to be of a political character and the number of times these are accessed and by whom; or she could examine the case of a few users of the Internet for their particular political action. While the former provides a general comprehensive overview of the phenomenon, the latter offers an in-depth understanding of how such a process takes place. Both approaches shed light on each other and can contribute to the full analysis in any research project.

The ethnographic approach is intrinsically sensitive to the subtlety and complexity of human social life in a way that a quantitative approach cannot be. A researcher basing her work on quantitative methods will miss many of the subtleties of human expression as she fits her findings into purpose-built categories, however well grounded they may be. Nuances, expressive silences and insinuations on the part of informants will be ignored by the quantitative researcher, judged as soft data and, therefore, dismissed as scientifically unreliable. Yet, as the study of people, their cultures and the complex constructions of meaning through which they communicate, the social sciences cannot confine themselves to quantifiable methods (Klandermans and Staggenborg 2002).

In the following section, we shall look at ethnography as an approach and explain its main characteristics as naturalistic and holistic, involving a research process of three interchangeable steps. We shall then expand on ethnographic methods and writing, before ending with a discussion of ethics as an integral part of the discipline of ethnography.

It is necessary, however, to stress that research drawing on ethnography is not necessarily restricted, as has been traditionally presumed, to the work of anthropologists and scholars of cultural studies. Ethnography is useful for students of all disciplines in the social sciences who may, throughout their research using other systematic methods, feel the need to back up or enrich their study with ethnography, particularly in those situations where some of their findings consist of hunches or impressions that are difficult to prove in a systematic frame (see Schmitter, ch. 14, Franklin, ch. 13, Vennesson, ch. 12, and Héritier, ch. 4). While ethnography has traditionally been associated with micro-studies, small-scale and marginal social groups, and single-case studies, we stress that it can be applied in a variety of different contexts and at different levels of comparison, in combination with other methods.

Ethnography as an approach

Naturalistic

The ethnographic approach is naturalistic, in that it attempts to work with society as it is, without trying to influence or control it. The goal is to understand behaviour in its habitual context, as opposed to an abstract or laboratory setting, and to interpret how people give meaning to their experiences.

While scientifically motivated, ethnographic research is carried out with a humanist emphasis, delving empathetically into the complexity of the culture and political world of people.

Thus, the ceremony observed by the researcher in the first vignette highlights codes of behaviour crucial to understanding the dynamics of this society. It turns out that this ceremony, on the occasion of the annual fiestas of a town close to the frontier with France in the Spanish Basque Country, was being acted out for the second time ever. It had been conceived and staged by a group of inhabitants defending the traditional enactment of a procession during the fiestas involving the parading of local men dressed as soldiers, and in which the only participation of women hitherto had been in the form of a sort of nurse and mascot, one for each military company. Opponents of this traditional approach argued that it was inadmissible for women in today's world not to be allowed to take part in the military procession on an equal footing with men, rather than in the demeaning role of beauty-pageant figure. Defenders of the traditional procession replied that tradition, for all the modernity and gender equality of today, could not be changed. If more participation on the part of women was required, then it had to be done in other ways which respected the tradition. So they created a new parade in which women could be the main protagonists, as witnessed by our researcher. In this parade, participants re-enact another scene said to have occurred at the same historical moment as that celebrated by the town inhabitants – their attack on a foreign enemy besieging their town. While local men took up arms, the women distracted the enemy with lanterns, leading them through and out of town. But this solution has not satisfied local contesters and over the years political parties have taken sides in the debate. Accusations have since flown in all directions, with the defenders of tradition being attacked as ultra-conservatives, and their opponents being accused of being outsiders, left-wing extremists and terrorist sympathizers. To make sense of such a complex conflict in which not only gender issues are at stake but also local and national identity politics and clashing experiences of globalization, the researcher must necessarily immerse herself in it. She can thus more easily observe the tensions acted out and the power at play.

Ethnographic research involves an exploration of a society's cosmogony, of the way in which people make sense of the world they live in and how, acting on the basis of their beliefs, they relate to each other and to people different from themselves. Through descriptive generalizations and the development of explanatory interpretations about how societies work, in particular contexts and time spans, the researcher seeks to account for the commonalities and variations among societies and their trajectories over time. By assuming an intrinsic link between what is observed objectively and the subjective interpretation given to it, the researcher explains how people give objects and actions meaning in accordance with their beliefs and the conventions of society. Reality is thus appreciated as inseparable from human experience, with knowledge deemed as existing only in a social context.

Holistic

Ethnographic research is holistic in that it is founded on the idea that something can only be more fully understood when looked at as part of its 'whole' system, and by assuming that a 'whole' is more than the sum of its parts. While the idea of 'whole'-ness is, of course, illusory (see also Schmitter, ch. 14), the general idea in ethnographic research is that, by studying a phenomenon in its own dynamic context, more can be intrinsically understood about it than by simply examining it in isolation – since everything exists in relation to other things – and reducing it systematically to a list of abstract formulae.

Ethnographers immerse themselves in the context of the phenomena they are studying. Someone carrying out a study about the behaviour of football fans, for example, would attend a match and pose open-ended questions to those present with a view to understanding the context of behaviour. Responses to these questions are likely to be different in the context of a match than in a neutral setting stripped of the emotion fuelling the football fans' self-expression. Similarly, in the case of our second vignette, the researcher may well pursue his study by observing the woman in the various different contexts among which she habitually shifts and which are therefore relevant to a fuller understanding of who she is as a member of a social, cultural and political reality. These observations and 'background knowledge' (Cicourel 1991) will complement the data obtained from his interviews with her. Meanwhile, a researcher employing more quantitative interview techniques such as questionnaires or closed-ended questions to study the same subject will obtain effective data on the mobility and actions of the woman and her family, but would not be able to account for some occasionally unclear answers, ambiguous statements or silences that may also be extremely telling. In those situations, the researcher will have hunches about the significance of these but no possibility of giving them voice in a rigid quantitative framework.

Theoretical openness and self-reflexivity

Much research is directed towards testing formal theories (see Schmitter, ch. 14, and Héritier, ch. 4). This means that the researcher approaches the object of study with expectations about what she will find and with a set of already defined concepts. Ethnographic research, by contrast, attempts to take an explicitly open-ended stance. This means that the researcher does not look for specific manifestations, following pre-formed ideas of what, for example, 'identity' is (Bray 2004, 2006). This preconceived treatment of identity is very common amongst researchers who continue to take it for granted as comprising a specific array of characteristics, rather than considering the mechanisms by which the concept is crystallized as reality. In the words of Brubaker and Cooper, they confuse identity as a category of practice and as a category of analysis (2000: 5). This preconception then marks the tone of much research, giving researchers a false start.

In ethnographic work, it is crucial that the researcher reflect, before engaging in research, on her self-awareness and cultural make-up and thereby on her capacity for interpretation in environments foreign to her. She seeks to venture into the field as a *tabula rasa*, with a willingness to be open to whatever she finds and take in facts on their own terms, rather than on hers. Only after an adequate amount of time spent gaining familiarity with the social environment can the researcher decide which courses of investigation are worth pursuing and which informants merit further analysis. Equally, the researcher has to eschew preconceived ideological notions that would lead her not only to impose her own set of values but also to favour the point of view and lifestyle of a certain group of people while neglecting those of others and remaining insensitive to the power games being played out. Such an approach would stunt the scope of interpretation and produce biased results.

A process in three steps

The ethnographic approach to research involves three fundamental steps: initial formulation of the research subject and identification of the object of research; data-gathering; and writing and analysis of empirical material. While the first leads to the next, each requires the researcher to reflect back and review his approach, thereby contributing to the final refinement of the study (see also Pizzorno, ch. 9).

In the first step, the researcher focuses on so-called 'sensibilizing concepts'. These stand in contrast with 'definitive concepts'. Instead of prescribing what should be looked at, as would be the case with definitive concepts, sensibilizing concepts indicate the direction in which the researcher could look.

In the data-gathering phase, the ethnographer attempts to get to know the object of study as well as possible, principally by spending a significant length of time exposed to various situations. Any preconceptions of the object that the researcher may have had are reconsidered accordingly and the processes of participant observation and interviewing adapted. Cardano calls this particularity of ethnographic research 'submissiveness to the object' (2003: 19) during the period of fieldwork. As this full immersion can be rather intense, the researcher is recommended to go in and out of the field at regular intervals in order to take a step back and reflect efficiently on the situation under study.

The ethnographic approach also calls for continuous attention to the presence of the researcher in the data-gathering and analytical process. The researcher must be aware that, in engaging in fieldwork, he becomes, in effect, an independent variable in the study being undertaken. People are aware of the researcher's presence. To continue, therefore, in the naturalistic *démarche*, the researcher needs to consider this factor. While in some cases the researcher's presence may eventually be forgotten or pass unnoticed – which may be to the researcher's advantage for his study, depending on the subject – it may also be interesting to observe how people react to the researcher's presence.

The researcher's culture and upbringing will also affect his relationship with his informants (Touraine 1981: 37). He cannot escape being subjected to identification with the cultural, social and historical contexts of the groups to which he belongs, any more than the individuals that he is studying can separate themselves from their groups. 'Understanding', wrote Gadamer (1979: 158), 'always implies a pre-understanding which is in turn pre-figured by the determinate tradition in which the interpreter lives and shapes his prejudices.' 'The history of the individual', according to Bourdieu (1977: 86), 'is never anything other than a certain specification of the collective history of his group or class.' He must therefore bear in mind that in the gathering and analysis of his data, however empathetic it will have been thanks to his efforts in the field, his interpretation will also be based on his own cultural background and personal inclinations.

This is where, in the third phase, ethnographic writing comes in. This process essentially involves both note-taking during fieldwork and a form of analytical writing for the final manuscript. The researcher records her findings and analyses them, always in an exploratory and self-reflexive fashion. The researcher's experience is objectified in the process of making notes and observations based on the initial exploratory phase of research. At this stage, it is imperative for the researcher to continue bearing in mind her position in the society under study and how her own sense of identity and capacity for interpreting the world around her plays a role in the work. From these writings, new questions often emerge, and the researcher will reflect and redirect her study accordingly. This flexibility, together with the self-reflexivity involved, is one of the principal features that characterize the value of ethnographic research.

Ethnographic methods

As the ethnographic approach to research is essentially naturalistic, so are its methods. Naturalistic observation involves looking at subjects in their natural habitats, as they evolve without external intervention. Participant observation and interviewing enable an understanding of the perspective of people within the context of their everyday life. Effective ethnographic research requires taking the time to gain awareness of subtle human expressions (Wolcott 1999). Thus it is also known as longitudinal research, whereby continuous long-term study of an area or group of people forms the basis of data-gathering. As the researcher also asks broad questions that allow respondents to answer choosing their own words, a longitudinal approach to fieldwork allows the researcher to qualify her understanding during the research process through further probing questions.

Participant observation

Participant observation is the main data-collecting technique in ethnographic research. It requires involvement on the part of the researcher with the community of people she is studying, in their natural environment and over an extended period (DeWalt and DeWalt 2002). The researcher studies people in their own space and time, thereby gaining a close and intimate familiarity with them and their practices (Rabinow and Sullivan 1987). A researcher might also consider it necessary to learn the local language in order to better understand people on their own terms and more effectively enter their frame of mind.

Originally developed as a fieldwork technique by anthropologists such as Malinowski and Boas, and by researchers in urban studies from the Chicago School of Sociology, this technique is now widely used in other disciplines in the social sciences because of its ability to delve into the complex expressions of human life in a non-quantifiable fashion. The sociologist Lichterman, for instance, found participant observation crucial for his investigation of individualism in environmental activism; thanks to this method, he was able to 'find out how people construct these identities in everyday milieux and create bonds of political community' (1995: 240). Regarding the vague data occasionally obtained in interviews because of the informant's confusion on how to explain herself as a political actor, he noted the 'need to understand speech in the context of everyday action and interaction if we want to see how commitments translate into group solidarities' (*ibid.*).

Participant observation may be done to varying degrees, from regular formal contact with some members of a community to lengthy full immersion. There is no standard way of doing it, as this depends on the researcher's experiences in the field, how his research itinerary is determined by decisions he makes and by chance encounters and events while out in the field. Methods of participant observation are thus necessarily plural (Dal Lago and De Biasi 2002: xvii), and in his fieldwork the researcher must necessarily adopt a flexible approach in order to sensitively detect the factors of interest.

These extended periods spent with the people under study enable the researcher to obtain detailed and accurate information about them. They permit elimination of the researcher's preconceived ideas and prejudices, which may have remained unconscious, and allow him to effectively enter his informants' minds and understand their actions, non-actions and mode of thinking. Observable details are better understood over a longer period, just as more hidden details, like taboo behaviour or the unravelling of some complexity, can be discovered only with time.

By taking part in social interaction, the researcher is able to make better sense of it. The researcher can also discover discrepancies between what participants say and believe should happen and what actually does happen, or between different aspects of the formal system. This contrasts with the quantitative method of carrying out one-time surveys of people's answers to a set of questions. While these may be consistent at a particular moment in time, they are likely to give only a partial view of reality because they may involve conflict between different aspects of the social system, or between conscious representations and less conscious behaviour in further exploration.

Going back to our first vignette, then, by participating in the ceremony, the researcher is able to make more sense of the interviews that she may have conducted with some of the participants. The interviews she will undertake afterwards will be better formulated than had she not taken part in the ceremony. Via her participant observation, she has acquired deeper knowledge of the issues concerning the society under study, enabling her to get closer to the root of her research study. Likewise, in the third vignette, the researcher observes a group of people discussing common issues of concern as a team. She observes them individually, while paying attention to how their interaction forms the dynamics of the group and their collective idea-exchanging and decision-making. A researcher interested in understanding social movements from the inside will gain significantly from such exposure. Some indices of the dynamics of such contexts are additionally revealed in this case by the use of different languages. By following up with several of the individuals after the meeting, in further participant observation work and interviewing, the patterns to this interaction can be better understood.

In the process of participant observation, the researcher necessarily develops a degree of empathy with the object of study. The endeavour is for the researcher to become '*part* of the community', rather than seeing it as a mere 'other' object of study, to better understand it. This issue, however, can easily involve a personal dilemma for the researcher: what does becoming part of the community actually entail? To what extent should the researcher fit in and 'go native'? The sociologist Bertaux gives this seemingly simple but very worthy piece of advice: 'be yourself' (1999: 76). It is not necessary for the researcher to undertake total mimesis and try to become like his informants, as such engagement risks the researcher losing his own identity and thus the ability to analyse rationally his object of study. For this reason, it cannot be stressed enough that the researcher must have a strong but open understanding of himself, of who he is and how to place himself *vis à vis* his informants in order to most effectively appreciate them, with empathy and sensitivity, without sacrificing independent thinking. It is crucial that the researcher preserve a degree of detachment so that he may eventually produce an impartial scientific analysis (Hastrup and Hervik 1994).

The ethnographer's perspective has effectively to become that of both an 'insider' (emic) and an 'outsider' (etic) (Agar 1996; Roper and Shapira 2000). By taking this emic and etic perspective, a balance between subjectivity and objectivity is sought (Bourdieu 1977) in order to develop a holistic understanding of the object of study. The researcher must be able to understand issues from the inside and empathize with people's experiences and points of view, at the same time analysing them critically and impartially from the outside.

During the course of fieldwork, the researcher will inevitably form friendships with certain people more than others, on account of personal affinities. It is difficult to provide external advice on such occurrences; it is for the researcher to judge how to manage particular relationships with various informants while considering the potential ethical and professional consequences. For example, when spending more time with certain people because of friendships formed, a researcher should not be surprised if other informants to whom he would have liked to have had equal access are no longer as willing to communicate with him as he would have wished (see also Whyte 1994). All of these situations will therefore have an impact, not only on the quality of the researcher's findings but also on the project's ultimate direction and focus (Adler and Adler 1987).

It may be useful for the researcher occasionally to take a break from long periods of fieldwork and return to an academic environment. This separation enables her to regain a sense of perspective and to minimize emotional involvement in the subject. The shifting from practice to theory enables the researcher adequately to re-evaluate each (Briggs 1986), to reflect on the observations made during fieldwork in an appropriately objective-subjective fashion and to reconsider her theoretical frames with a view to refining them. Coming back to the field at regular intervals also enables the researcher to see the object of study with a fresh eye, to notice aspects she may well have not noticed earlier or to observe the changes that will most certainly have taken place (Wengle 1988).

A variant of participant observation, observant participation, is often used to describe fieldwork in contexts in which the researcher is personally involved outside the immediate context of her academic work. This could be the case, for example, in relation to research relating to a minority community to which the researcher has links of affinity. Partial or full membership in the community or subculture that is the object of research allows a different sort of access to the community while shaping the researcher's perceptions in ways different from those of a full outsider. Such is the example of the social anthropologist Lila Abu-Lughod, who is of North American and Palestinian parents and who looks at the diverse experiences of women in the Muslim world today. Her status as a woman with a personal link to the Middle East meant that not only was she more easily able to get to the core of the issue, but she was also more rapidly admitted into its world and confided in by its members (Abu-Lughod 1988). Here, such a status is an advantage. However, there are other occasions when it risks being a disadvantage for the capacity to produce impartial research. Such is true, for example, for a researcher with nationalist sympathies studying either issues of identity and politics in a minority community, or immigration issues in his home country. In the first case, the researcher may be empathetic to certain expressions and plights of the community but remain insensitive to other, perhaps more subtle, expressions on the part of other community members whom the researcher may have not recognized as such. In the second case, he risks simply producing a normative and self-interested project.

What is crucial in this thoroughly personally engaging way of doing research is for the ethnographer to develop sensitivity and rationality, both necessary for the capacity to read impartially into situations. Because many aspects of social life cannot be broken down into bits, as in an ideal quantitative world, it is the work of the ethnographer to pick them out in the most scientific way possible. The unemotional hunches the researcher will have developed from her experience both in the field and in the academic environment will acquire value worthy of scientific consideration. Finally, as a human being herself, the researcher can only 'do (her) best' (again in the words of Bertaux) to be as attentive and open-minded as possible.

While out in the field, it is also recommended that the researcher make a pause in her academic literature reading to immerse herself thoroughly in the world she is studying and not be influenced by theoretical considerations. She is recommended to carry a notebook with her constantly, in which to note down all her observations and impressions.

Interviewing

Interviews serve to deepen the inside knowledge of the community under study. They help the researcher to obtain a thorough grasp of the role of the individual as social actor (Spradley 1979; Crapanzano 1992; Fowler and Hardesty 1994). Interviews complement participant observation in that they enable the researcher to check what people say they do against what they actually do (Spradley 1980; Burawoy, Burton, Ferguson *et al.* 1991: 20).

Interviews will take place at various moments in time during fieldwork, and different kinds may be used depending on the researcher's needs. In ethnographic research, the main form of interviewing is open-ended, either discursive or semi-directed. By discursive, we mean interviews such as the one in the second vignette, where the woman begins her personal account as she wishes, choosing freely what she considers important. This technique is most frequently used by researchers relying on biographical accounts or interested in personal history. It may also be used to help an informant to feel at ease and talk freely with the help of familiar references. Such an interview can become semi-directed as the researcher begins to ask more pointed questions, directing them towards the issues relevant to her study. They remain open-ended in that they do not require the interviewee to reply within a restricted frame, such as is found in a questionnaire-style interview.

The formulation, ordering and scaling of questions in open-ended and semi-directed interviews are critical for their success. It is important to bear in mind that the background of interviewees may affect their interpretation of the questions. Questions must be neutral as to intended outcome. A biased question encourages respondents to answer in one way rather than another; even questions without bias may leave respondents with expectations. The order or 'natural' grouping of questions is often relevant, as the nature of a previous question may affect the answer to a subsequent one. Wording should be kept simple, without technical or specialized jargon, and the meaning of questions should be clear. Ambiguous words, equivocal sentence structures and negatives cause misunderstanding, invalidating the interview results. Double negatives should be reworded as positives. Contingency or follow-up questions can be posed if a respondent gives a particular response to a previous question, enabling the researcher to avoid posing irrelevant questions. The researcher will also need to develop the capacity to improvise, judging for herself and from her previous observations how valid some of her questions may be to the particular interviewee.

Open-ended interviews are the main technique in ethnographic research precisely because they enable interviewees to say what they feel is relevant and important to them. Open-ended questions suggest no options or predefined categories. Respondents supply their own answers without being constrained by a fixed set of possible responses. Within this flexible format, it is nonetheless necessary for the ethnographer to impose some order on all the information she is gathering in order to manage the overload of information, the relevance of which she will eventually be able to judge as she progresses in her fieldwork.

There are various types of open-ended question. For example, completely unstructured questions could involve asking an interviewee's opinion on a certain issue, or exploring what was his important consideration in a moment of decision-making. The researcher works according to what the informants say, directing the discussion to the areas that she wants further explored and deepened. This directing is done in various ways, employing open-ended questions and following a pattern that replicates the experience, such as: 'What did you do when you arrived?' 'How did you feel then?' For example, a researcher interested in exploring the European discourse of regional politicians might begin in this way: 'What does the idea of Europe mean to you?' 'How is it important in your work?' 'What, in your opinion, makes the reference to Europe worthwhile, or not?' Following on from the answers received, the researcher can then proceed to more specific examples and explanations.

The selection of informants will depend on the research objective, but the range should be wide. To understand a local conflict, for example, it will be useful to observe not only those directly involved in it but also people who are not involved, thereby providing an outsider's experience. The researcher must also decide whether to select interviewees according to categories such as sex, age, economic class, social group and background, depending on their relevance to the issue under study. In the case of the second vignette, a study on immigration policy and here specifically on the experience of rural families who have migrated to the city, the researcher will have to decide for himself upon the relevance of focusing on the woman or/and the man as an informant. Ultimately, many of these issues will be solved depending on the flair of the researcher as he goes about exploring the terrain. The scientific value of his style and hunches will be judged based on how well he can justify his actions in the field and explain the situations he observed and his impressions. This will come in the form of ethnographic writing, which we shall explain later.

In carrying out the interview, the researcher adapts to the situation, taking account of how different people relax and open up according to circumstances. Thus, the researcher's interview technique might range from informal small talk to longer and more directed interviews that may be recorded *in situ*. In the vignette, the researcher asks the woman to tell her story in her husband's presence. Alternatively, the researcher might prefer to invite the woman to speak on her own, on the assumption that she might speak more freely without her husband beside her. The researcher has to bear in mind that the answers he obtains may change according to the context in which the interview takes place. In order to allow the informant to feel more at ease and less self-conscious, the researcher must find the situation most amenable to the interviewee and be ready to carry out informal interviews in informal settings (Kvale 1996).

Recording interviews is crucial, but it will be for the researcher to judge how necessary it is to record absolutely everything. It is vitally important to note down the conditions and circumstances in which an interview takes place and the general feelings she has during the interview. If the researcher can use a tape recorder, so much the better. Unless she is carrying out discourse or speech analysis, however, the scientificity will depend not so much on the exact recording of her informants' interviews as on the essentials of what they said, including the way in which they formulated their ideas, their choice of words and their expressions. The same applies to transcription of interviews. In my experience, a tape recorder has often hindered the spontaneity of verbal exchanges with informants, even if they may eventually have forgotten about its presence. I learnt rapidly to rely on my own discipline to note information and quotes as fast as I could, either *in situ*, or graved in my mind to write them more succinctly on my laptop later. Of course, it did mean that sometimes my citations of people were not precisely *ad verbum*; but the essence of what the informants said remained, and, embedded in my thick descriptions of the informant, their personal and social background and the context in which I had met them, enabled the quotes to conserve all their validity and legitimacy as data for my final analysis.

Finally, it is imperative for the ethnographer to develop a discipline of noting everything down quickly and succinctly, of mulling over his notes, practically 'sleeping with them' (Demaziere and Dubar 2000: 296). By scrupulously reviewing this data, constantly comparing it with other findings and, as far as possible, verifying it again with informants, the ethnographer effectively tackles data in a scientific fashion.

Ethnographic writing and analysis

Ethnography is derived from Ancient Greek words meaning 'writing on people' – although it can also take the final form of film documentaries and other audio-visuals. Ethnology is, then, the comparative synthesis of ethnographic information. Ethnography is the researcher's main mode of recording and analysing the data gathered during fieldwork. It is initially composed of field notes with a mix of quotations from informants, descriptions of events and informants' behaviour and personal impressions and questions (Sperber 1984: 13), all self-reflectively elaborated. This reflexive account is what renders the researcher's data-gathering process scientifically valid (Altheide and Johnson 1994). Ethnographic notes can also take the form of a diary. When quoting informants, it is imperative that the researcher explain the context in which the informants spoke. The ethnographic notes will also contain other material the researcher may have deemed relevant while in the field, including quantitative data such as statistics, but also artefacts, photographs and films.

Out of the field and back in an academic environment, the researcher begins to 'clean up' her ethnographic material, rewriting her descriptions and interpretations in a coherent style, backed up by self-reflexive references and regular reminders that the researcher's impressions are personal. This reveals the researcher's ability to relativize and, based on this self-reflexivity and the long period spent in the field, to produce a fair evaluation (Altheide and Johnson 1994; Richardson 1994). When constructing an interpretation of a text, it is necessary to explain why such an interpretation is appropriate, as well as why other alternative interpretations were discarded, or, in Gadamer's (1979) words, 'justify what is not correct'. As the researcher goes about giving her descriptions order as part of the analysis, she will do so on the basis of the sensibilizing concepts, placing them according to themes, actors, situations and whatever else emerges from the field.

The ethnographic manuscript ends up, after thorough reviewing and stylistic accommodation, as a critical and analytical account of the culture, society or community studied and particular issues related to it. This final ethnographic account will be composed of both thick and thin descriptions of the community examined by the researcher – that is, a process going from the general to the specific, describing the subject under study in its context.

There are different ways of doing this, depending on the writing style the researcher adopts – whether it is narrative (the researcher telling the story), discursive (the informant telling her story), or punctuated by illustrative vignettes or stories and corresponding analyses. Vignettes recount specific events, moments that reveal the issues addressed by the researcher. They may be about the behaviour and reactions of individuals to specific instances, and their relationships to other people and ideas. In these descriptions, the researcher must mention all those details that are revealing. Superfluous details must be left out. So describing the woman as wearing blue overalls and speaking different languages must be mentioned only if these details help the reader to situate the person in the analysis, if the researcher is concerned about symbols and their role in a particular cultural environment and if they are revealing of the interaction taking place among the various people gathered together. Finally, the writing style should bear in mind not only the general reader, but also the people who are the subject of the study.

Ethics

Ethics is a crucial aspect of the discipline of ethnography. As a person entering the lives of the people under study, the researcher holds an important responsibility to them. It is fundamental that he work transparently with respect to his research and his relationship with his informants. When delving into private aspects of their lives or making public some of his findings, the researcher must always ask permission. He must also be able to explain as clearly as possible the subject of his study and his interest in spending time with the community. Often, particularly in situations of conflict, the researcher may be solicited by informants to take sides, or asked to express an opinion on the local situation as a supposed 'expert' in the field. He must be able to respond in a neutral fashion, on the lines of the complexity of the situation at stake and his attempt simply to explore the different dynamics of interaction in this particular case and how they shed light on human relations in different circumstances.

In interviewing situations, questions should not be too intimate or indiscreet; but the researcher can probe according to his judgement of the level of trust that is developed with the respondent. The researcher has also the responsibility of assuring confidentiality. When describing the private, intimate life of some informants, it may be necessary to preserve their anonymity by using invented names. These names can nonetheless reflect the cultural aspect of the person so as to still evoke the relevant idea for the final ethnographic report.

Conclusion

We have described ethnography as an approach and a method. Aimed at acquiring a deeper knowledge of the social community and the individual as a member of society, ethnography does this by means of fieldwork, carrying out open-ended interviews and spending time interacting with members of the community. Ethnography refers also to the final writing up of the research.

Ethnography holds central place in the social and political sciences because of its inherently holistic and naturalistic character, which is fundamental for a thorough understanding of the human being as a social subject. It provides a methodology for data-gathering and data analysis in a flexible fashion that can account for the non-palpability and complex dynamics of the human social world that the researcher will encounter as she goes about her investigation.

While conventionally associated with anthropologists, ethnography is a research approach and method that is useful for social and political scientists of other disciplines to take into account. Alongside their principal methods of research, it can help them to provide further light on their findings and to illustrate their work more vividly.

Nowadays, we recognize that the representation of a social fact is a representation from a particular point of view. The advantage of ethnography as a research tool then becomes clear: thanks to its emphasis on context and self-reflexivity, ethnography explains the viewpoint from which the researcher makes her interpretation. A researcher's hunches and the nuances she will have picked up during her research either hold no validity or are uneasily integrated in other methods of research. With an ethnographic approach, on the other hand, with all that it entails – close empathetic observation and self-reflexivity – these findings are given their just scientific weight.

Comparing approaches, methodologies and methods. Some concluding remarks

Donatella della Porta and Michael Keating

Surveying the differences in approaches

As mentioned in the Introduction, this volume is a plea against the construction of impenetrable barriers between approaches. We believe that social science knowledge is a collective enterprise, built using various techniques, methodologies and methods.

Social science research is made from different tasks and different moments – from the selection of a problem for analysis, through the development of proper theories and concepts, to the choice of cases and units of analysis, data collection and data analysis. Although each research project has to give serious consideration to each of these tasks, single pieces of research usually privilege some of them. Some are more oriented towards the development of new concepts; some explicitly aim at theorization; some are field-oriented, producing new data; some use sophisticated techniques for data analysis; and some are geared to normative questions.

Even very good pieces of research are usually remembered because they gave a particularly original contribution to one (or a couple) of these tasks. Some contributions are often cited because of the systematization of new concepts (for example, Charles Tilly's concept of a repertoire of collective action), others because they put forward a new theory about a macro-phenomenon (such as Barrington Moore Jr's work on the origins of democracy). Some pieces of research are considered as particularly valuable because of the collection of new databases (for example in values surveys or electoral studies), while others use existing databases but aim at developing new instruments of data analysis.

Subdisciplines differ in their attention to the different steps of research. Political and social theorists reflect a great deal on concept development and deductive theorization, and methodologists stress the importance of data collection and data analysis. Even if American influence since the 1950s has had a homogenizing impact on sociology and political science, there is still some truth in the stereotypical vision of greater attention to empirical investigation in the Anglo-Saxon culture and to theory-building on the European continent. At the national level, such relatively young disciplines as sociology and political science still reflect the impact of the different disciplines that nurtured them: for example, philosophy in Italy versus law in France for political science (Favre 1985; Morlino 1989). Beyond the path-dependency from the past, the disciplinary proximity to other 'sister' disciplines also helps explain the ways in which some scholars developed general preferences. Methodological individualism is a basis for theorizing through modelling closely resembling economics. Attention to institutions and culture (see, respectively, Steinmo's and Keating's chapters) is more influenced by historical approaches. The epistemological assumption about the need to 'understand the world in order to change it' – as French political scientist Pierre Favre (2005) put it – finds support among normative theorists but also among administrative scientists, who are usually more interested in the policy (or political) relevance of the social sciences. Qualitative scholars usually give more attention to conceptualization in the form of the development of 'systematized concepts', while quantitativists focus their concerns on operationalization (that is, the choice of indicators) (Adcock and Collier 2001).

This also means that each good research project is indebted to the work of other scholars. We refer to other people's theories; borrow concepts that are developed (either inductively or deductively) by others; make use of previous debates on problems and solutions in data collection; apply techniques of analysis that have long histories of trial and error. Each piece of research usually only marginally improves on issues of theoretical clarity and empirical knowledge.

In sum, social science is a collective endeavour in which various skills and a large amount of communication between scholars are needed. This is not as obvious a statement as it seems. Method-driven research has the merit of improving methodological reflections, but it is far from producing reciprocal understanding among scholars using different methods. Scholars more explicitly concerned with methods ('method-conscious') often tend to radical and misleading criticism of their opponents. So on the one hand, 'interpretivist' approaches are depicted as unscientific subjective narratives, while, on the other, 'positivist' approaches are dismissed as illusionary mimicry of natural sciences. There is a recurrent tendency to present simplistic interpretations of the classical authors (Van Langenhove 2007). Occasionally, such misrepresentation is deliberate. More often, it stems from ignorance about the development of the other branch, its sophistication and its success in overcoming its own earlier shortcomings. Even the word 'theory' is used in different ways. For some, it means modelling social behaviour with a view to scientific explanation and prediction. For others, it refers to normative reflection, with its origins in philosophy and the humanities. 'Critical theory', in turn, is pitted against both.

With this volume we would like, instead, to facilitate communication and to overcome stereotypes through a respect for the plurality of approaches in the social sciences. Pluralism emerges first of all from the combination of chapters, with an attempt to cover the various steps of research according to different epistemological approaches. In this endeavour, as mentioned, we have been helped by the participation of scholars who work within different perspectives and who present 'from within' their experiences with approaches and methods. Second, during the writing of this volume (as in other social enterprises), a social capital of reciprocal trust has been activated facilitating the development, if not of complete agreement, at least of a mutual understanding of the concerns and challenges coming from other approaches. In the various processes of redrafting, the chapters started to talk more to each other.

The contributions in our volume are far from disproving the existence of cleavages in the understanding of the logic and practice of the social sciences. Important differences are visible in the tensions between the desire for generalization and the acknowledgement of complexity. Héritier is as explicit in the preference for the construction of (possibly) law-like statements as Kratochwil is in warning against the illusion of them. Even in the narrative style, Kratochwil's presentation of 'what constructivism is (and is not)' privileges a philosophical criticism of an ontological vision of reality as (more or less) easily captured by social science knowledge. It does not deny that the purpose of social science is understanding, but it conceptualizes the logic (and limits) of explanation proper to social sciences as different from the dominant one in some natural sciences. A similar diversity in the conception of the purpose of social science is visible if we contrast the logic of modelling in game theory as presented in Chwaszcza's chapter with an understanding of individual behaviour as based upon a search for recognition in Pizzorno's sociological analysis. If a recognition of the role of human agency is present in both approaches, the assumptions about what motivates people (as well as about how much these motivations should be subject to empirical scrutiny) differ widely. The conception of science as being neutral rather than normatively oriented also represents, as Bauböck stresses in his chapter a relevant difference in social science thinking and practices.

Different nuances are visible in how scholars working within different traditions address the steps in the construction of a research design. Whereas both Kratochwil and Mair recognize how crucial is the task of conceptualization, the former defines concepts as necessary filters between the world and our knowledge of it, recognizing their normative load (a point also made by Bauböck), while the latter is less interested in where the concepts originate and more focused on the construction of a common vocabulary that would make knowledge cumulative. In the development of the explanatory models that will guide empirical research, the very conception of causality shifts, between the (parsimonious) focus on relations between variables presented by Héritier and the historically dense process tracing used by Vennesson. In these different emphases, what is at stake is also the recognition of the understanding of specific (sometimes defined as 'single-N') events as a legitimate object for the social sciences, and whether descriptive analysis should always be hierarchically subordinate to causal inference. A similar difference in emphasis is visible in the way in which Schmitter and della Porta address the issues of case selection and, especially, 'casing' (that is, how cases should be conceptualized). More confident in generalization, Schmitter suggests increasing the number of cases, whenever possible, and especially 'substitut[ing] variables for proper names'. By contrast, della Porta defends the traditional distinction between comparison by variables and comparison by cases, considering the different (legitimate) assumptions that accompany the two strategies. Finally, with regard to contrasting methods, the chapters by Franklin on quantitative techniques and by Bray on qualitative ones make clear the differences, not only in how to treat empirical evidence, but also in how to conceive fieldwork and how it relates with theorizing.

Although these differences persist, we also noticed potential for dialogue between approaches and methodologies. Mair and Kratochwil both consider conceptualization as a basic step in research and theory; the chapters on game theory and recognition theory both emphasize individual motivations; causal analysis and case studies both develop process tracing as a methodological tool; Schmitter and della Porta agree on the legitimacy of starting and stopping at different moments on the 'research clock'; Franklin and Bray both stress the relevance of method-conscious work.

We can also identify meeting-points among the various approaches, even where they are not complementary across the board. Chwaszcza takes us through rational choice and game theory and ends up pointing to the importance of institutions, thus linking to the concerns of Steinmo and Héritier. Bray, looking at the perceptions and motivations of individuals in context, helps to open up Héritier's 'black box', although Héritier herself is more informed by rational choice assumptions. Keating brings in culture and values as a factor in motivation, helping to answer questions that rational choice and game theory do not themselves address – that is, why people want to do certain things. Venesson and Héritier both cover 'process tracing' as a way of connecting events and constructing causal links. Bauböck shows how normative questions arise in the course of empirical research and, while some social scientists insist that they should be excluded, shows how they can be incorporated into research design. It is often at these meeting-points between theories and approaches that the most interesting and challenging work in social science is done.

Where do we go and how?

An important issue remains. Is it possible to recognize all of the above differences and still believe in the possibility of a cumulative enterprise that makes use of the different approaches; or is the aim of a peaceful co-existence based upon a sort of 'pillarization' the only realistic one? One possibility, as Bauböck suggests, is to regard social science as cumulative, but not in a linear manner. Methodological triangulation may provide another way forward (see della Porta and Keating, ch. 2). Some scholars still consider a sort of methodological monism as healthier, regretting the attacks of general theorists and qualitative methodologists (from ethnographers to historical sociologists) against 'positivism' (Goldthorpe 2000: 5). In this perspective, different views are considered as incompatible and third ways that appeal to pluralism as misleading rhetoric (*ibid.*, especially ch. 4). It often depends on whether we are inclined to see scientific discoveries as dependent upon an ordered and well-structured process, or a contingent 'mess' (Law 2004); whether we search for 'the one true theory about the universe', or the acknowledgement that 'our preserved theories on the world fit together so snugly less because we have found out how the world is than because we have tailored each to the other' (Hacking 1992: 3).

To address these questions, it is useful to reflect on some trends that intensify the separation between exponents of different approaches and methods, but also on others that counter it. One is the growing methodological sophistication within each approach, requiring more and more investment in learning the basic technical skills, together with the growth of theories and empirical knowledge in every field. Professional knowledge increases exponentially, with the effect of requiring a degree of specialization. As political scientists and sociologists would acknowledge, were they to reflect on their own profession as a social system, politics (or power games) then serve to freeze the resulting 'social cleavages'. We have already mentioned some trends towards professionalization, with journals, associations, summer schools and specialized departments. All this creates many avenues for the consolidation of each approach, but less space for cross-fertilization among them. Conflict dynamics strengthen these 'identities' in the competition for scarce resources, and methodological debates escalate into holy wars within and between departments, journals and professional associations. The stereotyping of the 'other' leads to its stigmatization and, sometimes, to what criminologists call 'secondary deviance'. If specialization reduces the capacity to understand each other's work, conflictual dynamics reduce even the interest in communicating.

Fortunately, this dark image depicts only part of the debate in the social sciences, since there are some countertendencies that push towards cross-fertilization. Europeanization as well as the set of phenomena that go under the label of 'cultural globalization' have facilitated transnational communication, with some cross-border intellectual curiosity. This is particularly true in the European Union where, although academic power is still nationally structured, occasions for international encounters have increased at all stages of an academic career. Even sceptics would admit that new technologies have changed our conception of spaces. Whether or not globalization represents a new social reality or just a new understanding of old ones, it challenges acquired knowledge and the capacity of existing categories such as states or social classes (to cite just two concepts critical in political science and sociology). This calls for a convergence of efforts from different disciplines to reflect on the challenge to the welfare state in the face of demographic changes, the problems of representative democracies in dealing with the growing power of economic corporations, or the difficulties of the nation-states in addressing new configurations of power at multiple levels. Finally, *per amore o per forza*, these new challenges – to which problem-oriented scholars are especially sensitive – have pushed towards more cross-national research, often under the sponsorship of international organizations, thus providing occasions for interaction and communication.

The combination of different methods (especially qualitative and quantitative) in order to increase the validity and overcome the biases of each approach has been dismissed as naïve, given 'the different and incommensurate ontological and epistemological assumptions associated with various theories and methods' (Blaikie 1991: 115). It is true that mere eclecticism is a mistake and that accumulating evidence based on very different epistemological assumptions does not increase confidence in results. Yet, as we emphasized earlier (Chapter 2), there is scope for synthesis, triangulation, multiple perspectives and cross-fertilization. To return to the questions we raised there and in the Introduction (Chapter 1), different methods can be equally valid, depending on the question we are asking. So what is needed in order to 'bridge the quantitative–qualitative divide' (Tarrow 2004) is a recognition of the relevance of such different questions, for example structural impacts and individual perceptions of them, or continuities and changes. James Mahoney and Gary Goertz (2006) similarly acknowledge the legitimacy of two main approaches to explanation: the qualitative one – that is, searching for explanation of certain outcomes in individual cases (a 'causes-of-effects' approach to explanation) – and the quantitative one, looking for the general effects of various causes (an 'effects-of-causes' approach to explanation). From this main difference, others derive. The scope of generalization is limited (sometimes even just to the analysed cases) in the first approach, and as broad as possible in the second one. A deterministic logic, with its search for necessary causes and concern with lack of fit, features in the first approach, and a probabilistic one in the second. Social sciences, as we have emphasized, may have many goals. Rather than committing themselves to one methodology as a matter of principle or dogma, we believe that social scientists should choose an approach, a methodology and specific methods appropriate to the questions they are asking.

References

Abbott, Andrew 1992. 'What Do Cases Do? Some Notes on Activity in Sociological Analysis', in Ragin and Becker (eds.), pp. 53–82.

Abel, Peter (ed.) 1991. *Rational Choice Theory*. Aldershot: Edward Elgar.

Abélès, Marc 1989. *Jours tranquilles en 89: ethnologie politique d'un département français*. Paris: Éditions O. Jacob.

Abu-Lughod, Lila 1988. 'Fieldwork of a Dutiful Daughter', in Saraya Altorki and Camillia Fawzi El-Solh (eds.), *Arab Women in the Field: Studying Your Own Society*. Syracuse, N.Y.: Syracuse University Press, pp. 139–61.

Ackerman, Bruce and James Fishkin 2004. *Deliberation Day*. New Haven: Yale University Press.

Adcock, Robert 2005. 'What is a Concept?', Working Paper no. 1, Committee on Concepts and Methods, International Political Science Association.

Adcock, Robert and David Collier 2001. 'Measurement Validity: A Shared Standard for Qualitative and Quantitative Research', *American Political Science Review* 95: 529–47.

Adler, Emmanuel 1997. 'Seizing the Middle Ground', *European Journal of International Relations* 3(3): 319–63.

Adler, Patricia A. and Peter Adler 1987. *Membership Roles Field Research*. Newbury Park, Calif.: Sage.

Agar, Michael H. 1996. *The Professional Stranger: An Informal Introduction to Ethnography*. San Diego, Calif.: Academic Press.

Allais, Maurice 1953. 'Le comportement de l'homme rationnel devant le risque: critique des postulats et axiomes de l'école américaine', *Econometrica* 21: 503–46.

Allen, William Sheridan 1984. *The Nazi Seizure of Power. The Experience of a Single German Town 1922–1945* (1st edn 1965). New York: Franklin Watts.

Allingham, Michael (ed.) 2006. *Rational Choice Theory*, 5 vols. London: Routledge.

Allison, Graham T. 1971. *Essence of Decision: Explaining the Cuban Missile Crisis*. Boston: Little, Brown.

Almond, Gabriel A. 1990. *A Discipline Divided: Schools and Sects in Political Science*. Newbury Park, Calif.: Sage.

Almond, Gabriel A. and Stephen J. Genco 1977. 'Clouds, Clocks, and the Study of Politics', *World Politics* 4 (July): 489–522.

Almond, Gabriel A. and Sidney Verba 1965. *The Civic Culture: Political Attitudes and Democracy in Five Nations*. Boston: Little, Brown.

Almond, Gabriel A. and Sidney Verba (eds.) 1980. *The Civic Culture Revisited*. Boston: Little, Brown.

Altheide, David L. and John M. Johnson 1994. 'Criteria for Assessing Interpretive Validity in

Qualitative Research', in Norman K. Denzin and Yvonna S. Lincoln (eds.), *Handbook of Qualitative Research*. London: Sage, pp. 485–99.

Amenta, Edwin 1991. 'Making the Most of a Case Study: Theories of the Welfare State and the American Experience', in Charles C. Ragin (ed.), *Issues and Alternatives in Comparative Social Research*. Leiden: E. J. Brill, pp. 172–94.

Amin, Ash 1999. 'An Institutionalist Perspective on Regional Economic Development', *International Journal of Urban and Regional Research* 23(2): 365–78.

Anckar, Dag 1997. 'Nomination: A Note on the Cumulation Problem', *European Journal of Political Research* 31(1): 73–81.

Anderson, Benedict 1983. *Imagined Communities: Reflections on the Origin and Spread of Nationalism*. London: Verso.

Aoki, Masahiko 2001. *Towards a Comparative Institutional Analysis*. Cambridge, Mass.: MIT Press.

Arendt Hannah 1970. *Macht und Gewalt*. Munich: Piper.

Aristotle 1999. *The Politics and the Constitution of Athens* (ed. Stephen Everson). Cambridge University Press.

Arneson, Richard and Ian Shapiro 1996. 'Democratic Autonomy and Religious Freedom: A Critique of Wisconsin v. Yoder', in Russell Hardin and Ian Shapiro (eds.), *Political Order* (NOMOS XXXVIII). New York University Press, pp. 365–411.

Auyero, Javier 2007. *Routine Politics and Violence in Argentina*. Cambridge University Press.

Axelrod, Robert 1984. *The Evolution of Cooperation*. New York: Basic Books.

Bachelard, Gaston 1971. (Textes choisis par Dominique Lecourt). *Epistémologie. Textes choisis.* Paris: Presses universitaires de France.

  1986. *Le rationalisme appliqué* (1st edn 1949). Paris: Presses universitaires de France.

  1991. *Le nouvel esprit scientifique* (1st edn 1934). Paris: Presses universitaires de France.

  1993. *La formation de l'esprit scientifique. Contribution à une psychanalyse de la connaissance* (1st edn 1938). Paris: Vrin.

Bader, Veit 2005. 'The Ethics of Immigration', *Constellations* 12(3): 331–61.

Bagnasco, Arnaldo and Carlo Trigilia 1993. *La construction sociale du marché. Le défi de la troisième Italie*. Cachan: Éditions de l'Ecole Normale Supérieur de Cachan.

Ball, Terence 2002. 'Confessions of a Conceptual Historian', *Redescriptions: Yearbook of Political Thought and Conceptual History* 6: 11–31.

Banfield, Edward C. with Laura Fasano 1958. *The Moral Basis of a Backward Society*. Glencoe, Ill.: The Free Press.

Banting, Keith and Will Kymlicka (eds.) 2007. *Multiculturalism and the Welfare State: Recognition and Redistribution in Contemporary Democracies*. Oxford University Press.

Barry, Brian 1989. *A Treatise on Social Justice*, vol. I: *Theories of Justice*. London: Harvester Wheatsheaf.

Barthes, Roland 1972. *Mythologies*. London: Jonathan Cape.

Bartolini, Stefano 1993. 'On Time and Comparative Research', *Journal of Theoretical Politics* 5: 131–67.

  2000. *The Political Mobilization of the European Left, 1860–1980: The Class Cleavage*. Cambridge University Press.

  2006. *Restructuring Europe: Centre Formation, System Building, and Political Structuring between the Nation State and the European Union*. Oxford University Press.

Bartolini, Stefano and Peter Mair 1990. *Identity, Competition and Electoral Availability: The Stabilisation of European Electorates, 1885–1985.* Cambridge University Press.

2001. 'Challenges to Contemporary Political Parties', in Larry Diamond and Richard Gunther (eds.), *Political Parties and Democracy.* Baltimore: Johns Hopkins University Press, pp. 327–43.

Bates, Robert, Avner Greif, Margaret Levi, Jean-Laurent Rosenthal and Barry Weingast 1998. *Analytic Narratives.* Princeton University Press.

Bauböck, Rainer 1997. 'Notwendige Öffnung und legitime Schließung liberaler Demokratien', *Archives Européennes de Sociologie,* no. 1: 71–103.

Beitz, Charles 1979. *Political Theory and International Relations.* Princeton University Press.

Belkin, Aaron and Philip Tetlock (eds.) 1996. *Counterfactual Thought Experiment in World Politics.* Princeton University Press.

Bellah, Robert 1985. *Habits of the Heart. Individualism and Commitment in American Life.* Berkeley: University of California Press.

Bendix, Reinhard 1963. 'Concepts and Generalizations in Comparative Sociological Studies', *American Sociological Review* 28: 532–9.

Benhabib, Seyla (ed.) 1996. *Democracy and Difference.* Princeton University Press.

Bennett, Andrew 2004. 'Case Study Methods: Design, Use, and Comparative Advantages', in Detlef F. Sprinz and Yael Nahmias-Wolinsky (eds.), *Models, Numbers and Cases: Methods for Studying International Relations.* Ann Arbor: University of Michigan Press, pp. 19–55.

Bennett, Andrew and Colin Elman 2006. 'Qualitative Research: Recent Developments in Case Study Methods', *Annual Review of Political Science* 9: 455–76.

Bennett, Andrew and Alexander L. George 2001. 'Case Studies and Process Tracing in History and Political Science: Similar Strokes for Different Foci', in Colin Elman and Miriam Fendius Elman (eds.), *Bridges and Boundaries.* Cambridge, Mass.: MIT Press, pp. 137–66.

Beran, Harry 1984. 'A Liberal Theory of Secession', *Political Studies* 32: 21–31.

Berger, Peter and Thomas Luckmann 1967. *The Social Construction of Reality.* Garden City, N.J.: Doubleday.

Berlin, Isaiah 1969/1979. *Four Essays on Liberty.* Oxford University Press.

2002. 'Two Concepts of Freedom', in Isaiah Berlin, *Liberty* (ed. Henry Hardy). Oxford University Press, pp. 188–217.

Berman, Sheri E. 2001. 'Modernization in Historical Perspective. The Case of Imperial Germany', *World Politics* 53: 431–62.

Bertaux, Daniel 1999. 'L'approche biographique: sa validité méthodologique, ses potentialités', *Cahiers internationaux de sociologie* 64: 197–225.

Berthet, Thierry and Jacques Palard 1997. 'Culture politique réfractaire et décollage économique. L'exemple de la Vendée du Nord-Est', *Revue française de science politique* 47(1): 29–48.

Bevir, Mark and R. A. W. Rhodes 2003. *Interpreting British Governance.* London: Routledge.

Bicchieri, Cristina 2006. *The Grammar of Society: The Nature and Dynamics of Social Norms.* Cambridge University Press.

Biddle, Stephen 2006. *Military Power. Explaining Victory and Defeat in Modern Battle* (1st edn 2004). Princeton University Press.

Blaikie, Norman W. H. 1991. 'A Critique of the Use of Triangulation in Social Research', *Quality and Quantity* 25: 115–36.

Blyth, Mark 1997. 'Any More Bright Ideas? The Ideal Turn of Comparative Political Economy', *Comparative Politics* 29: 229–50.

2002. *Great Transformations: Economic Ideas and Institutional Change in the Twentieth Century*. Cambridge University Press.

2003. 'Structures Do Not Come with an Instruction Sheet: Interests, Ideas and Progress in Political Science', *Perspectives on Politics* 1(4): 695–706.

2006. 'Great Punctuations: Prediction, Randomness, and the Evolution of Comparative Political Research', *American Political Science Review* 100(4): 493–8.

Bohman, James 1996. *Public Deliberation, Pluralism, Complexity, and Democracy*. Cambridge, Mass.: MIT Press.

Boudon, Raymond 1976. 'A Theory of Justice', *Contemporary Sociology* 5: 102–9.

Bourdieu, Pierre 1977. *Outline of a Theory of Practice*. Cambridge University Press.

2004. *Science of Science and Reflexivity*. Cambridge: Polity.

Bourdieu, Pierre, Jean-Claude Chamboredon and Jean-Claude Passeron 1983. *Le métier de sociologue* (1st edn 1968). Paris: Mouton.

Bradshaw, York and Michael Wallace 1991. 'Informing Generality and Explaining Uniqueness: The Place of Case Studies in Comparative Research', in Charles C. Ragin (ed.), *Issues and Alternatives in Comparative Social Research*. Leiden: E. J. Brill, pp. 154–71.

Brady, Henry E. and David Collier (eds.) 2004. *Rethinking Social Inquiry. Diverse Tools, Shared Standards*. Lanham, Md.: Rowman & Littlefield.

Brady, Henry E., David Collier and Jason Seawright 2004. 'Refocusing the Discussion of Methodology', in Brady and Collier (eds.), pp. 3–21.

Bramber, Thomas, William Clark and Matt Golder 2006. 'Understanding Interaction Models: Improving Political Analysis', *Political Analysis* 14:63–82.

Brams, Steven J. 1990. *Negotiation Games. Applying Game Theory to Bargaining and Arbitration*, rev. edn. London: Routledge.

Brams, Steven J. and Alan D. Taylor 1996. *Fair Division. From Cake-cutting to Dispute Resolution*. Cambridge University Press.

Braudel, Fernand 1980. 'History and the Social Sciences: The *Longue Durée*', in Fernand Braudel, *On History*. University of Chicago Press, pp. 25–54.

Bray, Zoe 2004. *Living Boundaries: Identity and Frontier in the Basque Country*. Brussels: Peter Lang.

2006. 'Basque Militant Youths in France: New Experiences of Ethnonational Identity in the European Context', *Nationalism and Ethnic Politics* 12(3–4): 533–53.

Brennan, Geoffrey and Alan Hamlin 2000. *Democratic Devices and Desires. Theories of Institutional Design*. Cambridge University Press.

Briggs, Charles L. 1986. *Learning How To Ask: A Sociolinguistic Appraisal of the Role of the Interview in Social Science Research*. Cambridge University Press.

Brubaker, Rogers and Fred Cooper 2000. 'Beyond "Identity"', *Theory and Society* 29: 1–47.

Buchanan, Allen 1991. *Secession. The Morality of Political Divorce from Fort Sumter to Lithuania and Quebec*. Boulder, Colo.: Westview.

2004. *Justice, Legitimacy, and Self-Determination. Moral Foundations for International Law*. Oxford University Press.

Buchanan, James and Gordon Tullock 1965. *The Calculus of Consent: Logical Foundations of Constitutional Democracy*. Ann Arbor: University of Michigan Press.

Burawoy, Michael. 1998. 'The Extended Case Method', *Sociological Theory* 16(1): 4–33.

Burawoy, Michael, Alice Burton, Ann Arnett Ferguson, and Kathryn J. Fox 1991. *Ethnography Unbound: Power and Resistance in the Modern Metropolis.* Berkeley: University of California Press.

Campbell, Donald T. and Julian C. Stanley 1963. *Experimental and Quasi-Experimental Designs for Research.* Boston: Houghton Mifflin.

Campbell, John 2002. 'Ideas, Politics and Public Policy', *Annual Review of Sociology* 28: 21–38.
2004. *Institutional Change and Globalization.* Princeton University Press.

Campelli, E. 1996. 'Metodi qualitativi e teoria sociale', in C. Cipolla and A. De Lillo (eds.), *Il sociologo e le sirene. La sfida dei metodi qualitativi.* Milan: Franco Angeli.

Cardano, Mario 2003. *Tecniche di ricerca qualitativa.* Rome: Carocci.

Carens, Joseph H. 1987. 'Aliens and Citizens. The Case for Open Borders', *Review of Politics* 49(2): 251–73.
1996. 'Realistic and Idealistic Approaches to the Ethics of Migration', *International Migration Review* 30(1): 156–70.
2000. *Culture, Citizenship, and Community: A Contextual Exploration of Justice as Evenhandedness.* Oxford University Press.

Carnevali, Barbara 2004. *Romanticismo e riconoscimento. Figure della coscienza in Rousseau.* Bologna: Il Mulino.

Cassese, Antonio 1995. *Self-Determination of Peoples. A Legal Reappraisal,* Cambridge University Press.

Chauvel, L. 1995. 'Valeurs régionales et nationales en Europe', *Futuribles* 200: 167–201.

Checkel, Jeffrey T. 2006. 'Tracing Causal Mechanisms', *International Studies Review* 8(2): 362–70.

Cicourel, Aaron V. 1991. 'Semantics, Pragmatics, and Situated Meaning', in Jef Verschueren (ed.), *Pragmatics at Issue,* vol. I. Amsterdam: John Benjamins.

Coffé, Hilde 2005. 'Do Individual Factors Explain the Different Success of the Two Belgian Extreme Right Parties?', *Acta Politica* 40(1): 74–93.

Coleman, James 1986. 'Social Theory, Social Research, and a Theory of Action', *American Journal of Sociology* 91: 1309–35.
1988. 'Social Capital in the Creation of Human Capital', *American Journal of Sociology* 94 (Supplement): 95–120.
1990. *Foundations of Social Theory.* Cambridge, Mass.: Harvard University Press.

Collier, David 1990. 'Il metodo comparato: due decenni di mutamento', *Rivista Italiana di Scienza Politica* 20: 477–504.

Collier, David and Robert Adcock 1999. 'Democracy and Dichotomies', *Annual Review of Political Science* 2: 537–65.

Collier, David and Steven Levitsky 1997. 'Democracy with Adjectives: Conceptual Innovation in Comparative Research', *World Politics* 49(3): 430–51.

Collier, David and James E. Mahon 1993. 'Conceptual "Stretching" Revisited: Adapting Categories in Comparative Analysis', *American Political Science Review* 87(4): 845–55.

Collier, David and James Mahoney 1996. 'Insights and Pitfalls. Selection Bias in Qualitative Research', *World Politics* 49: 56–91.

Collier, David, Henry E. Brady and Jason Seawright 2004a. 'Critique, Responses, and Trade-offs: Drawing Together the Debate', in Brady and Collier (eds.), pp. 195–228.

2004b. 'Sources of Leverage in Causal Inference: Toward an Alternative View of Methodology', in Brady and Collier (eds.), pp. 229–65.

Collier, David, James Mahoney and Jason Seawright 2004. 'Claiming Too Much: Warnings about Selection Bias', in Brady and Collier (eds.), pp. 85–101.

Collier, David, Jason Seawright and Gerardo L. Munck 2004. 'The Quest for Standard: King, Kehoane and Verba's *Designing Social Inquiry*', in Brady and Collier (eds.), pp. 21–50.

Congleton, Roger D. and Birgitta Swedenborg (eds.) 2006. *Democratic Constitutional Design and Public Policy*. Cambridge, Mass.: MIT Press.

Connolly, William E. 2004. 'Method, Problem, Faith', in Shapiro, Smith and Masoud (eds.), pp. 332–49.

Conolly, John 1983. *The Terms of Political Discourse*, 2nd edn. Princeton University Press.

Cooke, Philip and Kevin Morgan 1998. *The Associational Economy. Firms, Regions, and Innovation*. Oxford University Press.

Corbetta, Piergiorgio 2003. *Social Research. Theory, Methods and Techniques*. London: Sage.

Crapanzano, Vincent. 1992. *Hermes' Dilemma and Hamlet's Desire: On the Epistemology of Interpretation*. Cambridge, Mass.: Harvard University Press.

Creswell, John W. 1994. *Research Design. Qualitative and Quantitative Approaches*. London: Sage.

Crouch, Colin, Patrick Le Galès, Carlo Trigilia and Helmut Voelzkow 2001. *Local Production Systems in Europe. Rise or Demise?* Oxford University Press.

Crozier, Michel 1964. *The Bureaucratic Phenomenon* (1st edn 1963). University of Chicago Press.

Dahl, Robert 1961. *Who Governs? Democracy and Power in an American City*. New Haven: Yale University Press.

1967. *Pluralist Democracy in the United States: Conflict and Consent*. Chicago: Rand McNally.

1971. *Polyarchy: Participation and Opposition*. New Haven: Yale University Press.

Dahrendorf, Ralf 1959. *Class and Class Conflict in Industrial Society*. Stanford University Press.

1995. 'Preserving Prosperity', *New Statesman and Society*, 13/29 December: 36–40.

2000. 'La sconfitta della vecchia democrazia'. *La Repubblica*, 12 January.

Dal Lago, Alessandro and Rocco De Biasi (eds.) 2002. *Un certo sguardo. Introduzione all'etnografia sociale*. Rome: Laterza.

Davis, James W. 2005. *Terms of Inquiry. On the Theory and Practice of Political Science*. Baltimore: Johns Hopkins University Press.

DeFelice, E. Gene 1980. 'Comparison Misconceived: Common Nonsense in Comparative Politics', *Comparative Politics* 13(1): 119–26.

Delanty, Gerald 1999. *Social Theory in a Changing World*. Cambridge: Polity.

della Porta, Donatella 1995. *Social Movements, Political Violence and the State*. Cambridge University Press.

Demazière, Didier and Claude Dubar 2000. *Dentro le storie. Analizzare le interviste biografiche*. Milan: Raffaello Cortina.

Denzin, Norman K. and Yvonna S. Lincoln 2000. 'Introduction: The Discipline and Practice of Qualitative Research', in Norman K. Denzin and Yvonna S. Lincoln (eds.), *Handbook of Qualitative Research*, 2nd edn. Thousand Oaks, Calif.: Sage, pp. 1–29.

Derrida, Jacques 1982. *Margins of Philosophy*, trans. Alan Bass. University of Chicago Press.

Descartes, René 1980. *Discourse on Method and Meditations on First Philosophy*. Indianapolis, Ind.: Hackett.

Dessler, David 1991. 'Beyond Correlations: Toward a Causal Theory of War', *International Studies Quarterly* 35: 337–55.

1999. 'Constructivism within a Positivist Social Science', *Review of International Studies* 25: 123–37.

DeWalt, Kathleen M. and Billie R. DeWalt 2002. *Participant Observation*. Walnut Creek, Calif.: AltaMira.

DiMaggio, Paul J. and Walter W. Powell 1991. 'Introduction', in W. W. Powell and P. J. DiMaggio (eds.), *The New Institutionalism in Organizational Analysis*. University of Chicago Press, pp. 1–38.

Dodd, Lawrence C. and L. Richard Schott 1979. *Congress and the Administrative State*. New York: Wiley.

Dogan, Mattei and Dominique Pelassy 1990. *How to Compare Nations*, 2nd edn. Chatham, N.J.: Chatham House Publishers.

Dore, Ronald 1973. *British Factory–Japanese Factory. The Origins of National Diversity in Industrial Relations*. Berkeley: University of California Press.

Downs, Anthony 1957. *An Economic Theory of Democracy*. New York: Harper.

Dryzek, John 2000. *Deliberative Democracy and Beyond: Liberals, Critics, Contestations*. Oxford University Press.

Dumont, Louis 1970. *Homo Hierarchicus. The Caste System and Its Implications*. University of Chicago Press.

Duncan, Otis D. 1975. *Introduction to Structural Equation Models*. New York: Academic Press.

Durkheim, Emil 1982. *The Rules of Sociological Method*. New York: The Free Press.

Dworkin, Ronald 2000. *Sovereign Virtue. The Theory and Practice of Equality*. Cambridge, Mass.: Harvard University Press.

Eatwell, Roger 1997. 'Introduction: The Importance of the Political Culture Approach', in Roger Eatwell (ed.), *European Political Cultures. Conflict or Convergence?* London: Routledge.

Eckstein, Harry 1960. *Pressure Group Politics: The Case of the Medical Association*. Stanford University Press.

1975. 'Case Study and Theory in Political Science', in Fred I. Greenstein and Nelson W. Polsby (eds.), *Handbook of Political Science*. Reading, Mass.: Addison-Wesley, pp. 79–138.

1992. 'Case Study and Theory in Political Science' (reprint of 1975 version with an introduction), in Harry Eckstein, *Regarding Politics. Essays on Political Theory, Stability, and Change*. Berkeley: University of California Press, pp. 117–76.

Eden, Lynn 2004. *Whole World on Fire. Organizations, Knowledge, Nuclear Weapons Devastation*. Ithaca: Cornell University Press.

Eisenstadt, S. N. 1968. 'Comparative Study', in David L. Sills (ed.), *International Encyclopedia of the Social Sciences*, vol. XIV. New York: Macmillan, pp. 421–9.

Eisenstadt, S. N. and Stein Rokkan 1973. *Building States and Nations*. Beverly Hills, Calif.: Sage.

Elman, Colin 1996. 'Horses for Courses: Why Not Neorealist Theories of Foreign Policy?', *Security Studies* 6(1): 7–53.

2005. 'Explanatory Typologies in Qualitative Studies of International Politics', *International Organization* 59 (Spring): 293–326.

Elster, Jon. 1979. *Ulysses and the Sirens*. Cambridge University Press.

1983. *Sour Grapes*. Cambridge University Press.

1989. *Nuts and Bolts for the Social Sciences.* Cambridge University Press.

1998. 'A Plea for Mechanisms', in Hedström and Swedberg (eds.), pp. 45–73.

2000. *Ulysses Unbound.* Cambridge University Press.

Esping-Andersen, Gøsta 1990. *The Three Worlds of Welfare Capitalism.* Cambridge: Polity.

Esping-Andersen, Gøsta and Walter Korpi 1983. 'From Poor Relief to Institutional Welfare States: The Development of Scandinavian Social Policy'. Paper read at ECPR workshop on the Comparative Study of Distribution and Social Policy, Freiburg, 20–25 March.

Evangelista, Matthew 1999. *Unarmed Forces. The Transnational Movement to End the Cold War.* Ithaca: Cornell University Press.

Falkner, Gerda 2000. 'Policy Networks in a Multi-Level System: Convergence towards Moderate Diversity?', *West European Politics* 23(4): 94–120.

Farrell, Henry and Adrienne Héritier 2003. 'Formal and Informal Institutions under Codecision: Continuous Constitution Building in Europe', *Governance* 16: 577–600.

Favell, Adrian and Tariq Modood 2003. 'The Philosophy of Multiculturalism: The Theory and Practice of Normative Political Theory', in Alan Finlayson (ed.), *Contemporary Political Philosophy: A Reader and Guide.* Edinburgh University Press, pp. 484–95.

Favre, Pierre 1985. 'L'histoire de la science politique', in Madeleine Grawitz and Jean Leca (eds.), *Traité de science politique.* Paris: Puf.

2005. *Comprendre le monde pour le changer. Epistémologie du politique.* Paris: Presses de Sciences Po-Références.

Feagin, Joe R., Anthony M. Orum and Gideon Sjoberg (eds.) 1991. *A Case for the Case Study.* Chapel Hill: University of North Carolina Press.

Featherstone, Kevin 2003. 'Introduction: In the Name of "Europe"', in Kevin Featherstone and Claudio M. Radaelli (eds.), *The Politics of Europeanization.* Oxford University Press, pp. 3–26.

Ferejohn, John 2004. 'External and Internal Explanations', in Shapiro, Smith and Masoud (eds.), pp. 144–65.

Ferguson, Adam 1966. *An Essay on the History of Civil Society* [1767]. Edinburgh University Press.

Feyerabend, Paul K. 1975. *Against Methods. Outline of an Anarchist Theory of Knowledge.* Atlantic Highlands, N.J.: Humanities Press.

Finnemore, Martha 2003. *The Purpose of Intervention. Changing Beliefs about the Use of Force.* Ithaca: Cornell University Press.

Fiorina, Morris 1995. 'Rational Choice and the New(?) Institutionalism', *Polity* 28(1): 107–15.

Fischer, Frank 2003. *Reframing Public Policy. Discursive Politics and Deliberative Practices.* Oxford University Press.

Flyvbjerg, Brent 2001. *Making Social Science Matter.* Cambridge University Press.

2006. 'Five Misunderstandings about Case-Study Research', *Qualitative Inquiry* 12(2): 219–45.

Formisano, Ronald P. 2001. 'The Concept of Political Culture', *Journal of Interdisciplinary History* 31(3): 393–426.

Fowler, Don D. and Donald L. Hardesty (eds.) 1994. *Others Knowing Others. Perspectives on Ethnographic Careers.* Washington, D.C.: Smithsonian Institution Press.

Franklin, Mark 2001. 'How Structural Factors Explain Turnout Variations at European Parliament Elections', *European Union Politics* 2(3): 309–28.

2004. *Voter Turnout and the Dynamics of Electoral Competition*. Cambridge University Press.

Frieden, Jeffry A. 1999. 'Actors and Preferences in International Relations', in David A. Lake and Robert Powell (eds.), *Strategic Choice and International Relations*. Princeton University Press, pp. 39–76.

Friedman, Jeffrey (ed.) 1996. *The Rational Choice Controversy*. New Haven: Yale University Press.

Frohlich, Norman and Joe A. Oppenheimer 1992. *Choosing Justice: An Experimental Approach to Ethical Theory*. Berkeley: University of California Press.

Fukuyama, Francis 1992. *The End of History and the Last Man*. New York: The Free Press.

Fuller, Steve 1991. *Social Epistemology*. Bloomington: Indiana University Press.

Gadamer, Hans-Georg 1979. *Truth and Method*. London: Sheed & Ward.

Gagnon, Alain-G. and James Tully (eds.) 2001. *Multinational Democracies*. Cambridge University Press.

Gallie, W. B. 1956. 'Essentially Contested Concepts', *Proceedings of the Aristotelian Society* 56: 167–98.

Galston, William A. 2002. *Liberal Pluralism: The Implications of Value Pluralism for Political Theory and Practice*. Cambridge University Press.

Galtung, Johan 1981. 'Structure, Culture, and Intellectual Style: An Essay Comparing Saxonic, Teutonic, Gallic and Nipponic Approaches', *Social Science Information* 20(6): 817–56.
  1988. *Methodology and Development*. Copenhagen: Christin Ejlers.

Gambetta, Diego 1988. 'Can We Trust in Trust?', in Diego Gambetta (ed.), *Trust Making and Breaking Cooperative Relations*. New York: Blackwell, pp. 213–37.

Gans, Chaim 2003. *The Limits of Nationalism*. Cambridge University Press.

Gauthier, David 1986. *Morals by Agreement*. Oxford University Press.
  1994. 'Breaking Up: An Essay on Secession', *Canadian Journal of Philosophy* 24(3): 357–72.

Gayon, Jean and Jean-Jacques Wunenburger (eds.) 2000. *Bachelard dans le monde*. Paris: Presses universitaires de France.

Geertz, Clifford 1973. *The Interpretation of Cultures*. New York: Basic Books.

Gellner, Ernest 1991. *Nationalism*. New York University Press.

George, Alexander 1979. 'Case Studies and Theory Development: The Method of Structured, Focused Comparison', in Paul Gordon Lauren (ed.), *Diplomacy. New Approaches in History, Theory, and Policy*. New York: The Free Press, pp. 43–68.

George, Alexander L. 1993. *Bridging the Gap. Theory and Practice in Foreign Policy*. Washington, D.C.: United States Institute of Peace Press.

George, Alexander L. and Andrew Bennett 2005. *Case Studies and Theory Development in the Social Sciences*. Cambridge, Mass.: MIT Press.

George, Alexander L. and Timothy J. McKeown 1985. 'Case Studies and Theories of Organizational Decision Making', in *Advances in Information Processing in Organizations. A Research Annual*. Greenwich, Conn.: JAI Press, pp. 21–58.

George, Alexander L. and Richard Smoke 1974. *Deterrence in American Foreign Policy: Theory and Practice*. New York: Columbia University Press.

Gerring, John 1999. 'What Makes a Concept Good? A Criterial Framework for Understanding Concept Formation in the Social Sciences', *Polity* 31(3): 357–93.
  2001. *Social Science Methodology: A Criterial Framework*. Cambridge University Press.

2005. 'Causation: A Unified Framework for the Social Sciences', *Journal of Theoretical Politics* 17: 162–98.

2007. *Case Study Research: Principles and Practices*. Cambridge University Press.

Gerring, John and Joshua Yesnowitz 2006. 'A Normative Turn in Political Science?', *Polity* 38(1): 101–33.

Giddens, Anthony 1976. *The New Rules of Sociological Method*. London: Hutchinson.

Gilbert, Margaret 1989. *On Social Facts*. London: Routledge.

Gilligan, Carol 1982. *In a Different Voice: Psychological Theory and Women's Development*. Cambridge, Mass.: Harvard University Press.

Giner, Salvador, Lluís Flaquer, Jordi Busquet and Núria Bultà 1996. *La cultura catalana: el sagrat i el profà*. Barcelona: Edicions 62.

Glaser, Barney G. and Anselm L. Strauss 1967. *The Discovery of Grounded Theory: Strategies for Qualitative Research*. Chicago: Aldine.

Goertz, Gary 2004. 'The Substantive Importance of Necessary Condition Hypotheses', in Gary Goertz and Harvey Starr (eds.), *Necessary Conditions. Theory, Methodology and Applications*. Lanham, Md.: Rowman & Littlefield, pp. 65–94.

2006. *Social Science Concepts: A User's Guide*. Princeton University Press.

Goetz, Klaus H. 2008. 'Government and Governance', *West European Politics* 31(1–2): 258–79.

Goffman, Erving 1971. *The Presentation of Self in Everyday Life*. Harmondsworth: Penguin.

1980. *Behavior in Public Places*. Westport, Conn.: Greenwood.

1990. *Asylums*. New York: Doubleday.

Goldthorpe, John H. 2000. *On Sociology. Numbers, Narratives and the Integration of Research and Theory*. Oxford University Press.

Goodin, Robert 1992. 'If People Were Money . . .', in Brian Barry and Robert E. Goodin (eds.), *Free Movement. Ethical Issues in the Transnational Migration of People and of Money*. State College: Pennsylvania State University Press, pp. 6–21.

Gourevitch, Peter 1986. *Politics in Hard Times: Comparative Responses to International Economic Crises*. Ithaca: Cornell University Press.

1999. 'The Governance Problem in International Relations', in D.A. Lake and R. Powell (eds.), *Strategic Choice and International Relations*. Princeton University Press, pp. 137–64.

Granovetter, Mark 1978. 'Threshold Models of Collective Behavior', *American Journal of Sociology* 83: 1420–43.

Green, Donald P. and Ian Shapiro 1994. *Pathologies of Rational Choice Theory: A Critique of Applications in Political Science*. New Haven: Yale University Press.

Gurr, Ted R. 1971. '*A Causal Model of Civil Strife: A Comparative Analysis Using New Indices*', in John V. Gillespie and Betty A. Nesvold (eds.), *Macro-Quantitative Analysis: Conflict, Development and Democratization*. Beverly Hills, Calif.: Sage, pp. 217–26.

Gutmann, Amy and Dennis Thompson 1996. *Democracy and Disagreement*. Cambridge, Mass.: Belknap Press.

Guzzini, Stefano 2000. 'A Reconstruction of Constructivism in International Relations', *European Journal of International Relations* 6(2): 147–82.

Habermas, Jürgen 1981. *Theorie des kommunikativen Handelns*, 2 vols. Frankfurt: Suhrkamp.

1983. *Moralbewußtsein und kommunikatives Handeln*. Frankfurt: Suhrkamp.

1992. *Faktizität und Geltung. Beiträge zur Diskurstheorie des Rechts und des demokratischen Rechtsstaates.* Frankfurt: Suhrkamp.

Hacking, Ian 1992. 'The Self-vindication of Laboratory Science', in Andrew Pickering (ed.), *Science as Practice and Culture.* University of Chicago Press, pp. 29–64.

1999. *The Social Construction of What?* Cambridge, Mass.: Harvard University Press.

Hadenius, Axel 1992. *Democracy and Development.* Cambridge University Press.

Hall, Peter A. 1989. *The Political Power of Economic Ideas.* Princeton University Press.

2003. 'Aligning Ontology and Methodology in Comparative Research', in Mahoney and Rueschemeyer (eds.), pp. 373–404.

Hall, Peter A. and Rosemary C. R. Taylor 1996. 'Political Science and the Three New Institutionalisms', *Political Studies* 44(5): 936–57.

Hampsher-Monk, Ian, Karin Tilmans and Frank van Vree (eds.) 1998. *History of Concepts: Comparative Perspectives.* Amsterdam University Press.

Hardin, Garrett 1968. 'The Tragedy of the Commons', *Science* 162/3859: 1243–8.

Hardin, Russell 1985. 'Individual Sanctions, Collective Benefits', in Richmond Campbell and Lanning Sowden (eds.), *Paradoxes of Rationality and Cooperation.* Vancouver: University of British Columbia Press, pp. 339–54.

Hargreaves Heap, Shaun P. and Yanis Varoufakis 2004. *Game Theory. A Critical Text,* 2nd edn. London: Routledge.

Hargreaves Heap, Shaun, Martin Hollis, Bruce Lyons, Robert Sugden and Albert Weale 1992. *The Theory of Choice.* Oxford: Blackwell.

Hastrup, Kirsten and Peter Hervik (eds.) 1994. *Social Experience and Anthropological Knowledge.* London: Routledge.

Hattam, Victoria Charlotte 1993. *Labor Visions and State Power: The Origins of Business Unionism in the United States.* Princeton University Press.

Hay, Colin 2002. *Political Analysis. A Critical Introduction.* Basingstoke: Palgrave.

Hedström, Peter and Richard Swedberg (eds.) 1998. *Social Mechanisms: An Analytical Approach to Social Theory.* Cambridge University Press.

Held, David 1995. *Democracy and the Global Order: From the Modern State to Cosmopolitan Governance.* Stanford University Press.

Held, David and Daniele Archibugi (eds.) 1995. *Cosmopolitan Democracy: An Agenda for a New World Order.* London: Polity.

Hempel, Carl 1965. *Aspects of Scientific Explanations and Other Essays.* New York: The Free Press.

Héritier, Adrienne 2007. *Explaining Institutional Change in Europe.* Oxford University Press.

Hobsbawm, Eric 1983. 'Introduction: Inventing Traditions', in Eric Hobsbawm and Terence Ranger (eds.), *The Invention of Tradition.* Cambridge University Press, pp. 1–14.

Höffe, Ottmar 1994. *Immanuel Kant.* Albany: State University of New York Press.

Hollis, Martin and Robert Sugden 1993. 'Rationality in Action', *Mind* 102(405): 1–35.

Homer-Dixon, Thomas F. 1999. *Environment, Scarcity, and Violence.* Princeton University Press.

Honneth, Axel 1992. *Kampf um Anerkennung.* Frankfurt: Suhrkamp.

Hopkin, Jonathan and Caterina Paolucci 1999. 'The Business Firm Model of Party Organisation: Cases from Spain and Italy', *European Journal of Political Research* 35(3): 307–39.

Huntington, Samuel 1982. 'American Ideals versus American Institutions', *Political Science Quarterly* 97(1): 1–37.

1996. *The Clash of Civilizations and the Remaking of World Order.* New York: Simon & Schuster.

2004. *Who Are We?: The Challenges to America's Identity.* New York: Simon & Schuster.

Immergut, Ellen 1992. *Health Politics: Interests and Institutions in Western Europe.* Cambridge University Press.

Inglehart, Ronald 1988. 'The Renaissance of Political Culture', *American Political Science Review* 82(4): 1203–30.

1990. *Culture Shift in Advanced Industrial Society.* Princeton University Press.

Jackman, Robert W. 1985. 'Cross-national Statistical Research and the Study of Comparative Politics', *American Journal of Political Science* 29(1): 161–82.

Jackson, Robert 1990. *Quasi States: Sovereignty, International Relations and the Third World.* Cambridge University Press.

Jervis, Robert 1990. 'Models and Cases in the Study of International Conflict', *Journal of International Affairs* 44(1): 81–101.

1997. *System Effects: Complexity in Political and Social Life.* Princeton University Press.

2006. 'Understanding Beliefs', *Political Psychology* 27(5): 641–63.

Johnston, David 1986. *The Rhetoric of the Leviathan.* Princeton University Press.

Jonsen, Albert R. and Stephen Toulmin 1988. *The Abuse of Casuistry. A History of Moral Reasoning.* Berkeley: University of California Press.

Jupille, Joseph H., James A. Caporaso and Jeffrey T. Checkel 2003. *Integrating Institutions: Rationalism, Constructivism, and the Study of the European Union.* Oslo: ARENA.

Kaase, Max and Kenneth Newton 1998. *Beliefs in Government.* Oxford University Press.

Kacowicz, Arie M. 2004. 'Case Study Methods in International Security Studies', in Detlef F. Sprinz and Yael Nahmias-Wolinsky (eds.), *Models, Numbers and Cases: Methods for Studying International Relations.* Ann Arbor: University of Michigan Press, pp. 107–25.

Kahneman, Daniel and Amos Tverski 1981. 'The Framing of Decisions and the Psychology of Choice', *Science* 211: 453–8.

Kalleberg, Arthur L. 1966. 'The Logic of Comparison: A Methodological Note on the Comparative Study of Political Systems', *World Politics* 19(1): 69–82.

Kant, Immanuel 1787. *Critique of Pure Reason.* Riga: Preussische Akademie Ausgabe.

Karagiannis, Yannis 2007. *Economic Theories and the Science of Inter-Branch Relations.* Florence: European University Institute.

Katzenstein, Peter J. 1978. *Between Power and Plenty: Foreign Economic Policies of Advanced Industrial States.* Madison: University of Wisconsin Press.

Katznelson, Ira and Barry Weingast 2005. 'Intersections between Historical and Rational Choice Institutionalism', in Ira Katznelson and Barry Weingast (eds.), *Preferences and Situations.* Cambridge University Press, pp. 1–26.

Katznelson, Ira and Margaret Weir 1985. *Schooling for All: Class, Race and the Decline of the Democratic Ideal.* New York: Basic Books.

Keating, Michael 2001. *Plurinational Democracy.* Oxford University Press.

Keating, Michael, John Loughlin and Kris Deschouwer 2003. *Culture, Institutions and Economic Development. A Study of Eight European Regions.* Cheltenham: Edward Elgar.

Keohane, Robert 1988. 'International Institutions: Two Approaches', *International Studies Quarterly* 32: 379–96.

Keohane, Robert O. and Elinor Ostrom (eds.) 1995. *Local Commons and Global Interdependence: Heterogeneity and Cooperation in Two Domains.* London: Sage.

King, Gary, Robert O. Keohane and Sidney Verba 1994. *Designing Social Inquiry. Scientific Inference in Qualitative Research.* Princeton University Press.

1995. 'The Importance of Research Design in Political Science', *American Political Science Review* 89(2): 475–81.

Kiser, Edgar and Shawn Bauldry 2005. 'Rational-Choice Theories in Political Sociology', in Thomas Janoski, Robert R. Alford, Alexander M. Hicks and Mildred A. Schwartz (eds.), *The Handbook of Political Sociology.* Cambridge University Press, pp. 172–86.

Klandermans, Bert and Suzanne Staggenborg (eds.) 2002. *Methods of Social Movement Research.* Minneapolis: University of Minnesota Press.

Klein, Peter D. 2005. 'Epistemology', in *Routledge Encyclopaedia of Philosophy Online.* www.rep.routledge.com/article/P059 (accessed 18 May 2005).

Knorr-Cetina, Karin 1981. *The Manufacture of Knowledge.* Oxford: Pergamon.

Kratochwil, Friedrich 2007. 'Of False Promises and Safe Bets', *Journal of International Relations and Development* 10(1): 1–15.

Kuhn, T. S. 1962. *The Structure of Scientific Revolutions.* University of Chicago Press.

Kukathas, Chandran 1992. 'Are There Any Cultural Rights?', *Political Theory* 20(1): 105–39.

Kymlicka, Will 1995. *Multicultural Citizenship. A Liberal Theory of Minority Rights.* Oxford University Press.

2007. *Multicultural Odysseys: Navigating the International Politics of Diversity.* Oxford University Press.

Lagrange, Hugues and Marco Oberti (eds.) 2006. *La rivolta delle periferie.* Milan: Bruno Mondatori.

Laitin, David 2003. 'The Perestroikan Challenge to Political Science', *Politics and Society* 31(1): 163–84.

Lake, David A. and Robert Powell (eds.) 1999. *Strategic Choice in International Relations.* Princeton University Press.

Lakoff, George 1987. *Women, Fire and Dangerous Things.* University of Chicago Press.

Lane, Jan-Erik and Svante Ersson 2005. *Culture and Politics. A Comparative Approach,* 2nd edn. Aldershot: Gower.

Lasswell, Harold D. 1968. 'The Future of the Comparative Method', *Comparative Politics* 1: 3–18.

Law, John 2004. *After Methods: Mess in Social Science Research.* New York: Routledge.

Lazarsfeld, Paul F. 1972. *Qualitative Analysis. Historical and Critical Essays.* Boston: Allyn & Bacon.

Lazarsfeld, Paul F. and Allen H. Barton 1951. 'Qualitative Measurement in the Social Sciences: Classification, Typologies, and Indices', in Daniel Lerner and Harold D. Lasswell (eds.), *The Policy Sciences.* Stanford University Press, pp. 155–93.

Le Grand, Julian 1982. *The Strategy of Equality: Redistribution and the Social Services.* London: Unwin Hyman.

Lehmbruch, Gehrhard 1967. *Proporzdemokratie: Politisches System und Politische Kultur in der Schweiz und in Oesterreich.* Tubingen: Mohr.

1974. 'A Non-Competitive Pattern of Conflict Management in Liberal Democracies: The Case of Switzerland, Austria and Lebanon', in K. D. McRae (ed.), *Consociational Democracy: Political Accommodation in Segmented Societies*. Toronto: McClelland & Stewart, pp. 90–7.

Lewis, David K. 1969. *Convention*. Cambridge, Mass.: Harvard University Press.

Lewis, Orion and Sven Steinmo 2007. 'Taking Evolution Seriously', European University Institute, Florence.

Lichbach, Mark Irving 1997. 'Social Theory and Comparative Politics', in Mark Irving Lichbach and Alan S. Zuckerman (eds.), *Comparative Politics. Rationality, Culture, and Structure*. Cambridge University Press, pp. 239–76.

Lichterman, Paul 1995. *The Search for Political Community*. Cambridge University Press.

2002. 'Seeing Structure Happen: Theory-Driven Participant Observation', in Bert Klandermans and Suzanne Staggenborg (eds.), *Methods of Social Movement Research*. Minneapolis: University of Minnesota Press, pp. 118–45.

Lieberman, Robert 2002. 'Ideas, Institutions, and Political Order: Explaining Political Change', *American Political Science Review* 96(4): 697–712.

Lieberson, Stanley 1994. 'More on the Uneasy Case for Using Mill-Type Methods in Small-*N* Comparative Studies', *Social Forces* 72(4): 1225–37.

Lijphart, Arend 1968. 'Typologies of Democratic Systems', *Comparative Political Studies* 1(1): 3–44.

1971. 'Comparative Politics and the Comparative Method', *American Political Science Review* 65: 682–93.

1975. 'The Comparable-Case Strategy in Comparative Research', *Comparative Political Studies* 8: 158–77.

1977. *Democracy in Plural Societies. A Comparative Exploration*. New Haven: Yale University Press.

Lin, Ann Chih 1998. 'Bridging Positivist and Interpretivist Approaches to Qualitative Methods', *Policy Studies Journal* 26(1): 162–80.

Lipset, S.M. and Stein Rokkan 1967. 'Introduction', in S.M. Lipset and Stein Rokkan (eds.), *Party Systems and Voter Alignments*. New York: The Free Press.

Little, Daniel 1991. *Varieties of Social Explanation: An Introduction to the Philosophy of Social Science*. Boulder, Colo.: Westview.

Luce, R. Duncan and Howard Raiffa 1957. *Games and Decisions*. New York: Dover.

Luhmann, Niklas 1997. *Die Gesellschaft der Gesellschaft*. Frankfurt: Suhrkamp.

MacCormick, Neil 2007. *Institutions of Law: An Essay in Legal Theory*. Oxford University Press.

Macedo, Stephen 2005. 'What Self-Governing Peoples Owe to One Another: Universalism, Diversity, and the "Law of Peoples"', in Christoph Eisgruber and András Sajó (eds.), *Global Justice and the Bulwarks of Localism: Human Rights in Context*. Leiden: Martinus Nijhoff, pp. 143–60.

MacIntyre, Alasdair 1971. *Against the Self-Images of the Age: Essays on Ideology and Philosophy*. London: Duckworth.

Mackie, John L. 1976. 'Causes and Conditions', in Myles Brandt (ed.), *The Nature of Causation*. Urbana: University of Illinois Press.

Mahoney, James 1999. 'Nominal, Ordinal and Narrative Appraisal in Macrocausal Analysis', *American Journal of Sociology* 104(4): 1154–96.

2000a. 'Path Dependence in Historical Sociology', *Theory and Society* 29: 507–48.

2000b. 'Strategies of Causal Inference in Small-*N* Analysis', *Sociological Methods and Research* 28(4): 387–424.

2003. 'Strategies of Causal Assessment in Comparative Historical Analysis', in Mahoney and Rueschemeyer (eds.), pp. 337–72.

Mahoney, James and Gary Goertz 2006. 'A Tale of Two Cultures: Contrasting Quantitative and Qualitative Research', *Political Analysis* 14(3): 227–49.

Mahoney, James and Dietrich Rueschemeyer (eds.) 2003. *Comparative Historical Analysis in the Social Sciences*. Cambridge University Press.

Mair, Peter 1996. 'Comparative Politics: An Overview', in Robert E. Goodin and Hans-Dieter Klingemann (eds.), *A New Handbook of Political Science*. Oxford University Press, pp. 309–35.

2006. 'Cleavages', in Richard S. Katz and William J. Crotty (eds.), *Handbook of Political Parties*. London: Sage, pp. 371–5.

2008. 'Democracies', in Daniele Caramani (ed.), *Comparative Politics*. Oxford University Press, in press.

Mansbridge, Jane J. 1990. 'The Rise and Fall of Self-Interest in the Explanation of Political Life', in Jane J. Mansbridge (ed.), *Beyond Self-Interest*. University of Chicago Press, pp. 3–22.

Maoz, Zeev 2002. 'Case Study Methodology in International Studies. From Storytelling to Hypothesis Testing', in Michael Brecher and Frank P. Harvey (eds.), *Millenial Reflections on International Studies*. Ann Arbor: University of Michigan Press, pp. 455–75.

March, James G. and Johan P. Olsen 1984. 'The New Institutionalism: Organizational Factors in Political Life', *American Political Science Review* 78: 734–48.

1989. *Rediscovering Institutions*. New York: The Free Press.

Marcussen, Martin 2000. *Ideas and Elites: The Social Construction of Economic and Monetary Union*. Aalborg University Press.

Mattei, Paola 2007. 'From Politics to Good Management? Transforming the Local Welfare State in Italy', *West European Politics* 30(3): 593–620.

Maturana, Humberto and Francisco Varela 1992. *The Tree of Knowledge: The Biological Roots of Human Understanding*. London: Shambhala.

May, Ernest R. 1973. *'Lessons' of the Past: The Use and Misuse of History in American Foreign Policy*. Oxford University Press.

Maynard Smith, John and George R. Price 1973. 'The Logic of Animal Conflict', *Nature* 246: 15–18.

Mayntz, Renate 2002. 'Zur Theoriefähigkeit makro-sozialer Analysen', in Renate Mayntz (ed.), *Akteure - Mechanismen - Modelle. Zur Theoriefähigkeit makro-sozialer Analysen*. Frankfurt: Campus, pp. 7–43.

Mayr, Ernst 2004. *What Makes Biology Unique? Considerations on the Autonomy of a Scientific Discipline*. Cambridge University Press.

McAdam, Doug, Sidney Tarrow and Charles Tilly 2001. *Dynamics of Contention*. Cambridge University Press.

McConnell, Grant 1966. *Private Power and American Democracy*. New York: Knopf.

McKeown, Timothy J. 1999. 'Case Studies and the Statistical Worldview: Review of King, Keohane, and Verba's *Designing Social Inquiry: Scientific Inference in Qualitative Research*', *International Organization* 53(1): 161–90.

2004. 'Case Studies and the Limits of the Quantitative World View', in Brady and Collier (eds.), pp. 139–67.

McNamara, Kathleen 1998. *The Currency of Ideas: Monetary Policy In the European Union*. Ithaca: Cornell University Press.

Mead, George Herbert 1934. *Mind, Self and Society*. University of Chicago Press.

Mercer, Jonathan 1996. *Reputation and International Politics*. Ithaca: Cornell University Press.

2005. 'Rationality and Psychology in International Politics', *International Organization* 59: 77–106.

Merton, Robert K. 1968. *Social Theory and Social Structure*. New York: The Free Press.

Meyer, John W. and Brian Rowan 1983. 'Institutionalized Organizations: Formal Structure as Myth and Ceremony', in John W. Meyer and W. Richard Scott (eds.), *Organizational Environments. Ritual and Rationality*. London: Sage, pp. 21–44.

Michels, Robert 1999. *Political Parties: A Sociological Study of the Oligarchical Tendencies of Modern Democracy* (1st edn 1911). New Brunswick, N.J.: Transaction.

Mill, John Stuart 1843. *A System of Logic*. New York: The Free Press.

1972. *On Liberty, Utilitarianism, and Considerations on Representative Government*. London: Dent.

1974. *A System of Logic, Ratiocinative and Inductive: Being a Connected View of the Principles of Evidence and the Methods of Scientific Investigation*, ed. J. M. Robson; introduction by R. F. McRae. London: Routledge & Kegan Paul.

Miller, David 1995. *On Nationality*. Oxford University Press.

Mills, Charles Wright 2000. *The Sociological Imagination* (1st edn 1959). Oxford University Press.

Molina, Oscar and Martin Rhodes 2002. 'Corporatism: The Past, Present and Future of a Concept', *Annual Review of Political Science* 5: 305–31.

Møller, Jørgen 2007a. 'The Post-Communist Tripartition 1990–2005: Contrasting Actor-Centered and Structural Explanations', PhD thesis, European University Institute, Florence.

2007b. 'The Gap between Electoral Democracy and Liberal Democracy Revisited: Some Conceptual and Empirical Clarifications'. *Acta Politica*, in press.

Monroe, Kristen Renwick 2001. 'Paradigm Shift: From Rational Choice to Perspective', *International Political Science Review* 22(2): 151–72.

Monroe, Kristen Renwick (ed.) 2005. *Perestroika! The Raucous Rebellion in Political Science*. New Haven: Yale University Press.

Moravcsik, Andrew 1993. 'Preferences and Power in the European Community: A Liberal Intergovernmental Approach', *Journal of Common Market Studies* 31: 473–524.

Morlino, Leonardo (ed.) 1989. *La scienza politica in Italia*. Turin: Edizioni della Fondazione Agnelli.

Morlino, Leonardo 1990. 'Problemi e scelte nella comparazione', *Rivista Italiana di Scienza Politica* 20: 381–96.

Mueller, Dennis 1989. *Public Choice II*. Cambridge University Press.

Munck, Gerardo L. 2004. 'Tools for Qualitative Research', in Brady and Collier (eds.), pp. 105–22.

Myrdal, Gunnar 1944. *The American Dilemma*. New York: Harper.

Nachmias, David and Chava Frankfort-Nachmias 1976. *Research Methods in the Social Sciences*. London: Arnold.

Nagel, Thomas 2005. 'The Problem of Global Justice', *Philosophy and Public Affairs* 33(2): 113–47.

Neurath, Otto 1913. 'Die Verirrten des Cartesius und das Auxiliarmotiv'. *Jahrbuch der Philosophischen Gesellschaft an der Universität zu Wien*, reproduced in Karl-Peter Markl (ed.), *Analytische Politikphilosophie und ökonomische Rationalität*, vol. II. Opladen: Westdeutscher Verlag, pp. 186–99 (1984).

Neustadt, Richard E. and Ernest R. May 1986. *Thinking in Time: The Uses of History for Decision Makers*. New York: The Free Press.

Nida-Rumelin, Julian 1993. *Kritik des Konsequentialismus*. Munich: Oldenbourg.

Njolstad, Olav 1990. 'Learning from History? Case Studies and the Limits to Theory-Building', in Nils Petter Gleditsch and Olav Njolstad (eds.), *Arms Races*. London: Sage, pp. 220–46.

Norris, Pippa 2002. *Democratic Phoenix: Reinventing Political Activism*. Cambridge University Press.

North, Douglass C. 2005. *Understanding the Process of Economic Change*. Princeton University Press.

  2006. 'What's Missing from Politicial Economy?', in Barry R. Weingast and Donald Wittman (eds.), *The Oxford Handbook of Political Economy*. Oxford University Press, pp. 1003–9.

Nozick, Robert 1974. *Anarchy, State, and Utopia*. New York: Basic Books.

O'Kane, Rosemary H. T. 1993. 'The Ladder of Abstraction: The Purpose of Comparison and the Practice of Comparing African Coups d'État', *Journal of Theoretical Politics* 5(2): 169–93.

Oberschall, Anthony. 1973. *Social Conflict and Social Movements*. Englewood Cliffs, N.J.: Prentice Hall.

Odell, John S. 2004. 'Case Study Methods in International Political Economy', in Detlef F. Sprinz and Yael Nahmias-Wolinsky (eds.), *Models, Numbers and Cases: Methods for Studying International Relations*. Ann Arbor: University of Michigan Press, pp. 56–80.

Okin, Susan Moller 1989. *Justice, Gender, and the Family*. New York: Basic Books.

Olson, Mancur 1971. *The Logic of Collective Action: Public Goods and the Theory of Groups*. Cambridge, Mass.: Harvard University Press.

  1982. *The Rise and Decline of Nations: Economic Growth, Stagflation, and Social Rigidities*. New Haven: Yale University Press.

Osborn, Martin J. and Ariel Rubinstein 1994. *A Course in Game Theory*. Cambridge, Mass.: MIT Press.

Ostrom, Elinor 1990. *Governing the Commons: The Evolution of Institutions for Collective Action*. Cambridge University Press.

  1996. 'Incentives, Rules of the Game, and Development', in *Annual World Bank Conference on Development Economics 1995*. Washington, D.C.: World Bank, pp. 207–34.

  1998. 'A Behavioral Approach to the Rational Choice Theory of Collective Action: Presidential Address, American Political Science Association, 1997', *American Political Science Review* 92(1): 1–22.

Palonen, Kari 2002. 'A History of Concepts as a Style of Political Theorizing: Quentin Skinner's and Reinhard Kosselleck's subversion of normative political theory', *European Journal of Political Theory* 1(7): 91–106.

Parisi, Arturo and Gianfranco Pasquino 1985. 'Relazioni partiti–elettori e tipi di voto', in Gianfranco Pasquino (ed.), *Il sistema politico italiano*. Rome: Laterza.

Parsons, Talcott 1968. *The Structure of Social Action*. New York: The Free Press.

Parsons, Talcott and Neil J. Smelser 1956. *Economy and Society: A Study in the Integration of Economic and Social Theory*. London: Routledge & Kegan Paul.

Pasotti, Elanora and Bo Rothstein 2002. 'In the Market for Ideas: A Quest For a Unified Conceptual Approach in Political Science'. Paper presented at the annual meeting of the American Political Science Association, Boston, 28 August.

Passeron, Jean-Claude and Jacques Revel 2005. 'Penser par cas. Raisonner à partir des singularités', in Jean-Claude Passeron and Jacques Revel (eds), *Penser par cas*. Paris: École des Hautes Études en Sciences Sociales-Enquête, pp. 9–44.

Pateman, Carole 1970. *Participation and Democratic Theory*. Oxford University Press.

Patomäki, Heikki 1996. 'How to Tell Better Stories about World Politics', *European Journal of International Relations* 2(1): 105–33.

Peters, B. Guy 2000. 'Governance and Comparative Politics', in Jon Pierre (ed.), *Debating Governance*. Oxford University Press.

  2005. *Institutional Theory in Political Science: The New Institutionalism*, 2nd edn. London: Continuum.

Pierson, Paul 1993. 'When Effect Becomes Cause: Policy Feedback and Political Change', *World Politics* 45: 595–628.

  2000. 'Increasing Returns, Path Dependence and the Study of Politics', *American Political Science Review* 94(2): 251–68.

  2004. *Politics in Time: History, Institutions, and Social Analysis*. Princeton University Press.

Pinkard, Terry. 2000. *Hegel. A Biography*. Cambridge University Press.

Platt, Jennifer 1992a. ' "Case Study" in American Methodological Thought', *Current Sociology – La sociologie contemporaine* 40(1): 17–48.

  1992b. 'Cases of cases . . . of cases', in Ragin and Becker (eds.), pp. 21–52.

Pogge, Thomas 1988. *Realizing Rawls*. Ithaca: Cornell University Press.

Poggi, Gianfranco 1983. *Calvinism and the Capitalist Spirit: Max Weber's Protestant Ethic*. London: Palgrave Macmillan.

  2000. *Durkheim*. Oxford University Press.

Polanyi, Karl 1944. *The Great Transformation*. New York: Farrar & Rinehart.

Polsby, Nelson 1968. 'The Institutionalization of the House of Representatives', *American Political Science Review* 62(1): 144–68.

Popper, Karl 1961. *The Logic of Scientific Discovery*. New York: Science Editions.

  1965. *The Logic of Scientific Discovery*. New York: Harper.

  1972. 'Epistemology without a Knowing Subject', in Karl Popper, *Objective Knowledge*. Oxford University Press, chap. 3.

Portes, Alejandro 2001. 'Social Capital: Its Origins and Applications in Modern Sociology', *Annual Review of Sociology* 24: 1–24.

Przeworski, Adam 2004. 'Institutions Matter?', *Government and Opposition* 39: 527–40.

Przeworski, Adam and Henry Teune 1970. *The Logic of Comparative Social Inquiry*. New York: Wiley-Interscience.

Putnam, Robert 1988. 'Diplomacy and Domestic Politics: The Logic of Two-Level Games', *International Organization* 42: 427–60.

  1993. *Making Democracy Work. Civic Traditions in Modern Italy*. Princeton, N.J.: Princeton University Press.

Quine, Willard Van Orman 1953. 'Two Dogmas of Empiricism', in Willard Van Orman Quine, *From a Logical Point of View.* Cambridge, Mass.: Harvard University Press, pp. 20–46.

Rabinow, Paul and William M. Sullivan 1987. *Interpretive Social Science: A Second Look.* Berkeley: University of California Press.

Ragin, Charles 1987. *The Comparative Method: Moving Beyond Qualitative and Quantitative Strategies.* Berkeley: University of California Press.

  1992. ' "Casing" and the Process of Social Inquiry', in Ragin and Becker (eds.), pp. 217–26.

  1994. *Constructing Social Research: The Unity and Diversity of Methods.* Thousand Oaks, Calif.: Pine Forge.

  2000. *Fuzzy Set Social Science.* Chicago: University of Chicago Press.

  2004. 'Turning the Tables: How Case-Oriented Research Challenges Variable-Oriented Research', in Brady and Collier (eds.), pp. 123–38.

Ragin, Charles and Howard Becker (eds.) 1992. *What Is a Case? Exploring the Foundations of Social Inquiry.* Cambridge University Press.

Ragin, Charles and David Zaret 1983. 'Theory and Method in Comparative Research: Two Strategies', *Social Forces* 61(3): 731–54.

Raiffa, Howard with John Richardson and David Metcalfe 2002. *Negotiation Analysis: The Science and Art of Collaborative Decision Making.* Cambridge, Mass.: Harvard University Press.

Rapoport, Anatol and Albert M. Chammah 1965. *Prisoner's Dilemma: A Study in Conflict and Cooperation.* Ann Arbor: University of Michigan Press.

Ratner, Steven R. 1996. 'Drawing a Better Line: *Uti Possidetis* and the Borders of New States', *American Journal of International Law* 90(4): 590–624.

Rawls, John 1971. *A Theory of Justice.* Cambridge, Mass.: Harvard University Press.

  1993. *Political Liberalism.* New York: Columbia University Press.

  1999. *The Law of Peoples.* Cambridge, Mass.: Harvard University Press.

Reiff, Karlheinz and Hermamm Schmitt 1980. 'Nine Second-order National Elections: A Conceptual Framework for the Analysis of European Election Results', *European Journal of Political Research* 8(1): 3–44.

Richardson, Laurel 1994. 'Writing: a Method of Inquiry', in Norman K. Denzin and Yvonna S. Lincoln (eds.), *Handbook of Qualitative Research.* London: Sage, pp. 516–29.

Riker, William H. 1962. *The Theory of Political Coalitions.* New Haven: Yale University Press.

  1997. 'The Ferment of the 1950s and the Development of Rational Choice Theory', in Kristen Renwick Monroe (ed.), *Contemporary Empirical Political Theory.* Berkeley: University of California Press, pp. 191–201.

Riker, William H. and Peter Ordeshook 1973. *An Introduction to Positive Political Theory.* Englewood Cliffs, N.J.: Prentice Hall.

Robinson, W. S. 1950, 'Ecological Correlations and the Behavior of Individuals', *American Sociological Review* 15(3): 351–7.

Rodrik, Dani (ed.) 2003. *In Search of Prosperity: Analytic Narratives on Economic Growth.* Princeton University Press.

Rogowski, Ronald 1995. 'The Role of Theory and Anomaly in Social-Scientific Inference', *American Political Science Review* 89(2): 467–70.

  2004. 'How Inference in the Social (but Not the Physical) Sciences Neglects Theoretical Anomaly', in Brady and Collier (eds.), pp. 75–84.

Rokkan, Stein 1970. *Citizens, Elections, Parties.* Oslo: Universitetsforlaget.

Rokkan, Stein *et al.* 1988. *Centre–Periphery Structures in Europe 1880–1978: An International Social Science Council (ISSC) Workbook in Comparative Analysis.* Ann Arbor: Institute for Social Research, University of Michigan.

Roper, Janice M. and Jill Shapira 2000. *Ethnography in Nursing Research.* Thousand Oaks, Calif.: Sage.

Rorty, Richard 1980. *Philosophy and the Mirror of Nature.* Oxford: Blackwell.

　　1994. 'Method, Social Science and Social Hope', in Steven Seidman (ed.), *The Postmodern Turn: New Perspective on Social Theory.* Cambridge University Press, pp. 46–64.

Ross, Marc Howard 1997. 'Culture and Identity in Comparative Political Analysis', in Mark Irving Lichbach and Alan S. Zuckerman (eds.), *Comparative Politics. Rationality, Culture, and Structure.* Cambridge University Press, pp. 42–80.

Roth, Philip 2004. *The Plot against America.* London: Jonathan Cape.

Rothstein, Bo 1982. 'Den Svenska byrakratins uppgang och fall [The rise and fall of the Swedish bureaucracy]', *Haften for Kritiska Studier* 15(5): 26–46.

　　1992. 'Labor Market Institutions and Working Class Strength', in Steinmo, Thelen and Longstreth (eds.), pp. 33–56.

Rousseau, Jean-Jacques 1959. *Oeuvres, Pleiade, I.* Paris: Gallimard.

Rueschemeyer, Dietrich 2003. 'Can One or a Few Cases Yield Theoretical Gains?', in Mahoney and Rueschemeyer (eds.), pp. 305–36.

Ruggie, John 1998. *Constructing the World Polity: Essays On International Institutionalization.* London: Routledge.

Rustow, Dankwart 1955. *The Politics of Compromise.* Princeton University Press.

Sabatier, Paul A. and Hank C. Jenkins-Smith 1999. 'The Advocacy Coalition Framework: An Assessment', in Paul A. Sabatier (ed.), *Theories of the Policy Process.* Boulder, Colo.: Westview.

Sagan, Scott D. 1993. *The Limits of Safety: Organizations, Accidents, and Nuclear Weapons.* Princeton University Press.

Sandel, Michael 1982. *Liberalism and the Limits of Justice.* Cambridge University Press.

Sangrador García, José Luis 1996. *Identidades, actitudes y estereotipos en la España de las Autonomías.* Opiniones y Actitudes, no. 10. Madrid: Centro de Investigaciones Sociológicos.

Sartori, Giovanni 1970. 'Concept Misformation in Comparative Politics', *American Political Science Review* 64: 1033–53.

　　1971. 'La politica comparata: premesse e problemi', *Rivista italiana di scienza politica* 1: 7–66.

　　1976. *Parties and Party Systems: A Framework for Analysis.* Cambridge University Press.

　　1984. 'Guidelines for Concept Analysis', in Giovanni Sartori (ed.), *Social Science Concepts: A Systematic Analysis.* London: Sage, pp. 15–85.

Satz, Debra and John Ferejohn 1994. 'Rational Choice and Social Theory', *Journal of Philosophy* 91(2): 71–87.

Savage, Leonard J. 1954. *The Foundations of Statistics.* New York: Wiley.

Scarrow, Susan E. 2000. 'Parties without Members: Party Organization in a Changing Electoral Environment', in Russell J. Dalton and Martin P. Wattenberg (eds.), *Parties without Partisans.* Oxford University Press, pp. 79–101.

Scharpf, Fritz W. 1988. 'The Joint Decision Trap: Lessons from German Federalism and European Integration', *Public Administration Review* 66: 239–78.

1991. 'Political Institutions, Decision Styles, and Policy Choices', in R.M. Czada and A. Windhoff-Héritier, *Political Choice. Institutions, Rules and the Limits of Rationality.* Boulder, Colo.: Westview.

Scharpf, Fritz W. (ed.) 1993. *Games in Hierarchies and Networks. Analytical and Empirical Approaches to the Study of Governance Institutions.* Boulder, Colo.: Westview.

Scharpf, Fritz W. 1997. *Games Real Actors Play. Actor-Centered Institutionalism in Policy Research.* Boulder, Colo.: Westview.

2006. 'Social Science as a Vocation – Are Max Weber's Warnings Still Valid?'. Inaugural Lecture, Max Weber Programme, European University Institute, Florence.

Scharpf, Fritz W., Bernd Reissert and Fritz Schnabel 1976. *Politikverflechtung: Theorie und Empirie des kooperativen Föderalismus in der Bundesrepublik.* Kronberg: Scriptor Verlag.

Schelling, Thomas C. 1960. *The Strategy of Conflict.* Cambridge, Mass.: Harvard University Press.

Schmitter, Philippe C. 1974. 'Still the Century of Corporatism?', *Review of Politics* 36.

2001. 'Parties Are Not What They Once Were', in Larry Diamond and Richard Gunther (eds.), *Political Parties and Democracy.* Baltimore: Johns Hopkins University Press, pp. 67–89.

Schmitter, Philippe C. and Gerhard Lehmbruch (eds.) 1979. *Trends toward Corporatist Intermediation.* Beverly Hills, Calif.: Sage.

Schumpeter, Joseph 1908. *Das Wesen und der Hauptinhalt der theoretischen Nationalökonomie.* Munich: Duncker & Humblot.

1942. *Capitalism, Socialism, and Democracy.* New York: Harper.

Scott, Allen 1998. *Regions and the World Economy. The Coming Shape of Global Production, Competition, and Political Order.* Oxford University Press.

Searle, John 2001. *Rationality in Action.* Cambridge, Mass.: MIT Press.

Seligson, Mitchell 2002. 'The Renaissance of Political Culture, or the Renaissance of the Ecological Fallacy?', *Comparative Politics* 34: 273–92.

Selznick, Philip 1949. *TVA and the Grass Roots : A Study in the Sociology of Formal Organization.* Berkeley: University of California Press.

Sen, Amartya 1977. 'Rational Fools: A Critique of the Behavioral Foundations of Economic Theory', *Philosophy and Public Affairs* 6: 317–44.

1990. 'Rational Fools', in Jane J. Mansbridge (ed.), *Beyond Self-Interest.* University of Chicago Press, pp. 25–43.

Sewell, William H. 1996. 'Three Temporalities: Toward an Eventful Sociology', in Terrence J. McDonald (ed.), *The Historic Turn in the Human Science.* Ann Arbor: University of Michigan Press, pp. 245–80.

Shapiro, Ian 2002. 'The State of Democratic Theory', in Ira Katznelson and Helen V. Milner (eds.), *Political Science. State of the Discipline.* New York: Norton, pp. 235–65.

2004. 'Problems, Methods and Theories in the Study of Politics, or: What's Wrong with Political Science and What to Do About it', in Shapiro, Smith and Masoud (eds.), pp. 19–41.

Shapiro, Ian, Rogers M. Smith and Tarek E. Masoud 2004a. 'Introduction: Problems and Methods in the Study of Politics', in Shapiro, Smith and Masoud (eds.), pp. 1–18.

Shapiro, Ian, Rogers M. Smith and Tarek E. Masoud (eds.) 2004b. *Problems and Methods in the Study of Politics*. Cambridge: Cambridge University Press.

Shue, Henry 1980. *Basic Rights. Subsistence, Affluence, and U.S. Foreign Policy*. Princeton University Press.

Sil, Rudra 2004. 'Problems Chasing Methods or Methods Chasing Problems? Research Communities, Constrained Pluralism and the Role of Eclecticism', in Shapiro, Smith and Masoud (eds.), pp. 307–31.

Simon, Herbert A. 1982. *Models of Bounded Rationality*. Cambridge, Mass.: MIT Press.

1985. 'Human Nature in Politics: The Dialogue of Psychology with Political Science', *American Political Science Review* 79: 293–304.

1986. 'Rationality in Psychology and Economics', *Journal of Business* 59(4): S209–S224.

1995. 'Rationality in Political Behavior', *Political Psychology* 16(1): 45–62.

Sjöblom, Gunnar 1977. 'The Cumulation Problem in Political Science: An Essay on Research Strategies', *European Journal of Political Research* 5(1): 1–32.

Skinner, Quentin 2002. *Visions of Politics*, vol. III: *Hobbes and Civil Science*. Cambridge University Press.

Skocpol, Theda 1979. *States and Social Revolutions: A Comparative Analysis of France, Russia and China*. Cambridge University Press.

Skocpol, Theda and Edwin Amenta 1986. 'States and Social Policies'. *Annual Review of Sociology* 12: 131–57.

Skocpol, Theda and John Ikenberry 1983. 'The Political Formation of the American Welfare State in Historical and Comparative Perspective', *Comparative Social Research* 6: 87–148.

Skocpol, Theda and Margaret Somers 1980. 'The Uses of Comparative History in Macrosocial Inquiry', *Comparative Studies in Society and History* 22(2): 174–97.

Skowronek, Stephen 1982. *Building a New American State: The Expansion of National Administrative Capacities 1877–1920*. Cambridge University Press.

Skyrms, Brian 2004. *The Stag Hunt and the Evolution of Social Structure*. Cambridge University Press.

Smelser, Neil J. 1976. *Comparative Methods in the Social Sciences*. Englewood Cliffs, N.J.: Prentice Hall.

Smith, Rogers M. 2004. 'The Politics of Identity and the Tasks of Political Science', in Shapiro, Smith and Masoud (eds.), pp. 42–66.

Smyrl, Marc 1997. 'European Policies, Regional Programs, Local Politics', PhD dissertation, Harvard University.

Snyder, Jack 1989. 'Richness, Rigor, and Relevance in the Study of Soviet Foreign Policy', in Sean M. Lynn-Jones, Steven E. Miller and Stephen Van Evera (eds.), *Soviet Military Policy*. Cambridge, Mass.: MIT Press, pp. 3–22.

Sperber, Dan 1984. *Il sapere degli antropologi*. Milan: Feltrinelli.

Spohn, Wolfgang 1982. 'How to Make Sense of Game Theory?', in Wolfgang Stegmüller, Wolfgang Balzer and Wolfgang Spohn (eds.), *Philosophy of Economics. Proceedings, Munich, July 1981*. Berlin: Springer-Verlag, pp. 239–70.

Spradley, James P. 1979. *The Ethnographic Interview*. Belmont, Calif.: Wadsworth/Thomson Learning.

1980. *Participant Observation*. New York: Holt, Rinehart and Winston.

Steinbruner, John D. 1974. *The Cybernetic Theory of Decision: New Dimensions of Political Analysis.* Princeton University Press.

Steinmo, Sven 1993. *Taxation and Democracy: Swedish, British and American Approaches to Financing the Modern State.* New Haven: Yale University Press.

2003. 'The Evolution of Policy Ideas: Tax Policy in the 20th Century', *British Journal of Politics and International Relations* 5(2): 206–36.

Steinmo, Sven, Kathleen Thelen and Frank Longstreth (eds.) 1992. *Structuring Politics: Historical Institutionalism in Comparative Analysis.* Cambridge University Press.

Storper, Michael 1997. *The Regional World: Territorial Development in a Global Economy.* New York: Guildford.

Streeck, Wolfgang and Kathleen Thelen 2005. 'Introduction: Institutional Change in Advanced Political Economies', in Wolfgang Streeck and Kathleen Thelen (eds.), *Beyond Continuity.* Oxford University Press, pp. 1–39.

Stretton, Hugh 1969. *The Political Sciences: General Principles of Selection in Social Sciences and History.* London: Routledge & Kegan Paul.

Strøm, Kaare, Wolfgang C. Müller and Torbjörn Bergman (eds.) 2003. *Delegation and Accountability in Parliamentary Democracies.* Oxford University Press.

Tamir, Yael 1993. *Liberal Nationalism.* Princeton University Press.

Tarrow, Sidney 2004. 'Bridging the Quantitative–Qualitative Divide', in Brady and Collier (eds.), pp. 171–80.

Taylor, Michael 1987. *The Possibility of Cooperation.* Cambridge University Press.

Taylor, Peter D. and Leo B. Jonker 1978. 'Evolutionary Stable Strategies and Game Dynamics', *Mathematical Biosciences* 40: 145–56.

Tetlock, Philip E. 2005. *Expert Political Judgment. How Good Is It? How Can We Know?* Princeton University Press.

Tetlock, Philip E. and Aaron Belkin 1996. *Counterfactual Thought Experiments in World Politics.* Princeton University Press.

Tetlock, Philip E., Richard Ned Lebow and Geoffrey Parker 2006. *Unmaking the West: 'What-if' Scenarios that Rewrite World History.* Ann Arbor: University of Michigan Press.

Thatcher, Mark and Alec Stone Sweet (eds.) 2002. *The Politics of Delegation: Non-Majoritarian Institutions in Europe.* Special issue of *West European Politics* 25(1): 1–219.

Thelen, Kathleen 2004. *How Institutions Evolve: The Political Economy of Skills in Germany, Britain, the United States, and Japan.* Cambridge University Press.

Thomas, George, John Boli, Francesco Ramirez *et al.* 1987. *Institutional Structure: Constituting State, Society and the Individual.* Beverly Hills, Calif.: Sage.

Thompson, E. P. 1980. *The Making of the English Working Class.* London: Penguin.

Tiles, Mary 1984. *Bachelard: Science and Objectivity.* Cambridge University Press.

Tilly, Charles 1984. *Big Structures, Large Processes, Huge Comparisons.* New York: Russell Sage Foundation.

1986. *The Contentious French.* Cambridge, Mass.: Harvard University Press.

Tilly, Charles and Gabriel Ardant 1975. *The Formation of National States in Western Europe.* Princeton University Press.

Tilmans, Karin 2004. 'The Concept of the Dutch Citizen', *Redescriptions: Yearbook of Political Thought and Conceptual History* 8: 146–71.

Tocqueville, Alexis de 1999. *Souvenirs.* Paris: Gallimard.

Todd, Emmanuel 1990. *L'invention de l'Europe*. Paris: Seuil.

Toulmin, Stephen 1950. *An Examination of Reason in Ethics*. Cambridge University Press.
  2001. *Return to Reason*. Cambridge, Mass.: Harvard University Press.

Touraine, Alain 1981. *The Voice and the Eye: An Analysis of Social Movements*. Cambridge University Press.

Trachtenberg, Marc 2006. *The Craft of International History. A Guide to Method*. Princeton University Press.

Truman, David 1951. *The Governmental Process*. New York: Knopf.

Tsebelis, George 1990. *Nested Games: Rational Choice in Comparative Politics*. Berkeley: University of California Press.

Ullmann-Margalit, Edna 1977. *The Emergence of Norms*. Oxford: Clarendon.

Van Langenhove, Luk 2007. *Innovating the Social Sciences: Towards More Useable Knowledge for Society*. Vienna: Passagen Verlag.

Vaughan, Diane 1992. 'Theory Elaboration: The Heuristics of Case Analysis', in Ragin and Becker (eds.), pp. 173–202.
  1996. *The Challenger Launch Decision: Risky Technology, Culture, and Deviance at NASA*. University of Chicago Press.

Verba, Sidney 1991. 'Comparative Politics: Where Have We Been, Where Are We Going', in Howard J. Wiarda (ed.), *New Directions in Comparative Politics*. Boulder, Colo.: Westview, pp. 31–42.

Verba, Sidney, Norman H. Nie and Jae-on Kim 1978. *Participation and Political Equality*. Cambridge University Press.

Vico, Giambattista 1999. *The New Science 1744*, trans. David Marsh. London: Penguin.

Vincent, Andrew 2004. *The Nature of Political Theory*. Oxford University Press.

Von Neumann, John and Oskar Morgenstern 1944. *Theory of Games and Economic Behavior*. Princeton University Press.

Von Wright, Georg Henrik 1971. *Explanation and Understanding*. Ithaca: Cornell University Press.

Voss, Kim 1993. *The Making of American Exceptionalism: The Knights of Labor and Class Formation in the Nineteenth Century*. Ithaca: Cornell University Press.

Wallerstein, Michael 2001. 'Does Political Science Need a "Theory of Everything"?', *Newsletter of the American Political Science Association Comparative Politics Section*, Winter 2001, 1–2, 31.

Walton, John 1992. 'Making the Theoretical Case', in Ragin and Becker (eds.), pp. 121–37.

Waltz, Kenneth 1959. *Man, the State and War*. New York: Columbia University Press.
  1979. *Theory of International Politics*. Reading, Mass.: Addison-Wesley.

Weber, Max 1949. *The Methodology of the Social Sciences*. New York: The Free Press.

Weber, Steven 1996. 'Counterfactuals, Past and Future', in Tetlock and Belkin (eds.), pp. 268–88.

Weibull, Jörgen W. 1995. *Evolutionary Game Theory*. Cambridge, Mass.: MIT Press.

Weingast, Barry 1996. 'Political Institutions: Rational Choice Perspectives', in Robert E. Goodin and Hans-Dieter Klingemann (eds.), *A New Handbook of Political Science*. Oxford University Press, pp. 167–90.

Wendt, Alexander 1999. *Social Theory of International Relations*. Cambridge University Press.

Wengle, John L. 1988. *Ethnographers in the Field: The Psychology of Research*. Tuscaloosa: University of Alabama Press.

Whyte, William Foote 1994. *Street Corner Society*. University of Chicago Press.

Wiarda, Howard J. 1991. 'Comparative Politics: Past and Present', in Howard J. Wiarda (ed.), *New Directions in Comparative Politics*. Boulder, Colo.: Westview, pp. 3–30.

Willms, Johannes and Ulrich Beck 2004. *Conversations with Ulrich Beck*. Cambridge: Polity.

Wilson, Graham K. 1994. 'The Westminster Model in Comparative Politics', in Ian Budge and David McKay, *Developing Democracy: Comparative Research in Honour of J. F. P. Blondel*. London: Sage.

Wilson, Woodrow 1891. *Congressional Government: A Study In American Politics*, 8th edn. Boston: Houghton.

Wolcott, Harry F. 1999. *Ethnography: A Way of Seeing*. Walnut Creek, Calif.: AltaMira.

Wunenburger, Jean-Jacques (ed.) 2003. *Bachelard et l'épistémologie française*. Paris: Presses universitaires de France.

Yin, Robert K. 1994. *Case Study Research. Design and Methods* (1st edn 1984). Beverly Hills, Calif.: Sage.

Zielonka, Jan 2006. *Europe as Empire: The Nature of the Enlarged European Union*. Oxford University Press.

Ziman, John 1978. *Reliable Knowledge*. Cambridge University Press.

Zintl, Reinhard 2001. 'Rational Choice as a Tool in Political Science', *Associations* 5(1): 35–50.

Zysman, John 1977. *Political Strategies for Industrial Order: State, Market, and Industry in France*. Berkeley: University of California Press.

Glossary

Abduction *See* Deduction

Adhocery An *ad hoc* explanation is one that is invented after the fact to explain a specific occurrence or to justify a specific normative claim, without use of a theory. Social scientists deplore such explanations, since explanation should be general and applicable at least to all cases in the same category.

Behaviouralism Behaviouralism has various meanings in psychology and philosophy. In political science it denotes an approach pioneered first in Europe, then in the United States in the 1940s; it entered the mainstream over the subsequent two decades. It moved the emphasis from the study of institutions to that of individuals (or sometimes groups) and their behaviour. Behaviouralists tend towards the view that individuals would behave in the same way in the same circumstances and aim for universal knowledge and laws. They are positivist in their approach and usually work with large datasets. Behaviouralism has been challenged by rational choice theory, the new institutionalism, the renewed interest in culture and the normative turn in social sciences.

Black box When one set of factors or variables seems to cause another but we do not know how this happens, the gap in explanation is known as a 'black box'. Several research methods are devoted to opening the black box.

Case A case can be defined as either a unit of observation or a unit of analysis. Cases feature in large-*N* studies, where there are many cases over which the value of a variable is measured. The 'case study' is a strategy of research that focuses on a single unit – an event, a country or a historical process. Cases do not define themselves. The delimitation of a case results, rather, from the researcher's act of conceptualization. Case studies are often considered stronger in hypothesis building than in hypothesis testing, and in the logic of discovery more than in the logic of theory testing. They are important in ethnographic research, which seeks understanding rather than explanation. Crucial cases or deviant cases are particularly fruitful for theory evaluation.

Causation Causation refers to the idea that social and political events can be attributed to prior causes, in a manner analogous to the natural sciences. A strict causal explanation requires that a particular combination of circumstances should produce the same result and that each occurrence of a specific event should have the same causes. More commonly in the social sciences, causal relationships are said to be probabilistic. Causation is usually established by correlation, showing that the same causes are associated with the same effects; but this does not strictly prove that one has caused the other. The connection may be established by the rational choice assumption (that people will always choose the best option for themselves) or by process tracing (q.v.). Many social scientists admit that a specific event may be produced by various combinations of causes. Critics argue that the social world is not analogous to the natural world and that social events are not caused, but are the product of human volition and learning or of chance.

Comparative method In a broad sense, the comparative method refers to social science based on comparison of cases. This includes variable-based and case-based approaches. Sometimes the term 'comparative method' is restricted to the latter. The term 'comparative politics' is often restricted to comparisons of countries, but in principle any social entity can be analysed comparatively.

Comparative statics Comparative statics involves examining one feature while holding constant all the other features of the selected cases, and assessing how this variation impacts upon the outcome.

Conditions Causal analysis often uses necessary and sufficient conditions. Where A is always associated with B (every A has a B irrespective of other factors), then A is a sufficient condition for B. Where B is always associated with A (there is no B without A), then A is a necessary condition for B. Necessary and sufficient conditions allow us to specify causes precisely. More complex and less determinate is the INUS condition, where the identified cause or causes is an insufficient but non-redundant element of a complex which is itself unnecessary but sufficient for the production of a result.

Concepts Concepts are the building blocks of the social sciences. They consist of *terms* used to classify the social world into categories. Realists (including positivists) tend to believe that concepts correspond to real categories. Nominalists, and to a certain extent constructivists, argue that they are merely convenient ways of representing reality; their utility derives not from their correspondence to reality, but from their ability to explain outcomes.

Concomitant variation If two variables tend to vary together, then we have concomitant variation. In statistical analysis, this is also known as correlation (q.v.).

Consequentialism Consequentialism is the idea that a course of action will be chosen with regard to its likely results rather than its intrinsic merits (*see* Utilitarianism).

Constructivism There are many varieties of constructivism. Their common characteristic is their focus on our conceptual construction of the world, rather than on a 'concrete reality'. In international relations, constructivists emphasize the role of norms, as compared to the 'realist' emphasis on states, interests and power.

Controls In order to isolate the effect of the key variables in comparative analysis, other variables may be controlled for. That is, they are held constant; only cases in which their values do not vary are included.

Correlation A correlation exists between two quantitative variables when their values move together (*see also* Regression). This may suggest a causal relationship between them, but a correlation in itself cannot be used to demonstrate causation.

Counterfactuals Counterfactuals are events that did not occur but might have, had circumstances been different. We often use counterfactuals in our reasoning when building hypotheses, such as when we invoke a *ceteris paribus* ('other things being equal') clause. In a more explicit way, they are used in historical analysis to trace the impact of specific factors by asking what would have happened in their absence or (where they were absent) their presence.

Cybernetics In natural sciences, cybernetics refers to the study of fluxes of liquids. In the social sciences, it refers to the study of self-regulating systems and to spontaneous and unregulated forms of social communication.

Deduction/induction Deduction is a process of deriving conclusions directly from their premises by logic alone. It is the characteristic method of mathematics and is also used in philosophy. Induction involves looking at real cases and drawing general conclusions. The term 'deduction' is often used in the social sciences to refer to the hypothetico-deductive approach: a hypothesis is derived deductively from theory and is then tested empirically. The term 'abduction' is sometimes used for a process that iterates between deduction and induction.

Degrees of freedom In statistics, degrees of freedom are calculated based on the relationship between the number of cases and the number of variables introduced in a model. In quantitative research, degrees of freedom must be limited in order to avoid an underdetermined research design – that is, one with too few cases to test for the impact of all relevant variables. In comparative case studies, it is less of a problem to analyse a large number of variables with a few cases.

Determinism In philosophy, determinism is the belief that social events are determined by prior causes, which can be fully discovered and specified. It is traditionally opposed to free will, which stresses the ability of individual humans to make their own choices. Few social scientists would describe themselves as determinists, since all recognize an element of uncertainty in the world; but the extent to which they give a role to human agency differs.

Diachronic Diachronic analysis is the examination of one or more cases across time. Synchronic analysis is the examination of several cases at the same time.

Ecological fallacy The ecological fallacy involves the assumption that relationships that hold at the aggregate level will also hold at the individual level. The individualistic fallacy involves the assumption that relationships that hold at the individual level will also hold at a higher level of analysis.

Empiricism Empiricists believe that the world can be discovered and explained through observation or measurement. They identify facts through common language rather than theoretical definition. More generally, empirical research is usually conceived as referring to the use of original sources, including data, records and interviews; it is contrasted with purely theoretical inquiry. Others would stress that the empirical/theoretical distinction has to do with the definition of the object of the research. In practice, a great deal of social science research mixes theoretical and empirical approaches.

Endogeneity In statistics, endogeneity is the error of having the same indicator on both the dependent and independent variables.

Epistemology Epistemology is the study of knowledge and justification. A complex branch of philosophy in the social sciences, it refers to how we know things. Two main epistemological positions are usually distinguished. Positivists believe that we can know the social world directly. Constructivists argue, rather, that our knowledge consists of concepts – that is, abstract representations of the world whose value is based on their usefulness rather than their correspondence with reality.

Equifinality Equifinality is the circumstance that different causes or sets of causes can produce the same outcome.

Ethnographic methods Ethnographic approaches in the social sciences seek to understand (q.v.) actors on their own terms rather than bringing pre-formed theoretical notions to bear. They are sensitive to context and to the varied meanings that actions can have. Ethnographic methods typically include unstructured interviews and participant observation.

Explanandum/explanans The *explanandum* is what is to be explained (also defined in some approaches as the 'dependent' variable). The *explanans* is what does the explaining (also the 'independent' or 'intervening' variable).

Foundationalism Foundationalism in philosophy is the idea that there are two types of knowledge: the foundational, which is the basis for all knowledge; and the non-foundational, which is derived from foundational knowledge. Foundationalism also refers to the argument that in order to understand the world we must always return to the foundations of knowledge; to share ideas, we must share the same ontological and epistemological assumptions. Most social scientists agree that the social sciences enterprise would become impossible if this were the case; much progress can be made without returning to the foundations.

Hermeneutics Hermeneutics is the science of interpretation. The term is often used in social sciences to refer to approaches that stress subjective interpretation over shared standards of knowledge.

Holistic approach A holistic approach looks at individuals and societies as whole entities, rather than breaking them down into variables or characteristics.

Hypothesis A hypothesis is an expected state of affairs, usually a relationship between factors in the form 'if x then y'. It is often used in causal analysis (*see* Causation) to postulate a determinate connection between the two factors. The connection can then be tested empirically. If the connection holds, the hypothesis is confirmed. If it does not, it is rejected. According to Popper, a hypothesis is falsified when there is one instance of a lack of conformity; we can never say that we have verified a hypothesis. In practice, empirical research usually serves to modify a hypothesis, which is then confirmed in its new form. Some social scientists insist that all doctoral theses must have hypotheses; but this is too strict, since not all theses seek to test causal relationships.

Idiographic approach An idiographic approach seeks to explain only the case in question, rather than to draw generalizations.

Indeterminate research design An indeterminate research design is one in which the outcome is open to several different explanations, since with the number of cases available we cannot control for the impact of all operational variables on the dependent variable.

Induction *See* Deduction

Institutionalism Institutionalism is the belief that institutions have an independent impact on social and political behaviour. Old institutionalism focused on the study of institutions before the behaviouralist revolution, emphasizing the formal and legal aspects of institutions. New institutionalism defines institutions more broadly, going beyond the state. Institutions are seen as providing incentives to actors; socializing individuals into patterns of behaviour; providing solutions to collective action problems; and establishing continuity through history. New institutionalism has been influential in political science, sociology and economics – although the terms used sometimes differ and the ideas have often been derived independently.

Interpretation All social scientists need to interpret their information, but the stress on this aspect differs. Empiricists tend to focus on facts, which have a given and fixed meaning. Historians emphasize that their work involves selecting from the myriad facts of chronological experience and giving them meaning over time. Interpretivists in the social sciences emphasize the importance of the concepts that we construct in giving meaning to social facts. Some post-modern interpretivists insist that we cannot know reality as it is, and therefore deny the possibility of shared knowledge or meaning.

Inter-subjectivity An objective perspective takes the social world as given and external to individuals. A subjective perspective starts with the individual and his/her conception of the world. Inter-subjectivity seeks to combine these approaches by showing how individuals' meanings and interpretations both influence and are influenced by other individuals, as well as by institutions and social practices.

Intervening variable An intervening variable is a factor intervening in the relationship between an independent and a dependent variable (q.v.) such as to change the normal relationship between them.

Meta-theory A meta-theory is a theory about theories, or one that specifies prior conditions for the relevance of a given theory.

Method of agreement Contemporary methodologists often refer to John Stuart Mill's distinction between the method of agreement and the method of disagreement. In the method of agreement, two cases are selected which have the same outcome, differing in every other aspect except one. Following the same logic as the most-similar systems design (q.v.), this factor must therefore be responsible for any difference in the outcome. In the method of disagreement, two cases are selected which have different outcomes, and are the same in every aspect except one. Again, this factor must be responsible for any difference in the outcome. This is also the approach of the most-dissimilar systems design. Mill recognized that it is difficult, in practice, to find situations in the social sciences that correspond to these demanding conditions.

Methodological individualism Methodological individualism is based upon the assumption that the only valid unit of social analysis is the individual person. Macro-processes are based on the aggregation of individual decisions. Ontological individualism holds that only individuals exist and that to talk of collectivities as actors is meaningless. Explanatory individualism holds that only individual actions can explain social outcomes. The two positions are distinct, and the scholar may espouse one without necessarily subscribing to the other.

Middle-range theory A middle-range theory is one that works across a limited number of contexts or seeks to explain only certain aspects of a phenomenon. It is to be distinguished from universal theory, which predicates the same relationship between variables everywhere; and from pure empiricism, which studies the world without a theoretical framework. Middle-range theory is widely used in the social sciences, either on pragmatic grounds or out of the belief that our social science knowledge is always context-bounded.

Models A model is an abstract representation of a phenomenon, containing only those aspects of interest to the researcher. Descriptive models attempt to replicate the empirical phenomenon as closely as possible. Ideal-type models represent a pure form of a specific phenomenon against which real-world examples can be measured. Prescriptive models provide guides to action by showing how the world could be.

Most-similar systems design This is a way of selecting cases such that they are similar in as many respects as possible, thus isolating the key factors that make them different. The aspects that are similar are controlled, or become parameters (q.v.). The aspects that differ are variables. Most-dissimilar systems designs take cases that have produced similar outcomes in the matter of interest, but are otherwise very different. The aim is then to seek out the common factor that has produced the outcome. Most-similar and most-dissimilar research designs resemble Mill's method of disagreement and method of agreement (q.v.), respectively.

Multicollinearity Multicollinearity occurs in regression analysis when two variables vary together, so that we cannot tell which is causing the effect. Perfect multicollinearity is usually caused by the fact that the variables are not independent of each other or are measuring the same thing.

Nomothetic approach A nomothetic approach aims at producing general laws rather than simply explaining individual cases. It is often contrasted with an idiographic approach (q.v.).

Ontology In philosophy, ontology refers to the study of the essence of a certain phenomenon (i.e. without considering its specific variation). In the social sciences, it refers to what we can know. Positivists and constructivists (q.v.) have different views on this. Ontology also refers to the units of which the social world is composed. For some, the only reality is individuals; others work with larger social units.

Operationalization Operationalization is the act of taking a concept and converting it into something that can be studied empirically. This can involve a more concrete definition and the search for indicators of its presence and extent.

Parameters Parameters are those aspects of a comparative research project that do not vary. Parameterizing may be achieved by selecting most-similar systems (q.v.) or by controlling (q.v.) in other ways for variables other than the ones of interest.

Parsimony Parsimony is the principle that outcomes should be explained using the fewest possible variables (q.v.) (or characteristics). There is often a trade-off between parsimony and completeness of explanation. Social scientists differ in the emphasis that they place on one or the other.

Positivism Positivism in philosophy is the doctrine that only statements about the world that can be verified or falsified can be accepted. According to logical positivists, there are two types of truth: contingent truths revealed by empirical inquiry; and necessary truths that are analytic and *a priori* (such as mathematical truths). All else is either metaphysics or non-scientific statements about reality. Normative concepts, in particular, are considered as nothing more than expressions of the psychological states/attitudes of the individuals who hold them; as such, they are seen as 'subjective' at best, rather than 'objective' or 'public'. The classical difficulty with the insistence on empirical inquiry is that the only things of which we are directly aware are our own sensory perceptions. Positivists in the social sciences tend to see social sciences as being similar to natural sciences: they take the natural world and large parts of the social world as given and really existing and focus on empirical investigation. They are opposed by constructivists and interpretivists (*see* Interpretation), who insist that we deal only with concepts, which are constructed according to purpose. There are few logical positivists left, but social scientists are more or less positivist in their orientations.

Post-modernism There is a huge range of post-modernist positions. Generally, they reject the idea that the modern era represents the culmination of historical progress, regarding it rather as just one social model among others. Post-modernists are sceptical about grand narratives and theories, stressing subjective interpretation. They also deny the superiority and universality of Western conceptions of liberalism and democracy as well as the possibility of value-free social sciences.

Process tracing Process tracing is used in causal analysis, to fill in the black box (q.v.) of explanation when one variable is seen to be associated with another. It involves examining events to identify steps in the causal process that leads to the outcome in a particular historical context. In interpretivist approaches, it is oriented to identify the actors' motivations. Analytical narratives and systematic process tracing express similar notions.

Qualitative methods A qualitative method is any method that is not quantitative. Sometimes the term is reserved for those methods based on interpretation (q.v.) – including ethnographic (q.v.) approaches – as opposed to those that seek explanation.

Quantitative methods A quantitative method is strictly any method involving numbers. Usually, the term is applied to studies with large numbers of cases (large-N studies).

Rational choice Rational choice models of social behaviour are usually based on methodological individualism. Individuals are assumed to know their own interests and to seek to maximize them in social interaction. Outcomes are therefore explained by the combined actions of self-seeking individuals. The principal objection is that the rationality and self-interest assumptions are wrong. Individuals may not act rationally; and they may not be guided by self-interest. Attempts to rescue the theory by saying that self-interest can include altruistic behaviour (since this gives gratification to the individual) merely make the theory tautological, since the possibility of not being self-interested has been defined away. In recent years, rational choice theorists have relaxed these assumptions and incorporated other forms of motivation in their models – for example, game theory incorporates the actions of other actors into the calculation. Rational choice has been influential in the study of public policy through the public choice school, which seeks to reorganize public services based on quasi-markets, letting individuals select their own mix of services as far as possible. (*See also* Utilitarianism.)

Regression Regression analysis in statistics allows one to quantify the graduated effect of an independent variable on a dependent variable. Multiple regression analysis measures the effects of several independent variables on a dependent variable.

Scientific method There are many scientific methods, and most social scientists insist that they obey the scientific canons of rigour, logic and proof. The term 'scientific method', however, is generally used by exponents of positivist social sciences who seek to approximate the methods of the natural sciences.

Serendipity Serendipity is making discoveries by accident rather than on the basis of a research design.

Spuriousness A spurious relationship is one that appears to be valid but is not. This may be because of poor specification of variables, poor measurement, or analytical errors such as the ecological fallacy (q.v.).

Subsumption Subsumption occurs when one theoretical account can be logically incorporated into (subsumed under) another, broader one.

Synchronic *See* Diachronic

Taxonomy *See* Typology

Teleology Teleology is the study of ends. In history, it is a mode of interpretation that sees events as leading to a specific outcome; this provides a framework for interpretation. In philosophy, it is the belief that human activity is goal-oriented. Teleological ethics are a way of judging actions by their effects (*see* Consequentialism), as opposed to deontological justification, in which actions are judged on their intrinsic worth. In the social sciences, teleology is a way of explaining events by their outcomes rather than their causes. It sometimes takes the form of functionalism – the argument that because a process serves a particular social function, that must be why it came about. This is widely considered a fallacious form of reasoning.

Theory Theories are sets of propositions going beyond individual cases and allowing us to generalize. *Empirical theories* are based on the study of cases and seek to establish causal relationships among variables. Their validity depends on the ability to test these causal relationships in concrete cases. These tests typically involve operationalizing the theory and proposing a hypothesis in the form of 'if x, then y'. If this relationship holds, the theory is validated (see Héritier, ch. 4). More abstract, or analytical, theories explain large-scale processes by reference to general concepts and processes. Their validity depends on their ability to make sense of what happens in the social world by providing a scheme of interpretation. (*See also* Middle-range theory.)

Deductive theories are examples of formal logic, as in mathematics. Their validity depends on their internal coherence, not on correspondence with the world of facts. In social science they usually take the form of making certain assumptions about a hypothetical world and then reasoning logically as to what follows. Game theory is an example (see Chwaszcza, ch. 8). Deductive theory is often seen as essentially different from empirical theory, although they are often combined.

Normative theories involve the articulation of values, which are then used to criticize social processes and institutions or point the way to better ones. In recent decades, the terms 'political theory' and 'social theory' have increasingly been used to refer to normative theory, which was previously the preserve of philosophy. This is generally held to be distinct from empirical theory, although some social scientists would argue against too strict a separation of the empirical or analytical from the normative (see Bauböck, ch. 3).

Typology A typology is a scheme for classifying cases or concepts under a limited number of headings and on various dimensions. Descriptive typologies help in highlighting the distinctive features of cases and those shared in common. Ideal types are abstract representations of phenomena, identifying their defining features; real cases can then be examined for their closeness to these. Typologies may also be of help in explanation when they are combined with hypotheses about the effects of specific combinations of features.

A taxonomy is an exhaustive classification of things or concepts. The word comes from the natural sciences, where it is used to refer, for example, to classification of species. In social sciences, taxonomies are often used to classify cases under headings. A taxonomic category is a form of descriptive typology and is therefore to be distinguished from an ideal type.

Understanding Understanding, or *verstehen*, is a term used by those who argue that we cannot explain social change by reference to causal processes (*see* Causation), as in the natural sciences. Social sciences, rather, should be concerned with understanding social processes, including the motivations of actors and elements of contingency.

Utilitarianism Utilitarianism is a social philosophy stating that social practices and public policies are to be valued, not for their own sake, but for what they contribute to human good (utility) (*see* Consequentialism). Often the good is described in hedonistic terms. Jeremy Bentham formulated the principle of the greatest happiness of the greatest number as the criterion of practice. Critics have noted that there may be different conceptions of the good, some of which may involve absolute values, irrespective of their impact on the majority. Utilitarian assumptions about utility maximization are widespread in rational choice (q.v.) theory.

Validity The validity rule relates to internal and external generalization. Internal validity concerns whether the indicators used to measure the empirical values of variables measure what they intend to measure. External validity concerns whether the claims made for one case can be generalized to other cases, and to what extent.

Variable A variable is a characteristic that varies in its incidence among cases. Variables are used in causal analysis to seek to establish which factors systematically cause others. The causal variables are known as independent variables and the effects as dependent variables. Dummy variables merely indicate the presence or absence of a specific characteristic. Ordinal variables have a series of values in ascending order. Interval variables have a series of values in steps of equal size.

Index